MEDIEVAL AND RENAISSANCE
SPANISH LITERATURE

MEDIEVAL AND RENAISSANCE SPANISH LITERATURE

SELECTED ESSAYS

by

Keith Whinnom

Edited by Alan Deyermond, W. F. Hunter & Joseph T. Snow

UNIVERSITY
of
EXETER
PRESS

with the Journal of Hispanic Philology

First published in 1994 by
University of Exeter Press
Reed Hall
Streatham Drive
Exeter EX4 4QR
UK

British Library Cataloguing in Publication Data
A catalogue record for this book is available from the British Library

ISBN 0 85989 219 0

Typeset in 11pt Garamond by Kestrel Data, Exeter

Printed and bound in Great Britain by
Short Run Press Ltd, Exeter

Contents

Preface

When Keith Whinnom died in March 1986, his publications on literature amounted to nine books, a pamphlet, thirty-six articles and notes, and forty-two reviews; three more articles have since been published, and more items are on the way. This, of course, was only one side of his scholarship: he was, as Ian Macpherson wrote in the Preface to *The Age of the Catholic Monarchs*, 'an accomplished linguist whose researches during spells in the Far East and the Caribbean had led to the elaboration of a new general theory of pidgins and creoles; a lexicographer whose *Glossary of Spanish Bird-Names* (1966) became a standard work' (p. vii). And his literary and linguistic research and publications were only a part of his professional life: his teaching of undergraduates in the University of Hong Kong, Trinity College Dublin, the University of the West Indies, and in his last twenty years the University of Exeter; his visits to other universities, whether for a semester (Emory University, 1965) or for a day or two to give a lecture; his contributions to national and international conferences, both in the giving of papers and in taking his share in discussion; his supervision of graduate students; his work as an exceptionally conscientious external examiner at both BA and PhD level; his headship of the Exeter Department of Spanish, which became under his guidance one of the best in the country; his administrative work in the University as a whole, as Dean of the Faculty of Arts and, in his last four years, as Deputy Vice-Chancellor; his founding editorship of Exeter Hispanic Texts and his work on the editorial committees of seven journals and series published in other universities; his presidency of the Association of Hispanists of Great Britain and Ireland in the last year of his life, when, although seriously ill, he made the hitherto largely ornamental office of President into a powerful political weapon in the defence of Hispanic Studies—all of this made him a central and irreplaceable part of British hispanism and a world leader in his chosen fields of research. So, too, did the help he gave to other scholars, both in conversation and by letter. Ian Macpherson's memoir calls him 'generous to those who sought his help or advice, a prolific correspondent, a painstaking editor and selfless contributor to the works of others' (*BHS*, 63 (1986), 265-67), and my own memoir comments that he 'was always patient, always generous, with young scholars. [. . .] No request for information or guidance ever went unanswered' (*C*, 14 (1985–86), 355-58).

The admiration and gratitude that Keith inspired, and the sense of loss at his death, led to the publication of *The Age of the Catholic Monarchs 1474–1516: Literary Studies in Memory of Keith Whinnom*, ed. Deyermond and Macpherson, Special Issue of the *Bulletin of Hispanic Studies* (Liverpool: University Press, 1989, xii + 211 pp.). Many scholars have expressed a wish to possess his most important articles in book form, and the present volume endeavours to meet that wish as far as literary studies are concerned. Some articles were clearly inappropriate for inclusion, usually because they had been superseded by other work of Keith's: for instance, B39 in the Bibliography (pp. xxxi-xxxviii, below), though written as a conference paper before the *Poesía amatoria* book [A11], was published after it, and the cover of an offprint is inscribed 'Not worth printing after *Poesía amatoria*'. In other cases, however, the choice was far from easy, and the editors hesitated for a long time before reluctantly deciding that Keith's textual studies on *El Abencerraje* [B6] and *Celestina* [B16], his polemical piece on the *kharjas* [B42], and a couple of others had slightly weaker claims than the twelve articles, one note, and one pamphlet that are reprinted here. The criteria that we applied, in addition to the obvious ones of importance of subject and scholarly excellence, were: (*a*) the influence that each study has had; (*b*) the representation of Keith's main areas of literary interest (sentimental romance, with Diego de San Pedro at its core; narrative religious verse of the late fifteenth and early sixteenth centuries; *cancionero* love-lyric; *Celestina*; the revision of literary history); and (*c*) the illustration of Keith's preferred approaches to literary research (detailed analysis of texts; study of the literary and intellectual traditions that nurture a work or group of works; study of the relationships of manuscripts and early printed texts, and the establishment of a critical edition; analysis of generic and cultural concepts). The criterion of influence explains—indeed, makes inevitable—the inclusion of a three-page note as Chapter 10: within a few weeks of its first publication, the majority of English-speaking *Celestina* specialists, and a substantial proportion of Spanish-speaking ones, had adopted Keith's way of referring to the text. Sentimental romances are the subject of Chapters 1, 8, 13, and much of 12; narrative religious verse is studied in Chapters 2–5 and 9, and *cancionero* lyric in Chapter 7; Chapters 10 and 12 deal with *Celestina*; and general issues of literary history are dealt with in Chapters 6, 11, and 14. In types of scholarship, Chapters 1, 7, 8, and 12 show Keith's talent for detailed textual analysis; textual criticism and codicology are the methodological basis of

Chapters 2, 3, and 9; the study of cultural traditions and literary influences informs Chapters 1, 4, 5, and 13; and Chapters 6, 10, 11, and 14 show Keith at work with concepts, generic terms, and titles. This classification, though useful as an initial guide to the contents of this volume, is inevitably somewhat misleading, since it suggests watertight divisions where none exist: most of Keith's scholarship uses a variety of approaches, and much of it covers more than one area of interest. His literary scholarship forms an unusually coherent body of work, dealing (with a few exceptions) with Spanish literature from the mid-fifteenth century to the late sixteenth, the main weight falling in the reign of the Catholic Monarchs, and studying as a necessary foundation the wider issues that affect our understanding of that literature.

The studies selected for this volume are printed in the order in which they were originally published, which corresponds roughly to the order in which they were composed (though not necessarily to the date on the cover of the journal concerned). The editors considered a thematic grouping, but decided that it was better to print the studies in an order that illustrated the development of Keith Whinnom's scholarship. We also thought it important that this volume should, as far as possible, give the original texts of his studies; for that reason, they are wherever possible edited from carbon copies of his typescripts or from his corrected offprints (details are given on pp. xxxix-xli, below). The two articles that were translated into Spanish for publication in the Buenos Aires journal *Filología* are now published, for the first time, in their original English form (Chapters 3 and 7); Chapter 5, which Keith wrote in Spanish, remains in that language—the principle of following original texts takes precedence over that of linguistic uniformity.

The three editors shared equally in the selection of material and in the decisions on criteria. I am responsible for the editing of the texts and for the introductory matter, W. F. Hunter for the correction of proofs and day-to-day contact with the University of Exeter Press, and Joseph T. Snow and W. F. Hunter for the preparation of a detailed subject-index. All of us, and the University Press, are grateful to the editors and publishers of the journals and homage volumes in which the articles first appeared for allowing us to reprint them, and to Professor Daniel Eisenberg, Editor of the *Journal of Hispanic Philology*, for his generous financial support for the volume.

Alan Deyermond

Abbreviations

BAE	Biblioteca de Autores Españoles
BH	*Bulletin Hispanique*
BHS	*Bulletin of Hispanic Studies*
BRAE	*Boletín de la Real Academia Española*
C	*La Corónica*
Cel	*Celestinesca*
EHT	Exeter Hispanic Texts
HR	*Hispanic Review*
JHP	*Journal of Hispanic Philology*
JOS	*Journal of Oriental Studies*
MLR	*Modern Language Review*
NBAE	Nueva Biblioteca de Autores Españoles
NRFH	*Nueva Revista de Filología Hispánica*
PL	Patrologia Latina, ed. J. P. Migne
PMLA	*Publications of the Modern Language Association of America*
RFE	*Revista de Filología Española*
RFH	*Revista de Filología Hispánica*
RLit	*Revista de Literatura*
ZRP	*Zeitschrift für Romanische Philologie*

Keith Whinnom's Literary Scholarship

Keith Whinnom's first article on a literary subject [B1 in the Bibliography, pp. xxxi-xxxviii, below] is on Molière, an author who had attracted his interest during his undergraduate course at Oxford. Not until four years later (seven years after he began research) did he publish on his principal area of literary research, the life and works of Diego de San Pedro and (increasingly) the works of San Pedro's contemporaries. There seem to have been two main reasons for the delay. One is that a year in Spain, 1950–51, as Laming Travelling Fellow of The Queen's College, Oxford, proved fruitful in the discovery of manuscript evidence but discouraging in Whinnom's encounters with the Spanish academic establishment of that time. He began research in October 1950, under the supervision of Dámaso Alonso, and soon discovered that Emilio Cotarelo y Mori, the recognized authority on San Pedro's life, had seriously misunderstood some of the documentary evidence. The first two chapters of Whinnom's 320-page thesis for the Universidad de Madrid, 'Contribuciones al estudio de Diego de San Pedro', deal with Cotarelo's errors—notably those that led him to decide that San Pedro belonged to a family converted from Judaism—and then try to construct a more reliable account on the basis of a new analysis of the documents. His first article on the subject [B4] is based on these chapters. The third and last chapter, on the style of *Arnalte y Lucenda*, led eventually to another article [B7 = Chapter 1, below]. The thesis, of which I hope to give a detailed account elsewhere, may be merely a first draft: each chapter is separately paginated (though the same could be said of one Spanish doctoral thesis submitted in 1991), and the references are not presented in the systematic form that Whinnom was soon to adopt. There is no clear evidence as to its fate; perhaps he was discouraged from submitting, perhaps it was submitted but rejected. What is clear is that he did not receive a Madrid doctorate, and that the experience was deeply wounding. His supervisor said later that the thesis was seen as an attack on one of the great figures of Spanish scholarship.[1] It is true that some of the references to

Cotarelo are tactless, and that even the most tactful wording would still have shown him as a careless investigator, but the quality of Whinnom's research is high, and it is hard to imagine such a thesis failing to win a doctorate in Spain today, when British graduate students find not only a cordial welcome but also willingness to engage in debate. Forty years ago, things were different. It is understandable that Whinnom did not, even decades later, wish to speak of this episode, but though it hurt him, it did not deter him from his chosen path of research, and it may well have made him determined to present his findings in a way that could not be overlooked, with detailed presentation of his evidence and a meticulous revision before publication. The eagerness with which young scholars in Spain sought his help in later years, the gratitude that they expressed, and finally his election in December 1985 as one of the first list of Socios de Honor of the Asociación Hispánica de Literatura Medieval, must have done much to heal the wound inflicted by an earlier generation.[2]

The other major factor in the delayed publication of Whinnom's first article on San Pedro is that, after a year back in Oxford, he was appointed to a lectureship at the University of Hong Kong. He may have been exaggerating when he alleged, years later, that the library contained only two Spanish books (a grammar and a translation of *Don Quijote*), but there is no doubt as to its inadequacy for research on fifteenth-century literature. Whinnom therefore devoted himself, during his three years in Hong Kong, to linguistic research, laying the foundations for his brilliant work on the origins of pidgins and creoles. It is interesting to note that his work on the Spanish contact vernaculars of the Philippines [A1] led ultimately to the same late-medieval Mediterranean world that San Pedro knew: he concluded that pidgins were formed on the model of the Mediterranean *lingua franca* [B14, B24], and this at first controversial hypothesis is now widely accepted.

Back in Europe, as lecturer at Trinity College, Dublin (1956–61), Whinnom had excellent library facilities and contact with other hispanists, and he responded immediately with a steady flow of major articles. His demolition of Cotarelo's view of Diego de San Pedro's biography [B4] has already been mentioned; he sets a new standard in San Pedro studies by his rigorous scrutiny of the documents, and shows that there is no clear evidence that the author of *Cárcel de Amor* was a *converso*. Further documentary research led to an attempt to fill a gap in the biographical data [B5], but it later turned out that both Cotarelo and Whinnom had been dealing with the wrong San Pedro, one of the generation before the *Cárcel* author and perhaps his uncle; the error is proclaimed with characteristic frankness, and its implications are assessed [B15]. The biographical chapter of Whinnom's book about San

Pedro [A7, pp. 17-28], which is the final statement of his views on this subject, is consequently devoted in large part to the aristocratic setting in which San Pedro's working life was spent, since that at least can be traced with some certainty in the documentary sources. No other investigator has taken the matter further, and it is likely that Whinnom's documentary research advanced as far as it was possible to go. Yet, as he said on another occasion, 'there is a limit to what can be achieved by systematic research on literary topics: much depends on chance finds' [C27, p. 180], and it remains possible that a chance find will yet shed light on San Pedro's obscure life.

The study of San Pedro's works, in contrast to that of his life, shows steady progress over virtually the whole span of Whinnom's working life. His first article in this area [B7 = Chapter 1] puts in a new light something that previous critics had noticed but misunderstood: the change from an obtrusively rhetorical style in San Pedro's first romance, *Arnalte y Lucenda* (composed in the early 1480s?), to the plainer style of his second, *Cárcel de Amor* (composed just before it was printed in 1492?). By careful analysis and a thorough study of rhetorical treatises, he is able to show that *Cárcel*'s style is indeed still rhetorical, but in the new fashion in which brevity, not amplification, is the stylistic ideal. His findings have been accepted as definitive, and the only other scholar to have dealt at length with the question of rhetoric in San Pedro's works, Joseph F. Chorpenning in 1977, is concerned not with style but with structure.[3] Another article published at the same time [B8] deals with San Pedro's poems, and in a quite different way: Whinnom begins to sort out the tangled relationship and the uncertain chronology of *Las siete angustias* and *La Passión trobada*, and soon afterwards he examines the first printings of the latter poem [B9]. At that time, the *Cancionero de Oñate-Castañeda*, lost for many years, was despite its rediscovery still not accessible to scholars (its purchaser refused access for some years). Since it contains the earliest extant manuscript version of the *Passión*, probably the sole witness to the poem's first version, this *cancionero* is clearly of fundamental importance to any editor.[4] Dorothy Sherman Severin was eventually able to obtain access, and used the manuscript for her critical edition;[5] a different edition, based on the printed texts, forms part of the complete edition of San Pedro's poems in which she collaborated with Whinnom [A10]. That volume, ready for publication in 1972 though it did not appear until seven years later, completed the Whinnom edition of San Pedro's works, the two volumes of prose works [A5 and A6] having been published in the early 1970s. Whinnom's introductions to those volumes fill 150 pages, and constitute a monograph on San Pedro and his romances that is the distillation of years of research, and remains the fundamental treatment of the subject in Spanish. There is inevitably overlap with the book [A7] in which Whinnom introduces San Pedro to an English-speaking public, but, as he points out in his Preface, the book is designed for a quite different audience, he has 'assumed no prior knowledge (or misinformation) on the part of the reader', and he has tried 'to present a coherent picture of the man, of his writings, and of the extraordinary period of history through which he lived' (p. 7). The book is a remarkable achievement: while observing the formal requirements of a series not in most cases committed to rigorous scholarship, Whinnom manages both to carry out his obligation to the intelligent general reader and to say something new to his fellow-specialists. (A comparable success is achieved in both respects by a pair of lectures, 'The Chivalric Idea in Spain' and 'Love in the Fifteenth Century', given in other universities and soon to be published in a volume of lectures on medieval culture. These lectures develop lines of thought from A5, A6, and A7.) In three years, therefore, San Pedro studies were transformed: at the beginning of 1972 there was no reliable edition of his works and—except for those who could read German—no book-length study to which one could turn with confidence;[6] by the end of 1974 students could buy inexpensive but impeccably presented editions of the prose works (with an edition of the poems in press) and an up-to-date book as valuable to the specialist as to the beginner.

Whinnom's edition of *Cárcel de Amor* appeared in a slightly revised second editon [A5a], and the text is unlikely to require major revision since no new witnesses have been discovered in the past twenty years. In the case of *Arnalte y Lucenda* (the volume also contains San Pedro's parodic *Sermón*) things are very different: in the mid-1970s the Biblioteca Nacional, Madrid, acquired a manuscript of the highest importance and hitherto unknown, containing full or partial texts of sentimental romances and similar works. One of these is *Arnalte*, of which the manuscript offers a better text than either of the extant early printings. The manuscript confirms many of Whinnom's conjectural emendations—a striking tribute to the quality of his edition—, but it makes a new edition necessary (the need is increased by the discovery of an aberrant but interesting sixteenth-century manuscript in an Italian library). The publishers of Clásicos Castalia asked Whinnom in the early 1980s to provide revised editions, but by that time he was heavily committed to administrative work as Deputy Vice-Chancellor and his health was poor, so, after consulting colleagues, he asked Ivy A. Corfis, who had critical editions of both works in press, to take over the project. She agreed, but before long Castalia decided that they did not after all want revised editions. This is a matter for great regret.[7]

Whinnom's interest in San Pedro was far from being exhausted with the publication of his editions, his English book, and two reviews [C27 and C39]. The Preface to the book ends: 'if I may be permitted a purely personal observation, I find that Diego de San Pedro wears well. Long after one has exhausted, through repeated readings and explanations, one's enthusiasm even for such a remarkable and popular work as *Celestina*, one finds that Diego de San Pedro retains his freshness' (p. 9). He underestimated *Celestina*'s hold on him, as we shall see, but he did not exaggerate that of San Pedro. He began to extend his interests to works and people connected with *Arnalte* and, especially, with *Cárcel*. He had already, in 1973, published an essay on Nicolás Núñez's sequel to *Cárcel* [B23 = Chapter 8], in which he compared Núñez unfavourably with San Pedro but wondered whether what he regarded as Núñez's trivialization of *Cárcel*'s uncompromising message may not have guaranteed the sixteenth-century vogue for the work. He went on to edit Núñez's *Cárcel*, together with a short work on the fringes of sentimental romance, *La coronación de la señora Gracisla* [A8]. (*Gracisla* was wholly unknown until the Biblioteca Nacional acquired its unique manuscript in the same codex as that of *Arnalte*.) The introduction and notes are necessarily fairly short, because of the length limits of Exeter Hispanic Texts, but they give all the essential information and many stimulating ideas. A few years later, Whinnom published a translation of San Pedro's *Cárcel* and of Núñez's sequel [A9]. Both romances had been translated into English by Lord Berners in the first third of the sixteenth century, but a modern translation was needed, and Whinnom's is excellent. Short articles fill gaps in our knowledge: one [B21] shows that a poem in praise of Lucrezia Borgia plagiarizes one in a lost edition of *Arnalte*; another [B22] identifies the Marina Manuel to whom San Pedro had sent his *Sermón*. A work that has good claims to recognition as a sentimental romance is the *Historia de duobus amantibus* of Enea Silvio Piccolomini, later to become Pope Pius II. It was translated into Spanish in the late fifteenth century, and Whinnom's article [B4 = Chapter 13] describes and evaluates it, speculating on its possible influence on fiction in the late fifteenth and the sixteenth centuries, though he concludes that the influence must have been negative: the remarkable innovations in narrative technique in Spanish during that period could have been a recognition that the *Historia de duobus amantibus* had taken traditional narrative patterns as far as they could go. Whether one work can bear this weight is, I think, doubtful, but Whinnom's contribution to critical evaluation of the work is beyond doubt.

In the last decade of his scholarly work, Whinnom's interests turned increasingly to questions affecting the whole genre of sentimental romance, and notably to the question of generic terminology. Frustrated, as many of us have been, by the difficulty of finding precise and consistent generic terms in medieval Spanish, he looked closely at 'tratado', which a number of scholars had regarded as meaning 'didactic treatise', and he showed that its meaning was much more general, indicating merely a prose work of some length [B38 = Chapter 14]. Only when the same work was called, on the same occasion, both 'tratado' and 'estoria' might it, he concluded, have a generic label. Given the strength with which the opposite view had been expressed, it is at first sight surprising that Whinnom has not been challenged on this issue, but one's surprise evaporates as one re-reads his carefully marshalled textual evidence and his closely reasoned argument. The only more recent study, by John Dagenais, confirms Whinnom.[8] The culmination —though not the end—of Whinnom's work on sentimental romance is his critical bibliography [A12], one of the few bibliographies that have established themselves as classics of scholarship. It is genuinely critical: the brief comments are not only informative but incisive, bearing an authority that derives from many years of research into the primary material and from careful scrutiny of all the secondary sources. The policy of Research Bibliographies and Checklists is to issue supplements, and Whinnom, realizing that his commitments and his health would not allow him to work unaided on this project, asked Ann Mackenzie to help him. He had even less time than he supposed, and when he died his share of the project had scarcely begun. The first supplement, now almost complete, is therefore the work of a Deyermond/Mackenzie/Severin team. Yet administrative burdens and ill health did not wholly obstruct further work in this field: the last article published in Whinnom's lifetime [B44] reopens the apparently closed question of the fictionalized biography of Juan Rodríguez del Padrón, author of the first sentimental romance. We had all accepted the verdict that this was a nineteenth-century forgery (or joke), but Whinnom shows that it is of considerable antiquity, and suggests that it may be 'a belated sentimental romance' (p. 143).[9] And even that late article is not the end of the story: among Whinnom's papers I have found two versions of an article re-examining a *Cárcel de Amor* problem, and an edited version will soon be published [B49].

An early study applies Whinnom's skills as textual critic to the puzzlingly different versions of a short fictional work from the mid-sixteenth century, *El Abencerraje* [B6]. Though this has been to some extent overtaken by the discovery of additional witnesses,[10] the article remains valuable for its fresh insights into the work's quality as well as its transmission, and it is a pity that Whinnom did not return to it in the light of his later work on sentimental romance.

Research on Diego de San Pedro's *Passión trobada*, mentioned above, led to a fruitful wider investigation of the narrative religious poems of the late fifteenth and early sixteenth centuries: Íñigo de Mendoza's *Vita Christi*, the Comendador Román's *Trovas de la gloriosa Pasión* and *Coplas de la Pasión con la Resurrección*, Ambrosio de Montesino's *Coplas sobre diversas devociones y misterios de nuestra santa fe católica* (all composed in the 1470s and 1480s, and all in print by 1492), and Juan de Padilla's slightly later *Retablo de la vida de Cristo*. He advanced on two fronts simultaneously: the textual tradition of Mendoza's *Vita Christi* and the religious traditions that shape the style and attitudes of all the poets mentioned. These two approaches are linked: one article concludes with the words 'Our knowledge of the Spanish 15th century is still woefully inadequate, and while some broad generalizations may be useful, they are going to be subject to continuous correction for as long as basic bibliographical problems are neglected' [B12, pp. 287-88 = Chapter 4, p. 67]. The study of the textual history of Mendoza's work has two phases, one concurrent with Whinnom's work on the *Passión trobada*, and the other a much later result of a bibliographical discovery. In the first phase, two articles deal with three editions of Mendoza's poems printed in the early 1480s and their implications for the preparation of a critical edition of the *Vita Christi* [B10 = Chapter 2], and with the important, long known, but hitherto insufficiently studied Escorial MS K-III-7 [B11 = Chapter 3]. The latter article shows that in this MS Mendoza's poems other than the *Vita Christi* are copied from a printed text, but that the text of the *Vita Christi* is that of a second and thoroughly revised redaction. The second phase of Whinnom's study of Mendoza's text arises from a discovery by F. J. Norton of an Italian moralizing work printed in 1517 which includes eight stanzas from the *Vita Christi*. I have already quoted from a sentence in C27; the sentence ends: 'much depends on chance finds, and the private contributions of cooperative colleagues' (p. 180). In the present case, both Norton's find and his generosity in drawing Whinnom's attention to it were necessary preconditions for the new phase of textual study, but of course they would not have been fruitful without Whinnom's background of meticulous research on Mendoza's text and his acute analytical intelligence. His comparison of the eight quoted stanzas with the previously known *Vita Christi* MSS and printed texts leads him to the conclusion that we must either postulate yet another redaction of this long poem or construct a simplified stemma in which there were only two redactions, with some minor revision before the printing of the second; and his argument for the second hypothesis is convincing [B29 = Chapter 9]. These three articles do not make easy reading; no classics of textual criticism are designed for that. But they show Whinnom's originality, maturity of judgment, and willingness to take immense trouble in order to get things right. These qualities are found again in his work on the text of *Celestina*, discussed below, and in the introduction to the as yet unpublished facsimile edition of the *Cancionero de Hurus (Zaragoza, 1495)*. Projects for a facsimile of this important *cancionero* (chiefly composed of long religious poems, but including at the end other types of poem also) were in hand from the early 1960s, when Whinnom lent Antonio Pérez Gómez his microfilm of the unique copy. They have been dogged by misfortune (see p. 33, n.16A below), but there are now hopes that the edition will soon appear. Whinnom's introduction, some sixty pages of typescript, gives a detailed description of the volume (including its woodcuts), carefully analyses its likely printed and manuscript sources, and argues persuasively that the compiler was the printer Pablo Hurus.

While working on Mendozan textual problems, Whinnom was also, in the early 1960s, much concerned with the background from which the *Vita Christi*, the *Passión trobada*, and poems by Montesino, Román, and Padilla sprang. In two articles that complement each other without substantial overlap [B12 = Chapter 4; B13 = Chapter 5], he shows the weaknesses of the generally accepted view that these narrative religious poems are inspired by the Devotio Moderna and specifically by Ludolph of Saxony's *Vita Christi*. There is, as he shows, no firm evidence that Ludolph's work was known in Spain before the 1490s, when Montesino translated it (though it had been translated into Portuguese fifty years earlier); Montesino's version was printed in 1502–03. Thus only the works of Padilla (to whom Whinnom briefly returned in C46) and the second redaction of Montesino's *Coplas* could have been affected by the Castilian translation, and Whinnom urges that another explanation must be found for the distinctive—and to modern eyes often shocking—features of San Pedro, Mendoza, Román, and most of Montesino. As to the more general influence of the Devotio Moderna (a movement now best known through the *Imitatio Christi* of Thomas à Kempis), Whinnom shows that the strong Marian elements in the Spanish poems make such an influence unlikely, and that their imagery and narrative approach owe much to the thirteenth-century *Meditationes vitae Christi* of pseudo-Bonaventure. His arguments, based on extensive reading of often obscure primary sources, have in large part been accepted. Julio Rodríguez-Puértolas's authoritative monograph on Mendoza's *Vita Christi*, which is accompanied by an edition of the text, devotes a dozen pages to the issues raised by Whinnom, and though he rightly observes that Whinnom's scepticism about Ludolph's influence is too strongly expressed (the work's approval by the Council of Basel in 1439 and its translation into Portuguese in 1446 make its influence in Castile possible), he comes down on balance with Whinnom: 'El juicio de Whinnom se confirma así una vez más'.[11] A recent study that returns to the question of Ludolph's influence does not try to reopen the question for the poets who are mentioned above, arguing only that a very different kind of poem from the late 1490s owes something to Ludolph.[12] Even Giuseppe Mazzocchi, whose excellent edition of Román's *Coplas de la Pasión con la Resurrección* came to hand as these pages were about to go to press, and who reacts more strongly against Whinnom's conclusions than Rodríguez-Puértolas, recognizes the strength of part of his case and does not attempt to return to the pre-Whinnom state of opinion.[13]

The study of another facet of Diego de San Pedro's poetry—his 26 *canciones*, *villancicos*, and other forms of court lyric—led Whinnom to a major investigation of the *canciones* in that vast repertory of court lyric from the mid-fifteenth century to the early sixteenth, the *Cancionero general* compiled by Hernando del Castillo and published in 1511. A careful analysis of their language, regarded by almost all other specialists in late medieval poetry as so restricted and abstract as to make them largely unreadable, led him to a startling conclusion: 'There is good reason to suspect that a good deal of *cancionero* love-poetry is a tissue of veiled eroticism and *double entendres*' [A3, p. 22 = Chapter 6, p. 106]. This view, outlined in four and a half pages of his inaugural lecture, is developed with detailed evidence in an article written a couple of years later [B19 = Chapter 7]. In that article, Whinnom shows conclusively that the court poets of the generations represented in the *Cancionero general* apply increasingly restrictive metrical rules to the *canción* and that there is a corresponding restriction of their lexicon; more debatably —but still, I think, convincingly—he identifies on metrical grounds eleven *canciones* that may be regarded as typical of the taste of the period, and, since Quirós wrote four of them, identifies him as the most representative *canción*-poet; and he produces evidence that makes it difficult to see all of this poetry as the expression of a pure, platonic love. Difficult, but not impossible: as Whinnom acknowledges, it is in the nature of euphemism that one can hardly ever prove conclusively that an innocent meaning is impossible [B19, p. 381 = Chapter 7, p. 127]. He continued to work on these and related questions, including a detailed analysis of San Pedro's *canción* 'El mayor bien de quereros', which he gave as a lecture in Durham in 1973 (revised as A11, Chapter 6). Poems which appear to have an obscene meaning, but at the last moment produce an innocent one (a device found in a variety of cultures), are studied in a conference paper given in 1980 (revised as A11, Chapter 5, so already superseded when published as B39). These studies and B19 were brought together with other material to form the basis of three lectures given in Santiago de Compostela in the summer of 1980, and the lectures underwent further revision for publication as *La poesía amatoria de la época de los Reyes Católicos* [A11], in which material from the 1970 article [B19] is used in the first four chapters (especially in Chapters 3 and 4). This book is the fullest expression of Whinnom's distinctive approach to *cancionero* poetry of the late fifteenth and early sixteenth centuries, and it has—like the closing section of his inaugural lecture and the 1970 article—been widely influential. Few if any scholars would now say, as used to be said regularly, that this poetry is too trivial to merit serious study; Whinnom's exercise in rehabilitation was rapidly successful, and many studies are in progress or already published.[14] Most of those now working on this poetry accept Whinnom's view that many of the poems are ambiguous or euphemistic; Ian Macpherson, for instance, has looked at other poems in this light and found that some not studied by Whinnom do indeed fit his hypothesis.[15] It was inevitable that some studies of this kind should push Whinnom's method further than it could safely go or than its originator thought prudent: parts of the brilliant but still, unhappily, unpublished MA dissertation by A. J. Foreman (see p. 132, n. 33, below) are a case in point. To say that a sexual reading of a poem is possible is, as Whinnom knew, not to say that it is certain or even probable. Many poems, especially those in which religious terms may have a sexual meaning, need to be thoroughly studied.[16] It was also inevitable that Whinnom's view should occasionally encounter strong opposition. This would have happened even had the view been diplomatically expressed, but although he wrote with impeccably scholarly caution ('the possible sexual connotations', 'the suggestive possibility', 'a hypothesis which may explain the alleged vagueness of some love-poetry', pp. 126-28 = B19, pp. 379-81), his irritation with those who could not or would not see possibilities that were to him obvious sometimes caused him to express himself in an unduly personal way. It was, for instance, unreasonable as well as imprudent to attribute contrary opinions to sexual inexperience [B19, p. 376 = p. 124, below]. Not surprisingly, the measured dissent of J. M. Aguirre was followed by A. A. Parker's angry rejection.[17] The debate continues, but it is clear that majority opinion is now with Whinnom, and that he achieved a fundamental and, it seems safe to assert, irreversible change in critical attitudes to the court lyric of the Catholic Monarchs' reign. That alone would guarantee him a lasting place in the history of scholarship.

Other aspects of the poetry of this period engaged Whinnom's attention, though not as insistently as the narrative religious verse or the *canciones*. His reading of poetry fused with his study of contact vernaculars in a collaborative article on the occurrence of *lingua franca* in a poem by Juan del Encina [B17]; he identified [B27] a probable reference to the *Libro de Buen Amor* in a poem found in a mid-sixteenth-century *cancionero*, but composed in 1476–77, thereby casting further doubt on an assertion he had made ten years earlier [A3, p. 9 = p. 98, below]; and he clarified the textual history of the *Coplas de la reyna de Nápoles* and their relation to the ballad on the same subject, the lament of a queen for the loss of her husband [B35]. His reading of a book on numerological structure in Juan de Padilla[18] led him to reflect on the very difficult question of where to draw the line in numerological interpretation, and the result was a lecture on 'Mathematics, Magic, and Medieval Literature', in which the theoretical question is tested against a structural analysis of Juan de Mena's *Laberinto de Fortuna*; this will form part of a volume of lectures on medieval culture. Half a dozen book reviews, the first published in 1967, the last—the last review he wrote—in 1984, deal with aspects of *cancionero* poetry [C14, 21, 23, 51, 54, 58]; most of them not only offer a discriminating appraisal of the book but offer original suggestions on the subject-matter. And in the last years of his life Whinnom wrestled with the intractable problem presented by an encoded rubric in the *Cancionero de Herberay des Essarts*, leaving near completion an article which is to be edited and published by Ian Macpherson.

This may be the best point at which to discuss Whinnom's most famous and influential piece: the inaugural lecture delivered in 1967 and published the following year [A3 = Chapter 6]. As all hispanomedievalists and many other scholars know, the lecture drew attention to the dangers of three features that Whinnom saw as endemic in histories of medieval and Golden-Age Spanish literature (and in many other studies of these periods). The third 'form of distortion', unwillingness to accept obscene writing as an integral part of literature, has just been considered in the discussion of Whinnom's work on *cancionero* lyric. The first distortion against which he warns is the neglect of 'the immense, connected mountain-range of medieval Latin literature', which is 'a barrier to all non-amphibious hispanists' [A3, p. 6 = p. 97, below], and the study only of the occasional 'islands in the sun', works in the vernacular (the images came naturally to one who had just returned after six years in the West Indies). Whinnom was beyond doubt amphibious: he read extensively in classical and medieval Latin. And there is no doubt that he is right in saying that a reading knowledge of Latin is essential for the hispanomedievalist, and in his insistence that for some genres before the fifteenth century continuity is to be found not in the relatively few works in Castilian but in medieval Latin literature. Doubts do, however, arise when one reads some other paragraphs in this first section. Space does not allow a full discussion, so three points must suffice. First, the statement that 'an extraordinarily high proportion of the major works [of medieval Spanish literature] are freely adapted translations, amplified glosses, amalgams of borrowed passages and *topoi*, and close imitations of medieval Latin (and in some cases medieval French or Arabic) works' (p. 7 = p. 97), though true, is likely to mislead the non-medievalist. It looks like a statement that is peculiarly true of medieval Spanish literature, whereas a similar comment could be made about most medieval vernaculars. I do not mean that Whinnom set out to give a false impression: the two sentences that follow the one quoted are general statements about medieval literary culture. Nevertheless, the overall impression given by this section of the lecture is that Spanish literature in the Middle Ages is abnormally lacking in originality, abnormally dependent on Latin. (A more balanced view is given in a lecture on 'Ovid in the Middle Ages', to be published in the volume of lectures; there, Whinnom speaks of strong and persistent Ovidian elements in medieval literature as a whole, Latin as well as vernacular.) A second reservation concerns Whinnom's remarks about the intellectual inferiority of medieval Spanish literature, summed up in the famous sentence: 'Medieval literature in Spanish is, *ipso facto*, literature for illiterates, designed to be recited aloud for the entertainment and edification of the uneducated' [A3, p. 11 = p. 100, below]. Berceo's *Sacrificio de la Misa*? The Alfonsine scientific translations? Pablo de Santa María's *Edades del mundo*? Enrique de Villena's *Doze trabajos de Hércules*? Any hispanomedievalist could prolong the list. And the footnote in which we are told that 'in the Middle Ages Spain has nothing to touch the writing of people like Peter Damian [. . .]' (p. 12 = p. 109, below) is concerned primarily—though the restriction is not admitted—with philosophical and theological writing. No one would dispute the superiority of Latin to any medieval vernacular in these and similar genres, but in lyric and drama the superiority of Latin is by no means as obvious, and in epic and romance the vernaculars are very clearly superior. Both these reservations were apparent when Whinnom's lecture was published, but a third only later emerged fully. Whinnom exemplifies the dangers of assuming vernacular continuity by examining the possibility of *Celestina*'s debt to the *Libro de Buen Amor* (pp. 7-9 = pp. 97-98, below). Having answered the arguments for such an influence, he concludes: 'It is scarcely conceivable that any writer at the end of the fifteenth century could have known the *Libro de buen amor*:

it vanished from the sight of educated men from 1449 to 1790.' This was, even then, a rash assertion, one of the exaggerations for rhetorical effect that are often found in inaugural lectures, and the evidence published by Lucius Gaston Moffatt some years earlier shows it to be exaggerated.[19] Since then, further evidence has appeared (one piece of it contributed by Whinnom himself [B27]); this is not the place to list it in detail, but reference must be made to the recent work of Pedro M. Cátedra.[20] Discussion of these three issues has already occupied considerable space, so I must be brief in dealing with Whinnom's second form of distortion (pp. 12-18 = pp. 100-04, below): 'an aesthetic bias in Spanish literary historiography' (p. 18). Anyone who has tried to write a history of literature, and many who have tried to read one, will know that the demands of literary history and of literary criticism often pull in opposite directions. There is, as Whinnom says, 'no necessary connexion between literary merit and historical importance' (p. 13 = p. 101); innovatory work 'tends to be marked by confusion and uncertainty' (p. 13; cf. B36 = Chapter 12). He points to the danger that what should be literary history may turn into a string of critical essays on a small number of texts that appeal to our taste (he returns to this question, with abundant documentation, in B34 = Chapter 11); he does not, however, comment on the equal danger that exclusive attention to the tastes of the period concerned will lead to the writing not of literary history but of a history of popular culture. In striving to correct one kind of imbalance, Whinnom is in danger of creating its opposite. And we should not lose sight of the fact that having dismissed popularity in favour of intellectual distinction in the first section of his lecture, he reverses the process in some parts of the second section. We should, therefore, read this essay as a series of salutary warnings, warnings that have raised the standard of hispanomedievalist scholarship in the quarter-century since they were uttered, rather than taking it as a body of entirely consistent doctrine—which, of course, Whinnom never intended it to be.[21]

The fourth main area of Whinnom's interest within the literature of the Catholic Monarchs' reign—alongside Diego de San Pedro, narrative religious verse, and *cancionero* lyric—was *Celestina* and its progeny. Its connection with San Pedro is not as direct and obvious as that between long religious and short amatory poems, but *Cárcel de Amor* is an important source for the last act of *Celestina*, Rojas's work is in some sense a reply to the sentimental romances, and its innovations in fiction are as striking as those of sentimental romance. It was, however, the request for a book review that triggered Whinnom's first *Celestina* publication. The review—of J. Homer Herriott's attempt to construct stemmata for the *Comedia* and *Tragicomedia* editions—

outgrew its original purpose and became an article [B16] in which he cogently (though sometimes with undue vehemence) demolished Herriott's arguments, offering instead his own far more convincing stemma. Two major *Celestina* projects soon came to occupy much of his time. One was the edition of *La comedia Thebaida* (a novel in dialogue, circa 1520, modelled on *Celestina*), which was being prepared by Douglas Trotter when he died at the age of 38 in 1966; the second was a major book on *Celestina*'s textual history, authorship, sources, and interpretation. The *Thebaida* edition was taken over by Whinnom, who had succeeded Trotter in the Exeter chair, as a tribute to him, and was published as a joint work [A4]. Whinnom's preface describes the work that Trotter had done and what he has contributed as second editor. Although Whinnom insists that this is far from being the definitive edition and study that Trotter had planned, it is a model of editorial care and clear exposition. The *Celestina* book was conceived as a Student's Guide, to be published by Tamesis Books (this was before the planning of the series Critical Guides to Spanish Texts, which have a quite different aim). Whinnom worked intensively on this book in the mid-1960s: he first mentioned it to me in a letter of 9 August 1966, when 120 pages were already written, but by the end of the decade he had put it aside, and he never returned to it.[22] It has not dated as much as one might suppose, despite the quantity of *Celestina* scholarship in the quarter-century that has elapsed, partly because the issues with which he deals in the completed part are less subject to rapid changes of fashion than is literary criticism, and partly because of his remarkable prescience. Just as some of his conjectural emendations in *Arnalte y Lucenda* were vindicated by the discovery of manuscript evidence (see p. xiv, above), so an article on the introductory *argumento* to *Celestina*, that he wrote in 1966 but did not publish, has been vindicated by the recent discovery of a partial manuscript of Act 1.[23] It is, therefore, worth publishing the part of the book that Whinnom had completed, and plans are in hand.[24] Whinnom wrote several brief pieces reacting to work on *Celestina* by other scholars [B26, B32, and B46], an obituary of the Venezuelan *Celestina* specialist Miguel Marciales [C53], seven fairly short reviews [C28, 30, 36, 40–42, and 52], and a long review of Stephen Gilman's *The Spain of Fernando de Rojas* [C37]. These dozen items show his view of scholarship and criticism as a continuing debate, and they contain—even in short reviews—many important observations. The review of Gilman is marred by an outburst of anger in its final lines and by a failure to recognize that Gilman's approach, so different from Whinnom's own and with characteristic and obvious weaknesses, has equally characteristic merits that have become fundamental to *Celestina* studies. Nevertheless, this review makes many points that needed to be made, and it is unwise to read Gilman's book without also reading the review.

As well as these contributions to debate, Whinnom's later *Celestina* work includes three major studies, the first being a brief but fundamental note [B30 = Chapter 10], that shows—as so often in his work—his ability to see points that are obvious once he has drawn attention to them but that we had all failed to notice. For over a hundred years *La Celestina* had been very widely accepted as the book's title, even though all the early editions that abandon Rojas's own titles use *Celestina*, and many scholars writing in English had been misled into referring to 'the *Celestina*' (even Whinnom, in A4, uses what he was later to describe as 'barbarism [. . .] a blatant hispanism [. . .] this gross solecism' [B30, p. 20 = p. 158, below]). By the mid-1970s he had realized that *Celestina* was the correct title (he uses it in B26) and was rightly indignant when editors (as in B36) or printers would not allow him to use it. The effect of B30 was rapid: most of Whinnom's fellow-specialists fell into line (most of us with embarrassed backward looks at our earlier publications), and the use of '*Celestina*' (or, for those writing in Spanish, 'la *Celestina*') is increasingly frequent even among non-specialists.[25] A full-length article on Rojas's motives and personality [B36 = Chapter 12] continues the argument with Gilman over the nature and significance of Rojas's *converso* status (his arguments, now more moderately expressed, are convincing), and he offers a salutary corrective to many critics' view of *Celestina* as a near-flawless masterpiece. It has, he argues, serious flaws, but it remains a masterpiece, and its immense influence may be due to 'its very imperfections, [. . .] its ambiguity and [. . .] its ambivalence, and [. . .] the complexity of Rojas's personality' [B36, p. 68 = p. 185, below]. This was his last major piece of work on *Celestina* itself, but only a year before his death, when he was already ill and hampered by administrative burdens, he addressed the Academia Literaria Renacentista in Salamanca on *Celestina*'s sixteenth-century imitators, in a paper full of scholarship and of sparkling ideas for generic reappraisal [B45].

The works that most consistently and most deeply concerned Whinnom as a literary scholar are the product of a relatively short period in Spanish literature: the first version of Mendoza's *Coplas de vita Christi* was composed in the late 1460s, and the expanded *Celestina* and the latest poems of the *Cancionero general* in the first decade of the sixteenth century. Whinnom sometimes, in conversation, exaggerated this chronological bunching: in response to one of my cries of despair about things I should have known but did not, while he had known them all along, he said, 'Yes, I know most of Spanish literature from 1492 all the way to 1511'. His intensive study of one of the richest and most innovatory forty-year periods in literary history made him, of course, an unequalled expert, but it did not confine him. As well as his brilliantly original and influential work on contact vernaculars (enough in itself to occupy a lifetime for most scholars), he ranged widely over medieval and Golden-Age literature in his teaching, contributed occasionally to controversies on earlier medieval works, and used his extraordinary command of his specialist area as a springboard for provocative and memorable reflections on the study of literary history. Of his three pieces on earlier literature, the second to be written though first to be published stresses the importance of the preaching context for medieval collections of *exempla*, at least until the fifteenth century [B33]. The most recent of the three [B42] is a comment, based on his experience with pidgins and creoles, on the debate on the *kharjas* conducted in successive issues of *La Corónica*. He gives reasons for scepticism about some of the reconstructions offered for *kharjas* in Arabic script, since their linguistic mixture can only be code-switching (a phenomenon often found in Chicano speech), yet they violate normal code-switching practice. The Arabic-script *kharjas* emerge from this article as even less safe ground for literary study than had been supposed (though Whinnom should have told his readers whether he could offer similar objections to the Hebrew-script *kharjas*). The longest and the earliest of the three pieces, an extraordinary polemical *tour de force*, is still unpublished, but will be in the volume of papers already mentioned. Written in 1970 for the British Hispanists' conference, it challenges neotraditionalist theory of the epic by seeing what happens if we invert the assumptions: for instance, if we see the extant poetic texts as versifications of episodes from the chronicles. As a series of warnings about insufficiently documented hypotheses and shakily constructed arguments, it is superb; if it were to be taken as a coherent set of alternative hypotheses it would run into difficulties.

I have dissented from some of Whinnom's opinions, and have pointed to what seem to me to be occasional technical flaws in his arguments, but I have realized afresh, rereading the whole range of his literary scholarship, how few the flaws are. As to dissent, I quote again from Ian Macpherson's Preface to *The Age of the Catholic Monarchs*: 'He was sharply aware of the provisional nature of all we claim to be knowledge, and not afraid to be contentious in the interests of provoking constructive thought and discussion. He became despondent only when he detected signs that his efforts might lead to the dreaded establishment of new dogma' (p. ix). The fourteen studies included in the present volume are representatives of an unusually coherent body of literary scholarship, based on painstaking and rigorous research. They are the product of much thought; they are highly original; they sparkle with new ideas; every one of them is of lasting importance. Their publication in a single volume shows even more clearly why Whinnom's reputation is so high, and how much we have lost by his early death.[26]

Alan Deyermond
Queen Mary and Westfield College, London

Notes

1. I owe this information to Professor P. E. Russell. Dr Norma Perry Whinnom recalls that her husband said in the early 1970s that political hostility to Dámaso Alsonso was the cause of opposition to his thesis. It is possible that both explanations are correct. The statement that Whinnom spent a year in Madrid on linguistic research, made both in my memoir (*C*, 14 (1985–86), 355) and in Ian Macpherson's (*BHS*, 63 (1986), 265), is an error.
2. Four Spaniards (Pedro Cátedra, Víctor Infantes, Carmen Parrilla, and Nicasio Salvador Miguel) contributed articles to *The Age of the Catholic Monarchs*, and others would have done so had it been possible to enlarge the volume. A number of recent studies by Spanish scholars have been dedicated to Whinnom or to his memory.
3. 'Rhetoric and Feminism in the *Cárcel de Amor*', BHS, 54 (1977), 1-8.
4. Julio Rodríguez-Puértolas was justifiably angry at the refusal of its then owner to allow him to consult it, and his editing of one of its texts suffered unnecessarily: see his *Fray Íñigo de Mendoza y sus 'Coplas de vita Christi'* (Madrid: Gredos, 1968), p. 9. He was later able, thanks to help from Dorothy Sherman Severin, and from Whinnom, to circumvent the refusal of access: 'El *Cancionero de Oñate-Castañeda*', *Boletín de la Biblioteca Menéndez Pelayo*, 45 (1969), 331-45, reprinted in his *De la Edad Media a la edad conflictiva: estudios de literatura española* (Madrid: Gredos, 1972), pp. 55-72. While his work was in press, the MS was given to the Houghton Library, Harvard University, and Michel Garcia was able to obtain microfilm and begin work on an edition: 'Le Chansonnier d'Oñate y Castañeda', *Mélanges de la Casa de Velázquez*, 14 (1978), 107-42; 15 (1979), 207-38; 16 (1980), 141-49. It is surprising that the *Vita Christi*'s next editor made no attempt to see the MS, which had been in the Houghton Library for ten years when his edition was published: Marco Massoli says that it is 'un manoscritto privato di pressochè impossibile consultazione' (Frey Íñigo de Mendoza, *Coplas de vita Christi* (Messina: D'Anna; Firenze: Istituto Ispanico, Università di Firenze, 1977), p. 114 n.). (I should add, in self-defence, that the

unreservedly favourable comment on Massoli's edition that I appear to give in *Edad Media* (*Historia y crítica de la literatura española*, ed. Francisco Rico, I, Barcelona: Crítica, 1980), p. 303, was added editorially after the typescript left my hands.) The *Oñate-Castañeda* text of the *Vita Christi* has at last been published: *El cancionero de Oñate-Castañeda*, ed. Dorothy Sherman Severin with Michel Garcia & Fiona Maguire, Spanish Series, 36 (Madison: Hispanic Seminary of Medieval Studies, 1990), pp. 259-97.

5. *La Pasión trobada*, Pubblicazioni della Sezione Romanza dell'Istituto Universitario Orientale di Napoli, Testi, 6 (Napoli: Ist. Univ. Orientale, 1974).

6. The exception is Regula Langbehn-Rohland's *Zur Interpretation der Romane des Diego de San Pedro*, Studia Romanica, 18 (Heidelberg: Carl Winter, 1970), reviewed by Whinnom in C27.

7. Corfis's editions are *Diego de San Pedro's 'Tractado de amores de Arnalte y Lucenda': A Critical Edition* (London: Tamesis, 1985), and *Diego de San Pedro's 'Cárcel de Amor': A Critical Edition* (London: Tamesis, 1987). Some addenda and corrigenda for A5 and A6 are included in A7, pp. 317-24.

8. 'Juan Rodríguez del Padrón's Translation of the Latin *Bursarii*: New Light on the Meaning of *tra(c)tado*', *JHP*, 10 (1985–86), 117-39.

9. See, however, Michel Garcia, '*Vida de Juan Rodríguez del Padrón*', in *Actas del IX Congreso de la Asociación Internacional de Hispanistas, 18-23 agosto 1986, Berlín*, ed. Sebastian Neumeister (Frankfurt am Main: Vervuert, for AIH, 1989), I, 205-13. Garcia views the *Vida* more sceptically.

10. See Francisco López Estrada's edition: '*El Abencerraje': novela y romancero*, Letras Hispánicas, 115 (Madrid: Cátedra, 1980).

11. *Fray Íñigo de Mendoza*, pp. 175-76, at p. 176.

12. Mercedes Vaquero, 'La Devotio Moderna y la poesía del siglo XV: elementos hagiográficos en la *Vida rimada de Fernán González*', in *Saints and their Authors: Studies in Medieval Hispanic Hagiography in Honor of John K. Walsh* (Madison: Hispanic Seminary of Medieval Studies, 1990), pp. 107-19.

13. Comendador Román, *Coplas de la Pasión con la Resurrección*, Pubblicazioni della Facoltà di Lettere e Filosofia dell'Università di Pavia, 61 (Firenze: La Nuova Italia, 1990), pp. 23-29.

14. Three are of particular methodological interest: Vicente Beltrán, *La canción de amor en el otoño de la Edad Media*, Estudios Literarios, 1 (Barcelona: PPU, 1989), and *El estilo de la lírica cortés: para una metodología del análisis literario*, Estudios Literarios, 2 (Barcelona: PPU, 1990); Jane Whetnall, 'Songs and *Canciones* in the *Cancionero general* of 1511', in *The Age of the Catholic Monarchs*, pp. 197-207.

15. 'Conceptos e indirectas en la poesía cancioneril: el Almirante de Castilla y Antonio de Velasco', in *Estudios dedicados a James Leslie Brooks presentados por sus colegas, amigos y discípulos* (Barcelona: Puvill, 1984), pp. 91-105; 'Secret Language in the *Cancioneros*: Some Courtly Codes', *BHS*, 62 (1985), 51-63.

16. See Jane Yvonne Tillier, 'Passion Poetry in the *Cancioneros*', *BHS*, 62 (1985), 65-78.

17. Aguirre, 'Reflexiones para la construcción de un modelo de la poesía castellana del amor cortés', *Romanische Forschungen*, 93 (1981), 55-81; 'Sobre una interpretación de "El mayor bien de quereros" de Diego de San Pedro', in *Estudios de folklore y literatura dedicados a Mercedes Díaz Roig* (México: Colegio de México, 1992), pp. 793-801. Parker, *The Philosophy of Love in Spanish Literature 1480–1680*, ed. Terence O'Reilly (Edinburgh: U.P., 1985), pp. 35-38 ('Appendix: The Courtly Love Poetry of Castile'). In a lecture given in 1968, Parker had criticized the final section of *Spanish Literary Historiography* for—among other things— failing to produce evidence in support of Whinnom's views (see *The Philosophy of Love*, p. 35). This was unfair: as much evidence was given as could be fitted into an inaugural lecture. Parker also, in his 1968 lecture, said that 'the implication [of Whinnom's words] was that the style and language of all these poems are exclusively of this kind [covertly sexual]' (summary on p. 35 of *The Philosophy*). I do not see how that implication can be derived from Whinnom's words: he refers to 'a good deal of *cancionero* love-poetry [. . .] a great many poems' [A3, pp. 22-23 = p. 106, below]. It is fair to disagree with Whinnom's view, but it is not fair to accuse him of implying 'all' when he explicitly says 'some'. At some point, perhaps in the early 1970s, Parker sent Whinnom copies of this and two other lectures, saying that they were to be revised for publication as part of a book. Whinnom, by that time believing that what he had seen was the definitive version of chapters already in press (he refers to 'un libro reciente' [A11, p. 21] and 'fotocopias de los primeros capítulos mecanografiados' [p. 93 n. 29]), devoted Chapter 2 of *La poesía amatoria* to an attack on the views that Parker had not yet published (and that were, as it turned out, by no means identical with the ones that Parker did publish). Thus misunderstandings, and the delayed publication of Parker's book, made the controversy between two of Britain's greatest twentieth-century hispanists less fruitful than it should have been.

18. Henk de Vries, *Materia mirable: estudio de la composición numérico-simbólica en las dos obras contemplativas de Juan de Padilla, el Cartujano (1467?–1520), con datos biográficos del poeta y apuntes sobre la composición numérica en otros autores* (Groningen: the author, 1972).

19. 'The Evidence of Early Mentions of the Archpriest of Hita or of his Work', *MLN*, 75 (1960), 33-44.

20. *Amor y pedagogía en la Edad Media: estudios de doctrina amorosa y práctica literaria*, Acta Salmanticensia, Estudios Filológicos, 212 (Salamanca: Universidad, 1989).

21. It was reworked as a lecture, 'The Approach to Medieval Spanish Literature', given at King's College London a few years later. This second version, to be included in the volume of Whinnom's lectures on medieval culture, modifies some elements and concentrates more closely on medieval literature. It was translated for publication in Spain, but never published.

22. 'I haven't touched it since Rodríguez-Moñino pressed me to do the San Pedro for Castalia' (letter to Professor L. P. Harvey, 4 October 1977).

23. For the manuscript, see Charles B. Faulhaber, '*Celestina* de Palacio: Madrid, Biblioteca de Palacio, MS 1520', *Cel*, 14:2 (Nov. 1990), 3-39; '*Celestina* de Palacio: Rojas's Holograph Manuscript?', *Cel*, 15:1 (May 1991), 3-52. The article has now been published [B47].

24. See Deyermond, 'Keith Whinnom's *Celestina* Book', in press in homage volume for Charles F. Fraker.

25. A cogently-argued case for using Rojas's original *Tragicomedia* [. . .] title, rather than *Celestina*, is made by Jeremy Lawrance, 'On the Title *Tragicomedia de Calisto y Melibea*', in *Letters and Society in Fifteenth-Century Spain: Studies Presented to P. E. Russell on his Eightieth Birthday* (Llangrannog: Dolphin, 1993), pp. 79-92.

26. None of the opinions expressed here is necessarily shared by the other editors; I have given an entirely personal view of Keith Whinnom's literary scholarship. I should, however, emphasize that the few criticisms of Whinnom's work that I have made were, to the best of my recollection, made to him in every case, either in correspondence or in conversation.

The Scholarly Writings of Keith Whinnom: A Revised Bibliography

This is a revised form of the 'Tentative Bibliography' published in *The Age of the Catholic Monarchs*, pp. 1-6. Its criteria are explained, and material still to be published is described, on pp. 1-2 of that volume. The present revision corrects some errors (e.g. in the date of item B11), adds some brief comments, and brings the record up to date by incorporating three posthumously-published articles and other work now in press. A further revision will be necessary when additional items have been published.

A. *Books and Pamphlet*
1. *Spanish Contact Vernaculars in the Philippine Islands.* Hong Kong: U.P.; London: Oxford U.P., 1956, xiv + 130 pp.
2. *A Glossary of Spanish Bird-Names.* Colección Támesis, A,3. London: Támesis, 1966, ix + 157 pp.
3. *Spanish Literary Historiography: Three Forms of Distortion.* An inaugural lecture delivered in the University of Exeter on 8 December 1967. Exeter: Univ., [1968], 24 pp.
3a. Repr. in A13, pp. 96-113.
4. (Edited, with G. D. Trotter) *La comedia thebaida.* Colección Támesis, B,8. London: Támesis, 1969, lxi + 270 pp.
5. (Edited) Diego de San Pedro, *Obras completas,* II. *Cárcel de Amor.* Clásicos Castalia, 39. Madrid: Castalia, 1972, 185 pp.
5a. 2nd edition, 1982.
6. (Edited) Diego de San Pedro, *Obras completas,* I. *Tractado de amores de Arnalte y Lucenda; Sermón.* Clásicos Castalia, 54. Madrid: Castalia, 1973, 199 pp.
7. *Diego de San Pedro.* Twayne's World Authors Series, 310. New York: Twayne, 1974, 172 pp.
7a. Pages 113-16 translated as 'La renovación estilística de Diego de San Pedro', by Carlos Pujol, in Alan Deyermond, *Edad Media* (*Historia y crítica de la literatura española,* ed. Francisco Rico, I, Barcelona: Crítica, 1980), pp. 386-89.

xxxi

8. (Edited) *Dos opúsculos isabelinos: 'La coronación de la señora Gracisla' (BN MS. 22020) y Nicolás Núñez, 'Cárcel de Amor'*. EHT, 22. Exeter: Univ., 1979, liv + 113 pp.

9. (Translated) Diego de San Pedro, *'Prison of Love' (1492) together with the Continuation by Nicolás Núñez (1496)*. Edinburgh: U.P., 1979, xxxix + 105 pp.

10. (Edited, with Dorothy S. Severin) Diego de San Pedro, *Obras completas*, III. *Poesías*. Clásicos Castalia, 98. Madrid: Castalia, 1979, 327 pp.

11. *La poesía amatoria de la época de los Reyes Católicos* [the variant title on the cover is an error]. Durham Modern Languages Series, Hispanic Monographs, 2. Durham: Univ., 1981, 112 pp.

12. *The Spanish Sentimental Romance 1440–1550: A Critical Bibliography*. Research Bibliographies and Checklists, 41. London: Grant & Cutler, 1983, 85 pp.

13. *Medieval and Renaissance Spanish Literature: Selected Essays*, ed. Alan Deyermond, W. F. Hunter, & Joseph T. Snow. Exeter: Univ. of Exeter Press & Journal of Hispanic Philology, 1994, xlii + 228 pp.

14. *The Textual History of 'Celestina'*, ed. Alan Deyermond, King's College London Medieval Studies (forthcoming).

B. *Articles, Notes, and Review-Article*

1. 'Molière, his Teachers and *L'Avare*', *Outlook*, 1 (1953), 20-22.
2. 'The Intercontinental Movement of Labour in the Nineteenth Century', *Ekonomi dan Keuangan Indonesia*, 7 (1954), 78-88.
3. 'Spanish in the Philippines', *JOS*, 1 (1954), 129-94.
4. 'Was Diego de San Pedro a *Converso*? A Re-Examination of Cotarelo's Documentary Evidence', *BHS*, 34 (1957), 187-200.
5. (With J. S. Cummins) 'An Approximate Date for the Death of Diego de San Pedro', *BHS*, 36 (1959), 226-29.
6. 'The Relationship of the Three Texts of *El Abencerraje*', *MLR*, 54 (1959), 507-17.
7. 'Diego de San Pedro's Stylistic Reform', *BHS*, 37 (1960), 1-15.
7a. Repr. in A13, pp. 1-17.
8. 'The Religious Poems of Diego de San Pedro: Their Relationship and their Dating', *HR*, 28 (1960), 1-15.
9. 'The First Printing of San Pedro's *Passión trobada*', *HR*, 30 (1962), 149-51.
10. 'The Printed Editions and the Text of the Works of Fray Íñigo de Mendoza', *BHS*, 39 (1962), 137-52.
10a. Repr. in A13, pp. 18-35.
11. 'MS Escurialense K-III-7: el llamado "Cancionero de Fray Íñigo de Mendoza"', *Filología*, 7 (1961 [1963]), 161-72. Translated anonymously from 11a.
11a. 'The "*Cancionero* of Fray Íñigo de Mendoza": MS Escurialense K-III-7', English original of B11. In A13, pp. 36-45.
12. 'The Supposed Sources of Inspiration of Spanish Fifteenth-Century Narrative Religious Verse', *Symposium*, 17 (1963), 268-91.
12a. Repr. in A13, pp. 46-71.

13. 'El origen de las comparaciones religiosas del Siglo de Oro: Mendoza, Montesino y Román', *RFE*, 46 (1963 [1965]), 263-85.

13a. Repr. in A13, pp. 72-95.

14. 'The Origin of the European-Based Creoles and Pidgins', *Orbis*, 14 (1965), 509-27.

15. 'Two San Pedros', *BHS*, 42 (1965), 255-58.

16. 'The Relationship of the Early Editions of the *Celestina*' [review-article on J. Homer Herriott, *Towards a Critical Edition of the 'Celestina': A Filiation of Early Editions*], *ZRP*, 82 (1966), 22-40.

17. (With L. P. Harvey and R. O. Jones) 'Lingua Franca in a *Villancico* by Encina', *Revue de Littérature Comparée*, 41 (1967), 572-79.

18. '*Tafanario*: problema etimológico', *Filología*, 12 (1966–67 [1969]), 211-17.

19. 'Hacia una interpretación y apreciación de las canciones del *Cancionero general* de 1511', trans. Elena Huber from 19b, *Filología*, 13 (1968–69 [1970]: *Homenaje a Ramón Menéndez Pidal*), 361-81.

19a. Excerpts included, as 'Constricción técnica y eufemismo en el *Cancionero general*', in Alan Deyermond, *Edad Media* (*Historia y crítica de la literatura española*, ed. Francisco Rico, I, Barcelona: Crítica, 1980), pp. 346-49.

19b. 'Towards the Interpretation and Appreciation of the *Canciones* of the *Cancionero general* of 1511', English original of B19. In A13, pp. 114-32.

20. 'Linguistic Hybridization and the "Special Case" of Pidgins and Creoles', in *Pidginization & Creolization of Languages*, ed. Dell Hymes (Cambridge: U.P., 1971), pp. 91-115.

21. 'Lucrezia Borgia and a Lost Edition of Diego de San Pedro's *Arnalte y Lucenda*', *Annali dell'Istituto Universitario Orientale di Napoli, Sezione Romanza*, 13 (1971), 143-51.

22. 'The Mysterious Marina Manuel (Prologue, *Cárcel de amor*)', in *Studia iberica: Festschrift für Hans Flasche*, ed. Karl-Hermann Körner and Klaus Rühl (Bern: Francke, 1973), pp. 689-95.

23. 'Nicolás Núñez's Continuation of the *Cárcel de Amor* (Burgos, 1496)', in *Studies in Spanish Literature of the Golden Age Presented to Edward M. Wilson*, ed. R. O. Jones, Colección Támesis, A, 30 (London: Tamesis, 1973), pp. 357-66.

23a. Repr. in A13, pp. 133-42.

24. 'The Context and Origins of Lingua Franca', in *Langues en contact—Pidgins—Creoles—Languages in Contact*, ed. Jürgen M. Meisel (Tübingen: Gunter Narr, 1977), pp. 1-18.

25. 'Lingua Franca: Historical Problems', in *Pidgin and Creole Linguistics*, ed. Albert Valdman (Bloomington: Indiana U.P., 1977), pp. 295-310.

26. ' "El plebérico corazón" and the Authorship of Act I of *Celestina*', *HR*, 45 (1977), 195-99.

27. 'A Fifteenth-Century Reference to Don Melón and Doña Endrina', *JHP*, 2 (1977–78), 91-101.

28. '*Alguie*: compositores viejos y editores nuevos', in *Libro-homenaje a D. Antonio*

Pérez Gómez, [ed. J. Pérez Gómez] (Cieza: . . . la fonte que mana y corre . . ., 1978), II, 269-73.

29. 'Fray Íñigo de Mendoza, Fra Jacobo Maza, and the Affiliation of Some Early MSS of the *Vita Christi*', *Annali di Ca' Foscari*, 16 (1977 [1979]), 129-39.

29a. Repr. in A13, pp. 143-55.

30. ' "*La Celestina*", "the *Celestina*", and L2 Interference in L1', *Cel*, 4, no. 2 (Nov. 1980), 19-21.

30a. Repr. in A13, pp. 156-58.

31. 'Creolization in Linguistic Change', in *Theoretical Orientations in Creole Studies*, ed. Albert Valdman and Arnold Highfield (New York: Academic Press, 1980), pp. 203-12.

32. 'Dr. Severin, the Partridge, and the Stalking-Horse', *Cel*, 4, no. 2 (Nov. 1980), 23-25.

33. 'La Littérature exemplaire du Moyen-Âge castillan et l'hispanisme britannique', *Mélanges de la Casa de Velázquez*, 15 (1979 [1980]), 594-601.

34. 'The Problem of the "Best-Seller" in Spanish Golden-Age Literature', *BHS*, 57 (1980), 189-98.

34a. Excerpts translated, as 'Manuscritos, impresos y mercado editorial', by Carlos Pujol, in Bruce W. Wardropper *et al.*, *Siglos de oro: barroco* (*Historia y crítica de la literatura española*, ed. Francisco Rico, III, Barcelona: Crítica, 1983), pp. 90-91.

34b. Repr. in A13, pp. 159-75.

35. 'Desde las coplas hasta el romance de la reina de Nápoles', in *Aspetti e problemi delle letterature iberiche: studi offerti a Franco Meregalli*, ed. Giuseppe Bellini (Roma: Bulzoni, 1981), pp. 371-83.

36. 'Interpreting *La Celestina*: The Motives and the Personality of Fernando de Rojas', in *Mediaeval and Renaissance Studies on Spain and Portugal in Honour of P.E. Russell*, ed. F. W. Hodcroft *et al.* (Oxford: Society for the Study of Mediaeval Languages and Literature, 1981), pp. 53-68 [the inclusion of '*La*' in the title, despite B30, is editorial].

36a. Excerpts translated, as 'Los motivos de Fernando de Rojas', by Jordi Beltrán or Eduard Márquez, in Alan Deyermond, *Edad Media: primer suplemento* (*Historia y crítica de la literatura española*, ed. Francisco Rico, I.1, Barcelona: Crítica, 1991), pp. 389-94.

36b. Repr. in A13, pp. 176-90.

37. 'Non-Primary Types of Language', in *Logos semantikos: studia linguistica in honorem Eugenio Coseriu 1921–1981*, V: *Geschichte und Architektur der Sprachen*, ed. Brigitte Schlieben-Lange (Berlin: Walter de Gruyter; Madrid: Gredos, 1981), pp. 227-41.

38. '*Autor* and *Tratado* in the Fifteenth Century: Semantic Latinism or Etymological Trap?', *BHS*, 59 (1982), 211-18.

38a. Repr. in A13, pp. 204-17.

39. 'La defraudación del lector: un recurso desatendido de la poesía cancioneril', in *Actas del Séptimo Congreso de la Asociación Internacional de Hispanistas celebrado en*

Venecia del 25 al 30 de agosto de 1980, ed. Giuseppe Bellini (Roma: Bulzoni, for AIH, 1982), II, 1047-52.

40. 'En los márgenes de la lengua: variedades no primarias del idioma', in *Actas del Cuarto Congreso Internacional de Hispanistas celebrado en Salamanca, agosto de 1971*, ed. Eugenio de Bustos Tovar (Salamanca: AIH, Consejo General de Castilla y León, and Universidad de Salamanca, 1982), II, 835-44.

41. 'The *Historia de duobus amantibus* of Aeneas Sylvius Piccolomini (Pope Pius II) and the Development of Spanish Golden-Age Fiction', in *Essays on Narrative Fiction in the Iberian Peninsula in Honour of Frank Pierce*, ed. R. B. Tate (Oxford: Dolphin, 1982), pp. 243-55.

41a. Repr. in A13, pp. 191-203.

42. 'The *Mamma* of the *Kharjas*, or Some Doubts Concerning Arabists and Romanists', *C*, 11 (1982–83), 11-17.

43. '*Cancionero general*', in *Dictionary of the Middle Ages*, ed. Joseph R. Strayer, III (New York: Charles Scribner's Sons, for the American Council of Learned Societies, 1983), 63. 'Diego de San Pedro', *ibid.*, X (1988), 645-46.

44. 'The Marquis of Pidal Vindicated: The Fictional Biography of Juan Rodríguez del Padrón', *C*, 13 (1984–85), 142-44.

45. 'El género celestinesco', in *Literatura en la época del Emperador*, ed. Víctor García de la Concha, Acta Salmanticensia, Academia Literaria Renacentista, 5 (Salamanca: Univ., 1988), pp. 119-30.

45a. 'El linaje de *La Celestina*' [the title is editorial], *Ínsula*, no. 490 (Sept. 1987), 3-4. Partial preprinting of 45.

46. 'Albrecht von Eyb's *Margarita poetica*: What Every *Celestinista* Should Know', ed. Alan Deyermond, *Cel*, 13, no. 2 (Nov. 1989), 45-47.

47. 'The *Argumento* to *Celestina*', ed. Alan Deyermond, *Cel*, 15, no. 2 (Nov. 1991), 19-30.

48. 'The Form of *Celestina*: Dramatic Antecedents', ed. Alan Deyermond, *Cel*, 17, no. 2 (Nov. 1993: *Studies in Honor of Peter Russell*, in press).

49. 'Cardona, the Crucifixion, and Leriano's Last Drink', ed. Alan Deyermond, in *Studies on the Sentimental Romance*, ed. Joseph J. Gwara & E. Michael Gerli (London: Tamesis, forthcoming).

C. *Reviews and Obituary*

1. Rev. of Watt Stewart, *Chinese Bondage in Peru. JOS*, 1 (1954), 230-32.

2. Rev. of Lily Abegg, *The Mind of East Asia. JOS*, 1 (1954), 237-38.

3. Rev. of E. R. Hope, *Karlgren's Glottal Stop Initial in Ancient Chinese, with Particular Reference to the hPhags-pa Alphabet and to Certain Points of Linguistic Psychology. JOS*, 2 (1955), 158-72.

4. Rev. of Stefan Wurm, *The Turkic Languages of Central Asia: Problems of Planned Culture Contact* and *Turkic People of the USSR: Their Historical Background, their Languages and the Development of Soviet Linguistic Policy. JOS*, 2 (1955), 182-83.

5. Rev. of T. Burrow, *The Sanskrit Language. JOS*, 2 (1955), 347-55.

6. Rev. of Joaquín de Entrambasaguas, *Miscelánea erudita: primera serie. BHS*, 35 (1958), 62.

7. Rev. of *Cuentas de Gonzalo de Baeza, tesorero de Isabel la Católica*, ed. Antonio and E. A. de la Torre. *BHS*, 35 (1958), 232-33.

8. Rev. of Juan Marichal, *La voluntad de estilo. BHS*, 36 (1959), 171-72.

9. Rev. of Manuel Alvar, *El español hablado en Tenerife. BHS*, 37 (1960), 259.

10. Rev. of William E. Bull, *Time, Tense, and the Verb: A Study in Theoretical and Applied Linguistics, with Particular Attention to Spanish*, and Henry Mendeloff, *The Evolution of the Conditional Sentence Contrary to Fact in Old Spanish. MLR*, 56 (1961), 313-14.

11. Rev. of Stanley L. Robe, *The Spanish of Rural Panama: Major Dialectal Features. BHS*, 38 (1961), 174-75.

12. Rev. of Fernán Pérez de Guzmán, *Generaciones y semblanzas*, ed. R. B. Tate. *BHS*, 44 (1967), 56-58.

13. Rev. of Lurline Coltharp, *The Tongue of the Tirilones: A Linguistic Study of a Criminal Argot. BHS*, 44 (1967), 137-38.

14. Rev. of Antonio Rodríguez-Moñino and María Brey Mariño, *Catálogo de los manuscritos poéticos castellanos (siglos XV, XVI y XVII) de The Hispanic Society of America. BHS*, 44 (1967), 288-91.

15. Rev. of Robert A. Hall, Jr, *Pidgin and Creole Languages. The American Anthropologist*, 69 (1967), 256-57.

16. Rev. of Emilio Lorenzo, *El español de hoy, lengua en ebullición. ZRP*, 83 (1967 [1968]), 620-22.

17. Rev. of St John of the Cross, *The Collected Works*, ed. and trans. K. Kavanaugh and O. Rodríguez. *Theology*, 71 (1968), 326-27.

18. Rev. of Paul Cornelius, *Languages in Seventeenth- and Early Eighteenth-Century Imaginary Voyages. ZRP*, 84 (1968), 119-21.

19. Rev. of *Litterae hispanae et lusitanae: Festschrift zum fünfzigjährigen Bestehen des Ibero-Amerikanischen Forschungsinstituts der Universität Hamburg*, ed. Hans Flasche. *BHS*, 46 (1969), 153-55.

20. Rev. of Richard E. Chandler and Kessel Schwartz, *A New Anthology of Spanish Literature. BHS*, 46 (1969), 176-77.

21. Rev. of F. J. Norton and Edward M. Wilson, *Two Spanish Verse Chap-Books: 'Romance de Amadís' (c. 1515–19), 'Juyzio hallado y trobado' (c. 1510): A Facsimile Edition with Bibliographical and Textual Studies. BHS*, 47 (1970), 150-53.

22. Rev. of *Abaco: estudios sobre literatura española*, ed. Antonio Rodríguez-Moñino, 1 and 2. *BHS*, 47 (1970), 250-52.

23. Rev. of Antonio Rodríguez-Moñino, *Poesía y cancioneros (siglo XVI). HR*, 39 (1971), 91-95.

24. Rev. of *Verdores del Parnaso*, ed. Rafael Benítez Claros. *BHS*, 48 (1971), 164-66.

25. Rev. of Francisco Aguilar Piñal, *Impresos castellanos del siglo XVI en el British Museum. BHS*, 48 (1971), 270.

26. Rev. of Otis H. Green, *The Literary Mind of Medieval and Renaissance Spain*, ed. John Esten Keller. *BHS*, 48 (1971), 350.

27. Rev. of Regula Langbehn-Rohland, *Zur Interpretation der Romane des Diego de San Pedro*. *BHS*, 49 (1972), 179-81.

28. Rev. of June Hall Martin, *Love's Fools: Aucassin, Troilus, Calisto, and the Parody of the Courtly Lover*. *MLR*, 68 (1973), 144-45.

29. Rev. of *Texas Studies in Bilingualism: Spanish, French, Czech, Polish, Serbian, and Norwegian in the Southwest*, ed. Glenn G. Gilbert. *BHS*, 49 (1972), 293.

30. Rev. of Dorothy Sherman Severin, *Memory in 'La Celestina'*. *BHS*, 49 (1972), 297-98.

31. Rev. of Rachel Blomberg, *Three Pastoral Novels: A Study of 'Arcadia', 'Diana', and 'Menina e moça'*. *BHS*, 49 (1972), 298-99.

32. Rev. of José Simón Díaz, *La bibliografía: conceptos y aplicaciones*. *BHS*, 50 (1973), 278-79.

33. Rev. of Charles Faulhaber, *Latin Rhetorical Theory in Thirteenth and Fourteenth Century Castile*. *MLR*, 69 (1974), 198-200.

34. Rev. of José Siles Artés, *El arte de la novela pastoril*. *BHS*, 51 (1974), 382-84.

35. Rev. of Jerónimo Arbolanche, *Las Abidas*, ed. F. González Ollé. *BHS*, 51 (1974), 384-85.

36. Rev. of James Mabbe, *Celestina or the Tragick-Comedie of Calisto and Melibea*, ed. Guadalupe Martínez Lacalle. *MLR*, 70 (1975), 202-03.

37. Rev. of Stephen Gilman, *The Spain of Fernando de Rojas: The Intellectual and Social Landscape of 'La Celestina'*. *BHS*, 52 (1975), 158-61.

38. Rev. of Gerhart Hoffmeister, *Die spanische 'Diana' in Deutschland: vergleichende Untersuchungen zu Stilwandel und Weltbild des Schäferromans im 17. Jahrhundert*. *BHS*, 52 (1975), 404-05.

39. Rev. of Armando Durán, *Estructura y técnicas de la novela sentimental y caballeresca*. *BHS*, 53 (1976), 61-62.

40. Rev. of Pierre Heugas, *'La Célestine' et sa descendance directe*. *BHS*, 53 (1976), 139-41.

41. Rev. of Gaspar Gómez de Toledo, *Tercera parte de la tragicomedia de Celestina*, ed. Mac E. Barrick. *BHS*, 53 (1976), 141-42.

42. Rev. of Ciriaco Morón Arroyo, *Sentido y forma de 'La Celestina'*. *BHS*, 53 (1976), 344.

43. Rev. of Bruno Damiani, *Francisco Delicado*. *BHS*, 53 (1976), 345.

44. Rev. of Francisco Delicado, *Retrato de la loçana andaluza*, ed. Bruno M. Damiani and Giovanni Allegra. *JHP*, 1 (1976–77), 243-45.

45. Rev. of R. M. Flores, *The Compositors of the First and Second Madrid Editions of 'Don Quixote' Part I*. *BHS*, 54 (1977), 246-48.

46. Rev. of Juan de Padilla (el Cartujano), *Los doce triunfos de los doce apóstoles*, ed. Enzo Norti Gualdani. I: *Studio introduttivo*. *BHS*, 54 (1977), 338-39.

47. Rev. of Roger Boase, *The Origin and Meaning of Courtly Love: A Critical Survey of European Scholarship*. *JHP*, 3 (1978–79), 223-24.

48. Rev. of Augusta Espantoso Foley, *Delicado, 'La Lozana andaluza'*. BHS, 56 (1979), 61-62.
49. Rev. of F. J. Norton, *A Descriptive Catalogue of Printing in Spain and Portugal 1501–1520*. BHS, 56 (1979), 246-47.
50. Rev. of D. W. Lomax, *The Reconquest of Spain*. BHS, 56 (1979), 332-33.
51. Rev. of Nicasio Salvador Miguel, *La poesía cancioneril: el 'Cancionero de Estúñiga'*. MLR, 74 (1979), 222-23.
52. Rev. of Orlando Martínez-Miller, *La ética judía y la 'Celestina' como alegoría*. Cel, 3, no. 2 (Nov. 1979), 25-26.
53. 'Miguel Marciales', *Cel*, 5, no. 2 (Autumn 1981), 51-53.
53a. Translated by J. G. Lobo, *Hoy Domingo* (Mérida, Venezuela?), Suplemento (30 May 1982), 14.
53b. Repr. of 53a, in Miguel Marciales, *El castellano, idioma milenario* (Mérida: Universidad de los Andes, 1982), pp. 45-47.
54. Rev. of Marqués de Santillana, *Poesías completas*, ed. Manuel Durán, I and II, and *Los sonetos 'al itálico modo' del marqués de Santillana: edición crítica, analítico-cuantitativa*, ed. Josep M. Sola-Solé. BHS, 58 (1981), 140-41.
55. Rev. of *España en Extremo Oriente: Filipinas, China, Japón: presencia franciscana, 1578–1978*. BHS, 58 (1981), 278.
56. Rev. of Oleh Mazur, *The Wild Man in the Spanish Renaissance and Golden Age Theater: A Comparative Study Including the 'Indio', the 'Bárbaro' and their Counterparts in European Lores*. BHS, 59 (1982), 338.
57. Rev. of Juan de Flores, *Triunfo de Amor*, ed. Antonio Gargano. BHS, 60 (1983), 61-62.
58. Rev. of Kenneth R. Scholberg, *Introducción a la poesía de Gómez Manrique*. C, 12 (1983–84), 293-94.

A Note on the Texts

In general, the fourteen items reprinted below have been adjusted to the norms set out in the *Modern Humanities Research Association Style Book*, 4th edition (1991). Thus, for example, single quotation marks are used throughout (except for quotations within quotations), volume numbers of journals and series are given in arabic numerals, italics for emphasis and quotation marks for non-quoted words have been reduced to the minimum, page-numbers are given in the form 123-27 (not 123-127 or 123-7), and omissions from quotations are indicated by bracketed ellipses. There are three reasons for this: the divergent practices in the original publication of these studies are much more often due to differing editorial and printing rules than to changes in Whinnom's own practice; it is desirable to have consistency in such matters throughout the volume; and it is also desirable to avoid practices that distract the reader by diverging sharply from current norms. I have not, however, tried to bring the footnotes into line with modern practice by adding details of monograph series or of publishers where these are lacking in the original, partly because this would have meant a much more extensive change than the regularization exemplified above, and partly because in a few cases a quite disproportionate amount of time would have been expended in tracking down the details.

Printers' errors have been silently corrected, as have a few errors of Whinnom's—for example, in B23 = Chapter 8, where Whinnom says that he quotes with 'minor editorial intervention' from the 1496 edition of Núñez's *Cárcel de Amor* (p. 358 = p. 134, below), which is also the base text for his edition in A8, a couple of folio references may be seen, by reference to A8, to be wrong. I have not, of course, corrected where there is any room for doubt.

In forms of reference to medieval Spanish works, I have followed what I believe to have been Whinnom's usage at the time when he wrote. Thus, in Chapter 1 [B7], 'the *Cárcel de Amor*' is allowed to stand, as is 'the *Celestina*' [A3], even though in later years he insisted on '*Cárcel de Amor*' and '*Celestina*'. For studies published after Whinnom changed his mind about the correct form of reference, in which editors or printers imposed an incorrect form on him (see his comment on p. 157, below), I have naturally restored the form he must have used in the typescript. It is impossible to be certain about the chronological frontier, but I believe that I have got it approximately right.

Quotations have been left as they are in the original publication, even though a better—even a much better—edition may have been published in the meantime. To substitute quotations from a more recent scholarly edition would, even assuming that I was competent to make the choice in all cases, have given a spurious air of modernity to studies written in the late 1950s and the 1960s, and would have gone some way towards a rewriting of the pieces. They are of their time, even though they have dated far less than most other studies written at that time. I have, however, added to all page-references to the Gili Gaya edition of Diego de San Pedro's *Obras* a bracketed reference to the Whinnom (for volume III, Severin & Whinnom) *Obras completas*, so that readers may if they wish compare the readings.

I had at first intended to add in brackets references to work published after the Whinnom study, but I soon realized that this would inevitably be patchy (because of the varying level of my competence in the different subjects covered), and would amount to extensive rewriting. I have therefore confined myself to supplying references, or explanations for non-appearance, when work is mentioned as in press or in preparation. Where further bibliographical information is needed, it is given in my account of 'Keith Whinnom's Literary Scholarship', above.

With one exception, the fourteen studies are here reprinted in their entirety. The exception is the first three paragraphs of Whinnom's inaugural lecture [A3 = Chapter 6], since these are concerned not with the topic of the lecture but with a tribute to his predecessor, Douglas Trotter. Their spirit has been preserved by the addition of a dedication to Douglas Trotter's memory. Similar dedications have been added to the three articles originally published in homage volumes (Chapters 8, 12, and 13) and to the two originally published in memorial volumes (Chapters 7 and 14).

I have tried, with the technical exceptions noted above, to offer in this volume what Keith Whinnom wrote, which in some cases differs from the original publication. Chapters 3 and 7 are edited from a carbon copy of the English texts that were published in Spanish translation, and an addendum sent out with offprints of B19 = Chapter 7 is incorporated. Chapter 5 is edited from a carbon copy and checked against Whinnom's manuscript corrections to an offprint. For Chapters 4 and 9 corrected offprints have been used. The remaining nine chapters (1, 2, 6, 8, and 10–14) are based directly on the printed text, since offprints bear no corrections or, where no offprints were available, the journal is one whose proof-reading practice minimizes the risk of error. Thus, while it would be excessive to claim that this volume offers a critical edition of the studies that it contains, I believe that it contains their authentic texts, and in some cases better texts than those previously available. Readers interested in the work of so meticulous a scholar deserve no less.

I

Diego de San Pedro's
Stylistic Reform

In his dedication of the *Cárcel de Amor* to the Alcaide de los Donceles, Diego de San Pedro wrote (p. 114, lines 2-7 [II, 80])[1] that he had written the novel

> porque de vuestra merced me fue dicho que deuía hazer alguna obra del estilo de vna oración que enbié a la señora doña Marina Manuel, porque le parescía menos malo que el que puse en otro tratado que vido mío.

Sr Gili y Gaya (p. 114, note) says that 'oración' can hardly allude to one of his poems, and suggests that San Pedro meant either the *Sermón de amores*, *Arnalte y Lucenda*, or some lost prose work; he does not venture to identify the 'tratado'. This caution is perhaps excessive. Only one of the works of San Pedro is labelled 'tratado', and that is *Arnalte*. (In the Burgos 1491 edition, the presumed *princeps*, it is entitled *Tractado de amores de Arnalte a* [sic] *Lucenda*, and in the second, Burgos 1522, edition, *Tratado de Arnalte y Lucenda*. Gili y Gaya himself uses 'Tractado de amores' as his running head.) If we then identify the 'tratado' as *Arnalte*, the 'oración' must be the *Sermón* or a lost prose work. But the evidence is not of a sort to justify the postulate that any major work of San Pedro has failed to come down to us (the 'lost eclogue' of the histories of literature was written by Diego de Guadalupe); for San Pedro gives us a catalogue of his works in the *Desprecio de la Fortuna* (composed in 1498 or 1501) and mentions—apart from *romances*, *coplas*, and *canciones*, of all of which we have samples—only 'aquella Cárcel d amor', 'un Sermón que escreuí', and 'aquellas cartas de amores / escritas de dos en dos' (pp. 236-37 [III, 276]). There is no reason to suppose that these 'cartas de amores' are anything other than *Arnalte y Lucenda*. The 'oración', therefore, must be identified as the burlesque *Sermón*. Internal evidence establishes the chronology of *Arnalte* and the *Sermón* (cf. p. 106, 18 [I, 179] and p. 27, 28-29 [I, 109]), and that agrees with this interpretation.

San Pedro, then, is contrasting the prose style of *Arnalte*, 'el estilo que puse en otro tratado', with that of the *Sermón* and the *Cárcel*. The implication is that, for reasons unstated, he had adopted to write the sermon a style noticeably different from that of his earlier prose, and that, having noted Marina Manuel's preference, he then proceeded to write the *Cárcel* in the approved style. Modern critics have agreed with Marina Manuel. Menéndez y Pelayo thought the style of the *Cárcel* was its principal merit, and called it 'casi siempre elegante, sentencioso y expresivo, y en ocasiones apasionado y elocuente', while Gili y Gaya has condemned the style of *Arnalte*. He writes (p. xxii) that the book 'da la impresión de un autor principiante', and protests that 'el retoricismo [. . .] viene a ensombrecer con su docta petulancia la intimidad que quisiéramos descubrir'. (The *Sermón* has also been censured, by Gallardo, Menéndez y Pelayo, and Gili y Gaya, but the condemnation refers to the content rather than the style.)

I want in this paper to examine the nature of San Pedro's stylistic reform by comparing the style of *Arnalte* with that of the *Cárcel*, less thoroughly with that of the *Sermón*, and, where relevant, with that of the prose preface to the *Desprecio*. The fact that it was a deliberate and conscious reform may have some bearing on the dating of San Pedro's works, since Gili y Gaya writes (p. xxiv) that the superiority of the later style argues a considerable time-gap between the two novels—implying that the difference is due solely to a slow evolution of technique. The fact that he should so adapt himself to the demands of his audience illustrates a characteristic aspect of the literary personality of San Pedro. And finally this reform is noteworthy as a symptom of the change of taste in the time of the Catholic Monarchs, as an aspect of that larger cultural evolution which Menéndez Pidal summed up as 'Del retoricismo al humanismo'.

Throughout the fifteenth century, and especially in the earlier part, there is a good deal of imitation of Latin syntax: postponement of the verb, hyperbaton (also, as *transgressio*, accounted a rhetorical figure), use of the present participle, and so on. I shall consider here only two of the more conspicuous of San Pedro's latinisms: the postponement of the verb, and, to illustrate his employment of the Latin subjunctive, the use of *como* with the subjunctive in narrative passages. (I deal separately with the absolute construction later.)

The placing of the verb at the end of the clause is perhaps the most obvious and persistent syntactical latinism of art-prose in the fifteenth and early sixteenth centuries. It is found at the beginning of this period in the Archpriest of Talavera, appears in rhetorically elevated passages in the *Celestina* (consider Calisto's first speech), and is a feature of Guevara's style. It is one of the points Gili y Gaya (p. xxii) singles out for condemnation in

Arnalte. The contrast between *Arnalte* and the *Cárcel* is in this respect very marked. San Pedro's early practice is well illustrated by this paragraph (p. 30 [I, 111]):

> Otras cosas muchas comigo mesmo fablé, las quales, por enojoso non ser, en el callar dexo. Y después que ya de mí despedido fui, con mis pensamientos el nauío de mis passiones a remar comencé. Pero como la tormenta de las ansias grande fuese, nunca puerto de descanso fallé, y como con el graue cuydado los deuidos pensamientos oluidase, muy poco el palacio seguía, nin al rey de ver curaua; y como él a mis amigos muchas vezes por mí preguntase, de yr vna noche a palacio acordé.

The postponed verb is, on the other hand, extremely rare in both *Sermón* and *Cárcel*, and wholly absent from the prose preface to the *Desprecio*. More precisely: in *Arnalte* the verb of the principal clause is postponed in about 50% of the cases, while the verb of the subordinate clause is postponed in 75%. In the *Sermón*, the *Cárcel*, and the preface to the *Desprecio*, there is not one example of an artificially postponed main verb; while the postponed verbs in subordinate clauses are to be found in under 3% of the cases in the *Sermón* and the *Cárcel*, and not at all in the *Desprecio*.

In fifteenth-century elevated style generally, the use of the subjunctive tends to follow Latin rules rather than vernacular practice. *Como* followed by the subjunctive is a latinism inasmuch as it seems certain that the usage derives from the Latin use of the subjunctive with temporal and modal *cum*. It occurs, especially in narrative style, in numerous fifteenth-century writers, but in few with the same repetitive insistence as in the San Pedro of *Arnalte*. In all the narrative passages linking the letters and set speeches, *como* is easily the most frequent conjunction—occurring indeed more often than all the other subordinating conjunctions put together. In the opening chapter of *Arnalte*, 'Comiença la obra' (pp. 3-9 [I, 89-93]), it occurs eighteen times, only once without the subjunctive: 'y como de comer acabamos' (p. 8, 28 [pp. 92-93]), and here Burgos 1522 reads 'acabássemos'. In the corresponding chapter, 'Comiença la obra' (pp. 115-21 [II, 81-88]), of the *Cárcel*, *como* is used thirteen times, but only twice with the subjunctive (p. 117, 16 [p. 82] and p. 118, 12 [p. 84]). However, this reform is not effected before the *Cárcel*, for in the tale of Pyramus and Thisbe at the end of the *Sermón*, *como* occurs five times and always with the subjunctive. I postpone further comment on these syntactical latinisms.

*   *   *

If one were to undertake to count and classify each colour of rhetoric and each figure of thought in San Pedro's prose works, it might be possible to demonstrate statistically that in his early or late style San Pedro showed a greater or less preference for certain figures. But the impression gained from a careful reading of the texts does not suggest that the difference in the frequency of any given figure—apart from those I deal with in this paper—is such as to indicate a deliberate change of stylistic policy. And with the unconscious maturation of San Pedro's style I am not here primarily concerned.

For a limited number of rhetorical devices, including what Curtius terms 'figures of sound' and 'acoustic conceits', an appreciable difference is noticeable between the two novels. The author of the *Rhetorica ad Herennium*,[2] after defining and giving examples of the rhetorical colours *similiter cadens*, *similiter desinens*, and *annominatio*, comments (fol. 59) that all three are to be used 'perraro', very rarely. The medieval preceptists edited and studied by Faral[3] make no such reservation, and the figures are defined and illustrated without further comment. In the case of all three, it is as though San Pedro—as I shall show—had, in the interval between writing *Arnalte* and starting the *Cárcel*, taken to heart the remarks of the *ad Herennium*.

The figure of *traductio* has close connexions with *annominatio*, and it is convenient to consider them together. It is ambiguously defined in the *ad Her.* (fol. 53[v]), but the examples given there match the more precise medieval definitions: the same word, noun or adjective, is repeated in different cases of its declension; or the identical vocable is employed in different functions, as *amare*, 'to love' and 'bitterly' (a favourite medieval conceit). *Annominatio* (termed *paronomasia* by the classical and Renaissance rhetoricians) is in the *ad Her.* divided into ten varieties. It consists of using two or more words which differ from each other by the change of one letter, or the addition or subtraction of a letter or syllable, or of letters or syllables. Some of its forms are not imitable in Spanish, but the other kinds are: *temporare/obtemporare*, *leones/lenones*, *deligere/diligere*, *vincit/vinciit*, etc. The figure also covers anagram: *navo/vano*, *laudator/adulator*, and obscurer forms.[4]

Of these kinds of figure there are innumerable examples in the early works of San Pedro. Two of the most highly wrought specimens are to be found in his verse.[5] In the panegyric on Isabella in *Arnalte* (p. 15, 16-25 [I, 99]) there occurs:

> Nunca haze desconcierto,
> en todo y por todo acierta,
> sigue a Dios, que es lo más cierto,

> y desconcierta el concierto
> que lo contrario concierta;
> nunca jamás sale fuera
> de aquello con que él requiere,
> y como su gloria espera,
> porque quiere que la quiera,
> siempre quiere lo que él quiere.

And one of his *canciones* (p. 228, 22 [III, 258]), singled out for praise by Gracián (*Agudeza, Discurso* XXIV), has in twelve lines four variations of *querer*, four of *ver*, and eight of *perder*. I have not space to cite all the examples of *traductio* and *annominatio* in *Arnalte y Lucenda*; they occur on the average twice per page. A peculiarity of San Pedro's use of the figure (I lump them together) is that he is rarely satisfied with using it once—he goes on for several lines. I quote two examples by way of illustration:

> Tiénesme, señora y hermana mía, tan aquexado con tu quexar, que es forçado que me fuerce para lo que mis señales señalan claramente declararte. (p. 38 [I, 118])
> Así que pues ver tu tormento con doble pasión el mío atormenta. Y grand merced recibiría que de mi cuydado te descuydes sin en quién me trabaja más trabajarte. (p. 40 [pp. 119-20])

Even counting such complex examples as single occurrences of the figure there are over a hundred and sixty of them in *Arnalte*; in many cases the constituent element is repeated more than once ('siruo-seruicios-seruida'); and even more often repetitions are grouped together as in the examples I have just quoted. In the *Cárcel* on the other hand—a novel half as long again as *Arnalte*—the device is always used once only at a time; on two occasions only is the constituent element repeated more than once (p. 142, 15-16 [II, 108], and p. 161, 22-23 [p. 126]); and even including all the possible accidents one is hard put to it to muster four dozen examples. Furthermore, in the *Cárcel* the device is almost always linked with a figure of thought, to point some kind of antithesis. It is no longer the idle jingle 'poco a poco te apocas' (p. 29 [I, 110]) but the meaningful 'yguales en cerimonia avnque desiguales en fama' (p. 152 [II, 118]). San Pedro has not wholly abandoned the trick, but he has begun to use it 'perraro'. Again the reform is effected in the *Sermón*, before the *Cárcel*, for there all the examples (eighteen in twelve pages of prose) are linked with figures of thought, as in 'Si un pensamiento le traxere desesperaciones, otro le traerá esperança' (p. 104 [I, 177]). Similarly, in the late preface to the *Desprecio* there are only two examples, both meaningful (p. 234, 6 [III, 272], and p. 235, 29 [p. 274]).

The colours of *similiter cadens* and *similiter desinens*, which the *ad Her.* groups with *annominatio*, are linked in San Pedro with a more important phenomenon which I deal with later.

Another 'figure of sound', which abounds in *Arnalte* and is almost wholly absent from the *Cárcel*, is that device known to the late Roman grammarians, and to the Renaissance theorists, as *parómoion*. The medieval rhetoricians called it *paranomoeon*. Matthew of Vendôme (Faral, p. 169) defines it: 'Paranomeon est per principia trium dictionum immediate positarum ejusdem litterae vel syllabae repetita prolatio.' He later quotes Isidore's warning: 'si ternarius numerus excedatur, non erit scema, sed scemati contrarium'; but this three-only rule was not observed by medieval writers in either Latin or Romance. And for Nebrija *paromeon* is merely 'cuando muchas palabras comiençan en una mesma letra'. It is in fact alliteration —though Curtius objects to 'alliteration' since it conceals the influence of the late antique grammatical term *parómoion*.[6] It would be fruitless, if not impossible, even to count all the examples of the figure in *Arnalte*. But, as illustrations, consider:

> E non de dicha me quexara si quando la mano en el papel puse, la gouernadora della peresciera: pues de libre, catiua quise ser, dándote prenda sin nada deberte. (p. 54 [I, 132])
>
>   porque el mal tan pressuroso ha sido, que avnque el espacio de padecerlo pequeño te parezca, ha fecho grande el daño. (p. 22 [p. 104])

There are about twenty-five examples in the one and a half pages of the 'Carta primera de Arnalte a Lucenda' (pp. 21-22 [pp. 103-05]), and three consecutive words in the same clause begin with the same sound (Matthew's *paranomeon*) four times (p. 21, lines 1, 11-12, 24, 25-26 [pp. 103-04]). In the 'Carta de Leriano a Laureola' (the first one also), of equivalent length (pp. 132-34 [II, 99-100]), there is not a single instance of 'pure paranomeon', not more than half a dozen alliterative phrases altogether, and only one really good example (p. 133 [p. 99]):

> y si porque lo hize te pareciere que merezco muerte, mándamela dar,
> que muy meior es morir por tu causa, que beuir sin tu esperança.

I cannot prove my point with statistics: the reader must check my conclusions for himself.

*   *   *

Various critics have pointed out the occurrence of lines of verse in fifteenth-century prose. Blecua and María Rosa Lida de Malkiel have written of *arte mayor* lines in the *Cárcel*.[7] But while San Pedro wrote some four thousand lines of verse, all but seven of these lines (the *quebrados* of *canciones*) are octosyllables. If one is looking for lines of verse in San Pedro's prose at all, it would be more logical to suppose they would be octosyllabic. It is also very much easier to find them. Consider this passage from *Arnalte* (p. 28 [p. 110]):

> era fuerça que los ojos deseando la cegasen: de manera que en grand manera disfigurándome yba. Y como viesse que yo mismo de mi mal era causa, estando en aquellos solos lugares donde sienpre para mis fatigas abrigo fallé, contra mí desta manera a dezir comencé: ¡Oh morada de desdichas, o edeficio de trabajos! ¿qué es de ti? ¿adónde estás? ¿qué esperas?

In this short passage there are some fine octosyllables: 'era fuerça que los ojos / deseando la cegasen', 'como viesse que yo mismo', 'contra mí desta manera', 'Oh morada de desdichas / o edeficio de trabajos'. One might even argue for an *arte mayor* line 'para mis fatigas abrigo fallé', or a hemistich 'a dezir comencé'. But merely to suggest that San Pedro is writing lines of verse into his prose misses the whole point. I believe that he was attempting in Spanish an imitation of the medieval Latin rhyme-prose.

The medieval preceptists placed rhyme, as *similiter cadens* and *similiter desinens*, among the colours of rhetoric. The *ad Her.* had listed the figures (fol. 57[v]) among the *exornationes* destined to become 'colours', and the technical distinction between them is observed by all the theorists of the twelfth and thirteenth centuries (and indeed by Nebrija, though he uses different labels). (*Cadens* is 'non-significant' rhyme: *virtutis/felicitatis, hablaban/trabajaban*; *desinens* does not depend on conjugation or declension: *invidiose/studiose, hermoso/glorioso*.) But since in

> Lloraua de lástyma, no sosegaua de sañudo, desconfiaua segund su fortuna, esperaua segund su iusticia (*Cárcel*, p. 176 [p. 140])

we have *similiter cadens* without any rhyme I may perhaps use the term *homoiotéleuton* for rhyme at the end of parallel clauses. That is what it meant to the Venerable Bede[8] although later, in its various barbarized forms, it usually meant to the Middle Ages no more than *similiter cadens* (but *desinens* to Nebrija). But if *homoiotéleuton* is the most striking feature of Latin art-prose and the hall-mark of the medieval elevated style,[9] the most important secondary feature of this rhyme-prose is the rhythm, which is so marked that such prose has even been mistaken for verse. Without attempting to pursue the history of Latin rhyme-prose I may point out that Thomas à Kempis was still writing it in the fifteenth century; and the *Imitation* offers an exact Latin analogue for San Pedro's style in *Arnalte*, at least so far as rhythm and rhyme are concerned. I should like to quote a longish sample:

> Qui sequitur me non ambulat in tenebris, dicit Dominus. Haec sunt uerba Christi quibus admonemur quatenus vitam eius et mores imitemur, si uelimus ueraciter illuminari et ab omne caecitate cordis liberari. Summum igitur studium nostrum sit in uita Iesu meditari. Doctrina Christi omnes doctrinas sanctorum praecellit, et qui spiritum Dei habent ibi manna absconditum inuenient. Sed contingit quod multi ex frequenti auditu euangelii paruum desiderium sentiunt, quia spiritum Dei non habent. Qui autem uult plene et sapide Christi uerba intelligere oportet ut totam uitam suam illi studeat conformare. Quid prodest tibi alta de Trinitate discutere, si cares humilitate, unde displiceas sanctae Trinitati? Vere alta uerba non faciunt sanctum et iustum, sed uirtuosa uita efficit hominem Deo carum. Opto magis sentire compunctionem, quam scire eius definitionem.[10]

Though most of the clauses have a *cursus*-like ending, it is clear that it is not *cursus* we have to do with here, but a metrical rhythm. The reader will have noted the fine '*arte mayor*' couplets—in fact the splendid swinging Goliardic measure of Walter of Châtillon, the Archpoet, and the rest—like 'Haec sunt uerba Christi quibus admonemur / quátenus vitam eius et mores imitemur'. And the rhythmic phrase óo oo óo of the Goliardic hemistich occurs again and again: 'ómne caecitáte', 'córdis liberári', etc. But the whole passage is not metrical: it is prose and not verse, for the rhythm is sporadic; and when the ornament is supplied by some other rhetorical colour, rhythm and rhyme may be entirely absent for a while. Thus in the same short opening chapter there is an elaborate piece of *repetitio* (six consecutive sentences open with 'Vanitas . . . est') in which rhythm and rhyme are temporarily forgotten.

I suggest that Diego de San Pedro, in a manner analogous with Thomas's use of the Goliardic rhythm, wrote rhythmic prose—I mean an imitation of the rhythmic rhyme-prose, and not of the rather unsatisfactorily named 'rhythmic prose', *prosaica modulatio*—by using the verse rhythms most familiar to him: the octosyllabic rhythm oo óo oo óo (or óo óo óo óo) which is by far the most frequent accentuation in all San Pedro's octosyllables, and also in the fifteenth century generally; the *arte mayor* rhythms like (o)ó oo óo oó oo óo, 'dándote prenda sin nada deberte', or óo oo óo oó oo ó(o), 'para mis fatigas abrigo fallé'; and—possibly—even the Goliardic measure.

Before looking at the rhyme there is one other aspect of the rhythmic structure of San Pedro's prose to consider: the rhetorical colour known as *compar*. For at least one medieval rhetorician *compar was* rhyme.[11] According to the *ad Her.* (fol. 57), the figure consists of parallel clauses having an equal or almost equal, 'fere par', number of syllables. The figure is of enormous importance in *Arnalte*.

While the octosyllable is easily the most frequent unit, the paired phrases or clauses may be each of any length from seven to twenty syllables —heptasyllables like (p. 30, 2-3 [I, 111]) 'e si no te valiere / a la razón requiere'; eneasyllables like (p. 24, 22-23 [p. 106]) 'Que dañas la condición tuya / y destruyes la salud mía' (where the second line, with contiguous accents on 7 and 8, does not have a Spanish verse-rhythm at all); decasyllables like (p. 39, 19-20 [p. 119]) ' porque el amor defiende con priesa / e ventura combate de espacio'. I cannot find a pair of hendecasyllables: a hendeca-syllable seems always to be matched with a dodecasyllable, and both are always explicable as *arte mayor*. With shorter and longer lines than these there are complications. There are four tetrasyllables (p. 48, 8-9 [p. 126]), 'que la ames / y la quieras / y la temas / y la rehuses' (the last line 'almost equal')—but perhaps they are better regarded as a pair of octosyllables. Pairs of hexasyllables do not constitute *compar*, for in all I have found there is no *membrum*;[12] they are simply *arte mayor* lines thrown in singly to help along the rhythm, like (p. 24, 30-31 [p. 107]) 'que en sola tu habla está mi consuelo'. Pentasyllables, on the other hand, never occur in pairs but in fours: they are pairs of decasyllables. Lines of more than twelve syllables normally have a completely irregular rhythm.

As for the rhyme, ignoring the distinction between *similiter cadens* and *similiter desinens*, it is in Thomas à Kempis of two kinds: a full consonance, like 'admonemur-imitemur', 'illuminari-liberari', 'compunctionem-defini-tionem', or a rhyme of the unaccented final syllable, like 'habent-inuenient', 'iustum-carum', etc. In *Arnalte* also there are these two kinds of rhyme. There is full consonance, in what looks like a verse couplet, in 'e si no te valiere a la razón requiere', but more often full rhyme is reserved for pairs of clauses in which the rhythm is less obvious, in which the clauses do not contain an exactly equal number of syllables, or for matching rhythmic clauses separated by intervening clauses. Thus (p. 28, 5-6 [pp. 109-10]) 'las bozes della su dormir de Lucenda recordar pudieron; pero los gritos de mis angustias nunca su galardón vieron' is, with eighteen and seventeen syllables, 'almost equal' *compar*. Consider also (p. 32, 12-16 [p. 113]):

> pero más con temor de su no
> que con esperança de su sí,
> no con menos dolor que acatamiento allegué,
> y con desigualados sospiros
> y con turbación conoscida,
> que quisiese comigo dançar le supliqué.

Or (p. 18, 8-11 [p. 101]):

> Pero quise por saber
> lo que sabes oyrte
> y porque en ella señalases,
> en plática tan fuerte
> quise ponerte
> y esto porque de mis pasiones
> quiero notorio hazerte.

When the rhymes are unaccented finals,[13] the fact that they are intended as rhymes is often pointed either by a marked rhythm, even if the clauses are not of exactly equal length, or by *compar* with *membra* of exactly equal length, e.g. p. 37, 3-5 [p. 117].

There is, therefore, considerable subtlety in San Pedro's rhyme-prose. There are various factors to consider. First of all there is a marked and recurrent rhythm of one of two main types: the 'trochaic' octosyllable, and, less frequent, the *arte mayor* (o)ó oo óo oó oo óo. There is *compar*, with clauses or phrases of almost every length from seven to twenty syllables. And there is rhyme. Rarely indeed do all three occur together. If there is fully consonant rhyme, the rhythm of the two clauses is different, or the number of syllables is unequal, or the clauses are separated by other clauses of distinct rhythmic structure; if there is perfect *compar*, full rhyme is very rarely used, and the rhythms are usually different; if a rhythm is continuous for several 'lines', it is not marked by rhyme, and will sometimes persist in spite of hypercataleptic syllables. San Pedro is writing prose, not verse.

In the *Cárcel* there is no consistent or marked rhythm; unless one ignores the natural phonic groups, *arte mayor* lines are not there more frequent than in any piece of modern Spanish prose; and there is no fully consonant rhyme. But there is *compar*; thus (p. 138, 17-18 [II, 104]): 'Iuzgándola me alegraua, oyéndola me entristecía' (eight and nine syllables, linked with the colour *contentio*, a highly specialized form of antithesis); or (p. 139, 27-28 [p. 105]): 'la dispusición en que estó ya la vees, la priuación de mi sentido ya la conoces, la turbación de mi lengua ya la notas' (twelve, fourteen, and twelve syllables); or (p. 138, 14-17 [p. 104]): 'Todas las señales de voluntad vencida vi en sus aparencias; todos los desabrimientos de muger sin amor vi en sus palabras' (twenty syllables each: they cannot be split into shorter units).

Before going on to examine another important difference between the style of *Arnalte* and that of the *Cárcel*, there are one or two points I should like to make here, in part recapitulating my argument. With regard to all the other colours of rhetoric, figures of thought, and methods of *amplificatio*, there is no striking difference between the two novels. The only colours San Pedro has virtually abandoned are the 'acoustic conceits' of *annominatio* and *traductio*, and *paranomoeon*—the meaningless jingle like 'poco a poco te apocas', and the alliterative 'espacio de padecerlo pequeño te parezca'—and along with these the rhyme of *similiter cadens* and *similiter desinens*. Rhythm, which is not discussed by the medieval theorists, is also abandoned. All these things hang together. In the *Cárcel* he is as concerned as ever with thought and balanced structure, but he is no longer concerned with the *sound* of his prose. Taking it a stage further, in the *Cárcel* San Pedro's figures of thought are more thoughtful. In *Arnalte*, for instance, his amplification is sometimes very weak: perhaps the best—or worst—example (one of the sub-divisions of *expolitio*, *aferre contrarium*) is (p. 22, 5-7 [p. 104]): 'por mayor bien auré por ti perderme que por nadie ganarme', where 'ganarme' is quite meaningless, except as a balance to 'perderme'. One might cite many more instances of San Pedro's weakening the force of what he intends for the sake of amplifying with *expolitio*, *oppositio* or *interpretatio*. *Amplificatio* in the *Cárcel* is never so weak or pointless.

My last point of difference: in the *Cárcel* San Pedro is brevity-conscious. This shows itself in two ways: in the frequent use of the *brevitas* topic, and in the employment of the techniques of *abbreviatio*. In the *Cárcel* San Pedro returns twenty-three times to the brevity-topic, usually to finish off a speech or a letter. He stops short because to go on would arouse the reader's or the character's interlocutor's distaste, for 'prolixity is tedious' ('si el alargar no fuese enoioso', p. 207 [p. 171]). There are many variations on the theme, and often it is combined with the *fastidium* topic. As an illustration: 'Y porque detenerme en plática tan fea ofenda mi lengua, no digo más' (p. 130 [p. 96]). There are eight letters in the *Cárcel* (not counting the challenge and reply) and five of them end with a *brevitas* formula. The topic (or trope: *significatio per abscissionem*) is, of course, a commonplace in fifteenth-century literature, but it is used in *Arnalte* only seven times in all (pp. 3 [88-89], 30 [111], 38 [118], 43 [122], 44 [122], 50 [127], 71 [146]).

But if the brevity-formula is often an excuse for saying no more on some subject, in other cases there is more to it than that; for instead of saying, 'Since prolixity is tedious, I shall *stop*', San Pedro sometimes says, 'Since prolixity is tedious, I shall *be brief*'. Thus Leriano, having discoursed on the 'quinze causas por que yerran los que en esta nación [i.e. women] ponen lengua' (pp. 192-95 [pp. 156-60]), then announces that, 'dexada toda prolixidad', he will tell Tefeo twenty reasons why men are obliged to women. Or again, having given various examples of virtuous women, he says (p. 205 [p. 169]) 'por la breuedad alegaré algunas modernas de la castellana nación'. The prolixity and brevity of which he speaks are to be understood in a special sense: 'dexada toda prolixidad' means that San Pedro is to write without using any rhetorical ornament or the techniques of *amplificatio*; 'por la breuedad', that he intends to employ the techniques of *abbreviatio*.

Faral devotes no more than half a page to *abbreviatio*. He remarks—and with all reason—that vernacular writers were not interested in the theory, in part because all its methods were not applicable in the vernacular, but mainly because brevity was not their aim. San Pedro's concern with brevity in the *Cárcel* is a further symptom of his attempt to follow the new rhetorical doctrines of the humanists.

Seven different methods are listed by the medieval preceptists. The classification of them is irregular and illogical, but for the moment I follow the order of John of Sicily and of Geoffrey of Vinsauf's *Poetria nova*. They are: *emphasis* or *expressio*; *articulus*, which is also one of the colours; the ablative absolute; the avoidance of *amplificatio* ('vitanda omnia quae prolixitatem inducant'); *intellectio*, which is also a trope (synecdoche to the Renaissance and later grammarians); *dissolutio* or *dissolutum*, which is a colour of rhetoric; and the present participle, *participans*.

Leaving aside synecdoche and the related figure of *expressio*, and the fourth method, 'dexada toda prolixidad', the remaining methods fall into two groups. *Articulus* and *dissolutio* are varieties of what we should now class as one figure, asyndeton; and it is convenient to consider the two participial constructions together. Adapting them to Spanish, there is the absolute construction with a past participle, corresponding with an ablative absolute, and the construction with the present participle (as English grammars have it) or *gerundio*. In San Pedro the contrast between the narrative passages in *Arnalte* and those in the *Cárcel* is striking: what is expressed by means of subordinate clauses in *Arnalte* is expressed in the *Cárcel* by participles.

Consider the narrative of the battle in the *Cárcel* (pp. 175-80 [pp. 140-46]). It contains seventeen examples of an absolute construction with a past participle, e.g. (p. 176, 14-16 [p. 141]) 'Finalmente, dexadas las dubdas, sabida la respuesta que Galio me dió, començó a proueer [. . .]', and sixteen examples of *participans*, e.g. (p. 178, 29-33 [p. 144]) 'començólo a hazer esforçando los suyos con animosas palabras, quedando sienpre en la reçaga, sufriendo la multitud de los enemigos con mucha firmeza de coraçón'. In narrative passages one of these absolute constructions occurs in the *Cárcel* on an average once in five lines. In *Arnalte* the picture is very different. There the devices are not unknown, but, not only are they used very much less often, they are employed inextricably confused with the techniques of *amplificatio*: they are used, not to abbreviate a narrative, but simply as another kind of ornament. As with *annominatio*, the absolute constructions occur in a rash: and though there are seven in seven consecutive lines on p. 72 [p. 147], one must search far for another example.

There is no example of *articulus* in San Pedro's prose works; but there are in the *Cárcel* numerous examples of *dissolutio*. Thus (p. 128, 15-19 [p. 95]):

> todos los males del mundo sostiene: dolor le atormenta, pasión le
> persigue, desesperança le destruye, muerte le amenaza, pena le secuta,
> pensamiento le desuela, deseo le atribula, tristeza le condena, fe no le
> salua.

Of course not all the examples are as elaborate as this—they consist usually of three or four clauses. In *Arnalte* the device is used scarcely at all.

To sum up, therefore: the principal features of San Pedro's stylistic reform are:

(a) the abandonment of syntactical latinisms such as the postponement of the verb and the use of the Latin subjunctive;
(b) the severe reduction of the use of such acoustic conceits as *annominatio* and '*paranomoeon*';
(c) the renunciation of the attempt to write Spanish rhyme-prose; and
(d) the employment of the techniques of *abbreviatio* in narrative style.

In all this—with the single exception of the use of the subjunctive with *como*—the *Sermón* agrees with the *Cárcel*. Thus in the *Sermón* there is no imitation of Latin syntax; there are only one or two examples of *annominatio*, and none of them elaborate; *parómoion* is rarer even than in the *Cárcel*; the prose is certainly not rhyme-prose; and as for the *abbreviatio*, in the one short piece of narrative in the *Sermón*, the *enxemplo* of Pyramus and Thisbe (pp. 109-10 [I, 181-83]), there are nine examples of an absolute participial construction (plus one with an adjective)—though it still tends to alternate with the *como*-plus-subjunctive formula of *Arnalte*. *Dissolutio* is used twice. (In every other respect, however, the *Sermón* is to be set against both novels, for they are written in art-prose, *sermo artifex*, while the *Sermón* employs *sermo simplex*.)

The ultimate explanation of this reform in San Pedro's art-prose is clearly to be sought, beyond the personal taste of Marina Manuel, in the changing intellectual climate of the period of the *Reyes Católicos*, and in particular in the advent of humanism. Nebrija, for instance, is the first of the Spanish Renaissance preceptists to censure the imitation of Latin syntax in Spanish and the use of rhyme in prose.[14] The *ad Her.* too, though it was the fountain-head of medieval rhetorical doctrine, repeatedly urges that 'figures of sound' be used very sparingly, and insists also (fols 5-7) on the virtues of brevity in narration. The medieval theorists so far forgot the caution of the *ad Her.* as to cite as ingenious achievements what the *ad Her.* had intended as horrid warnings; while the virtue of brevity was lost to sight, and its essence was seen to be in the use of particular devices. Even the reformed San Pedro does not confine himself to presenting the *purum corpus materiae* in his narrative, but links brevity with the techniques of *abbreviatio* and—at the very least—converts his verbs to participles. But, without going into further detail, the whole essence and intention of the humanist rhetorical reform may be summed up in the terms of Nebrija (p. 57: 'no de manera que sea la salsa más quel manjar') or Encina ('el guisado con mucha miel no es bueno'[15])—'More meat, less sauce'.

It may fairly be assumed that until Nebrija initiated his campaign against 'la barbaría, por todas partes de España tan ancha y luengamente derramada', the rhetorical treatises used in the Spanish universities would not differ greatly from the collection edited by Faral.[16] And that 'prerrenacentista' élite, who, like Mena, had visited Italy—or simply come under Italian influence —and paid homage to Cicero as 'el mayor orador', have no connexion with the *bachiller* Diego de San Pedro, who learned his rhetoric at a university, almost certainly Salamanca, and quite certainly long before the days of Lucio Marineo. Until, therefore, San Pedro was enlightened by the enlightened ladies of the court, his style was based on medieval rhetorical theory, and, perhaps even more important, on medieval models. We know that Nebrija, Gutiérrez, and the rest, following the Italians, by-passed the later theorists and went back to the late classical grammarians; that Nebrija's ideas may be taken as typical for that generation of Spanish humanists; and that the ladies of the court learned their Latin and rhetoric, and their notions of 'buen gusto', from Nebrija and his fellow-humanists. It is impossible to be more precise without indulging in pure speculation, for we know nothing of Marina Manuel, except that she was one of the 'damas de la reyna',[17] nor what exactly she said about the *Sermón* and *Arnalte*. There is one other problem which I cannot deal with here: in every respect but those I have noted the *Sermón* differs from both novels, being written in a wholly unpretentious, virtually unadorned style, while the novels are in art-prose. Clearly San Pedro's intention in the *Sermón* was merely to use *sermo simplex* for a comic work, which was moreover an imitation of a sermon. It would be curious—but typical of San Pedro—if he had misunderstood the reasons for Marina Manuel's preference.

The activities of Pietro Martire, Lucio Marineo, and other Italians in Spain; the work of the Italian-educated Spanish scholars; the advent of humanism, and its impact on Spain—that larger picture has been painted by many different hands. I offer this paper simply as a detailed description of one aspect of the impact of humanism on one writer of the time.

[*BHS*, 37 (1960), 1-15]

Notes

1. All page and line references to San Pedro's works are to the Gili y Gaya edition of his *Obras* (Madrid, 1950). [Page references in brackets are to the Whinnom edition of the prose works (1973, 1972) and to the Severin and Whinnom edition of the poems (1979).]
2. I have used the 1563/4 Aldine edition, corrected by Paulus Manutius: *Rhetoricorvm ad C. Herennium libri IIII incerto auctore* (Venice, 1563).
3. Edmond Faral, *Les Arts poétiques du XIIe et du XIIIe siècles* (Paris, 1924).
4. F. López Estrada, 'La retórica en las *Generaciones y semblanzas* de Fernán Pérez de Guzmán', *RFE*, 30 (1946), 310-52, defines *traductio* (p. 336) as 'la ayuda etimológica en la aclaración del sentido de una palabra'. This is quite incorrect: cf. *ad Her.* (fol. 53^v), Geoffrey of Vinsauf (Faral, pp. 231 and 322) or Eberhard the German (Faral, p. 351). His definition of *annominatio, ibid.*, 'la coincidencia homofónica entre un topónimo y una circunstancia determinada con la que se relaciona la palabra en la que se concentra el sentido' is also wrong. M. R. Lida de Malkiel, *Juan de Mena* (Mexico City, 1950) gives, *passim*, various examples of what she terms a 'figura etimológica' from different fifteenth-century writers,

all of which are in fact *annominatio*. Her definition of '*adnominatio*' (p. 446), 'que procede del latín escolástico y se limita a desarrollar por medio de un participio derivado del nombre en cuestión', is far too narrow.

5. The figures of *traductio* and *annominatio* used as rhymes in medieval vernacular verse receive separate treatment and special labels in the vernacular theorists, in Provençal, French, Portuguese, and Spanish. But not all the exotic varieties of rhyme will wholly account for verses like those I quote. The term *annominatio* is still necessary. I hope to publish elsewhere a note on this point.

6. E. R. Curtius, *European Literature and the Latin Middle Ages* (London, 1953), p. 284.

7. J. M. Blecua, ed., Juan de Mena, *El Laberinto de la Fortuna o las Trescientas* (Madrid, 1943), finds *arte mayor* lines in Lucena's *Tratado de vita beata*, and, note 220, p. xcii, suggests they are also to be found in the *Cárcel*. M. R. Lida de Malkiel, *op. cit.*, finds *arte mayor* lines (due to the influence of Mena, she believes) in Lucena, the *Celestina* (Menéndez y Pelayo had earlier suggested that octosyllables and *arte mayor* were to be found there), and the *Cárcel*. She lists thirty unconvincing examples from the first eleven pages, in over half the cases obtaining a dodecasyllable by ignoring any inconvenient words in the same natural phonic group; the rhythm of two thirds of her examples is not typically *arte mayor* at all; and on the same basis I find just as many in Gili y Gaya's preface.

8. cf. his *De schematis et tropis sacrae scripturae*, in Migne, PL, XC, col. 178.

9. So Eduard Norden, *Die antike Kunstprosa*, 3rd ed. (Berlin-Leipzig, 1915–18), p. 760.

10. The beginning of *Cap.* 1, *Liber* 1. I use a modern reprint; *Thomae a Kempis de imitatione Christi libri quattuor quos denuo recognovit Adrianus a Fortiscuto* (London, 1919).

11. Guillaume Molinier, *Flors del gay saber estier dichas las leys d'amors* (1356), ed. Gatien-Arnoult (Paris-Toulouse, n.d.). III, 331, he defines *compar* exactly as all the other medieval theorists, but adds: 'we call that parity of syllables "rim".' Earlier, I, 143, he complains of those who insist on consonance or assonance in defining rhyme.

12. The *ad Her.* definition demands *membrum*; but Matthew of Vendôme equates *compar* with *scesisonomaton*, which is a figure made up of parallel phrases consisting of noun and adjective. Similarly Molinier, *op. cit.*, does not insist on clauses in *compar*. But some syntactical parallelism is essential.

13. Many fifteenth-century Castilian poets make use of the final unaccented syllable in a kind of secondary rhyme (e.g. 'firmarme-firme-venirme-arrepentirme-apartarme'). See Pierre Le Gentil, *La Poésie lyrique espagnole et portugaise à la fin du moyen âge*, II: *Les formes* (Rennes, 1952), 150, for numerous examples.

14. Antonio de Nebrija, *Gramática de la lengua castellana* (Salamanca, 1492), ed. I. González-Llubera (Oxford, 1926), pp. 130 and 56-57.

15. Juan del Encina, *Arte de trobar*, in Menéndez y Pelayo, *Antología de poetas líricos castellanos* (repr. Santander, 1944), V, 46.

16. This comfortable assumption is customary, though highly unsatisfactory. But we do know that Geoffrey of Vinsauf was held in high esteem by the Marquis of Santillana ('perdimos a Dante, Gaufredo, Terençio, / Juvenal, Estaçio e Quintiliano' in his *Defunsión de don Enrique de Villena*), while Nebrija condemns Eberhard the German ('los Ebrardos [. . .] y otros no sé qué apostizos y contrahechos gramáticos', preface to his Latin-Spanish dictionary, Salamanca, 1492).

17. The lady is wrongly identified by Emilio Cotarelo y Mori, 'Nuevos y curiosos datos biográficos del famoso trovador y novelista Diego de San Pedro', *BRAE*, 14 (1927), 305-26, and in consequence by Gili y Gaya (p. 114). See my article 'Was Diego de San Pedro a *Converso*?', *BHS*, 34 (1957), 187-200. [See also B22 in the bibliography, p. xxxiii, above.]

2

The Printed Editions and the Text of the Works of Fray Íñigo de Mendoza

Fray Íñigo de Mendoza, reputedly Isabella's favourite preacher, is also one of the most important poets of the latter half of the fifteenth century; but no critical edition of his works exists, and no one to my knowledge has yet made a critical examination of the existing materials for it.[1] A recent article by Antonio Pérez Gómez[2] has cleared up some difficulties by unravelling the confusion of errors surrounding the first two editions of Mendoza's *Vita Christi*; but since these errors are all too liable to be perpetuated by the continued use of works such as the standard bibliographies, and since I have some comments to add, I shall not apologize for beginning again at the beginning while pursuing the story further.

A. The first known edition of the *Vita Christi* (together with Mendoza's *Sermón trobado*) is that printed in octavo by Centenera at Zamora, 25 January 1482. Only one copy is extant, that used for the Academy facsimile[3] (Biblioteca Nacional, *Cat. de incunables* 1290; Gallardo 3042; Salvá 132; Haebler 420; Palau 163762). It is notorious that this copy lacks leaf E1; but in the facsimile the missing stanzas are supplied on a tipped-in leaf. Pérez Gómez has shown that this has been done by photographing the missing stanzas from *C* (see below), arranging them on a specially composed leaf, and then reducing it from folio to octavo.[4] This gap would have been better filled from *B*. Amezúa appears to suggest that the reader might find a transcription of these texts in Foulché-Delbosc, *Cancionero castellano del siglo XV*, NBAE, XIX (Madrid, 1912), pp. 1-59; but Foulché-Delbosc's text, as the most cursory examination shows, is a transcript (with some serious inaccuracies) of *C*. It would seem that Gallardo and Salvá saw a copy of *A* bound together with a *pliego suelto* of Gómez Manrique's *Regimiento de príncipes*, a fact which started some odd hares (see Pérez Gómez, pp. 34-36).

B. What Pérez Gómez has argued to be the second edition of the *Vita Christi*[5] exists in two copies: the well-known Escorial text (Biblioteca de San

Lorenzo del Escorial, Cat. no. II-X-17; Gallardo 3043; Haebler 421, and see 'rectificación', p. 362; Vindel IV, 16; Palau 163764), and that in the Biblioteca Communale of Palermo, divided into two parts bound separately, recently discovered by Eugenio Asensio. It was printed at Saragossa, without imprint, possibly in 1482 by Paul Hurus and Hans Planck. This edition includes, as well as the *Sermón trobado* of *A*, the earliest known printing, in a distinctive but unacceptable version (see Pérez Gómez, pp. 38–41), of Jorge Manrique's *Dezir por la muerte de su padre*,[6] and Gómez Manrique's *Regimiento de príncipes* with its prose introduction. As Pérez Gómez has shown, *B* is, so far as Mendoza's contribution goes, a page-for-page (and, being verse, line-for-line) reproduction in folio of the octavo *A*, but skipping *A*'s B3^r, which leaves it short of six stanzas.

   C. Third in the series is the edition, again without imprint but Centenera, Zamora, 1483–84?, of which four copies are extant:[7] Bib. Nac., *Cat. de incunables* 1291 (apparently recently recatalogued as 897); Escorial 38-1-27; British Museum IB. 52920; Gallardo 3044-45; Salvá 182; Haebler 422 (the collation given is erroneous); Vindel II, 7; Palau 163763. This is the text transcribed in Foulché-Delbosc's *Cancionero*. The Escorial copy, bound together with the Comendador Román's *Coplas de la pasión con la resureción*, by Juan Vázquez of Toledo, led Amador de los Ríos[8] to start the phantom of the Toledo, Juan Vázquez, edition of the *Vita Christi*, a ghost laid by P. Benigno Fernández in 1911,[9] resurrected by Amezúa (see note 3), and now laid again—but who dare hope forever?—by Pérez Gómez. Sr Pérez Gómez, having established the sequence of these three editions, does not pursue further the problems of *C*.

   Rodríguez-Moñino,[10] for once misled by relying on earlier bibliographers, refers to three undated editions of the *Vita Christi* before 1490: Gallardo 3044 and 3045, and Salvá 182, and goes on (p. 14) to a discussion of their differing contents: thus Gallardo 3044 contains ten poems by Mendoza, three by Jorge Manrique, and one by Juan de Mena; Gallardo 3045 contains nine by Mendoza and six by other authors; and Salvá 182 contains ten by Mendoza and seven by other authors. There is in fact only one edition, *C*, and the table of contents will show how the varying counts arise. (Palau's list of contents omits five items.) Haebler, No. 422, shows that Gallardo wrongly made two editions of the two copies he saw, probably because the table of contents was bound at the beginning in one, and at the end in the other.[11] The contents of *C* are as follows (I abbreviate titles):

1. Mendoza, 'Vita Christi', A1^r-D6^v (Foulché-Delbosc, No. 1).
2. Mendoza, 'Sermón trobado', D6^v-E2^v (F-D No. 2).

3. Mendoza, 'Vituperio de las malas hembras', E2^v-E4^v (F-D No. 3).
4. Mendoza, 'Como es reparada nuestra Castilla', E4^v-F2^v (F-D No. 4).
5. Mendoza, 'Dechado', F2^v-F6^r (F-D No. 5).
6. Mendoza, 'Razón y sensualidad', F6^r-G8^v (F-D No. 6).
7. Mendoza, 'Gozos de Nuestra Señora', G9^r-G10^v (F-D No. 7).
8. Mendoza, 'La cena', G10^v-H4^v (F-D No. 8). *C*'s table of contents itemizes with the paragraph-sign which precedes the title of each poem '℞ luego tras ella enpieça la passion de nuestro redenptor', but in the text itself 'Comiença la passion de nuestro redemptor' is no more than a rubric within the poem of 'La cena'.
9. Mendoza, 'La Verónica', H4^v-I3^r (F-D No. 9).
10. Mendoza, 'Al spíritu sancto', I3^v-I4^r (F-D No. 10).
11. Jorge Manrique, 'Coplas a la muerte de su padre', I4^r-I7^r.
12. Anonymous, 'Lamentación a la quinta angustia', I7^v-I8^v (F-D No. 11, attributed to Mendoza).
13. Juan de Mena, 'Coplas contra los pecados mortales', L1^r-L7^v, and from there to M8^r, though not listed separately in the table of contents, Gómez Manrique's continuation of the poem, 'por fallescimiento del famoso poeta Juan de Mena'.
14. 'Pregunta' of Sancho de Rojas 'a un aragonés', and the 'respuesta', M8^r-M8^v, listed in the table of contents as one item.
15. Jorge Manrique, 'Coplas sobre qué es amor', M8^v.

It will be seen that one can arrive at varying totals, depending on the way one counts items 8, 12, 13, and 14. *C* contains in fact ten poems by Mendoza, two by Jorge Manrique, one anonymous item, one by Juan de Mena and Gómez Manrique, and the *pregunta* and *respuesta* of Sancho de Rojas and the Aragonese.

Of the series of *cancioneros* which contain works by Mendoza (there are more after *C*) it is *C* which contains the greatest number. Indeed the *Sermón trobado*, *Como es reparada nuestra Castilla*, *Al spíritu sancto*, and the dubious *Lamentación a la quinta angustia* are not again reprinted, so that *C* is the unique printed version (leaving aside Foulché-Delbosc) of all but the first.

One must here say a word about Foulché-Delbosc's transcription of Mendoza's *cancionero*. It is indubitably a transcript of *C*; this is the only possible source for certain poems, and that it is also his source for the *Vita Christi* and the *Sermón* is betrayed by the orthography and certain readings. It is, however, a seriously inaccurate transcript, for which Foulché-Delbosc may not be himself to blame, for it is presumably he who, as editor, has scrupulously marked verses he has realized are missing by inserting dotted lines—in a majority of cases where the transcriber's eye has simply jumped a line, or telescoped two. From one poem nine stanzas are missing. I point out the main errors of transcription later in this article.

D. There are two folio editions of a very different *cancionero* in 1492 and 1495. The 1492 edition *D* 1 is described by Méndez,[12] who had not himself seen it, but received the description from D. Gregorio Vázquez y Espina, who examined the copy belonging to Jovellanos. Salvá seems to have seen a mutilated copy of the same edition (No. 186), but he and the other bibliographers simply copy Méndez (Hain 4312; Haebler 423; Vindel IV, 50; Palau 163766). The 1495 edition, *D* 2, Méndez describes (Año 1495, No. 18, p. 142) as identical with that of 1492: 'De esta colección y sus Autores se puede ver en la pag. 134 no dudando ser la misma, pero ediciones diferentes. Esta segunda añade el Hymno del *Ave maris stella* en Español por Juan Guillardón, de quien no encuentro noticia: acaso estará también en la edición que no he visto.' But Méndez then goes on to say that the 1495 edition exists in the Bibliotheca Alexandrina in Rome, 'según refiere el Abate Diosdado',[13] from which Haebler inferred that Méndez had not seen the 1495 edition either. The 1495 edition is in fact extant (Biblioteca Universitaria Alessandrina, Inc. 382) and one or two problems present themselves.

Juan Guillardón's 'Ave maris stella' does not figure in the table of contents of *D* 1 as it is copied by Méndez; but it is clear that it exists in that edition, if not in the table of contents, for the indexed foliation of *D* 1 is identical with that of *D* 2: the story of the Virgen del Pilar (see item 10, below) still starts on fol. 78 in each.[14] Furthermore, Méndez himself speaks (p. 136) of 'las quince obritas comprehendidas en este cancionero' although he has listed only fourteen.

D 2 has at present no title-page (or preliminary leaves): fol. 1^r ($A1^r$) is blank; 1^v carries the *tabla*, and fol. 2 starts with the *Vita Christi*, as in *D* 1. Nevertheless Méndez cites a title-page for *D* 2, identical except for orthographic variants with that of *D* 1. The spelling proves nothing, for Méndez often modernizes, and resolves abbreviations, quite inconsistently. Nevertheless it is reasonable to suppose that this sumptuous edition did possess a *portada*, which ran 'Coplas de Vita Christi: de la Cena: con la Pasion: e de la Veronica: con la Resurreccion de nuestro Redentor: e las siete Angustias: e siete Gozos de nuestra Señora, con otras obras mucho provechosas' (Méndez), though probably spelled somewhat differently.[15]

Various bibliographers have appeared to suggest that one or other of the two editions described by Méndez was a phantom, and there was perhaps some justification for the suspicion. But *D* 2 is patently a reprint, since fol. 1^v, which carries the *tabla*, the poems being indexed correctly to their folios, is $A1^v$, and the text begins on $A2^r$ (fol. 2^r); and that the original edition was the 1492 *cancionero* described by Méndez, rather than some other lost edition, there would be little reason to doubt. That *D* 1 did exist is placed beyond doubt by the fact that Méndez, copying *D* 1, writes several abbreviations (q*ue*, virge*n*, jua*n*, etc.) which *D* 2 prints in full. It is conceivable, of course, that *D* 1 is itself a reprint, but since we do not have the collation we cannot tell.

D 2 is a page-for-page, line-for-line reprint of *D* 1 (but, obviously, not a reimpression from the same type). The colophon of each is identically worded, even to the odd 'emprentada', except for the date: *D* 1 is dated 27 November 1492, whereas *D* 2's colophon reads: 'Fue la presente obra emprentada enla / insigne ciudad de çarragoça de arrago*n* / por industria Շ expensas de Paulo / hurus de Co*n*stancia aleman A .x. dias / de octobre .M. cccc. xcv.' One recalls that it may have been Paul Hurus who made a page-for-page folio reprint (*B*) of Centenera's *A*.

D 2 is, like other products of the Hurus office, a handsome work, beautifully printed, with running headlines and foliation, and illustrated with large and very superior woodcuts. It is described (not always adequately or accurately) by Méndez, 1495, No. 18; Hain 4313; Haebler 424; Vindel IV, 67; Palau 163766*; and, according to Rodríguez-Moñino, by Juan M. Sánchez.[16] Since it is to be reproduced in facsimile by Sr Pérez Gómez (in late 1962) I shall not go into further descriptive detail here.[16A] The contents of the *cancionero* are as follows (I abbreviate the Mendoza titles):

1. Mendoza, 'Vita Christi', 2^r-31^r.
2. Mendoza, 'La cena', 31^v-35^v.
3. Diego de San Pedro, 'Coplas de la passión de nuestro redemptor', 35^v-53^v.
4. Mendoza, 'La Verónica', 54^r-60^v.
5. Pedro Jiménez ('peroximenes'), 'La resurreción de nuestro redemptor Jhesu Christo', 60^v-70^r.
6. Diego de San Pedro, 'Las siete angustias de Nuestra Señora', 70^v-74^v.
7. Mendoza, 'Los siete gozos', 74^v-77^r.
8. Ervías, 'Coplas en loor de Nuestra Señora', 77^r.
9. Juan Guillardón, 'Coplas sobre el *Aue maris stella*', 77^v-78^v.
10. Medina, 'Historia dela sacratíssima Virgen María del Pilar de Çarragoça', 78^v-81^v.
11. Juan de Mena, 'Coplas contra los siete pecados mortales' (with Gómez Manrique's continuation), 81^v-98^r.
12. Fray Juan de Ciudad Rodrigo, 'Los diez mandamientos, los siete peccados mortales con sus virtudes contrarias, y las quatorze obras de misericordia temporales y spirituales', 98^r-100^r.
13. Mendoza, 'Justa de la razón contra la sensualidad' (with its prose preface), 100^v-109^r.
14. Jorge Manrique, 'Coplas por la muerte de su padre', 109^r-112^r.
15. Fernán Pérez de Guzmán, 'Dezir gracioso Շ sotil dela muerte', 112^v-113^v.

I am here concerned only with Fray Íñigo,[17] but I cannot pass over the problem of *D*'s relationship with the *Cancionero de Ramón de Llavia*.[18] This religious anthology, selected and introduced with a prologue by Ramón de Llavia (or Llabia), was also printed in Saragossa, has been attributed to Hans (Juan) Hurus, Paul's father or elder brother, but cannot, on the typographical evidence, be assigned to a precise date before or after 1492.[19] It contains the *Dechado* and the *Coplas a las mugeres* (*Vituperio*) of Mendoza (in *C*, but not in *D*), almost inevitably Jorge Manrique's *Coplas por la muerte de su padre*, and also, more distinctively, his *Coplas sobre qué es amor* (as out of place here, among the 'muchas obras cathólicas puestas por coplas, las más esmeradas y perfectas', as in *C*), Ervías's *Coplas en loor de Nuestra Señora* (as in *D*), and Juan de Mena's *Pecados mortales* (as in *C* and *D*). There are in all twenty works in the collection, the most important poet being Fernán Pérez de Guzmán, who is represented by five, three more than any other poet. I would suggest that the logical position for this collection is between *C* and *D* (and so before 1492); but research could clarify the relationship of the Hans Hurus chrestomathy (Llavia) with that of Paul's (*D*), as also with the edition of the *Trescientas* of Juan de Mena (containing poems by Mendoza and others, which figure in earlier anthologies), printed by George Coci, who took over Paul's press in Saragossa.

As an anthology *D* is clearly superior to *C* and to the *Canc. de Llavia*. The poems are arranged in logical order: five on the life of Christ (the *Vita Christi* itself goes only as far as the Massacre of the Innocents), five on the Virgin, three moralizing works, and two poems on death. Rodríguez-Moñino writes of its 'perfecta unidad temática, religiosa', and goes on to speculate about the identity of its compiler, 'persona de criterio, conocimiento y buen gusto', suggesting the name of Fray Íñigo himself. The suggestion is also advanced, less cautiously, by Méndez ('puede sospecharse con algún fundamento'); but I think that the defects of the Mendoza texts would suggest that Mendoza was not involved, and that a much likelier candidate—who still fits Rodríguez-Moñino's description of the compiler—is Paul Hurus himself, who 'besides possessing artistic tastes was a man of literary ability',[20] and who had for models Centenera's *C* and Juan Hurus's *Canc. de Llavia*, and as his guide Llavia's stated, but not wholly fulfilled, intention.

One further incunable edition of the *Vita Christi* is recorded: [Seville] 1499, by Meinard Ungut and Stanislaus Polonus, in folio, an incomplete copy of which Vindel (V, 117; Palau 163767) saw in a bookshop in Barcelona; but I have been unable to see any copy of this edition. The same press produced also the first two sixteenth-century editions of the *Vita Christi*. The first of these, unrecorded by the bibliographers, in quarto, survives only as a fragment, a single gathering of eight leaves, signed E, bound at the end of an imperfect copy of a Toledo edition of the Marquis of Santillana's *Bías contra Fortuna* (Biblioteca Nacional R/12340). F. J. Norton, to whom I am indebted for this information, thinks that it was printed by Polono about 1502. The 1506 edition exists in a unique copy in the Biblioteca Nacional (R/11897) which is briefly noticed by Simón Díaz (III, No. 3783). A quarto of 36 unnumbered leaves by Jacobo Cromberger, Polono's successor, is presumably the 1506 Seville edition noted in the *Registrum* of Ferdinand Columbus (cf. Palau 163768). We know also of a further Seville edition by Cromberger in 1546 (Bib. Nac. R/12775), and two seventeenth-century editions, Seville 1611 and Valladolid 1615, cited by Nicolás Antonio and subsequently by other bibliographers, but seen by no one in modern times.

Some nine MSS of Mendoza's *Vita Christi* have been recorded, and they represent at least three distinct stages in the redaction of the poem. But there can be no doubt that it is the final version of this work that is to be found in the various printed editions.

Vita Christi

A, 'Uita chr*is*ti fecho por coplas por frey yñigo de me*n*doça a petiçion dela muy v*ir*tuosa señora doña iuana de cartagena',[21] is by no means a perfect text. It has sundry easily perceived and rectifiable literals: *dexomos*, *crarrera*, *eula* (*enla*), and a great many others, some less immediately obvious. Lines are missing: two in the 1st stanza of B2^r, one in the 5th of B7^v, and one in the 4th of C8^r, which are not supplied by any of the printed versions. (The rhyme-scheme in the second *quintilla* of the 3rd stanza on B6^r is ABBBA instead of ABAAB, but this error is to be found in the MSS and all printed versions, and must be Mendoza's mistake.) There are a number of faulty rhymes, some of which we may use to demonstrate the relationship of the printed editions: (1) 5th stanza, A1^v, fermosura/tuya; (2) 1st, A4^r, despedida-venida/criada; (3) 6th, B7^v, buena boca/cadena; (4) 1st, B8^r, boca/loco; (5) 3rd, C1^r, abominaçion/ladrones; (6) 4th, C1^r, vedada/gastado; (7) 2nd, C1^v, prejuras/portuguesas; (8) 4th, C1^v, mercadores/aferez; (9) 2nd, C4^r, entraro*n*/mira*n*do-mando; (10) 4th, C4^r, confirmara/esperaua; (11) 3rd, C8^r, a truncated line which does not rhyme: Pues sy toda causa/ordena-condempna; (12) 5th, D1^v, paresçe/condenaste; (13) 1st, D3^r, fauoreados/oydos-reçebidos; (14) 4th, D6^r, enemigo/daño-año; (15) 4th, D8^r, primeros/flores-señores. (Note that Mendoza apparently intended to rhyme *paz* with *mas*, 5th stanza, B6^v, and *mjraglo* with *diablo*, 5th, C8^r.) Finally we may add to this list one of the less obvious misprints: (16) 4th, D2^r, O pureza syn estoria.

B, as I have noted, is a page-for-page reprint of *A*, and, though it makes various obvious emendations (*dexemos*, *carrera*, *enla*, etc.) it does not correct a single one of the errors I have listed, though the reader will already have perceived, even without the assistance of the context, how some of them might be remedied. *B*, as I have also mentioned, omits the six stanzas of *A*'s B3^r; but these stanzas are not omitted in any other printed edition. *B* is, in short, a dead end as far as the *Vita Christi* is concerned, and is useful only for filling the gap of twelve stanzas left by the loss of E1 in the sole surviving copy of *A*.

C does venture to emend some of the errors of *A*, as follows: (2) creida, (3) boca buena, (8) mercaderes/aferes, (11) Pues si toda causa buena, (13) fauorecidos. But the missing lines are not supplied, and the persistence of misprints like 'entraron' (9) and 'estoria' (16) reveal its dependence on *A*; to account for the emendations effected one does not have to suppose anything more than a reasonably intelligent compositor. The reader may obtain a fair substitute for the original *C* by making the following emendations in Foulché-Delbosc's transcription.[22] 15b 3-1, 'cama', not 'carne'; 21b 5-5, 'indacielcis', not 'indaculcis'; 23b 2, the line *is* missing; 27a 4-1, 'Ouejas', not 'Quejas'; 31b 4, the line is not missing, read: 'toda nuestra fe ençierra / o quanto que meresçiste / o quanto que tu dixiste'; 33b 1-1, 'Yo so la que', not 'Yo sola, que', and 2-1, 'Yo so la que fue', not 'Yo sola, que fuy'; 36b 1, the line *is* missing; 48a 4, the line is not missing, read: 'aquesta saña tan biua / pues fue causa de poblarse / pues fue causa de alegrarse'; 48b 3-1, *C* has 'primeros', and Foulché-Delbosc has made the obvious emendation; 50a 1-3, 'o yra', not 'oyra'; 51a 1, the line is not missing, 'delante de sus entrañas'.

D. Paul Hurus emends five rhymes as in *C*: 2, 3, 8, 11, and 13 (the only emendations made by *C*), and introduces two more which had not occurred to Centenera: 'confirmaua' (10), and, a less easy one, 'promesas/portuguesas' (7). The other errors and lacunae of *A* and *C* remain unemended; though one should note that Hurus has made some rather unfortunate emendations in the story of the shepherds, restoring rustic forms in the dialogue to standard Castilian.[23]

The fragment of the Polono 1502? edition starts with the second *quintilla* of the 331st stanza of the *Vita Christi*, and represents a further stage of deterioration in the transmission of the text. Even in this brief fragment two further lines are lost, and of those surviving a dozen or so are turned to nonsense; but two of the original misprints are corrected: 'enemigo' replaced by 'engaño' (14) and 'primeros' by 'primores' (15). This edition must be in the first instance a reprint of Seville 1499, but there are no clues to indicate which of the previous printed versions served as the text for the Seville editions.

To sum up, *A* is the first edition; *B* and *C* derive from *A*; *D* almost certainly derives from *C* rather than *A*. A fair number of errors remain unchanged throughout this series of printings.

I have mentioned the various MSS of the *Vita Christi*. From these MS sources it is possible to supply the missing lines and emend many of the faulty rhymes of the printed texts.[24] Nevertheless it would appear that no MS can outrank the first printed edition, being either more recent in date, or representing a different and earlier redaction of the text. *A* must serve as the basis of a critical edition.

Other poems

Sermón trovado

In *A*, the 'Sermón trobado que fizo frey yñigo de mendoça al muy alto y muy poderoso prinçipe rey y señor el rey don ferna[n]do rey de castilla y de aragon sobre el yugo y coyundas que su alteza trahe por deuisa' has not more than half a dozen misprints, apart from a missing line in the 3rd stanza of E6[r]. *B*, making the obvious emendations, otherwise reproduces it exactly. So far as the text goes *C* might derive from *A* or *B*, but it is logical to suppose that Centenera followed his own *A*. The text is not again, so far as I am aware, reprinted. (Foulché-Delbosc transcribes *C*'s text without error.)[25]

Coplas a las mujeres

'Coplas que fizo frey yñigo de mendoça flayre menor doze en vituperio delas malas hembras que no pueden las tales ser dichas mugeres. E doze en loor delas buenas mugeres que mucho triumpho de honor merecen' is *C*'s title for this work. The poem is twice copied in the Escorial codex (from *C*), and reprinted (also from *C*) in the *Canc. de Llavia*.

Foulché-Delbosc's transcription should be emended: 61a 3 (nothing is missing), 'do los ombres sy pasean'.

Como es reparada nuestra Castilla

The 'Coplas conpuestas por fray yñigo de mendoça al muy alto Ƹ muy poderoso principe rey Ƹ señor el rey do*n* fernando de castilla Ƹ de leon Ƹ de cecilia al principe de aragon. E ala muy esclarescida reyna doña ysabel su muy amada muger nuestros naturales señores en q*ue* declara como por el aduenimie*n*to destos muy altos señores es reparada nuestra castilla' are printed only in *C*. It is copied in the Escorial MS.

Foulché-Delbosc's transcription should be emended: 66a 1 (the lines are not missing), 'con osado defensar / Ƹ no tienen lo ganado'; 72a 3 (the line is not missing), read: 'y su mal pueda curarse / dalde luego tal xaluegue / que por mucho q*ue* nauegue'. Nine stanzas are to be added to this poem.[26] They run as follows:

y luego con grand pujança
deshaziendo la cobdicia
hares syn otra mudança
el estante de esperança
y la gauia de justiçia
De templança la mediana
de caridad las entenas
por que v*uest*ra sabia gana
haga n*uest*ra vrca sana
para las mares agenas

Bonetas de fortaleza
los relingues de concierto
los castillos de firmeza
hares con alta sabieza
por que el daño quede muerto
sea el cumbre Ƹ ceuaderas
los seruientes Ƹ seruicios
vnas ganas verdaderas
de virtudes dela*n*teras
armadas contra los vicios

y para ma*n*dar las greyes
hares alto rey syn fallas
sus pendones de vnas leyes
que suelen hazer los reyes
para jamas no quebrallas

las escalas que son grados
de justicia sofridores
sean luego concertados
los pasos que estan quebrados
de sus mesmos socutores [*sic*]

Puesta eneste fundamento
la vrca que esta perdida
poblada con alto tiento
de vn suaue regimiento
con que su gente se mida
y asy tan syn emiendas
todos quantos la poblaren
ternan sanas sus haziendas
syn temor y syn contiendas
quanto enella nauegaren

para que el mal se desmalle
dela hurca recontada
es menester de buscalle
alto rey buen gouernalle
que la lieue concertada
que segund la mar ayrada
suele ser de nuestras ganas
enla primera jornada
puede ser por mal guardada
perder rocin ʒ mançanas

Rey de muy altos valores
para dar aqueste honor
estos grandes ʒ mayores
todos vos son seruidores
buscalde vos el mejor
por que mi seso liuiano
no sabria dar señor
pero ay esta vuestro hermano
ʒ sy no por vuestra mano
buscad vos el mas leal [*sic*]

La vrca de tal manera
sana del mal que le agrauia
alta reyna por cimera
como su propria heredera
vos seres dicha la gauia
para que asy la veles
que nola sobre el engaño
para que la gouernes
y mires y repares
como no reciba daño

Donde digo en conclusyon
segund la cabsa se muestra
que quiera esecucion
lo que ganare el patron
la mayor parte es la vuestra
uos señora soys fiel
heredera que esclaresce
el y vos y vos y el
señora soys el joyel
que en españa resplandesce

Fin
Reyes de grand poderio
de nuestros bienes los remos
perdonad mi desuario
y curad deste nauio
donde todos naueguemos
que segund esta perdido
sy le dexays oluidar
es el mal tan escogido
que el trabajo enuegecido
nunca se podra cobrar

Dechado

The 'Dechado que hyzo frey yñigo de mendoça ala muy escelente reyna doña ysabel nuestra soberana señora' is printed in *C*, the *Canc. de Llavia* (here based on *C*), and in a *pliego suelto* recorded in the *Registrum* of Ferdinand Columbus (No. 4108) and purchased by him in 1524. The Escorial MS copies it entire.

Foulché-Delbosc's transcript of this poem, obviously based on the British Museum copy, which lacks F2 and so the beginning of this piece, uses the *Canc. de Llavia* to fill the gap, as the orthography betrays. Llavia, and so Foulché-Delbosc, give the poem a different title: 'Dechado del regimiento de principes fecho ala señora reyna de castilla y aragon'.

Razón y sensualidad

After a prose preface addressed to Isabella, the title is given as 'Comiença a loor y seruicio de dios prouecho deletacion de los proximos la hystoria dela question y diferencia que ay entre la razon y [la] sensualidad sobre la felicidad Z bien auenturança humana. porque la sensualidad dize que enlos dulçores transitorios y tenporales consiste. y la razon que enlos spirituales y eternos. compusolo en metros fray yñigo de mendoça jndigno flayre menor dela obseruançia de sant francisco dirigela ala serenissima muy alta muy poderosa Z muy esclarescida reyna doña ysabel reyna de castilla Z de aragon que dios faga enperatriz monarcha'. A piece of it is copied in the Escorial MS. It appears in *D*, which calls it the 'Justa de la razon contra la sensualidad', and is also to be found in the *Trescientas* of Juan de Mena, printed at Saragossa by George Coci in 1506 and 1509.

Foulché-Delbosc's transcription should be emended: 81b 3 (the line is not missing), 'por ninguna pena es cara'; 93a 3 (the line is not missing), read: 'como vida que no yerra / fue cendrada y escogida / para que fuese medida'.

Los siete gozos

'Los gozos de nuestra soñora [*sic*] hechos por frey yñigo' appear in *C*, copied without the opening stanzas in the MS, in *D*, and in a *pliego suelto* without imprint now in the Bibliothèque Nationale, Paris.[27] This latter is perhaps the same as that registered by Ferdinand Columbus (No. 4110), though the *Registrum* mentions that this edition contained also 'other poems'. It was purchased by Columbus in 1524.

La cena

'Coplas hechas por frey yñigo de mendoça en que pone la cena que nuestro señor hizo con sus discipulos quando instituyo el sancto sacramento del su sagrado cuerpo.' *C*, Escorial MS (one and a half stanzas only), and *D*.

Foulché-Delbosc's transcription requires emendation: 100a 2, the line *is* missing, but it is the first and not the third, since a blank line is left against the initial paragraph-sign of the stanza, and the second line does not begin with a capital. 103b 2 (the line is not missing), read: 'que leuantan los manteles / se leuantan los temores'.

La Verónica
'Coplas que fizo frey yñigo de mendoça ala veronica.' This poem is in *C* and *D*.

Foulché-Delbosc's transcription requires emendation: 109a 4 (the line is not missing), read: 'la noche de tus tinieblas / y el morder de tus culebras'; 111b 3 (the line is not missing), 'seran las escuridades'.

There are two lacunae in the text of *C* (F-D 107b 5 and 115b 1) each marked by the printer's filling up with quads where his MS was illegible. *D* fills these gaps; but it is not necessary to postulate any other source for *D* than *C*. The blanks would call Hurus's attention to the missing line and missing word, and inspire him to one fairly easy emendation, 'al tu [mal d] espinadura', and one cliché line, 'tu mi dios omnipotente'. To drag in some other hypothetical text would involve us in extraordinary and finally indefensible complications. *D* derives from *C*.

Al espíritu santo
The 'Coplas fechas por frey yñigo de mendoça al spiritu sancto' exist in only one text, *C*.

La quinta angustia
The 'Lamentacion ala quinta angustia quando nuestra señora tenia a nuestro señor en los braços' is to be found only in *C*, where it is anonymous, and placed after Jorge Manrique's *Coplas a la muerte de su padre*. Foulché-Delbosc attributes it to Mendoza; no one to my knowledge has claimed it for Manrique, unless Gallardo may be said to do so implicitly, but there are clearly very few grounds for attributing it to either poet: its author is unknown.

Canción and *Invención*
A *canción* by Fray Íñigo, 'Para jamas oluidaros', is to be found in the *Canc. general* 1511, 182ᵛ. It is reprinted with the other poems of Mendoza by Foulché-Delbosc, No. 12, p. 120. A four-line *invención* to be found *ibid.*, 141ʳ, he omits.

Tratado de la misa
To complete the tale of the surviving works of Mendoza we must cite the work entitled 'Comiença vn tratado breue y muy bueno delas ceremonias dela misa con sus contemplaciones', [Seville] 1499, by 'tres alemanes compañeros' (Johann Pegnitzer, Magnus Herbst, and Tomas Glockner), and Alcalá de Henares 1541, copies of which are to be found in the Biblioteca

Nacional. The authorship of the work has been in dispute, being variously attributed to Íñigo López de Mendoza, Marquis of Santillana (Vindel), to Cardinal Mendoza (Nicolás Antonio), and to our poet (Palau). I have not investigated the matter.

Leaving aside the frivolities in the *Canc. general*, C is the primary text for all of Mendoza's poems except the *Vita Christi* and the *Sermón*, and when the necessary emendations have been made, Foulché-Delbosc's transcription will serve well enough. But the *Vita Christi* is Mendoza's major work, and a poem of far-reaching importance in the literary history of the period, and neither the facsimile *A* nor the transcription of *C* is satisfactory: a critical edition of the *Vita Christi* would fill a serious gap in fifteenth-century studies.[28]

[*BHS*, 39 (1962), 137-52]

Notes

1. I have used the facsimile of *A*, microfilms of the Palermo *B* (generously lent me by Sr Pérez Gómez), of the British Museum *C* (supplemented by photostats from the Biblioteca Nacional), and of the Rome *D* 2. (For explanation of the abbreviations see below.) I have assessed elsewhere the value of the Escorial codex K-III-7 [pp. 36-45, below]. Sr Julio Rodríguez Puértolas of the University of Nottingham is currently engaged with the problem of the various MSS of the *Vita Christi* [*Fray Íñigo de Mendoza y sus 'Coplas de Vita Christi'*: see p. 44, below, note 1].
2. 'Notas para la bibliografía de Fray Íñigo de Mendoza y de Jorge Manrique', *HR*, 27 (1959), 30-41.
3. *Vita Christi fecho en coplas por Fray Íñigo de Mendoza (Zamora, 1482)* (Madrid, 1953), with a preface, best ignored, by Agustín González de Amezúa.
4. In addition my copy has a faulty folding which results in the displacement of two leaves (the sequence as it stands is D6, 7, 4, 5—only D4 is signed), but this error does not exist in Pérez Gómez's copy and may not extend to others.
5. He has sufficiently demonstrated the sequence *A-B*, thus reversing the judgements of Menéndez y Pelayo (*Antología*), P. Benigno Fernández (see note 9), and Augusto Cortina (ed., Jorge Manrique, *Cancionero*, Madrid, 1944), and ending the uncertainty of sundry other scholars, such as Vindel and Amezúa. But the chronological sequence *B-C*, though probable, is not proven. 'Su

contenido va enriqueciéndose de una en otra, sucesivamente'; but Pérez Gómez himself recognizes (p. 33) that this is not a conclusive argument. The printing-dates are of course guess-work.

6. This version of the *Coplas* is reproduced in facsimile by Pérez Gómez in his *Tercera floresta de incunables*, VIII of the series Incunables Poéticos Castellanos (Valencia, 1959). Foulché-Delbosc's critical edition of the *Coplas* (in the Bibliotheca Hispanica, Barcelona-Madrid, 1905, with the preface in French; repr. Madrid, 1912, with the same preface in Spanish) records all the variant readings but fails to note the quite different ordering of the stanzas.

7. According to Palau, the fourth copy, in private hands, was offered for sale in 1951.

8. *Historia crítica de la literatura española* (Madrid, 1861–65), VII, 240.

9. In *La Ciudad de Dios*, 86 (1911), 59, *cit.* Pérez Gómez, p. 37.

10. In his invaluable *Cancionero general recopilado por Hernando del Castillo (Valencia, 1511)* (Madrid, 1958); introduction, indexes, and appendices by Antonio Rodríguez-Moñino, p. 13.

11. In consequence some bibliographers have included the unsigned table of contents in the last signature.

12. Francisco Méndez, *Typographía española o historia de la introducción, propagación y progresos del arte de la imprenta en España* (Madrid, 1796), Año 1492, No. 12, pp. 134-37.

13. i.e. Raymundo Diosdado Caballero, *De prima typographiae hispanicae aetate specimen* (Rome, 1793).

14. Méndez does not record the collation of *D* 1. The table of contents must have been placed at the beginning on fol. 1, or the foliation would differ from *D* 2. Fol. 1 could hardly have been A1 (as it is in *D* 2) but it could have been printed on a preliminary sheet without much difficulty.

15. The same wording, written in a modern hand, on fol. 1^r of the Rome copy may derive from Diosdado, Méndez, or the lost title-page itself.

16. [Juan Manuel Sánchez], *Bibliografía zaragozana del siglo XV* ('por un bibliófilo aragonés') (Madrid, 1908), pp. 113-14.

16A. [Pérez Gómez postponed, and eventually abandoned, this project. Keith Whinnom then prepared a facsimile edition with a long introductory study, but the Spanish publisher who commissioned the edition defaulted, and arrangements are now—through the good offices of Pedro M. Cátedra—being made with another publisher.]

17. On San Pedro's *Pasión* see my 'The Religious Poems of Diego de San Pedro: Their Relationship and their Dating', *HR*, 28 (1960), 1-15, written when I was unaware that this edition was extant, and my note, 'The First Printing of San Pedro's *Passión trobada*', [*HR*, 30 (1962), 149-51].

18. Repr. by the Sociedad de Bibliófilos Españoles (Madrid, 1945).

19. The guesses, which I shall not detail, range from 1485–95. Sir Henry Thomas, *Short-title Catalogue of Books Printed in Spain* [. . .] *before 1601 now in the British*

Museum (London, 1921), has with his habitual acuity placed it at 1490?, a date which admirably fills the bill. It is indubitably a product of the Hurus office, and at 1490 is probably to be attributed to Hans rather than Paul.

20. Konrad Haebler, *The Early Printers of Spain and Portugal* (London, 1896), p. 37.

21. In the British Museum copy of *C* a fifteenth- or sixteenth-century hand has added to this title the words 'su madre'. The same information is given in certain MSS of the *Vita Christi*, and Sr Rodríguez Puértolas informs me that he has documentary proof of its accuracy.

22. It should be noted also that Foulché-Delbosc inserts punctuation, which, though minimal, sometimes interferes with the sense and occasionally removes an ambiguity which might be otherwise resolved, expands all abbreviations, renders *R-* as *r*, sometimes omits the cedilla in words like *seruiçio*, and has made sundry other emendations which are quite unnecessary and indeed regrettable ('definicion' for 'difinicion', 'pobreza' for 'probeza', 'piedad' for 'piadad', etc.). My figures are to be interpreted: page, column, stanza (counting a fragment at the top of a column as the first), line of stanza (counting always from the beginning of the stanza).

23. There is, in fact, a steady trend from *A* to *D* towards correction of the rustic forms. It is clear that compositors were not yet used to the *sayagués* convention. I hope to pursue elsewhere some of the interesting implications of this fact: it means, for instance, that comparisons of the rustic dialect of Lucas Fernández and Juan del Encina, in the absence of holographic texts, are insecurely based.

24. I have indicated elsewhere, 'The *Cancionero* of Fray Íñigo de Mendoza', the assistance given by one of these MSS.

25. The *Sermón* and many other poems are to be found in the Escorial MS, but they are copied from *C*, and so this MS, except for its *Vita Christi*, is of no importance for an editor.

26. The transcriber has clearly used the British Museum copy, which lacks F2, which has the end of this poem and the beginning of the *Dechado*. Instead of turning to another copy of *C*, he has partially filled the gap by copying the beginning of the *Dechado* from the *Canc. de Llavia*. The first *quintilla* of the first of these nine stanzas is actually on F1^v, but was not transcribed by Foulché-Delbosc.

27. It is reproduced in facsimile by Pérez Gómez in his *Tercera floresta*, but in a preliminary note the editor makes it clear that its inclusion in the series does not mean he guarantees it an incunable. F. J. Norton informs me that it was certainly printed by Jacobo Cromberger at Seville, and on reliable typographical grounds cannot possibly have been printed before 1510. He thinks it was probably printed c. 1515, to within a year or two either way.

28. I wish to thank J. Rodríguez Puértolas of Nottingham, and F. J. Norton and Professor E. M. Wilson of Cambridge for their information and advice; I am grateful to J. S. Cummins of King's College for performing for me a number of chores in the British Museum; and I must record my enormous debt to D.

Antonio Pérez Gómez for his continued help, interest, and criticisms. [Julio Rodríguez-Puértolas was working on a critical edition of the *Vita Christi* when this article was written. It was completed in 1963, though not published until 1968: see n.1, above.]

3

The 'Cancionero of Fray Íñigo de Mendoza': MS Escurialense K-III-7

Of Fray Íñigo de Mendoza's *Vita Christi*, his major work, some eight manuscripts have been recorded. The *Cancionero de Castañeda* was sold by Pedro Vindel to a buyer whose name remains undisclosed, and the *Cancionero del obispo* has also been lost to view; but there are extant the *Cancionero de Vindel* in the Library of the Hispanic Society of America (New York), the MS in the Biblioteca de la Universidad de Salamanca, II-593 (formerly Bib. de Palacio, Madrid, VIII-A-3), of which Bib. Nac., Madrid, 3757 appears to be a copy (made in 1807), the two very important MSS, recently studied by Julio Rodríguez Puértolas,[1] British Museum Egerton 939 and Bibliothèque Nationale, Paris, Esp. 305, which represent the primitive version of the poem and of which the Paris MS contains the later excised stanzas 'contra la nobleza', and, finally, the Escorial codex K-III-7, which contains, besides the *Vita Christi*, most of Mendoza's other work in verse and is often referred to as the 'Cancionero de Fray Íñigo de Mendoza'.[2]

It is necessary, for purposes of comparison with K-III-7, briefly to list the contents of the *cancionero* printed, without imprint, by Antonio de Centenera in Zamora in 1483–84?,[3] the text of which served Foulché-Delbosc for the only modern edition of Mendoza's works:[4]

1. Mendoza, 'Vita Christi', A_1^r-D_6^v.
2. Mendoza, 'Sermón trobado', D_6^v-E_2^v.
3. Mendoza, 'Vituperio de las malas hembras', E_2^v-E_4^v.
4. Mendoza, 'Como es reparada nuestra Castilla', E_4^v-F_2^v.
5. Mendoza, 'Dechado', F_2^v-F_6^r.
6. Mendoza, 'Razón y sensualidad', F_6^r-G_8^v.
7. Mendoza, 'Gozos de Nuestra Señora', G_9^r-G_{10}^v.
8. Mendoza, 'La cena', G_{10}^v-H_4^v.
9. Mendoza, 'La Verónica', H_4^v-I_3^r.

10. Mendoza, 'Al spíritu sancto', I3^v-I4^r.
11. Jorge Manrique, 'Coplas a la muerte de su padre', I4^r-I7^r.
12. Anonymous, 'Lamentación a la quinta angustia', I7^v-I8^v.
13. Juan de Mena, 'Coplas contra los pecados mortales', with Gómez Manrique's continuation of the poem, LI^r-M8^r.
14. 'Pregunta' of Sancho de Rojas 'a un aragonés', and the 'respuesta', M8^r-M8^v.
15. Jorge Manrique, 'Coplas sobre qué es amor', M8^v.

The Escorial codex (inadequately described by Gallardo 3047) consists of 233 leaves of MS, of which the only foliation is a late pencil numbering in Arabic figures, 1-29, 29 [bis], 30-116, 116 [bis], 117-231. At the end are bound two short printed texts, 'Coplas [. . .] a reuerencia del nacimiento de [. . .] cristo',[5] and a poem beginning 'Con pena y cuydado, continuo guerreo' which has for title 'Estas coplas son de arte mayor [. . .]'. One leaf of the printed texts is missing: leaves 232 and 233 are AI and A3 of the *Coplas al nacimiento*; but in the MS itself there appear to be no missing leaves, despite various lacunae in the text of the *Vita Christi*, and more serious gaps in other poems.

The MS was executed by more than one hand, though it is not easy to determine how many, if more than one, were involved in the latter part (fol. 98^r on). They are habitually described as 'fifteenth-century', but it is not possible on the palaeographic evidence to affirm that they are not early sixteenth. The MS of the *Vita Christi* is in several ways different from the rest. It is, first of all, in a scrupulously regular script, which has at times the aspect of print; a large space is left for a coloured or illuminated initial *A* for the opening line; in general the copyist eschews abbreviations, and, unlike the later scribe or scribes, rarely uses capitals for the initials of stanzas. More important—and I anticipate—the text of the *Vita Christi* is here a distinct redaction, representing a half-way house between the MSS of the primitive version of the poem and the final corrected version of the printed texts. The contents of the codex are as follows:

1. 'Vita Christi', I^r-97^r (97^v is blank).
2. 'Sermón trobado', 98^r-111^r.
3. 'Vituperio de las malas hembras', 112^r-116 bis^v.
4. 'Como es reparada nuestra Castilla'.
5. 'Razón y sensualidad' (incomplete).
6. 'Gozos de nuestra Señora' (incomplete).
7. 'La cena' (incomplete: one and a half stanzas).

(I discuss the curious and complex foliation of items 4–7 below.)

8. 'Dechado', 146^r-156^v.
9. Juan de Mena, 'Coplas contra los pecados' (with Gómez Manrique's continuation), 157^r-213^v.
10. 'Pregunta de Sancho de Rojas a un aragonés', and the 'respuesta', 213^v-214^r.
11. Jorge Manrique, 'Coplas sobre qué es amor', 214^r-215^r.
12. Jorge Manrique, 'Coplas a la muerte de su padre', 215^v-229^r.
13. A more careful copy of the third item, 229^v-231^v.

It will be immediately obvious that this selection of texts, which, with omissions, duplicates that of the Centenera *cancionero* (which I shall call *C*), shows that the MS and the printed edition are intimately related; and the nature of the connexion can be established beyond doubt.

In the MS, items 4 to 7 are in confusion. *Como es reparada* (4) begins on 117^r, but the second *quintilla* of the second stanza on that page is the second *quintilla* of the fourth stanza of *Razón y sensualidad* (5), which then runs on to the bottom of 120^v, ending about an eighth of the way through, just after the eighteenth stanza (which begins 'Por mayor autoridad'). 121^r then begins in the middle of the *Gozos* (6) at the fourteenth stanza ('O quanta gloria sentiste'), and the *Gozos* then run on to their conclusion on 124^r, which also starts *La cena* (7), giving its title and first stanza. But 124^v carries on with *La cena* only for half a stanza, and joins this first *quintilla* of the second stanza of *La cena* to the second *quintilla* of the second stanza of *Como es reparada* (4), which then continues, from the point at which it was suspended on 117^r, to its completion on 145^v.

I have perhaps anticipated my argument in stating the facts in this way; but only the supposition that this part of the Escorial MS is a transcript of a mutilated copy of *C* can explain the relationship between them, for the anomalous junctures in the MS poems all occur precisely at the juncture of verso and recto pages in *C*. *C*'s E4^v finishes with the first one and a half stanzas of *Como es reparada*; *C*'s G1^r opens with the second *quintilla* of the fourth stanza of *Razón y sensualidad*, and G1^v closes with its eighteenth stanza; G10^r starts with the fourteenth stanza of the *Gozos*, and G10^v finishes with the first one and a half stanzas of *La cena*. That is to say, the MS sequence of stanzas and poems corresponds exactly, so far as these four items are concerned, with the *C* foliation E4, G1, G10, E5-8, F1-2^r. One should note too that it is unnecessary to suppose that any leaves are missing in the MS between the incomplete *Razón y sensualidad* and the acephalous *Gozos*.

The copying of *C* begins, in fact, with the *Sermón*. For this poem the scribe had a choice of printed texts,[6] but the remarkably close coincidence of the orthography between the MS and *C* (vocalic *i* or long *j* instead of *y*,

c before *e* and *i* instead of *ç*, *m* before *p* and *b* instead of *n*, and so on)
reveals—as might be expected—that *C* is once more the source. The copyist,
in short, transcribes *C* as follows: D6^v-E4^v, G1, G10, E5^r-F6^r, L1^r-M8^v,
I4^r-I7^r. He cannot have been unconscious that his text was seriously
mutilated, for, although he fell into hopeless confusion with some of the
Mendoza poems—pardonable inasmuch as there is no startling contrast of
content and all four are written in *quintillas dobles* (though in the *Cena* and
Gozos they have a final *quebrado*)—he did not, after concluding the *Dechado*,
go on to copy the opening of *Razón y sensualidad* on F6, and in copying the
Manrique *Coplas a la muerte de su padre* he ignored the scrap of *Al spíritu
sancto* on I4^r, and on I7^v the opening of the *Lamentación a la quinta angustia*.
All this, of course, deprives the latter part of the Escorial codex of any
authority: it is pointless to record its variant readings,[7] which, indeed, merely
spoil the sense, the octosyllable, and even, on occasions, the rhyme.

The text of the *Vita Christi*, at the beginning of this codex, is, however,
a very different matter.

A complete account of the primitive version of the *Vita Christi*, which can
be reconstructed by collation of the heavily Catalanized (and probably late)
Paris MS (which I shall now call *P*) and the defective British Museum
Egerton 939 (*Eg.*), may be found in the forthcoming article by Rodríguez
Puértolas [see note 1, below]. However, to understand the position of MS
Esc. K-III-7 in the sequence of revisions it is necessary to note here the
following points: (1) in the early version the plan of the entire work is
different; of the six sections of the printed version (Nativity, Circumcision,
Magi, Presentation, Flight into Egypt, Massacre of the Innocents) the
primitive version omits the Flight into Egypt, and telescopes the Circumcision and the Presentation, putting the Presentation before the episode of
the three Magi; (2) where in the printed version at the beginning of the
section on the Circumcision (*A* B7^r), Fray Íñigo 'dexa de hablar dela
conçepçion por no hazer cosquillas a ninguno', in the primitive version he
launches into a violent diatribe against the Dominicans who attacked the
Franciscan-held doctrine of the Immaculate Conception; (3) where in the
printed version, after describing the infant Christ in the manger, Fray Íñigo
(*A* B3^r) 'descúlpase del aver nonbrado enel primer trasunto / algunos
grandes', in the primitive version he has a long and violent attack on Enrique
IV, Alonso Carrillo, Juan de Acuña, Pedro Girón, Juan de Pacheco, Beltrán
de la Cueva, and Álvaro de Estúñiga;[8] and (4) between the primitive version
and the printed 'official' version there are innumerable minor differences
involving the suppression or insertion of entire stanzas, almost wholly

different redaction of certain passages, and abundant variant readings
plausibly attributable to the author's stylistic corrections. And it should be
noted at once that the Escorial MS is much closer to the printed text than
to the first version: in the plan of the whole work, in the omission of the
stanzas attacking the Dominicans and the grandees it agrees with the printed
texts. But in the actual redaction of the stanzas the Escorial MS is still quite
far, with well over a thousand significant variant readings, from the final
revised version represented by the printed texts.

K-III-7 gives the title of Mendoza's major work as: 'Comiença la vida de
n*uest*ro redenptor ih*esu* chr*isto* en estilo metrico conpuesta por vn frayre
menor de obseruancia a pedimiento de doña juana de cartajena'. Mendoza's
name does not appear, and the title is not *Vita Christi*. In *P* it is 'Vita christi
trobada por ffrayle enyeguo llopez de mendoça ffrayle menor de la
observança a pedimento de duenya joana de cartagena madre suya' and in
Eg. 'Vita christi trobado a pedimento de doña juana de cartagena conpuesto
por un frayle menor de observancia'. The title of *A* is 'Vita christi fecho en
coplas por frey yñigo de me*n*doça a petiçio*n* dela muy v*i*rtuosa señora doña
iuana de cartagena'. *P*, with its 'Llopez', is in error; but it is right with its
'madre suya' (which is also added in pencil to the BM copy of *C*). The
coincidence of the anonymity of the Escorial and Egerton MSS is suggestive,
for the Catalanized Paris MS is almost certainly late.[9] It would appear that
the primitive and first revised versions of the *Vita Christi* circulated anonymously.

The poem then begins as in *A*, showing only minor variants, but very
soon the texts diverge markedly. Here are the fourth, fifth, and sixth stanzas
in parallel: the topic of the rejection of the pagan muses and invocation of
the Christian, reinforced by the 'ciceronianus' anecdote about St Jerome
from the *Legenda aurea* (which Padilla in his *Retablo* later employs in the same
context):

MS K-III-7	*A* (1st edition)
despide las fiçiones poeticas	Despide las musas poeticas
por el conoscimjento de la	e in voca las cristianas
verdad chr*ist*iana	
dexemos las niñerias	Dexemos las poesias
de las musas jnuocadas	y sus musas invocadas
y las otras fantasias	por q*ue* tales ninirias
quen las huecas poesias	por humanas fantasias
suelen ser chimirizadas	so*n* cierto temorizadas
y biniendo ala verdad	y veniendo ala verdat

de quien puede dar ajuda
ala sola trinidad
que mana sienpre bondad
la supliquemos sin duda

da la razon de despedirlas

no digo que los poetas
los dagora y los pasados
no ayan obras muj netas
graçiosas dulces discretas
en sus renglones trobados
mas destas sciencias seglares
al fin de los entendimientos
que dan commo paladares
que sueñan dulces manjares
y al fin despiertan ambrientos

prueua lo por enxenplo

por auer mucho seguido
al poetico dulçor
fue de dios reprendido
açotado y desmentido
sant jeronimo doctor
asta que de sus entrañas
despidio la tal porfia
quedando varas estrañas
para los juegos de cañas
de la sacra theologia

de quien puede dar ayuda
ala sola trinidat
que mana sienpre bondat
gela pidamos sin duda

prosigue

Non digo quelos poetas
los presentes y passados
non fagan obras perfectas
graçiosas y bien discretas
en sus renglones trobados
mas affirmo ser herror
perdonen sy bien non fablo
en su obra el trobador
inuocar al dios de amor
para seruiçio del diablo

prosigue y prueua con sant
  iheronimo

Sant iheronimo acusado
por que en çiceron leya
en spiritu arrebatado
fue duramente açotado
presente dios que le dezia
si piensas que eres christiano
segund la forma deuida
es vn pensamiento vano
que eres çiceroniano
pues es çiceron tu vida

This degree of divergency is not typical of the differences between this MS and *A*, for after the eighth stanza there is no very substantial rewriting, in spite of the thousand-odd significant variants, which affect only three or four isolated words per stanza. In the opening stanza of the poem 'enciende la voluntad / repara nuestra memoria' is in *A* 'despierta la voluntad / endereça la memoria', and a large proportion of the variants are of this type, when there appears to be little or nothing to choose between them; but in general the readings of *A* will be found to be slightly superior (when the MS is not quite clearly wrong). The few stanzas which I have quoted will serve to show why we must accept that the MS represents a redaction earlier than that of *A*. The endings of the second and third stanzas quoted have acquired in *A* point which they lack in the MS. (The image of the disillusioned dreamer in the MS, second stanza quoted, is used later in the poem, *A* D3^v—it is, of course, a medieval preachers' commonplace—which is perhaps what prompted Mendoza to rewrite this particular *quintilla*.) In several instances (e.g. 2nd stanza, line 4; 3rd, lines 2-3) Mendoza has eliminated amplificatory devices, in accordance with his later expressed anti-rhetorical stylistic ideals.[10] In general the MS version is clumsier, less pointed, altogether less polished.

The Escorial MS has, as I have mentioned, certain lacunae compared with the printed text. They occur as follows: (i) two stanzas are missing between 33^v and 34^r (Nos 140 and 141 of the printed version, corresponding to stanzas 5 and 6 of *A*'s B4^r); (ii) a lacuna of three stanzas (Nos 143-45, *A*: 2-4 of B4^v) occurs between the two stanzas on 34^r; (iii) one stanza (No. 157, *A*: 4th of B5^v) is missing between 36^v and 37^r; (iv) seven stanzas (Nos 233-39, *A*: from the 2nd of C4^r to the 2nd of C4^v inclusive) are missing between the two stanzas on 55^v; (v) one stanza (No. 238, *A*: 4th of C8^r) is missing between the two stanzas on 66^v; and (vi) four stanzas (Nos 291-94, *A*: 6th of C8^v to the 3rd of D1^r inclusive) are missing between the two stanzas on 68^r. (A displacement of leaves at first sight suggests lacunae, but the order should be 89, 91, 90, 93, 92, 94.) All lacunae except (i) and (iii) occur in mid-page, but even in the two cases where they do not the gaps cannot correspond with a missing MS leaf, since this would have involved four stanzas in each case; and the irregularity of the numbers of missing stanzas in each gap does not suggest missing leaves in an earlier MS. Obviously the gaps could be accounted for by a copyist's carelessness, but an examination of *P* and *Eg.* suggests a more interesting answer.

The first three lacunae of K-III-7 occur in the episode of the shepherds at the end of the section on the Nativity. From 'Comie[n]ça la reuelaçion del angel alos pastores' (stanza 137) we have in *A* 34 stanzas (to 170) of rustic shepherd dialogue interrupted by brief snatches of narrative. The whole episode in *P* and *Eg.* is markedly different: only 14 stanzas of the final 'official' version are to be found in the primitive version; 8 stanzas are wholly missing; and 11 exist in a wholly or almost wholly different redaction.[11] Of stanzas 140-45, 143 and 144 exist in a very different redaction in *P* and *Eg.* and 145 is missing, as in K-III-7. Stanza 157, missing in the Escorial MS, is also absent from *P* and *Eg.* The absence of 140 and 141 from the Escorial MS may be due to a copyist's lapse, but these stanzas may have been forgotten or deliberately omitted by Mendoza while effecting his very substantial revision of the whole passage. It may be worth noting that there is some confusion in the dialogue between Juan Pastor and Mingo in K-III-7: the situation can be saved by attributing one speech to a third shepherd, but this is unnecessary both in the shorter primitive version, *P* and *Eg.*, and in the final version.

The next gaps occur in the episode of the Magi. Of stanzas 233-39, 233 and 234 are differently redacted in *P* and *Eg.*, but a copyist's lapse (perhaps jumping from the 'Comparacion' of stanza 232 to the stanza following the 'Comparacion' of 239) or a missing leaf in an earlier MS seem the most likely explanation of this gap in K-III-7. Stanza 283, however, missing in the Escorial MS, is in a quite different position in *P* and *Eg.*, placed after 173, so that it may have been omitted from Mendoza's first revision, and then reincorporated later in the final version. Stanzas 291-94 (the 'exclamaçionn [*sic*] delos reyes co*n*tra el tyrano rey herodes') are missing in all three MSS and must have been written only for the final version.

The *Vita Christi* is unfinished, ending quite abruptly after the Massacre of the Innocents, without even the usual prayer in the name of Doña Juana with which every other section is brought to a close. It is now clear that Mendoza twice revised his incomplete poem without ever bringing it to a conclusion. His first (and probably anonymous) version had a slightly different (and in its confusion of Circumcision and Presentation, incorrect) plan; in revising it (K-III-7) Mendoza cut out the diatribes against the Dominicans and the nobility, wrote in the Flight into Egypt, rewrote and expanded considerably the section on the Massacre of the Innocents, and in general corrected and expanded throughout; for the final official version he again began rewriting from the beginning, effecting very substantial changes in the opening stanzas, and thereafter emending two or three words in almost every stanza, and inserting one or two additional stanzas. But Mendoza completed neither the poem (even if it were never intended as a full *Vita* but only as an Infancy) nor his self-imposed task of revising it for the second time.

This MS of the *Vita Christi* is, as I have said, beautifully executed; but it abounds in errors. Its errors, however, do not coincide with those of *A* (except in one curious instance), and it proves most useful in correcting the printed text (from which *P* and *Eg.* stand somewhat distant). Four lines are missing from *A*, and they can be supplied from the MS as follows: (i) 1st stanza of B2^r, insert, after 'seraphines muy discretos', 'que los diuinos secretos', and, as the last line, 'en vn muy suabe modo'; (ii) 5th stanza of B7^v, insert as the penultimate line 'que en no estando exerçitadas'; (iii) 4th stanza of C8^r, insert as the penultimate line 'sieruen delo quela lunbre'. The

MS explains the origin of the curious non-rhyme *fermosura/tuya* (5th stanza, A1^v): for *A*'s 'ca te crio de no nada / doctada de fermosura' it reads 'ca te crio de no nada / ala sacra ymagen suya'; it would seem that in rewriting the stanza Mendoza forgot the rhyme in the last line. A further ten faulty rhymes in *A* can be satisfactorily emended on the authority of the MS. It is perhaps particularly useful for pointing to the errors of *A*, among them those simple literals emended in proof to the wrong sense, which it would probably not occur to an editor to change: thus 'parayso terenal', not 'eternal', B2^v 1st stanza; 'nuue liuiana', not 'nueua', D5^r 5th stanza; or 'tememos', not 'tenemos', D7^v 1st stanza. Sometimes both the MS and *A* are wrong, but collation of the texts reveals the correct reading: see, for instance, the 7th line of the 7th stanza (Esc. MS: 'que toda fuera el escoria'; *A*: 'quitada fuera la ystoria'), which should clearly read 'quitada fuera el escoria', and so on. There is one curious case in which *A* and the MS coincide in error. They have the non-rhyme 'fauoreados' (for an obvious 'fauorecidos'), *A* D3^r 1st stanza, although *C* makes the emendation.

We have still to examine in detail the text of the *Vita Christi* in the *Cancionero de Vindel*, and the Salamanca MS. Meanwhile the collation of *P* and *Eg.* with the printed text and MS Escurialense K-III-7 gives us a remarkable and unusual insight into the elaboration of one of the great works of the Spanish fifteenth century.[12]

[*Filología*, 7 (1961 [1963]), 161-72, in Spanish translation]

Notes

1. I am indebted to Sr Rodríguez for allowing me to see the typescript of his forthcoming 'Dos versiones de las coplas de *Vita Christi* de Fray Íñigo de Mendoza'. [Rodríguez-Puértolas's work appeared in a different form: the section headed 'Las versiones de la *Vita Christi* y fecha del poema', in Chap. 3 of his *Fray Íñigo de Mendoza y sus 'Coplas de Vita Christi'* (Madrid: Gredos, 1968), pp. 101-17. His book, completed in 1963 and revised before publication, includes the critical edition of the *Vita Christi* for which Whinnom was hoping (see p. 32, above).]

2. Charles V. Aubrun, 'Inventaire des sources pour l'étude de la poésie castillane au XVe siècle', in *Estudios dedicados a Menéndez Pidal*, IV (Madrid, 1953), 298-330, objects, p. 313: 'La désignation induit en erreur, puisqu'il s'agit d'un chansonnier collectif.'

3. There are copies in the Biblioteca Nacional, *Cat. de incunables* 1291, in the British

Museum, IB. 52920, and in the Escorial, 38-I-27. See Antonio Pérez Gómez, 'Notas para la bibliografía de Fray Íñigo de Mendoza y de Jorge Manrique', *HR*, 27 (1959), 30-41.

4. *Cancionero castellano del siglo XV*, I, NBAE, XIX (Madrid, 1912), and see my 'The Printed Editions and the Text of the Works of Fray Íñigo de Mendoza', *BHS*, 39 (1962), 137-52 [repr. pp. 18-35, above].

5. They are reproduced by Antonio Pérez Gómez in his *Segunda floresta de incunables* (Valencia, 1958), and are in fact by Fray Ambrosio de Montesino, and may be found in his *Coplas sobre diversas devociones y misterios de nuestra santa fe católica* (Toledo, c. 1485), reproduced in facsimile by Sir Henry Thomas (London, 1936) and more recently by Sr Pérez Gómez himself.

6. In the first edition of the *Vita Christi*, in octavo, by Centenera, Zamora, 1482 (facsimile Madrid, 1953), and in the folio edition, without imprint, but Saragossa, 1482?, possibly by Hurus and Planck. I shall call the first edition *A*.

7. As, for instance, R. Foulché-Delbosc does in his classic edition of the Manrique *Coplas* (Barcelona-Madrid, 1905, with the preface in French; repr. Madrid, 1912, with the same preface in Spanish).

8. The later excised stanzas are copied at the end of the Paris MS, with a note by the scribe indicating where they are to be inserted in the text.

9. By 'late' I do not mean to imply that it is necessarily later than the late fifteenth century (as Rodríguez Puértolas suggests). But this would place it long after the composition (between 1466 and 1474, as Rodríguez demonstrates), the final revision (before 1474), and a series of printings, from 1482 on, of the final version.

10. See my forthcoming article, 'El origen de las comparaciones religiosas del Siglo de Oro: Mendoza, Montesino y Román', [*RFE*, 46 (1963 [1965]), 263-85; pp. 72-95, below].

11. I work from Rodríguez Puértolas's table of concordances, [*Fray Íñigo de Mendoza y sus 'Coplas de Vita Christi'*, pp. 285-86].

12. I wish to record my gratitude to Sr Antonio Pérez Gómez, who lent me his microfilm of K-III-7.

4

The Supposed Sources of Inspiration of Spanish Fifteenth-Century Narrative Religious Verse

In the 1470s and '80s there appear in print for the first time in Spanish the long versified narratives of episodes from the life of Christ: Mendoza's *Vita Christi*, first printed in 1482 but probably first redacted in the reign of Enrique IV, Román's *Trovas de la gloriosa pasión* c. 1485 and *Coplas de la pasión con la resurrección* in 1486?, San Pedro's *Pasión trovada*, written probably in the period 1470–80 and first printed some time before 1492, and Montesino's *Coplas sobre diversas devociones y misterios de nuestra santa fe católica* c. 1485, comparatively much shorter pieces devoted mostly to isolated episodes of Christ's life, and with which I shall not be here much concerned.[1] That this new-style verse is ultimately connected with the ferment of new ideas in the second half of the fifteenth century it would be difficult to deny; but two of the theses advanced concerning the specific stimuli at work in this period fail to withstand detailed investigation.

Américo Castro suggested in 1940 that one of the factors creating the ambience in which narratives of the life of Christ flourished was the *devotio moderna*, 'cuyos reflejos a lo largo del siglo XV conocemos tan imperfectamente'.[2] Marcel Bataillon, in the preface to the Spanish translation of his great work on Erasmus, noted that, if he had the book to rewrite, he would go further back into the fifteenth century to trace the origin of certain spiritual currents, and marked the need for a close investigation of the history of the *devotio moderna* in Spain and elsewhere.[3] In Francisco López Estrada's manual we find a plain assertion that the *devotio moderna* explains the phenomenon of Mendoza, Montesino, and Padilla.[4] There are, however, *a priori*, certain objections to the thesis. Those who have studied the subject in detail appear unable to document a direct knowledge of the *devotio moderna* in Spain before Abbot Cisneros of Montserrat returned from Paris in 1496, having met there Standonck and Mombaer, with copies of Mombaer's *Rosetum exercitiorum spiritualium* and Gerard of Zütphen's *Tractatus de spiritualibus ascensionibus.*[5] Albareda, certainly, expresses (p. 65) the view that this would not be Cisneros's first acquaintance with the *devotio moderna*, and suggests that his predecessor Joan de Peralta may have introduced it to his monks. But Catalonia was in much closer contact with France than was Castile, and was, generally speaking, ahead of Castile in religious matters up to the end of the fifteenth century, both in the translation of foreign devotional works and in the writing of them: Francesc Eximeniç's *Vita Christi* antedates Mendoza's by perhaps a century. There were many reformers before the Reformation, and if one defines the *devotio moderna* only in general terms (hostility to traditional scholasticism, emphasis on a return to the Bible, a 'movement of obedient revolt from the stereotyped routine of passable salvation' in Previté-Orton's phrase), one is in some danger of confusing its manifestations with those of the Franciscan reform. We require some detailed and concrete evidence.

Bataillon, Chapter I, reaffirms his remarks of 1925[6] to the effect that the *Vita Christi* of Ludolph the Saxon (Ludolphus/Lodolphus Saxo/de Saxonia/ Carthusiensis, etc.) directly inspired Montesino, and that Mendoza owes a great deal to it. Pierre Le Gentil refers repeatedly to the influence of the work, remarking that Montesino's works are 'fortement influencées, comme celles de tous les poètes religieux du temps, par la *Vita Christi* de Ludolphe de Saxe'.[7] For López Estrada, Ludolph's *Vita* is the 'obra fundamental para la espiritualidad de la época'. But here lies the rub: the period to which they all refer is the early sixteenth century. All mention only the Toledo 1508 edition of Montesino's *Cancionero* (*Canc. de diversas obras de nuevo trovadas*, repr. BAE, XXXV), apparently unaware of the existence of the *cancionero* of 1485, of which Toledo 1508 is simply a revised and expanded version. The principal objection to the thesis of the influence of Ludolph's work before, say, the late 1490s is again the late-documented impact of Ludolph on Spain: the absence of MSS and of printed editions of the Latin text; the comparatively very late translation, by Montesino in 1501, published under the auspices of Cardinal Cisneros at Alcalá 1502–03;[8] the lateness of the unequivocal references to the work. There was indubitably a sixteenth-century vogue of 'el Cartuxano'; but one does not begin to find references to the work in Spain before the end of the fifteenth century.[9]

A further difficulty is that this vast work (which runs, on my calculation, close to three-quarters of a million words) is a mosaic structure which draws on a host of earlier writers, incorporating whole passages from other works, often without any kind of acknowledgment. Thus in his *Prooemium* Ludolph

copies his fellow-Carthusian Guigo's *De contemplatione* for its first third, takes
over almost entire the preface of the *Meditationes vitae Christi*, a chapter
of David of Augsburg's *De meditatione Domini Jesu*, and passages from
Burchardus de Monte Sion, St Bonaventure, and St Bernard. In fact just one
twenty-fourth of the preface (Bodenstedt, p. 29) is original Ludolph—or, of
course, some unidentified author. The features which Bataillon (*Erasmo*, pp.
51 ff.) singles out for mention are to be found in many another writer; so
to assert that Ludolph, rather than Ludolph's own sources—Bernard,
Bonaventure, the *Meditationes*, and so on—is the source and stimulus of some
Spanish writer in the fifteenth century must be, until we have a detailed
analysis and comparison of the texts in question, somewhat venturesome.

The third—and earliest—of the explanations adduced for the phenomenon
of Mendoza and Montesino is the Franciscan reform.[10] Both writers
were, of course, Franciscans of the new Observance. But Marcelino
Menéndez y Pelayo's statement that they 'conservan muchos rasgos de la
poesía tradicional de su orden'[11] needs considerable amplification: several
curious features of Mendoza's *Vita Christi* in particular are not to be found
in earlier Franciscan verse in Latin or Italian.[12] Even the debt of Montesino
to Jacopone da Todi, generally accepted by historians of literature since
Menéndez y Pelayo quoted a few parallel passages, must, I think, as Bataillon
suggested ('Chanson pieuse'), be reckoned rather doubtful. And in all these
theories we find no reference to the works of San Pedro or the Comendador
Román.

By concentrating here on certain aspects—still perhaps uncomfortably
broad for one paper—of this narrative religious verse, I hope to clarify some
details of the whole picture.

But first I must say something about one of the most important and
influential works of the later Middle Ages, written by an unknown
thirteenth-century Franciscan long thought to be Bonaventure himself, the
Meditationes vitae Christi.[13] Though it clearly owes much to the ideas of St
Bernard, who is quoted at every turn, it is novel in that it departs radically
from the earlier types of biblical exegesis. The pseudo-Bonaventure more
than once disclaims the role of commentator, for his purpose is not to
expound Scripture but to guide and assist the reader in devotional contemplation. He takes the Gospel narratives as his starting point and proceeds to
fill out the bare framework by the addition of circumstance, introducing
probable incident, amplifying sentences to speeches. The lacunae of the
biblical story (what happened to the gold given to the infant Christ?, see
Meditationes, Chapter IX) lead inevitably to this kind of speculation; and the

fact that language itself can never convey the reality entire leaves the imagination immense scope. The result is a kind of new apocryphal gospel. So, in Chapter XII, 'De fuga Domini in Aegyptum', which depends on the brief comment in Matthew 2: 14, we find detailed discussions of the journey, of how the Holy Family lived in Egypt, and so on. Here, he says with enthusiasm, we enter into a beautiful field of pious and tender contemplation, and a column of ratiocination leads us finally to a scene in which Jesus, delivering sewing to Mary's customers, 'must have met with' some termagant, 'mulier aliqua superba, rixosa, et loquax', who took the work and refused to pay for it, spoke to Christ harshly, and drove him away without the money. These and like points, he concludes, are exceedingly fit for meditation; and, despite the abundant detail he has supplied, he goes on to say that he has simply provided the reader with a clue, and that he must follow out the thought for himself.

The unknown author of the *Meditationes* starts from the premises that to know Christ is to love him, and that the love of Christ is the beginning and the end of all wisdom. He believes that the Christian, simply by focusing his attention on, 'meditating' upon, 'contemplating', the life of Christ, is drawn to holiness. Winding up his preface he tells the reader: 'Tu autem si ex his fructum sumere cupis, ita te praesentem exhibeas, his quae per Dominum Jesum dicta et facta narrantur, ac si tuis auribus audires et oculis ea videres, toto mentis affectu diligenter, delectabiliter, et morose.' In Chapter LI, enlarging on the contemplation of the humanity of Christ, he quotes Bernard: 'Haec meditari dixi sapientiam; in his justitiae mihi perfectionem constitui; in his plenitudinem sapientiae; in his divitias salutis; in his copias meritorum.' The passage concludes: 'Haec mea subtilior interiorque Philosophiae, scire Jesum, et hunc crucifixum' (cf. I Cor. 2: 2; Bernard, *Sermo XLIII in Cantic.*, PL, CLXXXIII, 995). The *Meditationes* include, Chapters XLV–LVIII, a treatise on meditation, compiled largely from the works of Bernard of Clairvaux. There are two kinds of active and one kind of contemplative life, which can be arranged in stages, but the final stage, the active life of the teacher, preacher, and saint, who 'vera sapientia imbutus et illuminatus, ad aliorem salutem intendat', he does not deal with, since his reader, a nun, will not require it: 'tuus status hoc non requirit' (Chapter XLVII). Similarly, though there are three kinds of contemplation, 'pro perfectis' the contemplation of the majesty of God and the contemplation of the Celestial Court, and 'pro incipientibus, imperfectis' the contemplation of the humanity of Christ, he makes it clear that his reader is a beginner, and does not long discourse on the third type 'quia totum hunc librum de ipso habes'. This is meditation for the ordinary man, the illuminating and purgative *contemplatio humanitatis Christi*: 'Christus intellectum illuminat, Christus affectum purgat' (Chapter LI). The *Meditationes* themselves are, in short, no mystical treatise; in the context, 'pro incipientibus', meditation and contemplation are interchangeable terms; and there is no suggestion of a *scala meditatoria*.

There are two points that require emphasis. First, despite the fact that the *Meditationes* are used in well over half the 181 chapters of Ludolph's *Vita Jesu Christi*, Ludolph, by including, but not otherwise imitating, the *Meditationes*, wrote a book very different from it. We have, as well as the meditative and mystic Ludolph (i.e. Henry Suso, James of Milan, etc.), Ludolph the theologian, Ludolph the preacher, and above all Ludolph the exegete, still interpreting his text *allegorice* or *mystice*, *tropologice* or *moraliter*, and, though not often, *anagogice*. Secondly, and again in marked contrast with Ludolph, the *Meditationes* are based almost exclusively on the New Testament: while they may describe innumerable apocryphal incidents (invented by the author) they never claim for them any validity beyond the obvious, and they make no use of the New Testament Apocrypha.[14] Ludolph, on the other hand, uses the *Pseudo-Matthaei evangelium*, the *Evangelium de nativitate Mariae*, and the *Evangelium Nicodemi* (*Gesta Pilati* and *Descensus Christi ad inferos*), as well as James of Voragine's *Legenda aurea*.[15]

I shall not here embark on a detailed study of the use of apocryphal material by the four poets with whom we are concerned, but it is necessary to say a word or two about the subject, since the invented details of the pseudo-Bonaventure's method of contemplation are not always easily distinguishable from genuine apocryphal matter. The back-to-the-Bible movement, an important aspect of the *devotio moderna* but by no manner of means exclusive to it, had its influence on San Pedro, Mendoza, and, to a much lesser extent, Montesino; but the Comendador Román remains innocent of such proto-Protestant ideas. From the evidence of his text, indeed, one might even begin to wonder whether he knew the Bible directly at all. He gives Matthew as his authority (E2^v) for the appearance of Christ to two disciples on the road to Emmaus, an incident recorded only by Luke; he again cites Matthew (E4^r) in place of Luke or John; E8^r he claims the authority of 'todos los euangelistas' for an episode reported by none of them; and when he admits (E10^v) that the Gospels are silent, 'callan los euangelistas', on the fate of the Virgin Mary, he appears to be tacitly claiming them for his source elsewhere, although the greater part of his narrative, and virtually all the Resurrection material, is apocryphal. Sir Henry Thomas (ed., *Coplas*, p. 15) has already noted that Menéndez y Pelayo's description of Román's work as a 'paráfrasis del texto evangélico' (*Antología*, III, 167) is far from accurate (he goes so far as to suggest that Menéndez y Pelayo had not read the poem), and has listed (pp. 13-15) a few of the many discrepancies between the Gospel narratives and Román's. Sir Henry mentions also 'minor incidents in the crufixion which may be attributed to the poet's imagination', citing specifically these details:

> (B8^v) fue desnudo y fue tendido
> en la cruz do le enclauaron
> la vna mano
>
> Con esta pasion tan braua
> por le penar mas entero
> visto por quien le enclauaua
> que tendido no llegaua
> con la otra al agugero
> los que siruen la sinoga
> con vna fuerça tan fiera
> que sobro
> trauaron con vna soga
> por su braço de manera
> que llego

and (C2^r) tiro la virgen su velo
> y cubriole lo que suele
> auergonçar

Both these details, however, are to be found in the *Meditationes vitae Christi*, Chapter LXXVIII, invented, so far as one can tell, by its author. I cannot, in fact, discover that Román has exercised his imagination at all in the invention of fresh incident. The *Gesta Pilati* is the ultimate source for most of the curious incidents of Román's 'Passion'—like the banners' bowing down to Christ, and again, after Pilate had ordered them held by stronger hands (B7); the *Legenda aurea*, Chapter LIII, provides most of the material for the 'Resurrection'; Román's version of the Veronica legend is a combination of the prevalent Roman tradition and the version which derives, via the *Golden Legend*, from the apocryphal *Mors Pilati*. For much of his material, of course, the Comendador is not necessarily drawing on any written source. That the crucified thieves were called Gimas and Gestas (Dysmas, Gestas in *Gesta Pilati* X; *Leg. aur.* LIII), that the soldier who pierced Christ's side with the spear was Longinus (*Gesta Pilati* XVI;

Meditationes LXXX; *Leg. aur.* XLVII and LIII) were facts universally familiar in the Middle Ages. Nor, despite the details I have quoted, is there any evidence that Román had read the *Meditationes*: it is extremely difficult to trace the direct influence of this work in the later Middle Ages, for topics from it become so widespread and popular, and innumerable themes, not only in books but in art and the medieval drama, derive from it, that there is no telling what chain of intermediate sources may have intervened.[16] But it is quite clear that in his approach to his subject Román has little in common with the author of the *Meditationes*.

Román's poem is analysed for us by the rubrication. The narrative proper is marked by the headings which summarize the story: 'Nota como mando pilato açotar a christo', etc., and the rubrics indicate clearly the four ways in which Román expands his text: he notes consistently—as indeed the Gospels and all the commentators do—how Old Testament prophecies are fulfilled ('Nota lo que prophetizo ysayas', etc.); he embroiders his tale with picturesque comparisons, which I have studied elsewhere [pp. 72-95, below], marked by the rubric 'Conpara'; he inserts at appropriate points prayers for the Reyes Católicos ('Rogatiua por los rreyes'); and he comments on his narrative under the rubric 'el auctor'. But these comments resolve themselves into no more than a series of stereotyped exclamations, at the same time unimaginative and almost irrelevant. When Christ is accused before Annas (B1^r) he says:

> Ued que obidiença tan biua
> ved que querer tan sin par
> venir el señor de arriba
> entre gente secutiua
> a quererse condenar

But this is not the urgent 'conspice', 'considera', 'vide', of the pseudo-Bonaventure, which call on the reader to concentrate all his attention on the person of Christ, in compassion, admiration, and love—almost to identify himself with Christ. The affective impulse seems lacking in Román. When, a few stanzas later (B1^v), he exclaims:

> O gloriosa humildad
> de nuestra holgança puerto
> que con tan gran caridad
> entre dios y humanidad
> posiste tanto conçierto

the Comendador himself does nothing to bridge the gap between his reader and God: he stands too far back from his subject. Román's is in fact a mediocre work, and it is interesting to find 'el Ropero' (*Canc. general* 1511, fol. 226ᵛ) accusing him of plagiarism: '(el) vellaco sermonero / chocarrero de roman / [. . .] / es el aue que no pone / mas hurta hueuos agenos'. If 'el Ropero' is in fact referring to Román's religious verse ('sermonero'), the only author who could have supplied the material is San Pedro; but if the Comendador did attempt to emulate San Pedro, he did so in a singularly unenlightened fashion.[17]

In contrast with Román, San Pedro has, leaving aside the introduction, only two kinds of rubric: 'el texto' (with such variants as 'Torna al texto euangelical') and 'el auctor'. If we abstract from the San Pedro *Pasión* those stanzas rubricated 'el texto', we find that we have what is for much the greater part simply a paraphrase of the Gospels, no less close to the original than any metrical psalm. As a sample:

El señor a sant pedro	Ait illi Jesus:
No te muestres tan constante	
pedro que no lo seras	Amen
que yo te digo que ante	dico tibi quia in hac
questa noche el gallo cante	nocte antequam gallus cantet
tres vezes me negaras	ter me negabis.
sant pedro lo que prosigo	
respondio con buena fe	Ait illi Petrus:
señor hare lo que digo	
y si conuiene contigo	Etiamsi oportuerit me
morir no te negare	mori tecum, non te negabo.
(A4ᵛ-A5ʳ [st. 26, pp. 118-19])[18]	(Matt. 26: 34-35)

San Pedro's translation suffers a minimum of amplification and distortion in its accommodation to the exigencies of his metre.

Details additional to the Gospel narrative derive primarily from the *Meditationes vitae Christi*, but whether directly or via some other text it is impossible to be sure. San Pedro, for instance, gives a long and very explicit account of the nailing of Christ to the cross, which occupies him for almost fifty lines. The pseudo-Bonaventure (and Ludolph, Chapter LXIII) describes the incident quite briefly: 'Qui autem retro crucem est, accipit manum eius dexteram, et eam fortiter cruci affigit. Quo facto, ille qui est in latere sinistro accipit manum sinistram, et trahit quantum potest, et extendit, et alium clavum immitit, percutit, et configit'. There are, of course, a prodigious number of meditations on the Passion between the *Meditationes* and San

Pedro, and each more gruesome than the last. San Pedro could have arrived
at the same result by accepting the opportunity given him by the author of
the *Meditationes* ('dedi tibi occasionem') and practising the meditative
technique demonstrated abundantly in the earlier chapters of that work. The
chain of circumstantial reasoning, the logical reconstructive technique (they
must have measured Christ on the cross first, and marked the places for the
holes; the impact of the first nail must have caused his 'neruios' to
'encogerse'; it would then have been necessary to pull on the other arm,
with, finally, the horrible results that San Pedro describes: 'sus pechos
descoyuntaron / las ternillas le sacaron / penetrando sus entrañas'): this is
precisely the kind of ratiocination by which the pseudo-Bonaventure has
Christ delivering sewing in Egypt. But whether San Pedro worked out the
details for himself, or used some other work, one cannot say. It is at least
worth noting that Ludolph is not the source in question.

Again it is the pseudo-Bonaventure who, reliving the Passion with intense
and obsessive sympathy, first realizes just what the casual comment
'induerunt eum vestimentis eius' (Matt. 27: 31; Mark 15: 20) implies:
'renouantur fracturae per pannos carni applicatos' (Chapter LXXVIII). San
Pedro expands this (C_1^v):

> [. . .] muy rezio le quitaron
> la su pobre vestidura
> mira si pena sintio
> quando se le fue quitada
> mira quien jamas penso
> mira quien jamas oyo
> crueldad assi [passada]
>
> Que al tiempo que se açoto
> la su carne delicada
> como toda se [le] abrio
> con la sangre que salio
> tenia la [ropa] pegada
> y como gela quitaron
> con yra muy furiosa
> como con fuerça tiraron
> los pedaços le sacaron
> de aquella carne preciosa
>
> [sts 166-67, p. 182]

It is possible that San Pedro has genuinely meditated upon the pseudo-Bonaventure's hint and made it his own, but the reminder that it was the scourging which caused the wounds is in Ludolph and must have been a commonplace.

Some details do seem to be San Pedro's own: so, for instance, reproaching Judas for his ingratitude, he recalls some curious domestic details of Mary's making his bed and cooking his food (A6ᵛ):

> di porque no te acordauas
> dela muerte que le dauas
> ala virgen madre triste
> en la qual fee verdadera
> de madre siempre hallaste
> acordarse te deuiera
> quantas vezes te hiziera
> la cama en que te acostaste
>
> Quanto bien recibimiento
> en su casa della ouiste
> lloro quando pienso y siento
> que te puso assentamiento
> y la mesa en que comiste
> como sierua te siruio
> y no como tu señora
> quantas vezes te guiso
> de comer y te lo dio
> de su mal no sabidora
>   [sts 49-50, p. 129]

These are the probable but unattested details of the *contemplatio humanitatis Christi*. Of apocryphal material proper, San Pedro makes only the most discreet use. Thus in his diatribe against Judas, he alludes to the legend of Judas's earlier life (A6ᵛ):[19]

> Mira si era gran pecado
> dalle la muerte a tu padre
> pues no era en menos grado
> aquel que falso dañado
> cometiste con tu madre [. . .]
> no deuieras oluidar

que te quito dela mar
porque tu vida viuiesse

Miraras que te quito
dela reyna y su poder [. . .]
miraras quanto te amo
y que en su casa mando
que fuesses procurador

[sts 47-48, p. 128]

Apart from this, and the episode of the frustrated intervention of Pilate's wife, from the *Gesta Pilati* in the first instance, there is no apocryphal matter except a one-line reference to the curing of blindness of the man who thrust the spear into Christ's side (i.e. St Longinus, though he is not named), and the Veronica story, which, though it is not to be found in the Gospels, was so firm a part of the Roman tradition, numerous Popes from Sixtus IV on confirming that the relic conserved in Rome was indeed her veil, that one cannot properly describe it as apocryphal. Indeed, though San Pedro elaborates the episode in curious fashion, it is noteworthy that, unlike Román, he ignores completely the truly apocryphal account, from the *Mors Pilati*, which was popularized by the *Legenda aurea*.[20]

There are numerous other points of contact between the *Meditationes* and San Pedro's *Pasión*. St Francis, as we know, mimed his sermons, and the Franciscan author of the *Meditationes* has the instinct of a dramatist: dialogue abounds. A feature of San Pedro's *Pasión* also is the enormous amount of direct speech, supplying, indeed, all the dialogue necessary for a dramatic performance.[21] In addition, the pseudo-Bonaventure, throughout the Passion, has his eyes firmly fixed on the Virgin. As with all the early Franciscans, the *Passio Christi* and *Compassio Mariae* are inextricably intertwined. As the sinner is urged to try to realize the inexpressible physical agony of Christ, so he is urged to attempt to appreciate the mental agony of Mary. In San Pedro's words (C1ʳ):

Los coraçones quebrauan
de compassion del señor
y su manzilla doblauan
quando enla virgen hablauan
conociendo su dolor

[st. 157, p. 178]

but now and again the emphasis on the suffering of the Virgin is a little disconcerting, as, among several possible examples, at the flagellation (B4^r):

> y assi lo començaron
> con tal fuerça y [con] tal gana
> y assi lo atormentaron
> que en su cuerpo no dexaron
> vna cosa sola sana
>
> Contempla lo que haria
> la madre desconsolada
> quando la carne veria
> del hijo que assi queria
> en viua sangre tornada
>
> [sts 120-21, p. 161]

All this is, of course, very Franciscan; but it is quite at odds with the attitude of the *devotio moderna*, with its proto-Protestant and, in a sense—for the Gospels assign Mary no such prominence—fundamentalist emphasis on the figure of Jesus.

San Pedro uses the term 'contemplate' in a sense exactly like that implied in the third type of contemplation in the *Meditationes*. On the agony in the garden (A5^{r-v}):

> O passo tan de notar
> para los contemplatiuos
> cosa digna de pensar
> y pensando la llorar
> todos quantos somos viuos
>
> [st. 31, p. 121]

or again (A6^r [st. 42, p. 126]), 'contempla qual quedaria / tu dios y tu saluador / contempla que sentiria', etc.; before Herod (B3^v [st. 113, p. 158]), 'Contempla con que humildad / aquestas cosas suffria / [. . .] / contempla [la] mansedad / y paciencia que tenia'; at the sentence of Pilate (B6^v [sts 148-49, pp. 172-74]), 'contempla anima deuota / la paciencia del señor / [. . .] / Contempla llora christiano / mira por ti que passaua [. . .]'; at the crucifixion (C6^r [st. 227, pp. 208-09]), 'qual es el que contemplando / enlo tal no ha compassion / qual es el duro que quando / este passo esta pensando / no quiebra su coraçon'. 'Contempla' may be replaced, and it often is, by 'piensa', 'mira', 'nota', and other expressions.

> (C1^v) nota agora si quieres
> cosa[s] de gran deuocion
> y enellas si me creyeres
> todo el tiempo que pudieres
> embuelue tu coraçon
>
> [st. 165, p. 181]

recalls St Cecilia, mentioned in the *Prooemium* of the *Meditationes*, 'quae cor suum repleverat de vita Christi'. San Pedro aspires no higher than this contemplation for beginners, and concludes his whole work (C6^v):

> contemplemos y pensemos
> en su passion muy gloriosa
> sospiremos y lloremos
> penemos porque gozemos
> de ver su gloria preciosa
>
> [st. 236, p. 213]

One final piquant parallel between the *Meditationes* and the *Pasión trovada*: the preface of each is addressed to a nun, who requested that the work should be written—but by San Pedro to a nun with whom he declares himself to be in love.

San Pedro's poem belongs in the tradition of the late medieval meditations on the Passion. It shares with the Latin prose works on the subject an almost morbid preoccupation with the physical sufferings of Christ, on which it dwells in harrowing detail—the kind of meditation to which Valdés objected: 'esotras ymaginaciones [. . .] que algunos tienen por contemplaciones, yo no se que se son, ni que fruto sacan dellas.'[22] As in the *Meditationes* one detects in the *Pasión* what at times might not unjustly be called a hysterical note, perhaps because of a kind of frustration before the age-old human paradox of 'videntes non videntes' (cf. Deut. 29: 4; Jer. 5: 21; Ezech. 12: 2; Matt. 13: 15-17); San Pedro and the pseudo-Bonaventure seem obsessed with the necessity of bringing home the words of the Gospel, making sure their readers receive the word as well as hear it. But regarded merely as literature, San Pedro's is a splendid poem; it is a pity that the limitations of my theme have precluded my quoting the finest passages, some of a startling, pathetic simplicity. Sincerity is not a virtue which the literary critic can reliably assess in any writer; but one cannot help suspecting that the immense and sustained popularity of the work, as well as its literary merit, derives in no small measure from the genuine emotional involvement of San Pedro with his theme, and to his active practising of the *contemplatio humanitatis Christi* according to the teaching of the *Meditationes*.[23]

Fray Íñigo de Mendoza is, of these four poets, the most complex. He is, after all, if I may be allowed the term, a professional where Román and San Pedro are amateurs. Since Mendoza begins his life of Christ at the beginning, and gets no further, after some four thousand lines, than the Massacre of the Innocents, we can make no comparison of passages in the *Vita Christi* parallel with the *Passions* of Román and San Pedro. Instead I shall examine one typical sequence, the forty stanzas dealing with the Circumcision (B7^r-C2^r),[24] and compare it with the treatment of the same episode in Ludolph[25] and the *Meditationes*.

In the first five stanzas Mendoza digresses from the proposition that Christ was not 'infected' by his mother, to speak of the Immaculate Conception, but does not pursue this long 'por no hazer cosquillas a ninguno'.[26] In the next seven stanzas he explains that Jewish law required that a child be circumcised on the eighth day, and goes on to state 'la cabsa prinçipal por que dios mando a los judios çircunçidarse', and then a second reason, illustrating the point with a comparison. In the fourteenth to seventeenth stanzas he gives two reasons why Christ was not obliged to submit to it, and then five reasons why he did. In the eighteenth stanza we find a scrap of narrative, but Mendoza at once embarks on three stanzas of exclamations (which he calls 'exclamaçiones', not 'contemplation'), following them with the 'exclamaçion llorosa de nuestra señora'. We have then, until the thirty-eighth stanza of the sequence, a series of hortatives and imperatives, also rubricated 'exclamaçion', which I shall examine in more detail later. He summarizes his message in a conclusion, stanza 39, and concludes with an 'oraçion en fin dela çircunçision en nonbre dela señora doña juana' (his mother, to whom the work is addressed).

The actual narrative is carried by only a few lines of the eighteenth and twenty-second stanzas of the sequence (B8^v):

> vn venerable varon
> segund la constituçion
> de aquel consejo eternal
> tomo su cultro enla mano
> para te çircunçidar

and

> Con vn tan triste dolor
> qual su gran lloro demuestra
> el viejo con grand temor
> te çircunçido señor [. . .]
> y la tu madre sagrada
> con la sangre que corria
> ençendida y ensañada
> la color toda mudada
> con grand angustia dezia [. . .]

The Circumcision is, of course, no more than a passing reference in Luke (2: 21): 'Et postquam consummati sunt dies octo ut circumcideretur puer, vocatum est nomen eius JESUS, quod vocatum est ab angelo priusquam in utero conciperetur.' Both Ludolph and the *Meditationes* point out that 'duo magna hodie facta sunt', and both discuss the name of 'Jesus', Ludolph at some length (Chapter X), quoting the opinions of Augustine, Bede, Anselm, and Bernard. Ludolph then describes the actual circumcision, incorporating in his text, verbatim but without any acknowledgment, part of the account given in the *Meditationes*, Chapter VIII: 'Plorauit autem puer Jesus hodie propter dolorem quem in carne sensit [. . .]. Sed eo plorante credis ne quod mater potuerit lachrymas continere? [. . .] Compatere et tu sibi et plora etiam cum eo [. . .].' Ludolph goes on to say that the Circumcision was the first of six occasions on which Christ's blood was spilled for us, and he lists the other five and explains the significance of each. He proceeds then to give five reasons for the institution of the rite among the Jews, following this with ten reasons why Christ should have submitted to it. He explains, citing Gregory and Bede, how the Jewish circumcision corresponds with Christian baptism. Then, quoting Bernard, he draws the moral lesson: we must circumcise ourselves, figuratively speaking, *exteriore* and *interiore*, in habits, acts, and speech, in thought, affection, and intention. Next he tells us that the Circumcision prefigures the Last Resurrection, discourses on the significance of the 'eighth day', quotes Pope Pius I's instructions to priests, and Bede on fornication and marriage, goes on to an exposition of the eight spiritual illuminations, and finally concludes with a prayer.

The pseudo-Bonaventure, having dealt with the name of 'Jesus', produces his usual imaginative reconstruction of the scene, describing the weeping of the infant, the tears of his mother, how she told him: 'Fili, si vis me a ploratu cessare, cessa et tu', and how the child, 'ex compassione matris', did so. He makes the point, but very briefly, that now we have baptism instead of circumcision, 'sed debemus habere circumcisionem spiritualem'. He mentions the virtue of poverty, but deals at length, citing Gregory, and then copying Bernard, only with the vice of loquaciousness and the value of silence for the religious.

We can divide Mendoza's sequence on the Circumcision into three parts: 1) the explanations, of why the rite was instituted, of why Christ submitted to it, etc.; 2) the narrative; 3) the moral lesson. All texts, of course, draw the same moral: 'nobis spiritualiter indicatur agendum' (Bernard, *Sermo III in Circumcisione Domini*, PL, CLXXXIII, 136), 'circumcidamus ergo corda nostra' (Hildebert, *In festo Circumcisionis Domini*, PL, CLXXI, 401), 'oportet nos circumcidi, non carne, sed spiritu' (Alcuin, *De divinis officiis*, Chap. II, PL, CI, 1176); but where the pseudo-Bonaventure goes on to deal only with the vice of loquaciousness, and Ludolph to treat the subject under abstract categories, Mendoza embarks on a long sermon, citing some very particular instances, as I shall show.

As for the narrative, Fray Íñigo's account coincides with the other two only in mentioning the Virgin's reaction, which, as I have pointed out, is a characteristically Franciscan trait. But the anger of the mother and the reluctance of the officiating priest are only in Mendoza. He omits both the 'cessa et tu' anecdote of the *Meditationes*, and mention of the *stone* knife, of which Ludolph makes much. So far we have no evidence of any contact whatsoever between Mendoza and either the *Meditationes* or Ludolph's *Vita Christi*.

But the reasons for the circumcision of the Jews and of Christ, which do not interest the pseudo-Bonaventure at all, run to some extent parallel in Ludolph and Fray Íñigo. Ludolph gives five reasons for the institution of the rite among the Jews: 1) in recognition of the merit of Abraham (who first circumcised Isaac at God's command, Gen. 21: 4); 2) to mark the Jews off from other nations; 3) to show to the Gentiles that they are descended 'de stirpe sancta'; 4) for the remedy of original sin and the repression of concupiscence; and 5) to fulfil in the Mosaic law the function of baptism. Mendoza begins by indicating, sixth stanza, that 'estonces por sacramento / les valia del baptismo'. This is not advanced as a reason; it is a passing remark, and a commonplace to be found in all the commentators at least from Augustine: 'Circumcisio baptismi vicem olim tenuit' (*De praesentia Dei*, Chap. XII, PL, XXXIII, 845). But Mendoza goes on to give the other reasons offered by Ludolph—not the first, but the second and third (stanza 7):

> La cabsa deste mandar
> enesta razon la fundo
> que fue querer señalar
> apartar santificar
> este pueblo en todo el mundo

and the fourth (stanza 8):

> fue medeçina del mal
> dela culpa original.

He elaborates this reason with an idea which Ludolph also advances, though not in the same context:

> [. . .] por çierto asi conviene
> porque justa cura aya
> que por el mienbro que viene
> quanto mal ombre sostiene
> por aquel mesmo se vaya.

Ludolph quotes Bede: 'In carne prepucii fiebat circumcisio quod in parte illa magis concupiscentia donatur per quam originale peccatum propagatur', but this is another commonplace, to be found in Augustine, and, in almost the same terms, long before Bede, in St Prosper of Aquitaine (*Liber sententiarum ex operibus S. Augustini delibatarum*, Chap. CCC, PL, LI, 472). Mendoza has a further four stanzas explaining that the Jews were 'gentes mal domadas' requiring, like a wilful hard-mouthed horse, this brutal discipline. This is not in Ludolph—at least in the section on the Circumcision.

 Ludolph does not give reasons why Christ might have been excused. Mendoza gives two (stanza 14):

> por no ser enfeçionado
> enel tienpo que engendrado
> y por ser diuinal rey

Bernard of Clairvaux gives the same reasons in his *Sermo I in Circumcisione Domini* (PL, CLXXXIII, 133).

 Mendoza gives five reasons why Christ submitted to the rite: 1) 'para que puedan mejor / [. . .] / conosçer [. . .] / su descomulgado error / manicheo y valentino.' This is Ludolph's 8°: 'vt in se veritatem carnis humane [o]fideret, et hereticos [. . .] confunderet'; 2) 'por demostrar / ala ley la obediençia': Ludolph 4°, 'vt obedientie [. . .] virtutem nobis suo comendaret exemplo preceptum legis'; 3) 'por aprouar / el legal çircunçidar': Ludolph 3°, 'vt legem veterem et circumcisionem quam deus instituerat approbaret'; 4) 'por [. . .] / demostrarles clara mente / que de aquellos desçendias / alos quales fue el mexias / prometido de su gente': Ludolph 1°, 'vt ostenderet se esse de genere abrahe [. . .] cui de christo repromissio facta est'; and 5) 'porque [. . .] / nos fueses ya descargando / la pesada legal carga': Ludolph 6°, 'vt legis onus in se sustinens alios a legis onere [. . .] liberaret'; 'fueses *ya*': Ludolph 7°, 'vt pro nobis sanguinem suum non solum in etate virili sed etiam in infantia funderet et tempestiue pati inciperet' (this last phrase is in the *Meditationes*).

But, as I have already noted, Ludolph's *Vita Jesu Christi* is a vast compilation which collects in one place virtually every orthodox idea ever expressed by the commentators of the New Testament. 'Cur voluit circumcidi Christus' is an inevitable topic, and Ludolph is able to give ten reasons in all. In the fifth century St Maximus of Turin gives Mendoza's first and fourth reasons (*Homilia XXXV de baptismo Christi*, VII, PL, LVII, 299); in the ninth, Alcuin gives Mendoza's second and fourth, and others (*De div. off.*, Chap. II, PL, CI, 1176); in the twelfth, Hildebert of Tours gives the second, fourth, and fifth (*Sermo XII de tempore*, PL, CLXXI, 399), while Bernard of Clairvaux, in his *Sermo in octava epiphaniae* and *Sermones I, II, III in Circumcisione Dei* (PL, CLXXXV, 153 and 131-38), gives precisely the same five reasons listed by Mendoza. As for Ludolph's remaining reasons, one has only to add to this list Raban Maur (PL, CVII, 561) and Prosper of Aquitaine (PL, LI, 472) to account for them all. And all this, of course, does not begin to scratch the surface of the literature on the Circumcision; leaving aside the written commentaries, and the *Breviary*, the number of sermons preached in the Middle Ages on the feast of the Circumcision must reach astronomical proportions.[27] Mendoza need not, in fact, have gone outside Augustine and Bernard for his information; but I should not for a moment think of suggesting that these writers were his sources. We have to do with a series of commonplaces, part of the medieval corpus of Christian knowledge, which, despite the elaborations, combinations, and subdivisions of individual authors, still presents a texture of belief so uniform as to frustrate any attempt to trace the specific source of specific topics in specific authors.

I have explained how certain coincidences between Mendoza and Ludolph can be accounted for; I have not proved, especially in limiting myself to the Circumcision, that Mendoza did not know Ludolph at all. But the argument can be carried further. It is not easy, as the reader will have gathered, to find anything omitted by Ludolph, but as I have already shown, Mendoza has material not to be found in Ludolph's *Vita Christi*. If, as certain critics have asserted, Mendoza did use Ludolph, he selected his material in such a way as almost to deny all sympathy with Ludolph's methods and intentions. In his narrative he rejects utterly all the apocryphal material from the *Pseudo-Matthew* and the *Gospel of the Birth of Mary* which fills Ludolph's early chapters, and confines himself strictly to the evangelical texts; in his commentary on the text he finds no place for the allegories and prefigurations in which everything stands for almost everything else, for the symbolic numbers, for the intellectual trapeze-acts performed high above the sober *sensus litteralis* of the Bible, for the huge volume of scholastic subtleties so carefully collected by Ludolph; equally he ignores the mystic treatises which the Carthusian copies, the material which, via Ludolph, was to have such influence on Spanish sixteenth-century devotional practice; and when Mendoza takes up the tropological meaning of his text, he does so, not in the arid categories and sub-categories of Ludolph, but in the vivid, concrete, topical, practical terms of the mendicant preacher. I do not believe that one can read Mendoza, and then Ludolph, and affirm that they have anything in common apart from the inevitable coincidences determined by their subject-matter and their common Christian background.

Almost half of Mendoza's disquisition on the Circumcision is taken up by the detailed interpretation of the tropological sense of the episode. He opens in fairly general terms:

> O castellana naçion
> çentro de abominaçion[es]
> o christiana religion
> ya de casa de oraçion
> hecha cueua de ladrones
> o mundo todo estragado
> o gentes enduresçidas
> o templo menospreciado
> o parayso oluidado
> o religiones perdidas

but quickly gets down to cases:

> Uenid y çircunçidad
> no la carne que es vedad[o]

mas las obras de maldad
la peruersa voluntad
el tienpo non bien gastado
los clerigos las simonias
el robar los caualleros
los frailes ypocresias
las henbras hechizerias
y los ricos sus dineros

and then proceeds to elaborate, not in diffuse generalities, but in very particular terms:

Çircunçiden los saluajes
el su maldito deporte
los galanes y los pajes
no çircunçiden los trajes
pues tan cortos son en corte
quanto yo sy se ronpiesen
las calças que andan de fuera
no syento que se cubriesen
sy commo adan no pusyesen
las dos fojas dela higuera

There follows a blistering and obviously well-informed attack on the ladies of the court, their gallants, the flirtatious nuns of the incredible convents before the Isabelline reform, and so on. The passage ends with a passionate lament, echoing *Mingo Revulgo*, on the wretched state of Castile, hastening to decay, the sheep straying while the negligent shepherds lie 'borrachos enbeueçidos / enel dulçor del peccado'. Passionate, unpretentious, fearless, direct, picturesque—even with a touch of humour at times—the tone of all this is unmistakably the tone of the vernacular Franciscan sermon. Mendoza's *Vita Christi* might, indeed, be regarded as a series of versified sermons: for the feasts of the Annunciation, Nativity, Circumcision, Epiphany, Presentation and Purification of the Virgin, and Holy Innocents (in the order of a *vita*, of course, and not of the Missal). In the vernacular mendicant sermons of the fourteenth and fifteenth centuries we can find precedents for most of the elements in Mendoza's poem: the ferocious social satire, the picturesque comparisons, the dramatic dialogue, the fervent devotion, the final prayer—even the fact that it is written in verse.[28] To elaborate this proposition now would take us too far afield. I would add, however, that the earlier *verse* of the Franciscan order, the mark of which Menéndez y Pelayo found on the work of Mendoza and Montesino, now seems to me, at least so far as Mendoza is concerned, to afford us much less close parallels than the vernacular sermon in prose.

We can dispose quite briefly of Fray Ambrosio de Montesino, at least with regard to the supposed influence of Ludolph the Saxon. His *Coplas sobre diversas devociones* are all—comparatively—short pieces. Leaving aside the special problem of the *romances* and *villancicos a lo divino*, they normally take the form of meditations on isolated episodes of Christ's life (though there are a few pieces on various saints) or even the separate instruments of the Passion (the ropes which bound Christ to the column, the crown of thorns, the nails, etc.) and consist of short passages of narrative or description interrupted by prayers or emotive exclamations in the style of the pseudo-Bonaventure, San Pedro, Mendoza (even the wretched Román!)—indeed in the tradition of Franciscan verse. I do not propose to argue the proposition that Ludolph had no influence on the *Coplas* of 1485. When Bataillon published in 1925 ('Chanson pieuse'), for the benefit of the *candidats d'agrégation* for whom the subject was set, his suggestions for research into the work of Fray Ambrosio, the existence of the 1485 *Cancionero* was not generally known, and, in view of the fact that Montesino's translation of Ludolph preceded his *Cancionero* of 1508, it was not implausible that the work should have had some influence on his poetry. (Indeed a careful examination of the changes Montesino made in his poems for the 1508 edition might yet reveal the effect of his translating experience—if only the influence of other writers through the medium of 'el Cartuxano'.) The coincidence of the titles of Mendoza's and Ludolph's works was no doubt suggestive —though one could draft a formidable list of late medieval *Vitae Christi*—but I am certain that Mendoza, if he did know Ludolph's work, owes nothing to him except a title. I should not at this stage attempt to deny—and I certainly have not proved—that the work of Ludolph the Saxon was unknown in Spain before, say, the 1490s, but I believe I have shown that the thesis of his influence on Mendoza and Montesino (in 1485) can be discarded without difficulty. There is still room for investigation into the dating of the first knowledge of this work in Spain. The *Vita* was, after all, approved by the Council of Basle, so that certain Spanish clerics must have heard of it in the first half of the fifteenth century.

Into all this the *devotio moderna* simply does not enter at all. Gerard Groote, reckoned by his contemporaries to be the founder of the movement (see Hyma, Chap. IV), was himself strongly influenced by the ideas of St Bernard of Clairvaux; St Francis, indeed, would have heartily approved of most of

Groote's reforming ideals. But the attitude of Román, San Pedro, Mendoza, and Montesino to the cult of the Virgin ranges them with the Franciscans rather than with the Brethren of the Common Life. No doubt Castro is right to protest ('Lo hispánico') that the origins of attitudes and ideas cannot always be precisely named or dated; but the fact remains that the *devotio moderna* is not necessary as an explanation for any of the attitudes he describes. Our knowledge of the Spanish fifteenth century is still woefully inadequate, and while some broad generalizations may be useful, they are going to be subject to continuous correction for as long as basic bibliographical problems are neglected.

[*Symposium*, 17 (1963), 268-91]

Notes

1. For these dates, which may appear arbitrary, see: for a demonstration that Zamora 1482 is the earliest of the known printed editions of the *Vita Christi*, A. Pérez Gómez, 'Notas para la bibliografía de Fray Íñigo de Mendoza y de Jorge Manrique', *HR*, 27 (1959), 30-41; for the earlier redactions, my 'The Printed Editions and the Text of the Works of Fr. Í. de M.', *BHS*, 39 (1962), 137-52 [pp. 18-35, above]; my forthcoming article 'MS. Escurialense K-III-7: el llamado *Cancionero de Fr. Í. de M.*', [*Filología*, 7 (1961 [1963]), 161-72; English original, pp. 36-45, above]; for some suggestions about the date of the first redaction, my forthcoming article 'El origen de las comparaciones religiosas del Siglo de Oro: Mendoza, Montesino y Román', [*RFE*, 46 (1963 [1965]), 263-85; pp. 72-95, below]; for Román's works, Sir Henry Thomas's introduction to his facsimile of the *Coplas* (London, 1936) and my 'El origen'; for San Pedro, my 'The Religious Poems of Diego de San Pedro: Their Relationship and their Dating', *HR*, 28 (1960), 1-15, and my 'The First Printing of San Pedro's *Pasión trovada*', *HR*, 30 (1962), 149-52; for Montesino, Sir Henry Thomas's introduction to the facsimile *Coplas*, also London, 1936.
2. 'Lo hispánico y el erasmismo', *RFH*, 2 (1940), 1-34.
3. *Erasmo y España* (Mexico City-Buenos Aires, 1950), p. xiii.
4. *Introducción a la literatura medieval española* (Madrid, 1952), pp. 131-32.
5. See Dom Anselmo María Albareda, 'Intorno alla scuola di orazione metodica stabilita a Montserrato dall'abate Garsias Jiménez de Cisneros', *Archivum Historicum Societatis Jesu*, 35 (1956), separately-paginated offprint, 65 pp.; Dom García M. Colombás, *Un reformador benedictino en tiempo de los Reyes Católicos: García Jiménez de Cisneros, abad de Montserrat* (Montserrat, 1955). The classic work

of Albert Hyma, published incomplete as *The 'Devotio Moderna' or Christian Renaissance, 1380–1520* (Grand Rapids, Michigan, [1924]), complete as *The Christian Renaissance: A History of the 'Devotio Moderna'* ([Grand Rapids], 1924), is still valuable as the only coherent account of the history of the whole movement, though it is superseded for Spain by the works cited above. A useful review-article, packed with facts and references is I. Rodriguez-Grahit's 'La *Devotio Moderna* en Espagne et l'influence française', *Bibliothèque d'Humanisme et Renaissance*, 19 (1957), 489-95. There is a considerable literature devoted to the indubitable influence of the movement in the sixteenth century in Spain.

6. M. Bataillon, 'Chanson pieuse et poésie de dévotion: Fray Ambrosio de Montesino', *BH*, 27 (1925), 228-38.

7. *La Poésie lyrique espagnole et portugaise à la fin du moyen âge*, I (Rennes, 1949), 297-337, at p. 313.

8. For details of MSS, translations, and printed editions, see Sister Mary Immaculate Bodenstedt, *The 'Vita Christi' of Ludolphus the Carthusian* (Washington, 1944), pp. 11-23, and Stanislas Autore, 'Ludolphe de Saxe', *Dictionnaire de théologie catholique*, IX (Paris, 1926), 1067-70. The details supplied with regard to Spain are unfortunately inaccurate (Montesino's translation is dated c. 1550); but one obtains from the information supplied a clear picture of the slow outward spread of Ludolph's work from Germany: e.g. almost two-thirds of the known MSS are in Germany, 25 in Munich alone; half the remainder are in northern France; the rest are distributed among England, Portugal, Switzerland, and Italy. The Dutch translation dates from 1400, was printed in 1487, and went through eight editions in thirty-two years; and so on. The Portuguese translation was done by Fr. Bernardo de Alcobaça in 1446, printed Lisbon, 1495; the Catalan by Joan Roís de Corella, Valencia, 1495–1500.

9. Among writers in the vernacular, the earliest that I know of to declare a debt to Ludolph is the Carthusian Juan de Padilla, in the preface to his *Retablo de la vida de Cristo*. No accessible text of this important work exists. Foulché-Delbosc, *Canc. cast. del siglo XV*, I, NBAE, XIX (Madrid, 1912), 423-49, merely reproduces, but suppressing Padilla's annotations, the brief extracts printed by Miguel de Riego in his *Colección de obras poéticas españolas* (London, 1842). A mutilated copy of the Seville 1505 edition exists in the Biblioteca Nacional, and a complete copy in the library of the Duke of Alba; see Duque de Alba, 'Un ejemplar de la primera edición del *Retablo de la vida de Christo*, desconocido de los bibliógrafos', *BRAE*, 30 (1950). The colophon of this edition declares that Padilla finished the poem in 1500. In 1501 we find Isabella having the prayers from the *Vita* copied out separately (*Cuentas de Gonzalo de Baeza*, ed. Antonio and E. A. de la Torre, Madrid, 1956, II, 528, 585).

10. On the Franciscan reform and establishment of the Observance in Spain see the *número extraordinario* of the *Archivo Ibero-Americano*, Nos 65–68 (1957): *Introducción a los orígenes de la Observancia en España: las reformas en los siglos XIV y*

XV, by PP. Fidel de Lejarza, Ángel Uribe, Alejandro Recio, and Diosdado Merino.

11. *Antología de poetas líricos castellanos*, III (Santander, 1944), 42.

12. On this early Franciscan verse a truly vast amount has been written. F. J. E. Raby, *Christian Latin Poetry*, revised ed. (Oxford, 1953), pp. 415-57, may serve as an introduction to the subject.

13. The text may be found in any of the older editions of the works of Bonaventure (not in Migne's Patrologia Latina). I have used *S. Bonaventurae Opera omnia*, XII (Venice, 1756).

14. In strict accuracy the *Meditationes* record the appearance of Christ to the Virgin after the Resurrection, before his appearance to the other three Maries, earlier justified in Catholic tradition by logical argument, and also the Harrowing of Hell, partly justified by Old Testament prophecies.

15. Among the voluminous literature on the voluminous New Testament apocrypha, I have found the clearest guide M. R. James, *The Apocryphal New Testament*, corrected ed. (Oxford, 1953). I have used the *Evangelia Apocrypha*, ed. C. Tischendorf (Leipzig, 1853), which contains all the texts to which I shall have occasion to refer, and, for the *Golden Legend*, Jacobus de Voragine, *Legenda aurea vulgo historia lombardica dicta*, ed. J. T. Graesse (Leipzig, 1850).

16. For the iconographical influence of the *Meditationes*, see Émile Mâle, *L'Art religieux de la fin du moyen âge en France*, 5th revised ed. (Paris, 1949), Part I, especially Chap. II.

17. There is a striking number of verbal coincidences between the poems of Román and San Pedro, although most of them prove to be clichés, or translations of biblical phrases.

18. I give the folio references to the only accessible text, that of Salamanca c. 1496 (British Museum G. 10958), transcribed by J. de Urquijo e Ibarra, 'La Pasión Trobada de Diego de San Pedro', *Revista Internacional de Estudios Vascos*, 22 (1931), separately-paginated offprint, 74 pp., printed as a photographic facsimile by Antonio Pérez Gómez (same title) in R*Lit*, 1 (1952), 163-82, and later included in his Incunables Poéticos Castellanos. I quote, however, from the much superior edition of c. 1516 (B.M., C. 63. f. 12), making any necessary corrections from the Salamanca 1496? text, and the even earlier, but incomplete, text in the Hurus *Cancionero* of 1495. [Stanza and page references in brackets are to the Severin and Whinnom edition of San Pedro's *Poesías* (1979).]

19. The innumerable legends concerning the earlier life of Judas are all designed to show that he was always a monster of iniquity. Most of the traditional elements are to be found in the life given in the *Golden Legend*, Chap. XLV, 'De sancto Mathia apostolo' (St Matthias replaced Judas). J. E. Gillet, 'Traces of the Judas Legend in Spain', *Revue Hispanique*, 65 (1925), 316-41, misses these references and in general quotes later material.

20. In San Pedro, Veronica, who does not know Christ, gives him her handkerchief to wipe his face; Mary appears, inquiring about her beautiful son; Veronica

assures her that the man she saw could not be he, since he was far from beautiful, but eventually remembers his face was impressed on her handkerchief, and shows it to Mary, who falls in a faint. There is no suggestion of a miracle. The apocryphal *Mors Pilati* and *Vindicta salvatoris* are the ultimate source of the account in the *Leg. aur.*, in which the Emperor Tiberius is cured by gazing on a portrait of Christ: when Christ was going about preaching (before the Passion), Veronica, 'deprived of his presence', decided to have his portrait painted; carrying the canvas to the painter, she met Christ, who caused his likeness miraculously to appear on the canvas. This is the version in the *Estoria del muy nobre Vespasiano emperador de Roma* (Lisbon, 1496?). In Román (B7ᵛ) Veronica, knowing Christ is to die, rushes to find a painter, but meets Christ, on the way to Calvary, who, somewhat ambiguously, 'le pinto su pintura'. There are many other versions: see the Comte de Douhet, *Dictionnaire des légendes du Christianisme*, vol. XIV of the *Troisième et dernière encyclopédie théologique* (Paris, 1855), 874-900.

21. It was actually performed at Lesaca in 1566; see Urquijo e Ibarra. There are various studies of the debt of the French authors of *mystères* to the *Meditationes*.

22. *Diálogo de la doctrina cristiana*, fol. 95ᵛ, facsimile of the Alcalá 1529 ed. by Marcel Bataillon (Coimbra, 1925).

23. For the numerous editions of the work, and the first just assessment of its literary merit, see Pérez Gómez, 'La *Pasión trobada* de D. de S. P.'. Critics have tended to parrot the judgment of Menéndez y Pelayo, who knew only an execrable eighteenth-century text, that reprinted in BAE, XXXV, No. 909.

24. I quote from the facsimile of the Zamora 1482 edition (Madrid, 1953), making any necessary emendations with the help of the later printed editions and MS Esc. K-III-7.

25. I quote from the *Vita Jesu christi domini ac saluatoris nostri*, corrected by Jodocus Badius, and printed at Paris in 1502. The most generally accessible text is that of Rome-Paris 1865.

26. For the background to this remark, the bitter controversies between Dominicans and Franciscans on the subject of the Immaculate Conception, see P. Alejandro Recio, O.F.M., 'La Inmaculada en la predicación franciscano-española', pp. 105-200 in the *número extraordinario* of the *Archivo Ibero-Americano*, Nos 57-58 (1955). P. Recio (pp. 118-19), exhibiting once more the odd persistence in misdating Mendoza's work, interprets the passage as a reference to the troubles in Valladolid in 1501.

27. For these references I have not gone outside the Patrologia Latina; but in the Library of Trinity College Dublin one finds shelf upon shelf of Latin collections of *sermones de tempore*, *in festis*, and *in sanctis*, printed in the fifteenth and sixteenth centuries, in most of which one can find several sermons on the Circumcision which produce varying totals of these 'reasons'.

28. Presumably Spanish vernacular sermons of the fifteenth century are preserved in some form somewhere in Spain; they have not been published, and there may be dangers in assuming that what holds good for the rest of Western Europe

must be true of Spain. With this reservation, G. R. Owst, *Literature and Pulpit in Medieval England* (Cambridge, 1933), is remarkably illuminating for Hispanist students of the fifteenth century, particularly since Mendoza's *Vita* (his sermons do not survive) correponds so closely with the general pattern. [Pedro M. Cátedra has shown that fifteenth-century vernacular sermons are indeed extant, and he and his pupils at the University of Salamanca are engaged in a catalogue, editions, and studies. See, for example, Cátedra, *Los sermones atribuidos a Pedro Marín: van añadidas algunas noticias sobre la predicación castellana de San Vicente Ferrer*, Corpus de la Predicación Hispánica Medieval, 1 = Acta Salmanticensia, Textos Recuperados, 1 (Salamanca: Univ., 1990).]

5

El origen de las comparaciones religiosas del Siglo de Oro: Mendoza, Montesino y Román

I

En los últimos decenios del siglo quince aparecen en español las *Pasiones* y las *Vidas de Cristo* versificadas. Casi seguramente la más temprana de las *Pasiones* es la *Pasión trovada* de Diego de San Pedro, la cual, impresa antes de 1492, no puede haber sido compuesta más tarde que 1480.[1] La *Vita Christi* de Fray Íñigo de Mendoza, que narra y comenta la vida de Cristo hasta el episodio de los Santos Inocentes, cuando se interrumpe bruscamente, se imprimió primero en Zaragoza en 1482,[2] pero apenas se ha considerado el problema de la fecha de su composición. Menéndez y Pelayo creía que debió de escribirse en los primeros años del reinado de los Reyes Católicos,[3] pero hay indicios de que su primera redacción remonta al reinado de Enrique IV, tales como la alusión al pavonearse de los cortesanos 'delante las portuguesas' (¿las damas de Juana?) (fol. C1^v), el ataque contra los privados reales (*ibid.*), y varias referencias despectivas a los monarcas en general y a las reinas en particular (cf. C7^r), que cuadran mal con las demás obras de Mendoza escritas durante el reinado de Fernando e Isabel, y que, a lo que sabemos de esta época, no pudieron escribirse durante aquel diluvio de poemas panegíricos.[4] Las *Coplas sobre diversas devociones y misterios de nuestra sancta fe cathólica* de Fray Ambrosio de Montesino son piezas más cortas, muchas de ellas consagradas a episodios del Nuevo Testamento, y fueron impresas, sin pie de imprenta, por Juan Vázquez, cuya producción tipográfica fechada cae entre los años de 1484 y 1486, de manera que se suelen fechar en 'hacia 1485'.[5] A pesar de algunas prometedoras alusiones a varios nobles en las dedicaciones de las coplas, no hay manera de establecer más exactamente la fecha de redacción de estas poesías, aunque es evidente que la mayoría se compusieron entre 1482 y 1485.

El Comendador Román, el menos estudiado de todos estos autores, se conoce mejor por sus poesías cortas, cómicas y satíricas, primero impresas en el *Cancionero general* de 1511, y luego reimpresas en el *Cancionero de Constantina* y el *Cancionero de obras de burlas*. Pero en este trabajo me atenderé únicamente a su obra más ambiciosa, de carácter muy distinto, su narración en verso de la Cena, la Pasión, y la Resurrección. La obra se compuso en tres etapas, y se imprimió en dos. Las *Trobas de la gloriosa pasión* (que empiezan con la Cena) fueron impresas en Toledo por Vázquez, y así se fechan hacia 1485. Las *Coplas de la pasión con la resurrección* son una reimpresión de las *Trobas*, aumentadas, como indica el título, por la narración de la Resurrección. El colofón nos informa, sin más, que el libro fue 'impreso en toledo', y ya que el segundo tipógrafo toledano, Antonio Téllez, adquirió una parte de los materiales de Vázquez, no es posible, a base de los indicios tipográficos, atribuirlas seguramente ni a Vázquez, en 1486 o más temprano, ni a Téllez en 1494 o más tarde. Debe notarse que la fecha acostumbrada de los bibliógrafos, 'hacia 1490', no es más que, en la frase de Sir Henry Thomas, 'a useful compromise', un término medio conveniente;[6] pero la verdad es que es completamente imposible que fueran impresas en 1490. La *Cena* y la *Pasión* se escribieron entre 1482 (hay una alusión a la guerra de Granada) y la fecha de su impresión, hacia 1485. Pero quisiera sugerir que Sir Henry Thomas debía haberse dejado convencer por sus propios argumentos basados en los indicios internos acerca de la fecha de composición de la *Resurrección*. En resumidas cuentas, una alusión a una victoria ganada contra los moros no sólo no se debe interpretar como una alusión a la toma de Granada,[7] sino que tiene que significar que esta ciudad todavía no había capitulado: del criado de los Reyes Católicos mismos se hubiera esperado, en otro caso, un hiperbólico canto de victoria. La *Resurrección*, pues, se compuso entre aproximadamente 1485 y 1492; y, puesto que Román, que vivía todavía en 1497, no vio la necesidad de enmendar lo que había escrito, la fecha más temprana sería la fecha más probable de su composición, así que la *Resurrección* sería escrita por los años de 1485–86.

Hasta que apareció la *Pasión* de San Pedro o la *Vita* de Mendoza, la poesía religiosa en España había quedado limitada a vidas de santos o milagros de Nuestra Señora, a largos poemas moralizadores sobre temas como el de los siete pecados mortales, y a poesías líricas, más cortas, generalmente dedicadas a la Virgen. Pero, a partir de los franciscanos del trescientos, que adoptaron con entusiasmo los temas de la Navidad y de la *Passio Christi–Compassio Mariae*, la vida de Cristo proporcionó material a los poetas narrativos de toda Europa, y no sólo en latín, sino también en inglés, francés, italiano, provenzal, y aun, dentro de la Península, en catalán. Tal vez el problema verdadero sea explicar cómo no se cultivó el género más temprano en Castilla; pero por lo menos es de suponer que la aparición, aun tardía, de esta clase de poesía, hay que destacarla contra el fondo de la reforma franciscana,[8] porque Mendoza y Montesino eran ambos franciscanos de la Observancia —es decir, miembros de las comunidades reformadas que en el curso del siglo XV se sintieron atraídas de nuevo a los ideales primitivos franciscanos de la pobreza y la humildad, y a una nueva desconfianza de la erudición y del intelecto mismo. Muchos elementos en la poesía de estos dos autores se pueden atribuir a la influencia de esta corriente de ideas, aunque no debíamos pasar por alto el hecho de que no todas las ideas y las actitudes identificadas por los críticos como franciscanas lo son exclusivamente, ya que muchas son características de toda la predicación mendicante por toda Europa en los siglos XIV y XV. Tal vez el rasgo más notable de esta nueva poesía religiosa sea que no tiene pretensiones; es de tanta sencillez e ingenuidad que, por lo menos, a un crítico le han parecido artificiales.[9]

Sin embargo, existen entre estos cuatro poetas tantas diferencias como semejanzas. He discutido en otro sitio sus distintos objetivos y métodos; tienen diferencias estilísticas también. San Pedro, a pesar de unos trozos espléndidos de retórica emotiva, especialmente en los lamentos de la Virgen (incorporados luego en las *Siete angustias de Nuestra Señora*), escribe sencillamente, en quintillas dobles, la estrofa menos complicada del siglo XV. Y, en contraste con sus demás obras, evita los *figurae* y *exempla* alegóricos. En toda la obra de San Pedro, escritor cuyo estilo, aparte de la *Pasión* y el *Sermón* burlesco, debe todo a los manuales medievales de retórica,[10] hay muchísimas metáforas dobles o sostenidas, pero no hay más de tres símiles (porque los teóricos, a pesar de Virgilio, de Homero, y de la Biblia, condenan este tropo);[11] y el hecho de que dos de estos símiles se presentan en la *Pasión* es algo muy significativo, aunque no pueden compararse con las imágenes de los otros poetas que estamos considerando.[12] En las estrofas preliminares dedicadas a la monja de quien está enamorado y a quien confiesa su 'pasión', jugando con esta palabra como se puede imaginar, compara su propia desgana de empezar la 'Pasión', mientras compone estrofa tras estrofa de prólogo, con la de unos reos a punto de ajusticiarse, que intentan diferir la hora inevitable pronunciando discursos prolijos. Y la *Pasión* misma empieza con la imagen más gastada de la Edad Media, el símil náutico: el piloto alejado de la tierra invoca la ayuda de los santos; y lo mismo hace el poeta, que luego, como Jorge Manrique, Mendoza, Padilla, etcétera, prosigue valiéndose del tópico igualmente vulgarizado, cuya historia anterior investigó Curtius, el de rechazar a las musas paganas.

El poema de Román, como dije arriba, se escribió en tres etapas, y en cada parte el empleo de las imágenes es distinto. La primera parte, la 'Cena' (A2^r-A5^v), se divide en dos secciones, de las que la primera y más larga, diecinueve estrofas de coplas de pie quebrado, es la 'Entroduçión alos rreyes' panegírica. La segunda sección, dieciocho estrofas de coplas reales, trata de la Cena. Empieza (A4^r) con una figura alegórica muy elaborada de la corte de Cristo, a la que volveré luego, y Román, después de apostrofar a Cristo, pidiéndole ayuda en componer el poema, sigue narrando, todavía haciendo uso del apóstrofe ('cenaste', 'lauaste los pies', etcétera), la historia de la Cena, terminando con algún comentario sobre el misterio de la Redención. Luego el Comendador explica en una rúbrica (A5^v) que, después de acabada esta sección, los reyes Fernando e Isabel le habían rogado que completase toda la historia de la Pasión, y así lo hace (A5^v-C8^r) en 178 estrofas de coplas de pie quebrado (no como las de la 'Entroduçión' sino como las del *Claro escuro* de Mena). En las *Coplas* sigue una tercera parte, la Resurrección (D1^r-E10^v), también escrita a petición de los Reyes Católicos, de 166 estrofas, otra vez de coplas de pie quebrado de la misma estructura que las de la Pasión. La narración está interrumpida por distintas variedades de comentario, entre ellas las comparaciones ilustrativas, que llevan la rúbrica de 'conpara'. En la Pasión hay cinco comparaciones así; en la Resurrección, compuesta más tarde, hay, aunque es más corta, quince.

La 'Cena' contiene una sola imagen, rubricada no 'conpara' sino 'comiença la contenplaçión dela çena por la corte que christo traya quando andaua enesta vida'. Se trata de una serie prolongada de correspondencias, una *figura* alegórica medieval completamente típica: así, en la corte de Cristo, los galanes eran los apóstoles, las damas las Marías, los brocados eran cilicios, los torneos la contemplación, y así sucesivamente. Algunos de los cotejos, que Román pone en paralelo por dos estrofas de diez versos, más o menos uno en cada verso, son desavenidos, y, aunque se pudiera considerar que yace implícito el contraste entre la corte de Cristo y la de la España contemporánea, la imagen entera carece de fuerza, porque Román no dice más que, para ser buenos cristianos, debíamos pensar en 'tales cortesanos' y 'aquel rrey'.

Al volvernos a las comparaciones de la Pasión y la Resurrección encontramos una diferencia marcada. Dos imágenes, una en cada parte, son metáforas: 'O pelicano syn par' (C5^r), y 'los terremotos tales / [. . .] / son trompetas y atabales' (D5^r); pero las demás son símiles. Así, en la Pasión, el Señor, compartiendo con nosotros sus virtudes, se parangona con un capitán generoso que divide los gajes de una guerra justa (A6^r); Jesús anda entre los judíos como un cordero entre lobos rapaces (B3^r); la Virgen, que se apresura a ver a su Hijo después de conocer la crucifixión, es como un hombre que lucha con el mar, 'echando el agua y beuiendo' (¿sus lágrimas?), sufriendo trescientas muertes antes de llegar a la tierra (C1^r); María sigue las huellas sangrientas de Cristo como una tigre que sigue la pista de sus cachorros (C1^v); y la última imagen de la Pasión es la metáfora ya mencionada, del pelícano que 'sacaste por nos librar / la sangre del coraçon' (C5^r).

En la Resurrección la frecuencia de las imágenes es tres veces más alta. A pesar del hecho de que cada una aparece en una estrofa bajo la rúbrica de 'conpara', son de una extensión muy variable, y todavía varias son cortas, comparaciones de uno o dos versos, que no sondan las implicaciones de la comparación. Por ejemplo: los apóstoles dejados solos después de la Ascensión de Cristo son 'como rreyes desconpuestos / esperando sus coronas' (E10^r), pero el resto de la estrofa describe a los apóstoles en términos aplicables sólo a ellos, y no a reyes que están esperando coronas; también la imagen de 'con pena tan jnfinita / como quando el sol se quita' (E9^r) no se persigue más adelante. A veces se mezclan los detalles de la imagen y de la realidad sin que haya correspondencia entre ellos, como cuando Román escribe (D3^r) que Dios entró en el mundo a quitarnos nuestros pecados, 'como rrey disimulado / en figura de rromero', andando mendigando de casa en casa para dejar la gloria abierta a todos. Una de las comparaciones es extremamente floja: la gracia de Dios es tan grande como una mina de oro inagotable (E7^r). Pero no es preciso detenernos en las comparaciones fracasadas. Román no siempre se bate en retirada apresurada de sus símiles ('retreats hastily from his similes', Thomas, p. 16), y tiene algunas comparaciones extensas en que se hermanan todos los elementos, como cuando el Cristo resucitado va visitando a sus amigos y discípulos (E5^v):

> Andaua dios visitando
> los suyos porque les preste
> como buen rrey peleando
> que anda sienpre rreparando
> la flaqueza de su hueste
> hablando muy amoroso
> por do quiere que se mueue
> sienpre en proa
> y al que siente mas dudoso
> porque haga lo que deue
> mas le loa

También nos complace la imagen (E7^r) de los apóstoles que esperan tristemente, después de irse Cristo, como niños cuyo padre se ha marchado, hasta que le vuelvan a ver: todos los elementos de la comparación son aplicables a las dos situaciones, aunque se pudiera poner reparos a lo banal de la comparación. Hay, sin embargo, algunas imágenes más llamativas: el Señor baja al infierno y (D4^r):

> por las cueuas de bolcan
> andaua como aliman
> entre gente de guinea

Después de una serie de apariciones y desapariciones milagrosas ('tropelías', las diría Cervantes), Román comenta (E4^v) que:

> andaua el señor sin fallas
> visitando a sus hermanos
> como jugador de manos
> quando pasa las agallas
> avnque lestauan mirando
> quando les aparescia
> sin conquista
> non sabien como ny quando
> se yva ny se venia
> de su vista.

Sir Henry Thomas encuentra el símil del capitán 'strange', el del alemán 'far-fetched' ('traído por los cabellos'), y en cuanto a Cristo como prestidigitador anota (p. 16): 'it would be in bad taste in anyone less naïve than the Comendador' ('en un autor menos ingenuo que el Comendador, sería de un gusto pésimo'). Sin embargo, estas comparaciones no son tan desafortunadas. Cristo entre los habitantes sombríos del infierno se destaca como un alemán rubio ('alemán' es casi sinónimo de 'roxo': véase Covarrubias s.v. ALEMANIA) entre los negros de la costa occidental de África. El 'ahora se ve, y ahora no' del prestidigitador describe justamente la serie extra- ordinaria de desapariciones y apariciones repentinas que ejecuta Cristo en los evangelios apócrifos. En cuanto al buen gusto, esto es otra cosa, y volveré sobre ello.

Fray Íñigo de Mendoza, al empezar su *Vita* versificada, paga el tributo acostumbrado a Juan de Mena, salvándole de la condenación general de la poesía profana (A1^v), utilizando el mismo argumento que emplea Mena en sus *Siete pecados*, pero el estilo de Mendoza en la *Vita Christi* es de lo más opuesto al de Mena—por lo menos del Mena del *Laberinto*. Fray Ambrosio de Montesino, como más tarde Padilla,[13] ataca el estilo elevado (*Coplas*, A2^r):

que lagrimas son meiores
en tal caso que alto estilo
pues con ellas los colores
y rretorecos primores
son pauilo

pero Mendoza, aunque está apuntando, claro está, al mismo marco de la comunicación sencilla y directa, parece menos seguro de su postura en rechazar el 'alto estilo' y adoptar el 'grosero', y hasta se disculpa del episodio de los pastores y su diálogo rústico,[14] empleando, para justificarse, una imagen típica, de largo abolengo (B6^v):[15]

Porque no pueden estar
en vn rigor toda via
los arcos para tirar
suelen los desenpulgar
alguna pieça del dia
pues razon fue declarar
estas chufas de pastores
para poder recrear
despertar y renouar
la gana de los lectores

En Mendoza, desde luego, no encontramos al mendicante puro; era un fraile cortesano, y ha sido tachado de hipócrita. Los ataques crueles lanzados contra él por Vázquez de Palencia ('¿cómo entiende y sabe tanto / del tracto de las mugeres?') y por otro galán anónimo ('lindo frayle de palacio', etcétera),[16] Menéndez y Pelayo los descartó como resultado del resentimiento de cortesanos heridos en lo vivo por su sátira. Pero se olvida de la poesía amorosa de Mendoza (*Canc. general* 1511, fol. 186^v) que para José Manuel Blecua (*Historia general de las literaturas hispánicas*, II) comprobaba su 'vinculación a los terrenales placeres'. Comoquiera que sea todo esto, Mendoza era predicador en la corte (es sumamente lamentable el que no nos haya llegado ninguno de sus sermones), y su *Vita Christi*, que se pudiera considerar como una colección de sermones versificados, está dirigida claramente a un público cortesano. No sólo se constituyen el blanco de su sátira las costumbres y los vicios de los cortesanos, su vestido, su lenguaje, su flirteo, y lo demás, sino que también hay que suponer que, a pesar de su estilo relativamente sencillo y directo, de su empleo del romance, forma métrica despreciada, y de sus 'chufas de pastores', pensó que esta misma clase culta leería la *Vita*, porque es digno de atención el hecho de que los *exemplos* de Mendoza aparecen raras veces como historias contadas por extenso, sino como alusiones indirectas.

A pesar de todo esto, Fray Íñigo, estilísticamente, es mucho más revolucionario que Fray Ambrosio. Los críticos suelen aparejar a los dos franciscanos y su 'poesía popular', pero, comparado con el Mendoza de la *Vita Christi*, Montesino es un poeta culto. Sigue empleando el hipérbaton de Mena y de Santillana ('ala ciudad boluiste / efesiana' (B2^v), etcétera), el participio de presente (las sesenta y seis estrofas de las *Coplas a sant juan euangelista* tienen el estribillo 'euangelista / más bolante' que trae por consecuencia casi sesenta y seis participios de presente para suplir las rimas), y estrofas y rimas bastante complicadas y difíciles. Hasta sus romances, que tanto comentario han excitado, son romances rimados.

Por encima, el empleo de las imágenes por los dos poetas es muy diferente. Montesino emplea mucho la *figura* alegórica, como, por ejemplo, en las *Coplas de sant juan*, A7^r-B3^v, donde se halla una alegoría elaborada de San Juan Bautista como su emblema, el águila: su alcándara es el Cielo, cada pluma es una piedra de firmeza, etcétera; está claro que Fray Ambrosio prefiere la metáfora al símil, de los que sólo hay tres o cuatro ejemplos en las *Coplas*; y está muy adicto a la *superlatio*, la comparación que depende de una fórmula como 'más [. . .] que' ('mas olias que ambar gris', 'diamantes no son tales / ni rrubis' (C6^r), etcétera). De imágenes que se pudieran equiparar con las que estamos considerando, tiene sólo éstas: el ruido de los golpes cuando se azotó a Cristo sonó 'como los delas canales / quando sobre losas llueue' (A4^r); el niño Jesús en los pechos de María es como una abeja que vuela entre las flores a chupar la miel (C2^r); los serafines bajan 'como los copos de nieue / espessos en çierço viento' (D5^r); y 'como cuerda de vallesta / que el azero doble el hilo / del cielo me traxo esta / a ser niño deste estilo' (B6^v). Su *Cancionero* de 1508 tiene muchos más símiles pintorescos, pero se había establecido la moda mucho antes de esta fecha.

Por el contrario, la *Vita Christi* de Mendoza no tiene ninguna *figura* alegórica, pero, mientras también utiliza los *exempla*, contiene en cuatrocientas tantas estrofas más de cincuenta imágenes, bajo la rúbrica de 'conparación',[17] lo cual significa que son dos veces más frecuentes que en Román, aun en la *Resurrección*. Algunas son vulgares: el ver la estrella que los conduce a Cristo destierra el 'vano ydolatrar' de los Reyes Magos como el despertar ahuyenta a las fantasías nocturnas (C3^r); cuando desapareció la estrella eran estos 'cristianos primeros' como navegadores en un mar tempestuoso, como guerreros cuando cae el portaestandarte (C3^v); el ofrecimiento de oro del tercer rey, después de los de los otros, es dulce como una manzana después de una purga, como la calma después de una tempestad en el mar, como el amanecer después de una noche oscura, como el tesoro para un pobre (C7^r); este mundo es como una barca averiada y peligrosa, como una casa que deja entrar la lluvia, como un licor dulce pronto bebido, como la canción falsa de la sirena, como un edificio sentado en arena, como una manzana que parece sana pero que está podrida dentro (D3^v); los bienes de este mundo son como la riqueza soñada que desaparece al despertarse el soñador (D3^v); la 'christiana color' de España es como el casco sano de una nuez podrida, como el color sano de la manzana que tiene dentro un gusano (D7^r).

Encontramos también en la *Vita* las comparaciones familiares sacadas de los bestiarios, tal vez las más usadas de todas las imágenes de los homilistas medievales. Hallamos los animales de la realidad circundante: la liebre (A2^r), que 'por no encobarse / a vezes pierde la vida' (amonestación a las vírgenes); el gallo encima del muladar (C4^v); el escorpión de aspecto inocente (C8^v); la anguila deslizadera (E1^v),

> que quanto con mayor gana
> apiertan y la detienen
> tanto mas es cosa llana
> que se desliza y desmana
> delas manos que la tienen

el perro con su presa, que intenta volver a ella, con 'saña doblada', cuando se le quiere apartar de ella, tirando por el collar (E1^v) (todas éstas imágenes de Herodes). A veces Mendoza elabora la comparación con detalles pintorescos: la mente humana, contemplando el misterio de la Encarnación, no puede jamás agotarlo, y todo lo que se ha escrito acerca de él (A4^r)

> es quanto lieua vn mosquito
> de muy grand cuba de vino
> que nunca le haze mella
> avnque beba quanto pueda
> sy mill vezes entra enella
> el sale borracho della
> mas ella llena se queda.

Los fieles españoles hacen sus preces (D7^r),

> como el tordo que se cria
> enla jaula de chequito

> que dize quando chirria
> ihesus y sancta maria
> y el querria mas vn mosquito

Los bienes de este mundo son traidores (D4^r),

> y con cara lisongera
> como mastin escusero
> halagan enla carrera
> porque con falsa manera
> nos muerdan mas de ligera

Los mismos animales familiares mirados a través de los anteojos del filósofo natural adquieren características extrañas: en la colmena sólo el rey de las abejas carece de aguijón (E2^v, un rey no debía pensar en la venganza); y hallamos también las criaturas semimíticas (como el pelícano de Román): la bestia maravillosa que es el elefante 'que se ensaña en sangre agena' (E5^v, el tercer rey, conmovido por pensar en la Pasión de Cristo), la sirena que adormece a los que oyen su canción (C7^r).

Nos encontramos con el aldeano dejado sin habla en un palacio al ver las cortinas (A4^v, véase abajo); con el paisano en casa de un gran señor, boquiabierto al ver los brocados (C3^v); con el esgrimador experto (C7^r); con el romero afligido por la erisipela, 'huego de sant marçal' (C8^v); con el sastre bueno (E2^r); con el contador fraudulento (E2^r); con la madre que descubre que el hijo dado por muerto está vivo (C4^v); y hay muchos más símiles inclasificables: el bocado del caballo (B7^v); el hombre que clava la vista en la lejanía para discernir algo ve menos bien que antes, y la vista 'despúes en sy tornada / apenas puede ver nada' (A5^r); la vela que alumbra a una reunión mientras se consume (los judíos que se abrasan en su religión, dando luz mediante los profetas); el anzuelo ocultado en el cebo (C8^v); los gritos que se oyen cuando el toro salta la barrera (D8^r); el pendón que 'queda colgado / do es vino vendido' (E2^r); y muchos más.

II

Esta clase de comparación no es completamente nueva aun en la poesía española del cuatrocientos; se presentan imágenes del mismo tipo—no tan realistas, ni tan memorables, ni tan elaboradas con detalles pintorescos, pero con todo esencialmente afines—en los versos de Hernán Mexía, Juan Álvarez Gato, Mena, Santillana, Pérez de Guzmán, Gómez Manrique, y de otros menos conocidos. Y estos a su vez no están haciendo más que tomar prestada la técnica, y hasta las imágenes mismas, del predicador medieval.[18] Ni siquiera es posible afirmar que cualquiera de las imágenes de Mendoza sea su propia invención. En uno de los más vulgarizados de los manuales de predicación de la Edad Media, el *Summa predicantium* de Juan Bromyard, del siglo catorce, se puede averiguar, s.v. CONSILIUM, que el tordo que chirría de Mendoza, que 'más querría un mosquito', no es más que una versión de la imagen del pájaro que habla inglés y francés sin entender palabra de ninguna lengua.[19] La presencia de esta imagen en Bromyard constituye una garantía adecuada de su empleo en varios millares de homilías medievales. En Bromyard también se puede hallar la cámara real con *sus cortinas* para asombrar al humilde aldeano,[20] el perro lisonjero y traidor, la muestra de una taberna, el mendigo apestado, la pesadilla, el soñador desilusionado al despertar,[21] el médico con sus purgas, el espejo deformador (y todas estas imágenes las emplea Mendoza), y varios centenares más, que van, como en Mendoza, del lugar común de origen inaveriguable, por la imagen bíblica y la sacada de las recopilaciones enciclopédicas de seudociencia zoológica, a la imagen más picante y sorprendente. Bien puede ser que Mendoza inventara alguna imagen de su propia cosecha—y el toro, por lo menos, parece español—pero la única originalidad que seguramente se le puede conceder es la de haber sabido adaptar, como todos los predicadores de la Edad Media, los *exempla* 'standard' (casi se pudiera decir clásicos), añadiendo color local, y elaborando los detalles. Este procedimiento puede traer como consecuencia una casi metamorfosis de la imagen: el mendigo se transforma en el romero afligido por una enfermedad distinta, el loro se hace estornino negro ('tordo'), las redes del cazador de aves se convierten en visco. Todo esto hace algo difícil la tarea del historiador de la literatura, tal como la define Kristeller: 'valorar los elementos tanto originales como tradicionales'.

Pero al intentar valorar la originalidad de estas comparaciones hay que tener en cuenta otra circunstancia. Cualquier *collatio aperta* consta de dos partes, la imagen, y la situación real a la que se aplica. Pero rastreando la historia de estos tópicos menudos, no se debe esperar encontrar la situación concreta, que ilustra la imagen, repetida de autor en autor. (La imagen del sol y la vidriera, que cito abajo, será casi única en ser aplicable a sólo dos situaciones.) La imagen del soñador desilusionado abarca cien situaciones de desilusión; la del anzuelo abraza cualquier engaño, cualquier triquiñuela, así que en Mendoza representa a Herodes diciendo a los Reyes Magos 'et cum inveneritis, renunciate mihi, ut ego veniens adorem eum' (*Matt.* 2. 8), mientras que en Montesino representa a la Encarnación de Cristo, imaginada como una trampa para coger al diablo. En la obra de Bromyard y las muchas recopilaciones semejantes, el predicador medieval encontraba un índice de tópicos (Adulatio, Amor, etcétera), y bajo cada rótulo algunas indicaciones de cómo se pudiera desarrollar el tema, juntas con anécdotas apropiadas y las imágenes que lo pudieran ilustrar. Es posible, luego, que en la poesía didáctica más temprana, Juan de Mena, por ejemplo, tomase prestadas, íntegras, *collationes* que oyó emplear en algún sermón, pero parece probable que predicadores de profesión como Mendoza y Montesino utilizaran las imágenes tradicionales en contextos originales. La diferencia más importante, en verdad, entre Fray Íñigo y los poetas didácticos anteriores es que Mendoza era predicador, y, según la opinión, el predilecto de la reina. Con Mendoza el fraile español se convierte en poeta.

El lector habrá notado ya que ninguna de las imágenes de Mendoza que he citado hasta aquí se aplicó a misterios de la fe o a la Persona Divina, y es precisamente un empleo de este tipo de imagen que, en obras posteriores, parece chocar a los críticos modernos. El comendador Román compara a la Virgen con un nadador que se ahoga, y con una tigre; a Cristo con un buen rey, el padre de una familia, un cordero entre lobos, el pelícano, el sol, un romero, un capitán generoso, un alemán, un prestidigitador. Mendoza tiene sólo cuatro imágenes así. El misterio del parto virginal queda aclarado con esta imagen (A3^r):

> Tu quedaras tan entera
> dela preñez del jnfante
> qual queda la vidriera
> quando enella Reuerbera
> el sol y passa adelante.

El padre jesuita Alonso Rodríguez observó en 1610: 'suelen traer un ejemplo natural[22] para declarar esto, aunque ninguno hay que cuadre del todo: así como el rayo del sol pasa por la vidriera sin quebrarla, antes queda ella muy entera.'[23] Esta imagen tiene, en realidad, dos aplicaciones: una, como en Mendoza, ilustrativa del parto virginal; o, en la tradición mística, otra ilustrativa del estado contemplativo, cuando el alma se siente invadida por Dios. La mayoría de los ejemplos del empleo de esta imagen reunidos por los estudiosos modernos del tópico[24] hay que fecharlos después de Fray Íñigo, aunque se ha notado su existencia en Berceo y en Juan Manuel. Pero los estudios eruditos que he citado dan la impresión de que, tras alguna aparición esporádica en la Edad Media española, la imagen se hace, en el

Siglo de Oro, un tópico preferido. Ya que no cabe duda de que se trata de un lugar común medieval en latín, en francés, y en inglés, ¿no nos debiéramos preguntar si esta impresión, aunque presta apoyo a la tesis de la llegada tardía a Castilla y la floración en el Siglo de Oro de mucha materia medieval, quedaría con valor después de una investigación minuciosa de los sermones medievales castellanos, que, a diferencia de las homilías medievales en latín y los sermones del Siglo de Oro, son accesibles sólo en los archivos y quedan por la mayor parte por investigar?

En cuanto a las imágenes aplicadas a la Persona Divina, Mendoza tiene (A7^r):

> en cas del boticario
> el buen fisico prudente
> escudriña en el almario
> el xarope que es contrario
> ala passyon del paçiente

El buen físico es Dios; el jarope que escoge es Cristo. Es una maña guerrera llevar las tropas por montañas despobladas, para que la sorpresa de la arremetida, y por consiguiente la victoria, sea mayor; así el Señor ocultó su divinidad en la humilde cuadra (D4^v). La carne de Cristo era cebo para el diablo, como la carne puesta en la buitrera, que al buitre, que no se fija en el ballestero, le cuesta la vida (D5^r). No he encontrado en la literatura anterior la imagen de la buitrera (aunque en la *Celestina*, Auto XII, Pármeno habla de Melibea como 'carne de buitrera'—y también 'ceuo de anzuelo'); pero se pudiera oponer que la imagen misma no es más que una variación local del conocido cazador de aves (cf. el diablo como cazador de aves en San Agustín, *Homiliae in S. Joann.*, LVII), mientras en su aplicación corre parejas con muchos otros reclamos, lazos, y trampas (cf. el anzuelo de Montesino).[25] En cuanto a las otras comparaciones, Dios el médico (cf. Roberto Basevorn, *Forma praedicandi*, p. 269: 'Medicus est Christus, nos infirmi'), y varias imágenes militares que figuran la lucha de Cristo con el diablo, son lugares comunes en los sermones medievales y la literatura religiosa.

En Román lo que interesa es el cambio progresivo en el empleo de las imágenes: un poema muy rutinario sobre la Cena (y muy corta si se le quita el material superfluo) no contiene ni un símil pintoresco; aumentado, a petición de Fernando e Isabel, una Pasión propiamente narrativa tiene cinco imágenes de este tipo, y, concluido, al tercer intento, la Resurrección contiene una comparación por cada diez estrofas. Sería difícil negar que Román, también cortesano, quedase sin influir por el éxito de la *Vita* de Mendoza, que pasó por tres ediciones antes de 1485. Se nos presenta luego un problema: ¿es posible que Román, poeta mediocre que entendió mal o pasó por alto tantas de las nuevas ideas religiosas entonces en boga, tal vez no se diera cuenta, al equiparar a Cristo con un jugador de manos, de que Mendoza sólo raras veces aplica esta clase de imagen a la Persona Divina? Fácilmente se pudiera concluir que la torpeza explica estas comparaciones chocantes mejor que una consciente voluntad de ser raro o un intento premeditado de despertar a los lectores. Sin embargo ambas explicaciones serían falsas. La novedad de las imágenes de Mendoza estriba en el hecho de que se presentan en la poesía religiosa narrativa en español; la novedad de Román, en que parece estar sin paralelo anterior en cualquier poesía española. Pero la novedad consiste sólo en la introducción de este tipo de comparación en la poesía, como ahora intentaré demostrar.

III

Los poetas frailes después de Mendoza casi unánimemente condenan el empleo del estilo ornado, el *sermo artifex* de la teoría retórica medieval, en las obras religiosas. Bien puede ser que la idea se hallase reforzada por la reacción hacia el buen gusto que motivaron las ideas de los humanistas en la época de los Reyes Católicos; pero en el cuatrocientos español encontramos la misma idea mucho más temprano, en obras didácticas como la de Pérez de Guzmán.[26] Parece ser eco de las nuevas ideas religiosas, porque el punto de vista tradicional (manifestado claramente en San Agustín, *De doctrina christiana*, IV) es que el predicador no debía despreciar la ayuda de la retórica (cap. 2),[27] aunque tampoco debía dejarla ofuscar su intento (cap. 10); el predicador elocuente ni se olvida de los colores retóricos ni los emplea indebidamente (cap. 26). Los teóricos de la Baja Edad Media definen el ideal de la misma manera, por referirse a los extremos; en el empleo de la retórica tanto como en el vestido del predicador, sus gestos, y la sonoridad y la rapidez de su dicción, etcétera.[28] Pero San Agustín distingue entre la predicación a los fieles y la dirigida a los neófitos y los paganos susceptibles de evangelización. El objeto y el arte del homilista que predica a los fieles—y es digno de notarse que el sermón ya está considerado como un género artístico—son la instrucción, el agrado, y la persuasión de los oyentes (*De doct. christ.*, IV, 26); pero en el *De rudibus catechizandis* donde San Agustín trata de la predicación misionera, menciona la retórica sólo para insistir en que el catequista deba convencer a su alumno culto de que el contenido de un sermón es más importante que el estilo. También al catequista misionero se le puede permitir, tan a menudo como necesita hacerlo para volver a captar el interés del alumno, que cuente un chiste inocente (*De rud. cat.*, 13), mientras en el sermón latino de la Edad Media, dirigido a los fieles, se permite emplear una *opportuna jocatio* 'ad plus ter in uno sermone' (Roberto Basevorn, cap. 50).

Con el advenimiento de los frailes mendicantes aparece también un nuevo tipo de predicación. Es evangélica y misionera. Es como si toda predicación estuviese dirigida a gentiles y paganos, porque en realidad el objeto de esta predicación era convertir a los oyentes y despertar en ellos el verdadero amor a Cristo. Se dirige, pues, al vulgo, en la lengua vernácula, en el propio idioma de la gente (en el sentido más amplio de 'idioma'); es una predicación 'llena de los hechos crudos y sencillos de la vida diaria, con pocos remilgos en cuanto al estilo—clara, franca, y enérgica',[29] que no desdeña ningún modo de reforzar su eficacia. Los elementos cómicos, hasta verdaderas payasadas, la crítica a menudo brutal de los ricos y los grandes, la declamación dramática con gestos mímicos, el explotar la experiencia diaria de la congregación mediante el empleo de las comparaciones y los ejemplos basados en la vida cotidiana, todo esto es típico de la predicación vernácula de los postreros siglos de la Edad Media, y es evidente que los predicadores mendicantes reaccionaron violentamente ante el sermón latino decadente con sus reglas increíblemente complejas, el que buscaba la justificación de estas reglas precisamente pretendiendo que desde los tiempos de los Padres de la Iglesia el arte homilético se veía abandonado por la inspiración. No cabe duda de que el echar mano a objetos familiares para deducir una moraleja es algo muy antiguo; pero son los frailes, que escogen una gran parte de sus imágenes de las escenas de la vida diaria, quienes vulgarizan esta clase de ilustración homilética. Los frailes del siglo XV nunca hubieran concedido la razón a Huarte de San Juan que afirmó que 'hoy, *recibida la fe* y de tantos años atrás, bien se permite predicar con lugares retóricos'.[30] Que sus oyentes creían, esto lo daban por entendido; pero que sus creencias guiaran su conducta diaria, esto no se notaba. Y así aspiraron no a la conversión intelectual sino a una conversión de alma y vida. Tal vez ningún predicador mendicante se salve del todo de alguna formación retórica, pero sí se puede afirmar que cuando utiliza recursos retóricos su propósito no es nunca puramente estético. En esta tradición mendicante debemos asentar tanto el 'estilo grosero' de Mendoza como las imágenes de Mendoza y Román.

La interpretación habitual del porqué de estas imágenes es que refuerzan una moraleja ('point a moral', Owst) o que 'hacen más inteligibles a los simples los misterios de la fe' ('make the mysteries of religion more intelligible to the simple', Wilson, p. 40); pero al examinarlas más de cerca, nos encontramos con el hecho de que, aunque algunas tienen algún mensaje moral (la liebre, el rey de las abejas), es rarísima la imagen que se emplea para hacer inteligible un misterio (el sol y la vidriera). Estas comparaciones pintorescas resultan innecesarias: comparar al tercer rey cuando habla con la Virgen con un esgrimador experto (Mendoza) o a la Virgen con una tigre que sigue la huella de sus cachorros (Román) no refuerza ninguna moraleja ni hace inteligible ningún misterio, no explica nada. Escribe el profesor Wilson que mediante estas imágenes la experiencia corriente de la vida diaria fue puesta en contacto con la experiencia religiosa; la analogía de la religión se percibía por todas partes y a todas horas; la religión no se vio cerrada en un compartimiento aislado del que se excluyeran los sentimientos y las acciones cotidianos.[31] Y hasta cierto punto el profesor Wilson tiene razón; no se puede negar que un tópico favorecido y una suposición básica del cristianismo medieval es la idea de que toda la naturaleza es el libro de Dios, el *liber naturae*, en que están escritas, para que las lean todos, las verdades de la religión (cf. Tomás de Kempis, *De imitatione Christi*, II, 4: 'omnis creatura speculum vitae et liber sanctae doctrinae esset'). Pero no creo que me equivoque en pensar que para el lector moderno estas imágenes pintorescas constituyen los trozos más vivos de la obra, y sin querer caer en un subjetivismo anacrónico e injustificable quisiera insinuar que tal vez no fuese tan distinto de nosotros el lector del cuatrocientos. Es decir, me parece que el motivo principal del predicador en emplearlas es 'recrear / despertar y renouar / la gana de los lectores'. No son ilustraciones útiles, ni siquiera un intento de dorar la píldora, sino sencillamente recursos para volver a ganar la atención, 'quando auditores fastidiunt' y 'dormire incipiunt' (Basevorn, cap. 50). (Y no creo tenga importancia el que tanto Mendoza como Basevorn se están refiriendo al humor y no a las imágenes.)

Los símiles no son, según los teóricos, *colores rhetorici* (*comparatio* es uno de los métodos de *amplificatio*), y, aunque son, claro está, en cierto modo ornamentales, durante el siglo XV y más tarde se salvan de la condenación general del estilo retóricamente ornado. Vale la pena de insistir en el hecho de que nadie se dio cuenta de que había cierta contradicción en esto. Otis H. Green (véase la nota 30) ha compilado un pequeño florilegio muy interesante de ideas referentes a la técnica de los predicadores y los escritores religiosos, sacadas de las controversias del Siglo de Oro. Una multitud de escritores se adhieren al ideal del estilo sencillo en la predicación: Fray Diego de Velades (1579), Francisco de Medina (1580), Fray Diego Pérez de Valdivia (1588), P. Juan Bonifacio (1589), Pedro Simón Abril (1589), y varios más, hasta bastante entrado el siglo XVII. Pero encontramos en la misma compañía a Fray Pedro Malón de Chaide, que choca a su editor comparando a Cristo con un burro y con un elefante,[32] pero que se alía con los defensores del estilo sencillo, mediante la antigua imagen de la carne y la salsa, 'guisado con mil salsillas' (II, 36).[33] La verdad es que estas imágenes pintorescas y aun chocantes están repartidas tanto entre los predicadores y moralistas que creen que 'la verdad no necesita colores postizos' (Velades, *cit.* Green) como entre los que creen que el predicador debe vestir las ideas universalmente recibidas de conceptos nuevos y brillantes.

El lenguaje figurado de los contemplativos del siglo XVI, objeto de numerosos estudios, complica el cuadro, ya que en varios aspectos importantes se diferencia del de Mendoza o de Román.[34] Las imágenes del Siglo de Oro verdaderamente análogas a las de estos dos autores se encuentran en los sermones y las obras didácticas del siglo XVI, en las obras de los que adoctrinan y persuaden. Allí, este mismo tipo de imagen ha provocado en los críticos modernos expresiones de disgusto,[35] tantas veces como tales imágenes hacen caso omiso del decoro, o, en las palabras del profesor Wilson (p. 51), 'echan abajo todas las barreras y cadenas de la elegancia italianizante, de Escalígero, y de la doctrina de los tres estilos'.[36] Sin embargo, quisiera sugerir que nos desviaremos al intentar clasificar las imágenes de los moralistas como comparaciones convencionales o rutinarias, imágenes sacadas de la vida diaria, símiles chocantes en que 'tal vez reciba daño la reverencia' ('reverence, perhaps, suffers', Wilson, p. 40). Es cierto que las comparaciones basadas en los objetos y los incidentes de la vida cotidiana y las escenas domésticas, las 'homely comparisons', son características de cierta tradición, pero yo no he topado con ningún predicador o moralista medieval que las emplee exclusivamente: es decir, el homilista que habla del ama de casa que barre de la cocina las cagadas de las gallinas (véase Owst, p. 35) utiliza no menos frecuentemente que este tipo de imagen las basadas en la mitología clásica o sacadas de los bestiarios fantásticos de la Edad Media.[37] Quiero decir que la imagen chocante de la época medieval no obedece a ninguna teoría de *admiratio*, sino que refleja tan sólo el empleo de los símiles libre del prurito moderno de considerar lo que reclama la unción. Con el advenimiento de los franciscanos, el acento con respecto al misterio de la Encarnación se traslada del Dios remoto y terrible de la temprana Edad Media al Hijo de Dios hecho hombre, al Niño en los pechos de su madre, al Hombre atormentado y sangriento, al 'vir dolorum sciens infirmitatem' (*Isaias* 52. 3); y en la atmósfera cargada de emoción de la predicación mendicante, que insiste en el Amor y en el Verbo hecho hombre, que nos avisa de la inminencia de Dios, la formalidad y el temor templado apenas tienen importancia. Las emociones que trata de despertar la predicación franciscana son la ternura, el espanto, el amor, la compasión, la alegría, y estas emociones triunfan del decoro. Y padeció daño la reverencia, como todavía lo sufre a veces en España por 'la intimidad con lo divino', como ha anotado María Rosa Lida.[38]

Todo esto no resuelve del todo nuestro problema en cuanto al decoro. María Rosa Lida (*ibid.*) investiga la boga cuatrocentista de las extrañas comparaciones blasfemas de los reyes y los grandes con Dios, Cristo, y la Virgen (boga que se presenta también en Francia según Huizinga, *El otoño de la Edad Media*, cap. 12). Así Montoro le dice a Isabel que si ella hubiera nacido antes de 'la hija de sant ana / de vos el hijo de dios / recibiera carne humana'. Escribe (p. 130) de su 'entronque con la irrupción de los conversos en la sociedad cristiana';[39] comoquiera que sea esto, Mendoza también, en su *Dechado*, se dirige a la reina empleando la misma comparación hiperbólica, 'a remediar nuestros males / desiguales / por gracia de dios venida' (descripción tradicional de la Virgen), mientras evita 'la equiparación desembozada con la Virgen'. Sugiere que le constriñe a Fray Íñigo el 'decoro isabelino'. En la *Vita Christi* encontramos la comparación poco decorosa de la carne de Cristo con la carne puesta en una buitrera, pero es imposible pasar por alto el contraste general entre las imágenes de Mendoza y las de Román, y tal vez hemos de admitir que Mendoza sí sintiera algún constreñimiento que se pudiera llamar el del decoro o del buen gusto. Pero lo sintió, y de ahí viene la dificultad, mucho antes de que adquisieran valor corriente en la corte isabelina las nuevas nociones acerca del buen gusto.

Dos nuevas ideas importantes aparecen en la teoría literaria de los humanistas, que son el *decorum* y la *admiratio*. Cómo relacionar a estas ideas con las imágenes chocantes de ciertos predicadores y moralistas del Siglo de Oro, lo dejo para otra mano; pero por lo menos espero haber demostrado que un escritor como Fray Domingo de Valtanás (*Doctrina christiana*, Sevilla, 1555) podría ser colocado a la zaga de una amplia tradición medieval. El profesor Wilson ha insinuado (p. 45) que a medida que pasan los años, y escritores nuevos intentan decir las mismas cosas con todavía más fuerza, las comparaciones se transforman en metáforas dobles o sostenidas; y sitúa a Ledesma en el extremo de un proceso evolutivo que empieza con autores como Valtanás. Por otra parte los historiadores de la literatura suelen mirar a Ledesma desde otro punto de vista y considerarle como el iniciador del conceptismo. Los dos puntos de vista son complementarios; pero después de examinar las imágenes de Mendoza y de Román, creo que se puede afirmar que la novedad de las imágenes en la poesía conceptista religiosa del siglo XVII, en Valdivielso, Bonilla, y Ledesma, quizás haya sido exagerada a causa de la falta del debido aprecio de lo que heredan estos autores de cierta tradición religiosa. Mi propósito principal era describir la primera aparición de este tipo de comparación en la poesía religiosa española; queda patente que otro fenómeno más del Siglo de Oro se ha de explicar mediante referencia al siglo XV, y al fin y al cabo a la Edad Media europea.⁴⁰

[*RFE*, 46 (1963 [1965]), 263-85]

Notes

1. Véanse mis artículos 'The Religious Poems of Diego de San Pedro: Their Relationship and their Dating', *HR*, 28 (1960), 1-15, y 'The First Printing of San Pedro's *Pasión trovada*', *HR*, 30 (1962), 149-51.
2. Véase Antonio Pérez Gómez, 'Notas para la bibliografía de Fray Íñigo de Mendoza y de Jorge Manrique', *HR*, 27 (1959), 30-41. Cito según el facsímil de esta edición publicado por la Real Academia Española (Madrid, 1953).
3. Todas las citas de Menéndez y Pelayo se refieren al cap. 22, 'La poesía religiosa en tiempo de los Reyes Católicos', de su *Antología de poetas líricos castellanos*, III (Santander, 1944), 42-75.
4. Véanse mis artículos 'The Printed Editions and the Text of the Works of Fray Íñigo de Mendoza', *BHS*, 39 (1962), 137-52 [pp. 18-35, *supra*], y 'MS. Escurialense K-III-7: el llamado "Cancionero de Fr. Í. de M." ', *Filología*, 7 (1961 [1963]), 161-72 [el original inglés, pp. 36-45, *supra*]. El trabajo por publicar de Julio Rodríguez Puértolas, 'Dos versiones de las coplas de *Vita Christi* de Fr. Í. de M.' [publicado en otra forma: véase la p. 44, *supra*, nota 1], demuestra claramente que la primera redacción pertenece al reinado de Enrique IV. Es, desde luego, insostenible la sugestión del P. Alejandro Recio en 'La Inmaculada en la predicación franciscana', *Archivo Ibero-Americano*, 15 (1955), 105-200, p. 118, de que Fray Íñigo se refiriera en la *Vita Christi* a algo que ocurrió en Valladolid en 1502.
5. Facsímil por Sir Henry Thomas (Londres, 1936). El texto del *Cancionero de diversas obras de nuevo trovadas* (Toledo, 1508) de Montesino fue reimpreso por Justo de Sancha en su *Romancero y cancionero sagrados*, BAE, XXXV. Muchas poesías son comunes al *Cancionero* y a las *Coplas* anteriores, pero en casi todos los casos las poesías del *Cancionero* revelan algunos cambios.
6. Facsímil de las *Coplas* (Londres, 1936), p. 12. Existe otro facsímil por Antonio Pérez Gómez, en Incunables Poéticos Castellanos, IV (Valencia, 1955). Cito de Román, como de los demás poetas, resolviendo las abreviaturas y corrigiendo las erratas sin más indicio.
7. Fue Plácido Aguiló y Fuster, *Apuntes bibliográficos acerca de cuatro incunables*

españoles desconocidos (Barcelona, 1888), cit. por Thomas, quien primero sostuvo que Román hablaba de la toma de Granada.

8. Véase mi 'The Supposed Sources of Inspiration of Spanish Fifteenth-Century Narrative Religious Verse', *Symposium*, 17 (1963), 268-91 [pp. 46-71, *supra*].

9. Pierre le Gentil, *La Poésie lyrique espagnole et portugaise à la fin du moyen âge*, I (Rennes, 1949), 314: 'La simplicité, le pittoresque, n'est ici, le plus souvent, que le pieux artifice d'un éducateur.'

10. Véase mi 'Diego de San Pedro's Stylistic Reform', *BHS*, 37 (1960), 1-15 [pp. 1-17, *supra*].

11. Cf. Quintiliano, *De inst. orat.*, VII, 3. Los teóricos medievales o insisten en que se empleen muy poco las comparaciones (Mateo de Vendôme, *Ars versificatoria*, IV, 3; Eberardo el Alemán, *Laborintus*, v. 313), o indican su preferencia por la metáfora (Gofredo de Vinsauf, *Poetria nova*, vv. 241-63). Los textos se pueden ver en Edmond Faral, *Les Arts poétiques du XIIe et du XIIIe siècle* (París, 1924). Faral señala el hecho de que las versiones medievales tardías de la *Eneida* suprimen las comparaciones virgilianas. La teoría retórica del sermón latino medieval es idéntica, salvo en el caso de un tipo de imagen (*v. infra*), con la de las *artes poeticae*: véase T. M. Charland, *Artes praedicandi: contribution à l'histoire de la rhétorique au moyen âge* (París-Ottawa, 1936), y especialmente el prólogo excepcionalmente valioso de M.-D. Chenu.

12. El tercer símil es una parodia de la imagen de los ríos confluentes de Mena, *Laberinto*, estr. 162, utilizado en su canción obscena 'A vna señora a quien le rogó que le besasse', *Canc. general* 1511, fol. 236^v.

13. *Retablo de la vida de Cristo* (Sevilla, 1505), Cántico primero: 'Cómo la vida de Cristo se debe escribir simple y devotamente, sin los altos estilos de los oradores y vanos poetas.' La realidad es que la actitud teórica de Padilla está mucho más cerca que su práctica al ideal mendicante: en el estilo se parece mucho más a Mena que a Mendoza.

14. La hipótesis de que se deriven los pastores rústicos de la *Vita Christi*, y así los de la tradición entera, de los de Virgilio, como volvió a afirmar recientemente Fernando Lázaro Carreter, *Teatro medieval* (Valencia, 1958), p. 50: 'procede del renacimiento de Virgilio en las aulas salmantinas', ya no se puede sostener: véase Marcial José Bayo, *Virgilio y la pastoral española del Renacimiento* (Madrid, 1959), pp. 9, 10 y 272. Frida Weber de Kurlat, haciendo la reseña del libro de Lázaro Carreter, *NRFH*, 13 (1959), insinúa que *Mingo Revulgo* representa la secularización de la predicación eclesiástica, y que en esto también *Mingo* influyó con Mendoza. Quisiera sugerir que hay que decir específicamente la predicación *mendicante*, y que no hay que recurrir a *Mingo Revulgo* para explicar la influencia de ésta en Mendoza.

15. Se trata de una *sentencia* clásica, que en Fedro, *Fabulae*, III, 14, 10, se presenta bajo la forma de 'Cito rumpes arcum, semper si tensum habueris', aunque tiene antecedentes griegos, por ejemplo Heródoto. La utiliza Juan Casiano, *Coll. pat.*, XXIV, 21; ocurre en una carta de San Bruno (impresa por A. Wilmart, 'Deux

lettres concernant Raoul le Verd, l'ami de saint Bruno', *Revue Bénédictine*, 51 (1939), 257-74); y Santo Tomás de Aquino, *Summa theol.* II-2, 168, *art.* 2, recuenta, de Casiano, una larga anécdota acerca de la respuesta que dio San Juan Evangelista a ciertos críticos: concluye con el *exemplum* vivo del arquero que dijo que 'si hoc continue faceret, arcus frangeretur; unde B. Joannes subintulit quod similiter animus hominis frangeretur, si numquam a sua intensione relaxeretur'. (Debo la cita de Santo Tomás al profesor Edward M. Wilson.) Habrá sin duda otros centenares de ejemplos.

16. Vázquez de Palencia, 'Contra Fray Yñigo de Mendoça sobre las coplas de vita christi', *Canc. general* 1511, fols 168^V-169^V, y 'Otra obra de otro galán contra Fray Yñigo de Mendoça', *ibid.*, fol. 170.

17. En otro sistema de clasificación, por ejemplo Roberto Basevorn, *Forma praedicandi* (1322), ed. Charland, *Artes praedicandi*, estas comparaciones se llamarían *exempla in natura* o *in arte* (véase la nota 22), mientras lo que nosotros y Mendoza solemos entender por *exemplum* se diría *exemplum in historia*.

18. Complica la cuestión el símil homérico, la 'larga imagen' de Mena, como la llama María Rosa Lida de Malkiel, *Juan de Mena* (México, 1950), que introdujo, de Dante, Francisco Imperial; Rafael Lapesa, *La obra literaria del Marqués de Santillana* (Madrid, 1957), p. 170, indudablemente tiene razón en considerar como faltas, 'imágenes de irredimible realismo', algunas de las excursiones realistas de Santillana: es una cuestión de tono. Sin embargo habría que pensar en la posible influencia con el Marqués de las imágenes de los predicadores medievales. Llama la atención el que ambos eruditos (y otros muchos) no se sirven, al discutir obras medievales, de la terminología crítica medieval. Al ocuparse de las imágenes de Mena, María Rosa Lida de Malkiel evita el término de 'símil', probablemente porque en su sentido moderno implica alguna conjunción que enlace las dos partes de la imagen; pero el símil medieval, *collatio aperta*, puede conformarse con la expresión paralela de la imagen y la realidad (cf. 'Las propiedades que las dueñas chicas han', del *Libro de Buen Amor*). Lapesa agrupa con las comparaciones auténticas las que emplean la fórmula de 'más [. . .] que', *aut simil*, que los teóricos consideran como una figura distinta, la hipérbole (*superlatio*). Por encima, María Rosa Lida, 'La hipérbole sagrada en la poesía castellana del siglo XV', *RFH*, 8 (1946), 121-30 (artículo al que volveré), pasa por alto el sentido técnico de 'hipérbole' en el siglo XV.

19. Harry Caplan, *Medieval Artes Praedicandi: A Hand-List* (Ithaca, Nueva York, y Londres, 1934) registra ediciones impresas de Bromyard de Basilea (s.a.), Nuremberg (1485, 1518), París (1500, 1518), Lyon (1522), Venecia (1586), etc., pero ninguna impresa en España. Existe una bibliografía extensa sobre los sermones medievales y los *artes praedicandi* que sería inútil citar aquí; pero uno de los libros más provechosos es G. R. Owst, *Literature and Pulpit in Medieval England* (Cambridge, 1933), ya que dedica muchas páginas, citando numerosos ejemplos, a estas imágenes pintorescas.

20. Vuelve a presentarse esta imagen en Juan del Encina, pero no es preciso postular,

como han hecho varios críticos, la influencia directa de Mendoza en Encina, aunque esto es posible.

21. Edward M. Wilson en su trabajo muy sugestivo 'Spanish and English Religious Poetry of the Seventeenth Century', *Journal of Ecclesiastical History*, 9 (1958), 38-53, empieza por citar la siguiente imagen: 'like the dreame of a hungry or thyrstie man, who in his slepe dreameth that he is eatinge and drinckinge; but after he is awaked, his pain continueth, and his soul is unpacient and nothing eased', de Juan Knox, *Comfortable Epistle to Christ's Afflicted Church* ('como el sueño de un hombre hambriento y sediento, que dormido sueña que está comiendo y bebiendo; pero luego al despertarse, continúa su angustia, y su alma sigue impaciente y nada satisfecha'), y la califica Wilson de 'memorable'. Pero se trata de un lugar común medieval; se encuentra en Román ('como quien se sueña rrey / y se falla mendigante', E6^{v}), en Mendoza (ya citado), otra vez en una versión anterior de la *Vita Christi* (MS. Escurialense K-III-7: véase mi trabajo, pp. 36-45, *supra*). Esto quiere decir que la inspiración de Knox en este caso no es sencillamente 'la vida cotidiana', sino la vida diaria tal como la refleja una larga tradición homilética.

22. Es decir, un *exemplum in natura*; cf. la nota 17.

23. *Pláticas de la doctrina christiana*, cit. por Robert Ricard, 'Paravicino, Rabelais, le soleil et la "vidriera" ', *BH*, 57 (1955), 327-30.

24. Dámaso Alonso, *La poesía de San Juan de la Cruz* (Madrid, 1942), pp. 262-63; Fernando de Castro Pires de Lima, 'No ventre da Virgem Mãe', *Brasília* (Coimbra), 2 (1943), 394-97; Robert Ricard, 'Cristal, vidrio, vidriera', *MLR*, 40 (1945), 216-17, y 41 (1946), 321; Jean Dagens, 'La Métaphore de la verrière', *Revue d'Ascétique et de Mystique* (1949), 524-31; Ricard, 'Paravicino'. La verdad es que empieza a ser frecuente esta imagen desde el siglo IX en adelante, y ya en el siglo VII Venancio Fortunato escribe: 'Lumina plena micans, imitata est aula Mariam / illa utero lucem, clausit et ista diem', *Analecta hymnica medii aevi* (Leipzig, 1886), p. 263; véase Yrjo Hirn, *The Sacred Shrine* (Londres, 1912, reimpr. 1958), pp. 244-46.

25. Un ejemplo clásico del anzuelo se halla en Marcial, IV, 56, 5: 'Sic avidis fallax indulget piscibus hamus.'

26. Véase Francisco López Estrada, 'La retórica en las *Generaciones y semblanzas* de Fernán Pérez de Guzmán', *RFE*, 30 (1946), 310-52.

27. La literatura posterior defiende la acogida dada a este producto de la erudición pagana mediante el 'spoliabitis Aegyptum' (*Exodus* 3. 22), que en el siglo XV en España servía para justificar la poesía vuelta 'a lo divino'.

28. Cf. Tomás Waleys, *De modo componendi sermones*, cap. 1, ed. Charland, *Artes praedicandi*.

29. 'Full of the raw and simple facts of daily life, with little restriction of style—direct, candid, forceful' (Owst).

30. Citado en Otis H. Green, ' "Se acicalaron los auditorios": An Aspect of the Spanish Literary Baroque', *HR*, 27 (1959), 413-22.

31. 'By it ordinary experience of every-day life was brought into touch with religious experience. The analogy of religion could be perceived in all places and at all times. There was no shutting off of religion into an isolated compartment from which ordinary feelings and actions were excluded.'

32. P. Félix García, ed., Malón de Chaide, *La conversión de la Magdalena* (Madrid, 1930), I, xxxvi, escribe de las 'imágenes que hieren desagradablemente la sensibilidad del lector'.

33. Cf. también Antonio de Nebrija, *Gramática de la lengua castellana* (Salamanca, 1492), ed. I. González-Llubera (Oxford, 1926), p. 57: 'no de manera que sea la salsa más quel manjar'; Juan del Encina, *Arte de trobar*, ed. Menéndez y Pelayo, *Antología de poetas líricos*, V (Santander, 1944), 46: 'el guisado con mucha miel no es bueno'; y Quintiliano, VI, 3, 19.

34. Los símiles de los escritores místicos están empleados principalmente para ilustrar y explicar el progreso de la meditación a la contemplación, y así abrazan una esfera de experiencia totalmente distinta de la que hemos estado considerando. Casi nadie disentiría de la tesis generalmente aceptada de que los místicos están obligados a emplear un lenguaje figurado para intentar comunicar su experiencia; a ningún crítico moderno, que yo sepa, le han ofendido estas imágenes, y nadie ha calificado a los místicos de irreverentes. Como dice Helmut Hatzfeld, 'El estilo nacional en los símiles de los místicos españoles y franceses', *NRFH*, 1 (1947), 43-77, p. 77: 'Los españoles, en este terreno sagrado, se abstienen por completo de toda agudeza.' También hay que reconocer que existe una tradición independiente de imágenes místicas, aunque es posible que tengamos un cuadro algo falseado por el empeño de los investigadores en buscar fuentes sólo en los místicos anteriores.

35. Sería fácil demostrar que no tenía razón María Rosa Lida, 'La hipérbole sagrada', p. 122 ('los conceptos de Ledesma y Bonilla son los que más han sobresaltado a la crítica extranjera') en insinuar que son sólo los extranjeros a quienes chocan estos conceptos; se pudiera recopilar toda una serie de juicios españoles referentes al 'pésimo gusto' de Ledesma.

36. 'Bursts open all the bonds and bars of Italianate elegance, Scaliger, and the doctrine of the three styles.'

37. La literatura clásica siguió siendo para los predicadores, incluso Mendoza, una mina de *exempla* (*in historia*); veintitrés autores clásicos, desde Homero en adelante, están citados en un manual homilético, el *Speculum laicorum* (traducción española, después de 1477, *Espéculo de legos*, BAE, LI), aunque está claro que la mayoría de ellos deben de citarse a segunda mano, de escritores tales como San Isidoro y Rabano Mauro, y de las varias recopilaciones anónimas.

38. 'La hipérbole sagrada', p. 122. Va todavía más lejos Erich Auerbach, *Mimesis: The Representation of Reality in Western Literature*, trad. Willard R. Trask (Princeton, 1953), en sostener que toda la doctrina cristiana, pero sobre todo la Encarnación y la Pasión, está opuesta al principio de los tres estilos (*passim*, pero especialmente pp. 41, 63, 72, 151, 162, y 554-57). Cita (p. 151) a San Bernardo

de Claraval, *Epistolae*, 469, 2, PL, CLXXXII, 674, donde insiste en que la vida de Cristo abarca la *sublimitas* y la *humilitas* juntas; pero el hacer explícita tal idea en la Baja Edad Media es algo característicamente franciscano.

39. R. O. Jones, 'Isabel la Católica y el amor cortés', *RLit*, 21 (1962), 55-64, rechaza completamente esta hipótesis: 'no hay la más leve justificación para echar mano a los conversos en este asunto' (p. 58), y demuestra con abundante documentación de los cancioneros que el concepto del decoro isabelino, tal como lo entiende María Rosa Lida, 'requiere alguna modificación' (p. 64).

40. Tengo que expresar mi agradecimiento a los profesores P. E. Russell de Oxford y E. M. Wilson de Cambridge por su crítica utilísima del borrador de este trabajo.

6

Spanish Literary Historiography: Three Forms of Distortion

in memory of Douglas Trotter[1]

The topic that I have pitched on for this evening's lecture is linked with certain problems in Spanish literary history which have been engaging my attention, intermittently, for some time. On one level it is a question of modifying certain accepted ideas about certain works of Spanish literature composed between the twelfth and the seventeenth centuries; but on another level all these problems involve questions of perspective; so that what I want to do is to treat them as so many case-histories, illustrative of three major types of distortion in the writing of the history of Spanish literature—which, incidentally, is what I mean by that possibly ambiguous 'Spanish literary historiography'.

I am not primarily concerned about the histories of literature as such, which are, for obvious reasons, particularly vulnerable to criticism—mainly because no-one can be fully competent in all parts of as vast a field as the literature of the Spanish people. But there is a good deal of other activity going on in the discipline which can only be termed 'the history of Spanish literature': there are a dozen reputable journals devoted exclusively to it, and a good dozen more which devote a fair proportion of their pages to the subject. And I am not concerned (here and now) about the factual accuracy of the histories of literature or of the articles in the journals. What interests me more—and worries me, a little—is the vision of Spanish literary history and the attitudes and assumptions of the historians and critics which seem to me to govern, and distort, both the general historiography and the investigation of the minutiae.

The first form of distortion with which I want to deal arises from the fact that people devote themselves to the study of 'Spanish' literature at all. They are blinkered, from the outset, by this concept 'Spanish'. The resultant distortion is a good deal less important for modern literature, where linguistic barriers, though permeable, do tend to wall off the literatures of Europe one from another, but for Renaissance literature, and even more for medieval literature, it is momentous. If I may offer you a three-dimensional analogy, we are faced in the Middle Ages with a phenomenon akin to an archipelago, an island-chain. The historians of Spanish literature pay attention only to those islands in the sun, the works written in the vernacular. But under the surface of the water, a barrier to all non-amphibious hispanists, lies the immense, connected mountain-range of medieval Latin literature. It would be an inaccurate generalization to affirm that all the substantial works of Spanish medieval literature are translations. But an extraordinarily high proportion of the major works are freely adapted translations, amplified glosses, amalgams of borrowed passages and *topoi*, and close imitations of medieval Latin (and in some cases medieval French or Arabic) works.[2] This is because the medieval writer's task was to pass on the work of the authorities of the past. As C. S. Lewis put it: 'The typical activity of the medieval author consists in touching up something that was already there'.[3] Now each individual investigator is well aware of this; but there persists (it seems to me) a kind of double vision: a readiness to seek the sources of medieval Spanish works in Latin or French or Arabic, but, simultaneously, a view of Spanish medieval literature as an organic continuum.

One instance of this form of distortion concerns the sources of the *Celestina*. I shall pass over the question of the customary listings of huge numbers of authors, Greek, Latin, Italian, and Spanish, though I should just like to get in the suggestion that Fernando de Rojas need not have read more than half a dozen books, if one of them were one of those medieval compendia of wise sayings from the philosophers.[4] What I want to discuss now is the alleged indebtedness of the *Celestina* to the *Libro de buen amor*, a commonplace of *Celestina* criticism and of Spanish literary history.

The *Celestina*, the first version of which dates from the late 1490s, is indubitably one of the great works of Spanish literature, on account both of its intrinsic merit and of its enormous influence on Spanish and European literature generally in the sixteenth and seventeenth centuries. The dominating character in the work, though it would lead to errors of interpretation to call her the protagonist, is the procuress Celestina. The *Libro de buen amor*, composed a hundred and fifty years earlier, is a goliardesque compendium of narratives and lyrics, in one section of which (itself an amplified version of the twelfth-century Latin elegiac comedy *Pamphilus de amore*) we find a procuress Trotaconventos. I could cite dozens of critics and historians who take it as demonstrated that Trotaconventos is the direct antecedent of Celestina. Even critics who show that they are

abundantly aware of the Latin literary tradition of the go-between, which
runs from classical drama through elegiac comedy to humanistic comedy,
accept, explicitly, the debt of the *Celestina* to the *Libro de buen amor*. Properly
to dispose of this notion would entail examining, among other things, the
list of alleged verbal reminiscences, and this is not the occasion to do so in
any detail. But I can and should say that these so-called verbal reminiscences
are very easily disposed of. The most wide-ranging of the *Celestina* source-
hunters has displayed the evidence exhaustively in parallel columns.[5] I have
nowhere seen it noted in print that every single passage in which the parallel
is not so trivial as to be wholly inconclusive figures earlier in the same book
as evidence of Rojas's debt to Ovid.[6] And I need scarcely say that Ovid is
undoubtedly a common source for both works.

But it would be idle for me to complain of an error of fact. Every issue
of every journal corrects some mistake of detail and modifies old mis-
conceptions. What concerns me more is the vision of Spanish literary history
which led in the nineteenth century to the assumption of a relationship,
subsequently to the production of evidence to support the assumption, and
then to the fossilization of the dogma. Because *a priori* one should not expect
to find any connexion at all. It is scarcely conceivable that any writer at the
end of the fifteenth century could have known the *Libro de buen amor*: it
vanished from the sight of educated men from 1449 to 1790;[7] there is the
very telling evidence that it was not printed; and it would have been
psychologically quite wrong for an amateur humanist like Rojas, whose
literary hero is Petrarch, to look for literary inspiration in any writer earlier
than Juan de Mena.

Although the case of the *Celestina* and the *Libro de buen amor* seems to me
a particularly cogent instance, I could adduce a number of other examples
of this kind of thing. The concept of the organic continuity of Spanish
medieval literature pervades most writing on the subject and lies implicit in
all histories of Spanish literature. And it needs to be replaced by a different
concept: of a vast European literature in Latin of which there are occasional
manifestations distinguished by their being written in Spanish. Obviously
there are some continuous traditions in medieval Spanish literature: formal
traditions certainly exist, of which versification is the most obvious example,
and there are undoubtedly continuities in popular poetry and to some extent
in the chronicles. But it is a question of where one looks for the evolutionary
mainstream. And if we fail to take medieval Latin literature into account,
Spanish medieval literature becomes a series of miracles.

At some point, of course, Spanish writers did become conscious of a native
tradition and were influenced primarily by their Spanish predecessors,

beginning to accept the notions and conventions and rhetoric and common-places of a Spanish rather than a European Latin tradition. And clearly the date at which they did so cannot be fixed with any precision. But it could hardly have happened before the volume of creative work produced in Spanish outweighed the volume of creative work in Latin consumed by Spaniards, and the balance did not tip towards Spanish until the sixteenth century.[8] The discontinuity of the native tradition is well illustrated by an analysis of Spanish book-production in the fifteenth and sixteenth centuries. To fifteenth-century readers not one line of Spanish verse from the thirteenth or fourteenth centuries was available in print. And the only medieval poems to find their way into print in the sixteenth century were the fourteenth-century rhymed Proverbs of Solomon and the rhymed catechism of Pedro de Veragüe.[9] The medieval works in Spanish which were printed before 1500 were largely para-literary: legal works like the *Fuero juzgo*, or the *Siete partidas* and *Fuero real* of Alfonso X, and a few of the fourteenth-century chronicles—but not the thirteenth-century *Primera crónica general* or *General estoria*.

If we leave the histories and legal codes on one side, the only works of pre-fifteenth-century Spanish literature to be printed in the fifteenth and sixteenth centuries were: the two pieces of verse I have mentioned, the collection of aphorisms and lives of famous men known as the *Bonium* or *Bocados de oro*, a very odd collection of scraps of oriental 'wisdom' known as the *Libro de los doce sabios*, two well-known collections of oriental apologues: *Calila y Dimna* and *Sendebar*, that strange pseudo-chivalresque tale *El caballero Cifar*, and, with certain reservations (since it was extensively rewritten), *Amadís de Gaula*. And that is all.[10] What Renaissance Spanish writers could have known of Spanish medieval literature was only a fraction of the work extant in manuscript form and lying forgotten in various archives, libraries, and private collections. And this does not mean that there was any kind of rupture with medieval traditions—for a host of medieval Latin works were reprinted freely throughout the sixteenth and seventeenth centuries—but simply that no continuity of vernacular literature, leaving aside popular oral poetry, is established before the fifteenth century.[11]

I have made, I suppose, part of the case for a School of Medieval Studies, or at least for the non-compartmentalization of the study of medieval European literature. But I should be satisfied if hispanists showed themselves more conscious of the existence of this vast literature in medieval Latin, and readier to acknowledge that it is in Latin that we find the genuine evolutionary continuum on which the bulk of the vernacular literature depends. Of course part of the reason for the neglect of medieval Latin—and

this will lead me to my second form of distortion—is a modern aesthetic
bias. There cannot really be any argument about the enormous disparity in
intellectual quality between medieval Latin and medieval Spanish writing.
Medieval literature in Spanish is, *ipso facto*, literature for illiterates, designed
to be recited aloud for the entertainment and edification of the uneducated.
The vernacular literature is intellectually inferior. Because of linguistic
limitations—it simply does not possess the lexical or syntactic resources of
Latin—it cannot handle fine distinctions; and because it is directed to a
popular and unlettered audience it lacks subtlety and sophistication. Whether
it is also inferior aesthetically is no doubt arguable: we find in Spanish
medieval literature a wealth of picturesque detail, a lively concrete fore-
ground, which is often lacking in Latin. And of course it is not easy
objectively to appraise the elusive quality habitually designated as 'naive
charm'. If I may put it this way: turning from Spanish to Latin medieval
literature is like turning from a diverting conversation with a West-country
farm labourer to a conversation with a fellow-academic—duller, no doubt,
because of the absence of the rustic picturesque, but, by and large, on a
more demanding intellectual level. What bothers me here is the scarcely
queried modern hispanist assumption that the concrete and colourful is
aesthetically superior to the abstract and 'colourless'.[12] And this brings me
to my second form of distortion.

This distortion arises from the fact that people try to write histories of
'Literature'. It is impossible objectively to define either literature or poetry.
The concepts 'literature' and 'poetry' embrace a more or less definable
semantic area—writing of a certain kind, or verse, respectively—plus an
expression of approval. There are those who will tell you that a given piece
of verse is not poetry: the White Goddess was not present.[13] All this means
is that they do not approve of it. Now I have no intention of contending
that all value-judgements are *per se* invalid, but I am increasingly doubtful
of their relevance and suspicious of the way they have been arrived at. We
may have given to the question 'What is a classic?' some reasonably
acceptable answers (like 'a work that has stood the test of time'), but we
have been asking the wrong question.[14] Let me attack this another way.
    Every age, every culture, every individual is bound, trapped even, in a
series of conventions and uncritically accepted notions which are, it would
appear, invisible to all but the most argus-eyed of the observers enclosed
within them. And nowhere are the restrictions of convention more clearly
exhibited than in the history of art and literature.[15] The more primitive the
art, the more rigid are the prescriptions which bind it. And the history of

the evolutionary process in literature, as in the plastic arts, has been very largely the history of fresh insights, of a breaking out from old conventions and exploiting added possibilities. And here we at once come up against a small problem. Clearly a work which breaks through a set of old conventions is, if the example is followed, a work important in the history of literature. But since the early revolutionaries rarely succeed in emancipating themselves completely from the discarded traditions, their work tends to be marked by confusion and inconsistency; and so, though there are exceptions, the acknowledged classics of Spanish literature stand, perhaps not far removed from, but not often at, the beginning of a new tradition. In other words, there is no necessary connexion between literary merit and historical importance. But it's worse than that.

The concept of a 'classic' which by some magic combination of ill-defined qualities breaks through the ruck of outdated literature to achieve a status of 'timelessness' is not merely unhelpful but can be positively pernicious. In literature, as in other things, there has been evolution, not progress, and there have been numerous evolutionary dead-ends. The mainstream of the literatures of Europe has drifted in the direction of emancipation from restrictive conventions, and towards what is loosely termed 'realism'; and our classics tend to stand in that main stream. But there have been, repeatedly, counter-currents, when writers imposed on themselves ever more restrictive conventions, and pushed a trend to its logical conclusion and ultimate extinction. Some such writers have been rescued. Góngora, for instance, who now holds a fairly secure place as one of the greatest of Spanish poets, is a difficult, highly intellectual, deliberately obscure, artificially ingenious poet, who was resurrected from neglect and derision in the 1920s. A proper reappraisal of Calderón—again a writer who accepted a series of self-imposed restrictions[16]—has had to wait until this century: in the nineteenth century he was criticized for being un-Shakespearean. And the rescue of works from oblivion is not complete. But of course it is not simply a question of reprinting a text, nor even of proclaiming loudly that some forgotten work is a lost masterpiece. In cases such as these a whole process of re-education is involved. A tradition which ultimately proves sterile is not, in literature, to be regarded as worthless. It represents the conquest of a new aesthetic area, and if it no longer forms a part of our living literary heritage, *we* are missing something, losing something, by our inability to appreciate it.

One criterion which the modern critic almost consistently ignores and which he ought never to neglect to apply is the esteem in which a writer was held by his contemporaries. If, for example, for a period of thirty or forty years, two generations of poets bend their best efforts to producing

verse of a certain clearly definable kind, moving quite distinctly in the
direction of reduced metrical freedom, ever more limited vocabulary, and
greater concentration of conceptualization, and if this kind of verse is
regarded by all the poets' contemporaries as the aesthetic ideal in this period,
I cannot help feeling that it is really incredibly smug of modern critics to
dismiss it as quite meaningless for us, as 'unrealistic' and 'artificial'. (The
use of the term 'artificial' is, indeed, almost always an indication of a modern
failure.) Now this is precisely the case of the so-called *cancionero* poetry of
the late fifteenth and early sixteenth centuries,[17] and particularly of its most
typical form, the *canción*.[18] The majority of modern critics have a complete
blind-spot where *cancionero* verse is concerned; and it could easily be shown
that the odd pieces which do occasionally find their way into modern
anthologies are precisely those least typical of this kind of poetry.[19] There
are, certainly, barriers of various kinds to a sympathetic appreciation of this
verse. I have yet to find a student take to it in the way students do take at
first sight to other works of the same period, such as the *Celestina* or the
ballads. But the students are educable, and a research student can become
enthusiastic. In fact I like the stuff myself. But what I am saying now is
simply that if an intelligent, literate, sensitive man tries hard to say something
within a certain literary convention, polishing and repolishing his work, the
result is *a priori* unlikely to be valueless, and that one would do well to be
suspicious of a set of modern aesthetic values which declares it to be so.

But it is still more complicated than that. What are we to do in the case
of the converse distortion, when a work or a writer disdained or ignored
by contemporaries happens to appeal to modern taste? There are again
numerous examples I could cite, but perhaps the most glaring case is that
of the *Cantar de mío Cid*, the Spanish national epic, composed, in the form
we know it, probably towards the beginning of the thirteenth century. I
have no wish to denigrate the literary quality of this work; but I strongly
suspect that all the objective evidence ought to lead us to the conclusion
that it was an artistic failure in its own time.

It is a critical cliché to contrast Spanish with French epic, to point out
that the heroes of French epic are demi-gods, unrealistic supermen who
inhabit a world of visions, magic, and monsters, who single-handed slay
thousands in one battle, whereas the Cid is a modest and believable hero,
who inhabits a world which gives at least the illusion of historical accuracy,
and who plausibly slays fifteen in a major encounter. There is a stark
romanesque quality about the epic of the Cid which is pleasing to modern
taste. But the available evidence seems to suggest that, except for the *Cid*,
Spanish epic was exactly like French epic.[20] And a warrior-hero who is

not a superman conforms to no canon of medieval rhetorical theory. Furthermore, it cannot be demonstrated that the *Cantar del Cid* had any influence on the course of Spanish literary history. The fact that the Cid, around whose figure there accrued subsequently a mass of legendary, often supernatural, material, should have become the Spanish national hero, celebrated in many another literary work, has contributed to the distortion of the perspective. I do not mean that our enjoyment of the work is in any way spurious. But I do believe that one cannot write an accurate and intelligible history of Spanish literature if one accords to this atypical work the space and position which it is habitually accorded as the first great Spanish literary monument.

The trouble is that we write our histories of literature with an almost total disregard for history, highlighting the works which happen to appeal to us. I should like to spend a few minutes more on one special aspect of this form of distortion, on what might be summed up as the problem of the best-seller, the work which, while popular, may represent the debasement of standards. Examples abound: for instance, it is a fact that the greater part of the plays consumed by the Spanish theatre-going public in the seventeenth century were comedies, often of the most frivolous kind. It is also a fact that except for a handful by one or two of the major dramatists (Lope, Tirso, Calderón) hardly any attention has been paid to them.[21] One has only to glance at a bibliography of critical writing on the theatre[22] to see that for a century now the critics have preferred to direct their attention to the tragedies.[23] Now why tragedy should be regarded as superior to comedy and whether this judgement is justifiable is not my concern now. The point is that an aesthetic bias in Spanish literary historiography has given generation after generation of students a quite false picture of what Spanish seventeenth-century drama was really like.

Another area of massive neglect, and one in which I am particularly interested, is that of the chivalresque romance. It is indisputable that for almost the whole of the sixteenth century the romances of chivalry (which derive ultimately from the tales of the Knights of the Round Table and the legends of Charlemagne) were the dominant form of fiction in Spain. *Amadís de Gaula*, which went through nearly thirty editions in eighty years and gave rise to numerous sequels and imitations, has received some attention; but there are dozens and dozens of others, most of which one can read only in the sixteenth-century editions, which have received no attention at all. And yet they formed the staple literary diet of Spaniards for a century. Charles V was an insatiable addict who commissioned private translations of French chivalresque works; Cortés described Mexico City as 'just like the cities in

Amadís'; they gave Ignatius of Loyola the inspiration to found the Jesuit Order; California was named after an island in a sequel to *Amadís*; the severer humanists, like Vives, deplored the hours they had compulsively wasted in earlier years following the adventures of the knights-errant; the moralists who condemned them betray a detailed knowledge of them. No Spanish writer in the sixteenth century could have escaped reading several of them. Certainly they are curious works to the modern mind, with their colourless cardboard heroes, their rambling plots which rely on coincidence to an improbable degree, their innumerable and interminable descriptions of knightly encounters . . . but, again, it is by no means impossible to recapture some experience of the pleasure of the sixteenth-century audience or to begin to appreciate their compulsive readability, and, rather more important, I ask—simply—how close can we get to the minds of other sixteenth-century Spanish writers without knowing these novels? And can the histories of literature that we have, which devote more space to Fray Luis de León— whose private poetry was not even available in print—than to all the romances of chivalry put together, and you can even add in two hundred almost wholly neglected heroic poems as make-weight—can such histories make any pretence of reflecting accurately the historical reality?

My third form of distortion is perhaps a subdivision of the second. It concerns what is customarily labelled 'obscenity' and 'pornography'. Puritanism set in in Spain in the late fifteenth century and became more virulent in the time of Philip II and the Counter-Reformation.[24] And except for a brief interlude in the nineteenth century it really has not relaxed its grip yet. One consequence is that a whole tradition of writing, very nearly extinguished in the sixteenth century, has continued to be ignored by modern Spanish editors and critics, as well as by the almost equally prudish foreign hispanists. So that you could read, easily, the pious poems of Alfonso X, but not the filthy comic verse he also produced;[25] the entire works of Diego de San Pedro were readily accessible—except for one of the most ingeniously obscene poems in Spanish.[26] And similar examples could be multiplied *ad nauseam* if not *ad infinitum*. And it is, of course, a brave man who tries to remedy the situation.[27] Now you may think that the fact that a quantity of dubious material is rapidly glossed over or simply left out of account in the histories of literature is not of any great moment. The critics who have had something to say about the tradition of obscenity in medieval literature tend to throw in the phrase 'the reverse of the medal';[28] it suggests that there are two rigidly separate kinds of writing, and that the historian can, without prejudicial consequences, ignore the matter which disturbs and embarrasses him. The traditions, I believe, are more integrated than this image suggests, and the ignoring of the obscene produces consequential distortions.

A certain amount of attention has been paid to the astonishing irreverence which accompanies medieval religious piety;[29] virtually none has been paid to the obscene verse which in Spanish accompanies the poetry of courtly love. The *Cancionero general* of 1511, a huge anthology of fifteenth- and early sixteenth-century verse, has a whole section at the end, later reprinted separately, of obscene and comic verse,[30] composed by poets whose love-poetry appears in the earlier sections. But in spite of this, the love-poetry has been persistently regarded as the expression of some rarefied, high-minded, 'pure', strictly non-physical passion. And there are critics who have clung to this belief in the face of the most obvious evidence to the contrary. The royal manuscript of the *Cancionero de Palacio*, for example, is decorated with a series of erotic drawings of animals and nude human figures. Someone, doubtless one of those friars who painstakingly censored other books in the sixteenth century, was obliged discreetly to blot these figures with ink. Time has made the ink-veil transparent; its modern editor, Francisca Vendrell de Millás, does not fail to perceive 'cierta libertad', a certain freedom, in the ornament; but she can still write, in so many words, that this love was 'Platonic'.[31] Now there have been other writers on the subject who have known that this poetry was not 'Platonic', and who have accepted that *cancionero* verse stands in the tradition of so-called 'courtly love', which stems from the Provençal poets of the twelfth century; but they have argued that in Spain the tradition was much modified, rather as it was modified by Andrew the Chaplain, with perhaps the occasional survival of parts of the older tradition.[32] This is broadly the position of Professor Otis Green, who *has* drawn attention to some of the poems which earlier commentators studiously ignored: poems in which the poet asks to see his lady nude, or begs her, in so many words, to sleep with him.[33] But I think it may go further than this.

The vocabulary of this poetry is, as I have said, a limited one, and there is a most marked tendency for it to exclude the concrete and adventitious and to depend on a series of abstract terms: death and life, pain and desire, heart and reason, glory and service, and so on. Now, in a significant number of texts there is no possible doubt that the connotation of some of these terms is sexual. The word *gloria*—in Juan del Encina, in the *Celestina*, in the *Comedia Thebaida*—is a euphemism for sexual possession. In Italian poetry of this period *morire* is an erotic metaphor.[34] There is one particularly good example of what I am talking about, pointed out by Professor R. O. Jones, in an *esparsa* by Guevara.[35] The poem uses this seemingly anodyne abstract vocabulary, but the rubric reads: '*Esparsa* to his mistress, being in bed with her'. There is good reason to suspect that a good deal of *cancionero* love-poetry is a tissue of veiled eroticism and *double entendres*. It may not be an entirely satisfactory test, I suppose, that a great many poems can be read in this way and acquire rather startling point. But I do not believe it is an interpretative hypothesis which can be dismissed out of hand. I have no time here to argue the case in detail—and, of course, some of the things I should need to quote are unquotable in the conventions within which *we* are all now confined—and I am perfectly ready to concede that I may be wrong. But I do think it is an extraordinary comment on hispanist literary historiography that this interpretation, in spite of numerous clues, should not have been put forward earlier, and I should remind you that it will surprise no-one who has done any work in the field of medieval and Renaissance English, French, Italian or Latin literature.[36]

I should try briefly to sum up what I have been saying. I have been complaining that, because of distortions imposed by *a priori* attitudes and assumptions, we have no history of Spanish literature based on historical criteria. It may not be easy to define the objective criteria on which we should rely in assessing a writer's historical importance—as distinct from his literary merit—but clearly one should pay some attention to his initial impact and continued influence, judged at least as much by what people read as by what other writers wrote.[37] The distortion of literary historiography by literary appreciation and the awful Victorian high-mindedness of so much hispanist criticism has at least two consequences which I believe are deplorable. One is the encouragement of hero-worship and the creation of sacred cows. We must get rid of the 'hero theory' of history in literary historiography: it is morally unhealthy. The 'great' writers have had far less influence on the course of literary history than is commonly supposed; they depend to an extent not properly appreciated on a host of unjustly neglected writers who created a viable medium for them and transmitted to them the bulk of their notions and attitudes; and the literary horizon is less accidented than critics lead the student to imagine.

The other consequence of not looking objectively at the facts of literary history is that what could and should be a liberating experience, a communication with minds trapped, certainly, in their own conventions, but subscribing to a—for them—valid set of values, a communication which can assist us to perceive our own blinkers and extend our sympathies and discover the pleasure of other aesthetic *mores*—becomes a mirror in which we see only ourselves, esteeming most highly the writers who seem least foreign to us.

I am prepared to concede that I may have painted the picture in rather blacker colours than the reality warrants. Góngora was rescued. *Cancionero* poetry is being actively reassessed by a number of workers. Progress is being made. With a little less dogmatism around it would be made a good deal faster, and doubtless, as Professor Trevor-Roper recently pointed out, it will not be achieved in one direction without a corresponding darkening of some other quadrant of the sky. But at least one can feel that in hispanic studies there is a very great deal of useful work still to be done.

[An Inaugural Lecture delivered in the University of Exeter on 8 December 1967. Exeter: Univ., 1968]

Notes

1. The first three paragraphs of this lecture—p. 5 in the 1968 pamphlet—were an appreciation of Douglas Trotter (1928–66), Keith Whinnom's predecessor in the Chair of Spanish at Exeter. They are omitted in this reprinting because they were specific to the occasion of the lecture, and fall outside the scope of the present volume, but the dedication evokes the spirit in which they were spoken.
2. Without even needing to argue the proposition one might mention Berceo, the *denuestos* and *debates*, the *Historia troyana*, the *Libro de Apolonio*, the *Libro de Alexandre*, the collections of fables and apologues, the early chronicles, the *Gran conquista de Ultramar*, the *Historia del caballero Cifar*, Juan Manuel, Juan Ruiz, etc., etc.
3. *The Discarded Image: An Introduction to Medieval and Renaissance Literature* (Cambridge, 1964), p. 209.
4. I intend to publish elsewhere, in a book on the *Celestina*, detailed support for what, as it stands, may be felt to be a highly unorthodox assertion.
5. F. Castro Guisasola, *Observaciones sobre las fuentes literarias de 'La Celestina'* (Madrid, 1924), still an invaluable arsenal, despite these strictures, of basic information.
6. This was pointed out long ago by Professor P. E. Russell of Oxford in an unpublished lecture. The late María Rosa Lida de Malkiel, in that amazing *tour de force*, *La originalidad artística de la 'Celestina'* (Buenos Aires, 1962) comes very close at times to the position I take. She frequently seems doubtful about or rejects outright some alleged parallels; she inquires (p. 544, note) whether the familiarity of 'los literatos españoles de nuestros días' with the *Libro de buen amor* has not led them to underestimate the Latin sources, and points out that the prestige of the Latin sources would be much greater; but in the section on

Trotaconventos and Celestina (pp. 557-65) she accepts the validity of Castro Guisasola's 'verbal reminiscences' and concludes that 'el aporte de Juan Ruiz a la creación de Celestina es evidente' (p. 565).

7. Obviously its eclipse cannot be dated with such precision, but the last clear reference to it is in the Marqués de Santillana's *Carta prohemio al Condestable de Portugal* (1449). Although it was first printed in 1790, there are some imprecisely dated eighteenth-century manuscript copies.

8. The analysis of Spanish book-production in the first decades of the century, made by F. J. Norton, Chapter X, pp. 125-37 of *Printing in Spain 1501–1520* (Cambridge, 1966), would seem to indicate that the balance had just tipped towards the vernacular in that period. But if one includes the 'non-fiction' —theology, philosophy, history, law, medicine, etc.—and if one thinks of the numerous works in Latin printed outside Spain but available to Spaniards, the tipping of the scales towards Spanish must be placed even later.

9. *Proberuios en rimo del sabio Salomón*, without date, place or imprint, dated by Salvá c. 1520, but omitted from Norton's list; and *Tratado llamado espejo de dotrina*, again without date, place or imprint, and similarly dated, by Gallardo, c. 1520, but also omitted by Norton, and so, without doubt, later.

10. These observations derive from an analysis of José Simón Díaz's *Bibliografía de la literatura hispánica*, III, 1, 2nd ed. (Madrid, 1963), supplemented from Norton: the *Libro de los doze sabios*, for instance, printed by Diego de Gumiel in Valladolid in 1502, is not recorded by Simón Díaz. It may well be that this very brief list could be expanded, but not, I believe, to an extent which would seriously prejudice my argument.

11. Of the continuity of the medieval Latin tradition there can be no doubt. The classic work of E. P. Goldschmidt, *Medieval Texts and their First Appearance in Print* (London, 1943), has conclusively shown that 'a great proportion of the surviving writings of the Middle Ages were not only known but in current use and circulation till about 1600' (p. 2), though we might still complain, as he complained a quarter of a century ago, that 'it is [. . .] quite striking to observe how little notice the historians of literature seem to have taken of the bibliographical material [i.e. relating to medieval Latin] made accessible to them' (p. 1). While he is concerned with Europe as a whole (England, France, Germany, the Netherlands, Italy), he makes almost no reference to the Peninsula; but he has amply demonstrated the availability of medieval Latin material and most of his conclusions are undoubtedly valid for Spain. E. R. Curtius, *European Literature and the Latin Middle Ages*, trans. Willard R. Trask (London, 1953), speaks of 'such a country as Spain which had preserved the medieval tradition uninterruptedly and in all its strength' (p. 296). No one who has studied either work would contest the validity of these conclusions: we must be careful to distinguish between medieval Latin material and medieval material in Spanish.

12. Comparisons of medieval Spanish texts with their Latin sources almost invariably result in a verdict in favour of the vernacular text; so, for example,

María Rosa Lida de Malkiel writes, '[. . .] como si cupiese sombra de duda acerca de la superioridad del *Libro* [*de buen amor*] sobre el *Pamphilus*' (*Originalidad*, p. 544). But even if all works of medieval Spanish literature could be demonstrated to be superior to their immediate Latin antecedents, I should still contend that in the Middle Ages Spain has nothing to touch the writing of people like Peter Damian, Anselm, Bernard of Clairvaux, Adam of St Victor, the other Archpriest [this is almost certainly a slip: read 'the Archpoet'], Walter of Châtillon, and scores of others. I find the reluctance of most hispanists to concede what seems to me self-evident (and surely not, *a priori*, implausible) quite astonishing. The crucial factor does appear to be that, as is generally conceded, the vernacular literatures abound in concrete details and 'local colour' lacking in Latin. Dr Lida de Malkiel tries to explain this: 'el impulso a la representación concreta y prolija, vedada en latín por las convenciones heredadas en esa lengua, se da rienda suelta en el medio expresivo no codificado que constituyen las lenguas romances' (p. 551); but she does not attempt to explain *why* the one should be regarded as aesthetically superior to the other.

13. There can be few men better equipped to speak of the experience of writing 'poetry' than Mr Robert Graves; but I am baffled by the use he makes of the terms 'Muse' and 'Goddess' in such works as *The White Goddess*, revised ed. (London, 1959), *The Crowning Privilege* (London, 1955), or *Mammon and the Black Goddess* (London, 1965). Taken literally they are (surely?) self-evident nonsense, and if they are taken as metaphors, it is not easy to know what they stand for. The role he attributes to 'inspiration' ('the genuine afflatus', 'the poetic trance', 'the miracle of the Muse-Goddess's appearance', etc.) inflates a trivial psychological phenomenon (the 'aha experience' is a notoriously unreliable guide to the value of an idea) into a dangerously subjective test of literary value: a good critic can 'smell' its presence.

14. Most critics would not seriously quarrel with the answer given by T. S. Eliot in his lecture to the Virgil Society, *What is a Classic?* (London, 1945). He refers, inevitably, to 'maturity', 'amplitude', 'catholicity', 'comprehensiveness', and 'universality'. I do not contest these criteria (though for 'universal' I would suggest we might read 'European'). What I am saying is that qualities of 'universality', i.e. general acceptability to those educated in a certain tradition, do not constitute an adequate test of literary merit. One can be reeducated in a different tradition.

15. The limitations of the artist's vision are beautifully demonstrated by E. H. Gombrich, *Art and Illusion* (London and New York, 1960, new ed. London, 1962), a book which ought to be compulsory reading for all students of literature.

16. A. E. Sloman, in *The Dramatic Craftsmanship of Calderón: His Use of Earlier Plays* (Oxford, 1958), has shown how Calderón improved earlier plays and analysed the ways in which he did so. But while the changes may have been beneficial, it is also clear that Calderón was accepting the restrictive conventions of neo-classicism. See Duncan Moir, 'The Classical Tradition in Spanish Dramatic

Theory and Practice in the Seventeenth Century', in *Classical Drama and its Influence: Essays Presented to H. D. F. Kitto* (London, 1965). It is, moreover, notorious that critical attention has focused itself primarily on the earlier (more 'Shakespearean') plays at the expense of the really mature and developed Calderón.

17. Professor Otis H. Green, in an epoch-making article, 'Courtly Love in the Spanish *Cancioneros*', *PMLA*, 64 (1949), 247-301, was the first seriously to challenge the verdict of Menéndez Pelayo, the weight of whose authority still lies heavy on hispanic studies. But despite the intelligent efforts of such scholars as Dr J. M. Aguirre or Professor R. O. Jones, the general consensus of opinion, even among those who have approached this kind of verse with initial sympathy, like Pierre Le Gentil, still seems to support Menéndez Pelayo. Certainly all secondary sources are unanimous. That the *New Cambridge Modern History*, I (Cambridge, 1957) should inform its readers that this verse is 'artificial, uninspired, but elegant and highly polished' (p. 179) is indicative of the ubiquitousness of an opinion which will be changed, if at all, with difficulty. I imagine that the argument I have advanced is what D. Dámaso Alonso meant when he wrote, perhaps a little too succinctly: 'Ninguna época se equivoca estéticamente', preface to Dámaso Alonso and José M. Blecua, *Antología de la poesía española: poesía de tipo tradicional* (Madrid, 1956), p. ix.

18. I hope to publish elsewhere a study of the *canciones* of the *Cancionero general* which will demonstrate: (a) the successive restrictions on metrical freedom, something which does not clearly emerge from the specialist studies of Pierre Le Gentil, *La Poésie lyrique espagnole et portugaise à la fin du moyen âge*, II: *Les formes* (Rennes, 1953), Tomás Navarro, *Métrica española* (Syracuse, NY, 1956), or even Dorothy Clotelle Clarke, *Morphology of Fifteenth Century Castilian Verse* (Pittsburgh, 1964); (b) the extraordinary pruning of the vocabulary, to the degree that twenty-five nouns account for 50% of the occurrences of all nouns; (c) the simultaneous elimination of the concrete in favour of the abstract; and (d) a rather less uniform tendency towards a certain pattern of conceptual structure. [See pp. 114-32, below.]

19. It can be clearly demonstrated (as I shall show elsewhere) that the anthologizers prefer those pieces in which there is some concrete vocabulary, like Nicolás Núñez's *canción* about the rose or Florencia Pinar's about the partridges (*Cancionero general*, fols 124^v and 125^v). In other words, they reveal again the same bias which prefers Spanish to medieval Latin literature.

20. To what extent the 'orthodox' view of Spanish epic can be directly attributed to the overwhelming authority of one man, D. Ramón Menéndez Pidal, would form an interesting topic of discussion. Certainly every critic and historian who quotes a date of 1140 for the *Cid* (and they are legion) betrays his dependence on Pidal. And we have now—unfortunately—reached a point at which any criticism of the views of Don Ramón is regarded by patriotic critics as akin to an attack on God. As long ago as 1927 Ortega y Gasset had this to say about

Pidal's hypervaluation of 'realism': 'En el pensamiento que dirige toda la producción de Pidal no hay más que dos puntos débiles. Un hombre tan cuidadoso, tan rigoroso, tan *científico* en el tratamiento del detalle, parte siempre de dos enormes supuestos que contrajo en la vaga atmósfera intelectual de su juventud, y que usa sin previo examen, sin precisión. Uno es la creencia, perfectamente arbitraria, de que lo español en arte es el realismo. A esta creencia va aneja la convicción no menos arbitraria de que el realismo es la forma más elevada del arte', in *Espíritu de la letra*, in *Obras* (Madrid: Espasa-Calpe, 1943), p. 1058. I have one qualification to make: though the supposition that Spanish epic was 'realistic' may be attributable to the influence of Pidal, he is by no means alone in the aesthetic hypervaluation of 'realism'.

21. The point is made by Professor R. O. Jones in '*El perro del hortelano* y la visión de Lope', *Filología*, 10 (1964 [1967]), 135-42.

22. I mean, of course, Warren T. McCready's superb *Bibliografía temática de estudios sobre el teatro español antiguo* (Toronto, 1966). Though he stops short at 1950, I do not have the impression that the work of the last seventeen years shows any radical shift of emphasis.

23. Hispanists will doubtless deplore the looseness of the terminology I employ. While it has even been denied that Spanish drama possesses any real tragedies (the view is popular in Spain), Professor A. A. Parker has surely demonstrated that it does, 'Towards a Definition of Calderonian Tragedy', *BHS*, 39 (1962), 222-37. But I am not concerned with the finer points of the definition of 'tragedy': I mean only the plays in which people get killed, whether justifiably executed for their misdeeds, as martyrs, as victims of the honour-code, or whatever. I might not be prepared to defend this definition of 'tragedy', but death is not funny, and, *faute de mieux*, I use it for the plays not comic comedy.

24. Obviously any generalization of this kind needs careful shading and more attention than I can give it here. It might be possible to maintain that there is some evidence of it in the Middle Ages in Spain: Menéndez Pelayo, *Orígenes de la novela*, I (repr. Madrid, 1962), in comparing Juan Manuel and Boccaccio (pp. 143-45), comes close to defending the otherwise ludicrous position that Juan Manuel is superior to Boccaccio, on the grounds that he shows none of the 'lubricidad' of the Italian. There are certainly grounds for arguing that what is later a dominant attitude has its origins with the Isabelline reform. There is evidence that early Spanish translations of French chivalresque romances eliminated 'lascivious' passages. But I think the all-important factor must have been the Inquisition and the Index: 'Libri, qui res lascivas seu obscoenas tractant, narrant aut docent [. . .] prohibentur'. The nude, simultaneously, almost disappeared from Spanish painting. In all this, of course, the Counter-Reformation was not very different from the Reformation, but the Inquisition and the Index constituted a machine for the effective suppression of printed 'pornography'.

25. It has recently been made available by M. Rodrigues Lapa, *Cantigas d'escarnho e*

de mal dizer (Coimbra, 1965). A prize example is No. 23 (pp. 42-43) on the Dean of Cádiz. Though many of the poems in this anthology (by various poets) are simply satirical (of the pretensions of the lesser nobility, of doctors, of other poets), a very large number are not only 'obscene' but deal with what to modern sensibilities are particularly scabrous sexual themes, like incest, homosexuality, lesbianism, venereal disease, etc.

26. D. Samuel Gili y Gaya, ed., Diego de San Pedro, *Obras* (Madrid, 1950), notes (p. xxv): 'También hemos suprimido una breve poesía que figura a su nombre en el *Cancionero General*, a causa de su carácter obsceno, que nada añadiría a la reputación del autor'. It is 'Más hermosa que cortés', *Canc. gen.* 1511, fol. 226^V.

27. Professor O. H. Green is one of the few who has tackled scabrous matter with dry academic authority, treating the topic as though it were a matter of course, in 'On Juan Ruiz's Parody of the Canonical Hours', *HR*, 26 (1958), 12-34, and in Chapter II, 'Medieval Laughter', in *Spain and the Western Tradition*, I (Madison, 1963). Professor Frank Pierce, in 'The Role of Sex in the *Tirant lo Blanc*', *Estudis Romanics*, 10 (1962), 291-300, makes an eloquent *apologia* in more reverent tones than I intend to employ myself: 'The general subject of this article is a universal one, and yet it has more often been ignored by students of literature than explicitly referred to—and, it should be said, for reasons some of which meet with the approval of the present writer. [. . .] Yet as a basic aspect of human experience and of the understanding of man—and, it can be said, of his understanding of himself and God—it would be most surprising if it did not play a large and necessary part in poetry and prose alike of all ages and of all cultures' (p. 291). Professor Sturgis A. Leavitt has dealt with a startling and neglected aspect of seventeenth-century drama in 'Striptease in Golden-Age Drama', *Homenaje a Rodríguez-Moñino* (Madrid, 1966), I, 305-10, in what must have claims to be the most facetiously written academic article ever printed. Most critics, when they are not censorious, seem to feel obliged to adopt a defensive position. I myself resent the need to offer any apology, but cannot help feeling that one is necessary, and I have more to say on the subject in the Introduction to the Trotter edition of the *Thebaida*. And, of course, there is the same suppressive machinery at work in lexicography and linguistics: for a recent confrontation of the problem see Camilo José Cela, 'Papeleta para un diccionario', and *idem*, 'Segunda entrega', *Papeles de Son Armadans*, 44 (1967), 131-57 and 336-48.

28. So Rodrigues Lapa: 'Havia que patentear o reverso da medalha', *Cantigas*, p. vii.

29. I mean, for instance, the blasphemous and obscene parodies of sections of the liturgy, the application of divine comparisons to mortal men (as in the extraordinary poem of Montoro to Isabella, *Canc. gen.*, fol. 75^V, in which he says that if Mary had not been born first, Isabella would have been chosen as the mother of Christ, and which has received comment from María Rosa Lida, 'La hipérbole sagrada en la poesía española del siglo XV', *RFH*, 8 (1946), 121-30,

from F. Márquez Villanueva, *Investigaciones sobre Juan Alvarez Gato* (Madrid, 1960), p. 227, and, with important corrections to the earlier comments, from R. O. Jones, 'Isabel la Católica y el amor cortés', *RLit*, 21 (1962), 55-64), and the introduction of homely and often quite indecorous comparisons in dealing with religious matters (Christ as a thimble-rig manipulator, etc.) where, as Lida put it (p. 122), devoutness suffers by 'intimacy with the divine'. See also E. M. Wilson, 'Spanish and English Religious Poetry in the Seventeenth Century', *Journal of Ecclesiastical History*, 9 (1958), 38-53, and my 'El origen de las comparaciones religiosas del Siglo de Oro: Mendoza, Montesino y Román', *RFE*, 46 (1963), 263-85 [pp. 72-95, above].

30. D. Antonio Rodríguez-Moñino, in the invaluable introduction to his fascimile reproduction of the 1511 *Cancionero general* (Madrid, 1958) deals sensibly with the notorious *Obras de burlas* and the incredible *Carajicomedia*, pp. 22-23. He makes the point that a 'veta alegre y libertina' has always existed in Spanish literature, but that it has been confined to a manuscript tradition, without, however, mentioning the Inquisition and the Index. He makes an eloquent plea against prudery in literary historiography, but uses, somewhat disingenuously, a statement of Menéndez Pelayo to support it: Don Marcelino, great scholar though he was, lost all sense of proportion when confronted with obscenity, as witness his intemperate assault on the *Thebaida* (which I deal with elsewhere), and his enormous authority has been, in this sense, unfortunate.

31. 'Platónico era el amor', p. 87 of *El cancionero de Palacio* (Barcelona, 1945). This was pointed out by Otis Green in the article 'Courtly Love in the Spanish *Cancioneros*'.

32. As to the meaning of the Provençal verse itself, Moshé Lazar, *Amour courtois et fin' amors dans la littérature du XIIe siècle* (Paris, 1964), has surely left us in no doubt that the 'pure love' of the Provençal poets was not the *amor purus* of Andrew.

33. So, for instance, *Cancionero de Palacio* No. 234, or *Cancionero musical*, ed. F. Asenjo Barbieri (Madrid, 1890), No. 14. Cited in Otis Green, 'Courtly Love'.

34. See Alfred Einstein, *The Italian Madrigal* (Princeton, 1949), II, 541-43. I am indebted to Professor R. O. Jones for this reference.

35. In 'Bembo, Gil Polo, Garcilaso: Three Accounts of Love', *Revue de Littérature Comparée*, 40 (1966), 526-40, p. 535, note. The poem itself is in the *Canc. gen.*, fol. 105[r].

36. It is, for instance, taken for granted by Peter Dronke, *Medieval Latin and the Rise of European Love-Lyric* (Oxford, 1965-66).

37. In the Taylorian Lecture, *Some Aspects of Spanish Literary History* (Oxford, 1967), Professor E. M. Wilson recently made the same point, arguing that literary historians have paid too much attention to change: 'we neglect the great continuities', 'the unchanging things are important too' (pp. 11-12).

7

Towards the Interpretation and Appreciation of the *Canciones* of the *Cancionero general* of 1511

in memory of Ramón Menéndez Pidal

The *Cancionero general* (Valencia, 1511) contains 220 *canciones*, distributed as follows: 155[1] in the section devoted wholly to *canciones* (folios 122^r-131^r); 41 in the section of 'Glosas de motes' (143^v-146^v)—the *motes* are glossed only by *canciones*; 25 glossed by various poets, and printed with the gloss and the remainder of the glossing poets' work in the appropriate sections,[2] although from the figure of 25 we must deduct five, for one *canción* not quoted in full (211^r), one quoted and glossed by two poets, Rodrigo Dávalos (95^v) and Pinar (187^r), and three which also figure in the section of *canciones*; and, finally, four others which occur in miscellaneous contexts: one in the 'Obras de devoción' (17^r), one quoted by Francisco Vaca in order to attack it (75^v), and two used as conclusions to longer poems ('Haze fin con esta canción', 172^r, and 'Acaba con esta canción', 174^r), which are therefore not indexed separately by Hernando del Castillo or Rodríguez-Moñino.

In the *Cancionero general* the *canción* is a fixed form which permits a number of minor variations within very narrow limits. We have from Pierre Le Gentil a detailed study of the versification of the *canción* in the Peninsula in the fifteenth century;[3] but the variations exhibited by the form at the end of the fifteenth and beginning of the sixteenth centuries are much fewer than those recorded by Le Gentil. He has emphasized in his study (especially pp. 275-77, and table, p. 276) the tendency to reduce the number of stanzas in the *canción* (unlike the *villancico*); and in the *Canc. gen.* there is in fact only one poem with the rubric 'canción' which has additional stanzas.[4] But Le Gentil does not note the corresponding reduction of a number of other permissible variations. Nor does Tomás Navarro Tomás examine this aspect of the evolution of the *canción*.[5] Some figures may prove illuminating. The 220 *canciones* of the *Canc. Gen.* exhibit the following metrical patterns.

> *Canciones* in quatrains (4 4 4): total 152
> Regular: 139
>> abba cddc abba : 57
>> abab cdcd abab : 37
>> abba cdcd abba : 23
>> abab cddc abab : 22
>
> Irregular: 13
>> abba cdcd baba : 2
>> abab cddc baab : 2
>> abba cddc baba : 1
>
> With reversed rhymes in the final couplet
>> abab cdcd baba : 5
>> abab cdcd abba : 1
>> abab cddc baba : 1
>> abba cddc abab : 1
>
> *Canciones* in *quintillas* and *sextillas*: total 68
>> 555 : 33
>> 545 : 29
>> 544 : 1
>> 556 : 1
>> 565 : 1
>> 666 : 2
>> 656 : 1

From the permissible variations in the form of the *canción* as they are listed by Le Gentil we can deduct, for the *Canc. gen.*, several important freedoms.

(1) In the *vuelta* there is invariably reprise of the rhymes of the *pie de la canción*, the opening quatrain or quintuplet (contrast the examples from the Marqués de Santillana, Juan de Mena, and other early poets quoted by Le Gentil, pp. 266-68).

(2) There are never more than four rhymes in the whole *canción* (again contrast Le Gentil's examples).

(3) The cases in which the *vuelta* fails to reproduce the rhymes in the same order as in the opening statement (a variation which Le Gentil does not

examine: 'Laissons de côté les pièces où l'ordre des rimes est inverti, ce qui a peu d'importance', p. 266) are, while still sufficiently frequent to fall within the concept of 'permissible variation', considerably rarer than in earlier poets. In the table above I have called them 'irregular'.[6]

(4) The five *canciones* with sextuplets are quite untypical, and at least two of them belong to other traditions: the 565 (quintuplet, sextuplet, quintuplet), which also has *pies quebrados*, is a religious poem by Juan Rodríguez del Padrón (17[r]), and one of the 666, also with *quebrados* (aab etc.) is by Juan Manuel (122[r]), who is almost certainly João Manuel, the Portuguese.[7]

(5) The *canciones* are written invariably in octosyllables, and the incidence of *quebrados* is almost negligible. Apart from the *canciones* by Rodríguez del Padrón and João Manuel which I have mentioned, they are to be found in only two other instances: in a three-*quintilla canción* by Tapia (123[v]), and in one using the most frequent of the rhyme-schemes, but again by a Portuguese, Juan (João) de Meneses (125[v]).

It is clear that the poets of the period of the Reyes Católicos not only willingly accepted the restrictions of the *canción*-form, but also ignored certain freedoms traditionally allowed. They evince a clear preference for the shorter, twelve-line, form, with restriction of the number of rhymes. And metrical restrictiveness goes hand in hand with the cult of the conceit.

In the *canciones* of the *Canc. gen.*, but not in, for instance, those of the *Cancionero de Baena*, there is invariably reprise of the rhymes of the *pie de la canción* in the *vuelta*. But the cases in which one finds no more than reprise of the rhymes are in a minority: about one in eight. In most cases there is repetition of the rhyme-words and of whole lines. The frequencies of the different kinds of reprise may be analysed as follows [Table 1]. The symbols are to be interpreted: r, repetition of the rhyme-word only; rr, repetition of the rhyme-word plus some of the other words in the same line (for example 'que ser solo el pensamiento / el testigo de mi mal', 'porque solo el pensamiento / es testigo de mi mal'); R, exact word-for-word repetition of a whole line.[8]

The most frequent pattern (2R), which accounts for almost a quarter of all the cases, is a simple restatement, at the end of the poem, of the last two lines of the opening quatrain or *quintilla* (the complete repetition of three lines or more occurs more usually in *canciones* using *quintillas* or sextuplets). The next most frequent pattern (R + rr) is almost the same thing, but the couplet is accommodated to the syntax by a small adjustment which involves altering a word or two (for example, in a *canción* by Diego de San Pedro, 122[v], 'que después de muerto yo / vuestr'alma dará la cuenta / [. . .] / mas

Table 1

No repetition, except of rhymes: 26 *canciones*
Repetition of rhyme-words and other words: 194 *canciones*

No. of lines affected							Totals
1	—	—	R: 10	—	rr: 9	r: 24	43
2	R + rr: 29	R + r: 8	2R: 53		2rr: 10	2r: 16	116
3	2R + rr: 5	2R + r:11	3R: 9	2rr + r: 2	3rr: 1		28
4	3R + rr: 1	3R + r: 1		2rr + 2r:1	4rr: 1	4r: 2	6
5	4R + rr: 1						1
							194

temo que muerto yo / vuestr'alma dará la cuenta'). One might note that, although there is no way of showing it by this kind of analysis, in virtually all cases the repetition is a simple repetition of the opening statement: it has been expanded and illuminated by the intervening gloss, but the slight verbal twists which do occur do not produce any kind of peripateia.

The vocabulary employed in these *canciones* is also extremely restricted. On any standard, the vocabulary is numerically small, and a count of the nouns in the section devoted to *canciones* (excluding the last one, for reasons I shall explain) reveals that out of a total of 297 different nouns, twenty-five account for over one half the total number of occurrences of nouns: specifically 882 occurrences out of 1630. These top-ranking nouns, with their frequencies, are:

vida (98)	mal (80)	dolor (74)	muerte (58)	amor (52)
pena (52)	razón (43)	passión (41)	gloria (41)	esperança (40)
coraçón (35)	fe (29)	ventura (26)	alma (23)	desseo (20)
plazer (20)	tormento (19)	remedio (18)	bien (18)	memoria (17)
temor (17)	tristura ⎱ (16)	morir (16)	causa (15)	pensamiento (14)
	tristeza ⎰			

This list already hints at another restriction: the bulk of the remainder of the vocabulary also, in fact, refers to emotional states and faculties of the mind.[9] This poetry is limited conceptually to abstractions, and there are

singularly few concrete terms. It is all love-poetry, but it is not amorous
verse of the 'tus bellos ojos' brand. Although theoretically it is the lady's
beauty which awakens the poet's desire and is the prime cause of love, the
lady's 'merit' (*merescimiento* or *merescer*) is mentioned far more frequently than
her beauty (beldad: 1, belleza: 1, hermosura: 3). The last *canción* in the section
(which I omitted from the vocabulary-count) is for this reason quite
untypical: by Mosén Crespí de Valdaura to Doña María de Aragón (131^r),
it praises her *virtud, lindeza,* and *real sangre,* using terms which are not
employed in any other *canción* in this section.

Equally untypical, though frequently included in anthologies, is the *canción*
by Florencia Pinar, 'A unas perdizes que le embiaron bivas' (125^v-126^r). It
is quite clear that modern sensibility tends to seize, from amidst this poetry
of abstractions, precisely the least typical examples—those pieces which offer
concrete images.[10] Even the much-quoted 'Ven muerte tan escondida' of the
comendador Escrivá (128^v) contains, quite untypically, a concrete simile:
'ven como rayo que hiere', etc. It may be worth emphasizing, however, that
even in a *canción* with an extraordinarily high frequency of concrete as against
abstract terms, such as Nicolás Núñez's 'Porque su amiga le dio una rosa'
(124^v), the same abstract vocabulary recurs (dolor, muerte, gloria, esperança,
coraçón, alma, temor), and the conclusion is expressed in conceptual
abstractions.

The high frequencies of a restricted number of abstract words ought to
indicate a low semantic content. I shall return to this point.

Few of the modern critics who have done any serious work on *cancionero*
poetry would subscribe to the views of Menéndez Pelayo on the subject:

> [. . .] coplas fútiles, coplas de *cancionero*, versos sin ningún género de
> pasión, devaneos insulsos que parecen imaginarios, conceptos sutiles y
> alambicados, agudezas de sarao palaciego tan pronto dichas como
> olvidadas, burlas y motejos que no sacan sangre: algo, en suma, que
> recrea agradablemente el oído sin dejar ninguna impresión en el alma.[11]

But the reluctance of modern critics to re-echo these despective epithets
would appear to be due to a very proper hesitation to condemn what is
merely aesthetically foreign, rather than because any positive and detailed
rebuttal of these charges has been formulated. In the course of the past
twenty years or so, students of the poetry of the late fifteenth century have
repeatedly urged its merit and importance; but we have as yet done no more
than begin to clear the way for a proper reappraisal of a considerable corpus

of verse. Professor Otis Green, in his analysis of the conceptual content of the *cancioneros*,[12] registered his disagreement with the assessment of Don Marcelino, expressed the opinion that *cancionero* poetry has been 'condemned to unjust neglect', and abundantly justified his proposition that 'this poetry is not a mere jumble of far-fetched superficialities'; but he did not himself attempt a revaluation of this verse in aesthetic terms. Similarly, Pierre Le Gentil, in his extended examination of the themes and forms of fifteenth-century lyric verse, claimed that late medieval poetry has been undervalued —though in somewhat lukewarm terms:

> Faut-il aller jusqu'à dire que leurs vers conservent encore aujourd'hui une pleine efficacité? Personnellement nous ne sommes pas éloigné de le croire. (pp. 476-77)

But he conceded (p. 491) that, while he had compiled a 'grammar' of this poetry, the measure of how successfully it was employed remained to be realized.

I have confined myself here, in examining the *canciones* of the *Cancionero general* of 1511, to one very narrow but still quite substantial area of late medieval verse. (Indeed there are numerically more poems in the form of *canciones* than in any other verse form.) Obviously Hernando del Castillo's collection is convenient; but, more than that, it represents, with some exceptions, a restricted and coherent period, and the climax of the development of the *canción* before the Italianizing revolution. Furthermore, as is well known, Hernando del Castillo seems to have exercised little personal selectivity, but to have aimed at collecting and publishing all the lyric material he could lay his hands on: the verse of aristocratic amateurs as well as that of semi-professional poets (Lope observed that the *Canc. gen.* was formed 'a bulto' and Rodríguez-Moñino calls it a 'biblioteca en pequeño'); and it is possible that we can come closer to appreciating the governing aesthetic ideals of the late fifteenth century when our literary samples are not passed previously through the sieve of the personal taste of one individual.

I have been proposing, implicitly, a method of approach to this poetry: one in which the exercise of aesthetic appreciation is postponed to the statistical determination of the contemporary aesthetic ideal. It is useless, I would suggest, for the modern reader to rely on his modern sensibility: in what seems to him a desert of abstractions he will seize, like Menéndez Pelayo (and many another much less perceptive critic), on the one piece which offers him some concrete image to cling to: partridges, a rose, or a lemon.[13] Ideally one would prefer to know which *canciones* were most popular in the period; and indeed this vast task is being undertaken by Professor Brian Dutton.[14] But, while waiting for the invaluable information which the computer-analysis of over 20,000 cards will provide, I would suggest that the good late fifteenth-century Spanish *canción* has a severely restricted metrical pattern (most usually octosyllables rhyming abba cddc abba), repeats in the *vuelta* the last two lines of the opening statement (sometimes with minor modifications), and employs a highly restricted vocabulary of abstract terms, among which partridges, roses, and lemons stand out as glaring anomalies. Our problem is to educate ourselves to respond to the typical *canción*.

As I have indicated, 57 *canciones* have the most frequent of the possible rhyme-schemes, and 53 repeat, word for word, the last two lines of the *pie de la canción*. If we look then for *canciones* which conform to both these requirements, we find we have just eleven 'typical' ones: one each by Diego de San Pedro ('Quien se viere cual me veo', 123[r]), Nicolás Núñez ('Llevo un mal qu'está sin medio', 124[v]), Juan Fernández de Heredia ('Puso tanto sentimiento', 128[v]), Vargas ('Quien alegre no se vido', 128[v]), and an anonymous author glossed by Rodrigo Dávalos ('Desconsolado de mí', 95[v]); two by Soria ('Bivo porque vuestro vivo', 129[r], and 'Nunca m'olvida dolor', 129[v]); and four by Quirós (to which I shall return). There are four more *canciones* which come very close to this pattern. In three of the cases one might suspect that we have to do with compositors' errors, since there is no reason for the change in the repeated lines. So (as I have mentioned), in a *canción* by Carasa (126[r]) 'los casos de amor' becomes in the *vuelta* 'las cosas de amor'; in one by Quirós (128[r]) 'ni yo quiero' becomes, repeated, 'no quiero yo', and in another by the same poet (129[r]) 'mis ojos que me perdieron' becomes 'mis ojos que me prendieron'. And it is interesting that the nearest of the near-misses within this particular metrical pattern, having the repetition-formula 2R + rr, is yet another *canción* by Quirós ('Porque razón lo desprecia', 145[v]).

Doubtless this method is arbitrary, the procedure barely justifiable. But if, just for the sake of the argument, we entertain the hypothesis that Quirós is the most typical composer of *canciones*, in that four of his compositions represent perfectly the aesthetic ideal of the period, and three more come very close, we might see where this reasoning leads us.[15] The four 'perfect' *canciones* are these: 'Enojaros no es razón', 128[r]; 'Bien fue bien de mi ventura', 129[r]; 'No bivo sin esperança', 129[r]; and a gloss on the *mote* of Gabriel el músico ('No hay lugar teniendo vida'), 'La fe de amor encendida', 145[v]. They read as follows.[16]

(1)
Enojaros no es razón
y es gran peligro esperaros
y por no descontentaros
nunca os pido galardón.

Tenésme vos sojuzgado
yo muero por más serviros
sin merced voy a pediros
en veros torno espantado.
No aprovecha la razón
en el mucho dessearos
y por no descontentaros
nunca os pido galardón.

(2)
Bien fue bien de mi ventura
con tales penas penarme
amores que quieren darme
por su gloria mi tristura.

Y fue tanto bien ser vuestro
que no sé cuál me consuele
no meresceros que duele
o merescer lo que muestro.
Assí que por mi ventura
comiençan en acabarme
amores que quieren darme
por su gloria mi tristura.

(3)
No bivo sin esperança
ni muero desesperado
que cuanto Dios ha criado
lo hizo sobre mudança.

Mudarse puede ventura
con el espera del cielo
mas en tal buelta recelo
que no reciba tristura.
Ni bivo sin esperança
por no morir en pecado
que cuanto Dios ha criado
lo hizo sobre mudança.

(4)
Otro mote de Graviel
No hay lugar teniendo vida.

La fe de amor encendida
me tiene tan encendido
que al remedio que se ha vido
no hay lugar teniendo vida.

Pues ved agora si quiera
que tan mal por vos me quiero
que ni con morir espero
lo qu'en vida no s'espera.
Assí que con tal herida
me tenéis tan mal herido
que al remedio que se ha vido
no hay lugar teniendo vida.

The reader acquainted with this kind of verse will immediately appreciate that these *canciones*, besides conforming to the metrical norm, are also entirely typical in language, in their use of rhetorical devices, and in their theme and content. And they are, I would suggest, initially disappointing. Whether or not one is justified in employing adjectives like 'insípido' and 'insulso', the very first thing we are obliged to take into account is that the mind—the modern mind, at least—tends to slide over these poems, failing to register anything of note. In reading through the whole section of *canciones* in the *Canc. gen.* it is a relief to come across a partridge or a lemon, something

which stands out with concrete distinctness and which is easily retained in
the memory. This is the direct effect, I would suggest, of the employment
of a vocabulary which is predominantly abstract and which contains a small
number of frequently used items. The constant repetition of a handful of
words (for what is true of the nouns extends to the rest of the vocabulary
also) diffuses their semantic content; or, in the terms of information-theory,
the statistical frequency of the signal lowers the amount of information in
the message. One might conclude—prematurely—that the poet has nothing
to say, that these poems do not mean very much, that they are all alike, and
that they are eminently forgettable ('tan pronto dichas como olvidadas'). But
this is puzzling, since it is obvious that the *cancionero* poets have taken a great
deal of trouble to polish their verses, as even the most hostile critics concede.
As Menéndez Pelayo notes (III, 219): 'Aun en los poetas más triviales de la
colección [el *Canc. gen.*], en los que no lucen más que un artificio huero y
una mera facilidad de versificar, hay por lo menos condiciones técnicas muy
estimables: casi todos versifican bien, y en los metros cortos quizá no han
sido superados nunca.' Are we simply to conclude that a generation of
cultured and intelligent men have expended their talents on achieving formal
perfection at the expense of the content of their poetry? It is the traditional
verdict.

But the problem can be presented in another way: are we simply failing
to perceive something in this poetry? I have in this paper just one suggestion
to make relating to the interpretation of this verse. Let us look more closely
at the fourth of the *canciones* by Quirós, on the *mote* of Gabriel, *cantor de la
capilla del rey*, which uses the terms of living and dying—terms of particularly
high frequency in the vocabulary of the *canciones* as a whole.[17] The poet is
in love, and says that there is no remedy for his wound while he lives. The
association of love and death is an old theme and a very familiar one.[18] But
there are various ways in which Love is associated with Death. (1) Unrequited
love may induce grave illness, insanity, and, in extreme cases, death. There
were to be several Golden-Age sceptics who commented cynically that no
one ever died of love; but it is worth insisting again, in the face of repeated
assertions that this verse deals in insincere exaggerations, that serious medical
opinion did concede that the mental disease of being in love could
occasionally produce death.[19] (Quirós himself has a long poem, 'Es una muy
linda torre', 206^v-207^v, to a lady who 'se burlava de los que dizen que se
mueren de amores'.) (2) Unrequited love is itself a state of suffering and
despair so painful as to be labelled, hyperbolically, 'death'. (3) Being in love
involves 'dying', figuratively speaking, to everything else. (4) In the eyes of
moralists or recanting truants, Love is, figuratively, a state of moral 'death'.

(For a combination of 3 and 4 see Boscán, *Canción* X, 'amor [. . .] aquella muerte'.)[20] (5) The poet in love may claim, simply inverting the third and fourth propositions, that a life without love is death ('Ben es mortz qui d'amor no sen / al cor calque dousa sabor').[21] Or, finally (6), the physical act of love may be regarded as a kind of dying.

The first five propositions require no further comment, but the last point clearly does, since in all hispanist writing on 'courtly love' one looks in vain for any such interpretation. I need not, however, labour the point, which in any event I put forward only as a possibility. That *morire* is a euphemism for the sexual act in the contemporary Italian madrigal is demonstrated by Alfred Einstein.[22] Perhaps more important, the image is used in medieval Latin, and I need quote no more than one example, from the fourteenth-century MS Escurialense O-III-2, fol. 101[r]:

> Alternant animas, laqueataque corpus in unum
>   corpora spiritibus pervia corda parant.
> Corpora spirituum transfusio languida reddit,
>   dumque sibi moritur vivit uterque pari.[23]

There are other possible examples, but I have found none in which the interpretation of *mori* is so unequivocal.[24]

With this in mind, we might note that several other items of our list of nouns also have, in certain contexts, sexual connotations. *Deseo* is always in this context physical desire; but *voluntad* can mean, as well as 'libre albedrío', 'deseo' and 'delectación'.[25] In several texts, *gloria* is a euphemism for sexual consummation,[26] and, indeed, I should like to suggest that it covers almost the same range of meanings as Provençal *joi*.[27] Whether *servir* may have similar connotations is less clear; but in view of its usage in a sexual sense in English, Medieval Latin, and Provençal, the suspicion cannot be said to be lacking in foundation.[28] Is it possible, then, that we may be able to say of the *canciones* of the *Canc. gen.* what Moshé Lazar said of the poetry of Provence? —'Évidemment, le troubadour n'exprime pas toujours ses désirs charnels à voix haute et d'une manière transparente, mais s'abrite derrière des périphrases, derrière des métaphores voilées [. . .] Bien des associations d'images, qui pourraient passer pour des formules usées, sont en réalité l'expression d'un brûlant désir de la possession physique.' Are we faced with a kind of *trobar clus* of ambiguous vocabulary?

There are dangers here,[29] and before inquiring whether any Spanish fifteenth-century verse will bear such interpretation, there are clearly two preliminary questions which present themselves. Is there justification for dismissing the traditional view of Spanish fifteenth-century love-poetry as 'platonic' (in the secondary sense of the term)? And, are we justified in looking for hidden meaning in a medieval text? To the first, one can reply that it is now becoming increasingly obvious that we have been misled for some time (a) as Otis Green pointed out, by failing to perceive that Spanish fifteenth-century poetry is to be placed in the tradition of so-called 'courtly love', (b) by regarding the treatise of Andrew the Chaplain as something more than a statement of his own personal and peculiar views, and (c), not least, by a series of puritanical critics who have refused to perceive the blatant sensuality of Provençal verse and, if I may be forgiven the observation, who seem curiously ingenuous and inexperienced where love is concerned.[30] And to the other question, one can reply that there is ample precedent in medieval rhetorical theory (via such devices as *ambiguitas*, *metaphora*, varieties of euphemism, *allegoria*, and *figura*) for a text to carry secondary meanings.

The long poem by Quirós to which I have referred, 'Es una muy linda torre', employs the imagery of a besieged citadel to refer to the lady, and it is almost impossible, I believe, that anyone should read it without finding the symbolism suggestive. The 'puerta escondida' in which the poet 'quiere entrar' can be read (must be read) on two levels: as a military image, and as the figurative expression of the poet's desire to conquer the lady's affections. But it is hard to believe that this imagery ('guardas el portillo', etc.) was not intended to provoke and evoke the possibility of reading it on a third level, in concrete sexual terms.

If we return now to the fourth of the *canciones* of Quirós, we see that there are several meanings that could be read into it. On the most superficial level the poet seems to be saying that only death can end the anguish caused by, one assumes, his unrequited love. But 'remedio' gives us a clue. Certainly death is the cure for all ills, but there are other remedies for the disease of love, of which the first and most obvious is 'quod detur sibi illa quam diligit'.[31] In the *Comedia Thebaida* Veturia tells Claudia that love-making is 'el médico y çurujano que tú has menester' (line 6858). So the poet is also expressing his despair of ever possessing his beloved. But this is linked with a further veiled statement about the nature of the remedy, which will involve his 'dying' ('no hay lugar teniendo vida'), and there seems to be the further suggestion that even this will not end his pain. But this poem is perhaps not the most convincing of examples. If *remedio* and *morir* will bear the interpretations I have suggested, this is the way to read it; but the fact that it might be read in this way is not an adequate test of the hypothesis.

The second of the *canciones* is a little clearer. On the more superficial level, the poet is speaking of the mixed joy (*gloria*) and sorrow of love. But if *gloria* has the double meaning of the Provençal *joi*, then he is again repeating the theme of the fourth *canción*: the paradoxical statement that even the ultimate *gloria* is accompanied by *tristura*, in this case occasioned by his unworthiness. 'Ser vuestro' is equivocal, but could clearly be construed as a euphemism. The 'typical' *canción* by Vargas deals, in still clearer terms, with a similar theme (128^v):

> Quien alegre no se vido
> lexos está de ser triste
> porqu'el dolor no consiste
> sino en llorar lo perdido.
>
> Y de aquesta conclusión
> nos queda determinado
> qu'el perder de lo ganado
> es lo que nos da passión.
> Que lo que no es posseído
> no dexa el coraçón triste
> porqu'el dolor no consiste
> sino en llorar lo perdido.

There can be little doubt that Vargas is saying that the lover who has not known true joy ('quien alegre no se vido') by possessing his beloved ('posseído'), cannot know what real unhappiness is.

It is in fact easier to be sure of the presence of 'métaphores voilées' in some of the poems by other poets. The rubrics of the 'Canción que hizo un gentilhombre a una dama que le prometió si la hallasse virgen de casarse con ella y él después de haverla a su plazer gelo negó' (126^v) or of the *esparsa* by Guevara, 'A su amiga estando con ella en la cama' (105^r) make it plain that there is no question there of a 'platonic' love; and there is no possibility of misreading the 'Justa que hizo Tristán de Stúñiga a unas monjas porque no le quisieron por servidor ninguna dellas' (222^{r-v}). In many others, there can also be little doubt that the poet is writing not about some soulful, 'platonic', 'pure' love, but about overwhelming and unbearable physical desire. So don Diego López de Haro (using *gloria* in two senses as 'sexual consummation' and a kind of semi-religious martyrdom) writes (130^r):

Quando acierta el dessear
donde gloria no s'espera
aquesta pueden llamar
la gloria más verdadera.

Qu'el mal con buena esperança
da dolor mas no mortal
y mal que consuelo alcança
no se puede dezir mal.
Assí que más lastimera
es la pena del pesar
do esperança desespera
siendo bivo el dessear.

Surely the *gloria* which 'no s'espera' can mean only the physical possession of the beloved.

If one is alive to the possible sexual connotations and implications of *esperança, remedio, galardón, desseo, voluntad, gloria, servicio, morir*, etc., one can hardly fail to receive the impression that the *canciones* of the *Canc. gen.* are, like the poetry of the troubadours, impregnated with sensuality. Professor Otis Green, while emphasizing that the poetry of the *cancioneros* is based on physical desire, writes that it 'is not a love of consummation'. But what about Guevara in bed, or Vargas, who has possessed his mistress, or the 'gentilhombre' who refused to marry the lady? What about *Amadís* and *La Celestina*? Is it really plausible to distinguish between 'amor caballeresco' and 'amor cortés' (a term devised on the basis of one medieval occurrence by Jeanroy)? Certainly it must be conceded that one cannot always find a clear secondary sexual interpretation for terms like *gloria*. When Quirós writes (in the first *canción* quoted) 'yo muero por más serviros', to construe the line in a sexual sense is to ignore the context. At the same time these ambivalent euphemisms (of whose ambivalence contemporary readers must have been aware) also infect the context, so that the ambiguous *galardón* referred to—the reward which may range from the smile of approval to total surrender —carries more clearly in this *canción* the suggestive possibility of its having the fullest meaning. It may well be true that the *canciones* are not a poetry of consummation. As Lope de Estúñiga complains (49^r): 'bondad / no te consiente hazer / mi voluntad [. . .] honestidad / te hace palacio ser / de castidad'. This verse does not, in general, celebrate a mistress's complaisance, and one suspects that perhaps some poets have discovered the perverse pleasures of perpetual frustration. But there is little doubt that the *cancionero* poets are obsessed with physical desire and the tantalizing prospect of its consummation rather than with the nebulosities of semi-mystical neoplatonic ideas.

The indisputable facts are, I think, these: (1) the technical expertise of the composers of *canciones* is considerable; (2) the poets of the end of the fifteenth century accept in the *canción* a series of technical restrictions which make the *canción* at once a more exacting and a more concise form; (3) simultaneously they restrict their vocabulary to a very limited range of abstract terms; (4) the majority of modern critics who have looked at this verse have either dismissed it as vacuous and insipid or have singled out for enthusiastic approval poems which in form or content are quite untypical, and cannot be taken as representative of the aesthetic ideal of the period; (5) some of these poems are in fact extremely difficult to paraphrase or to make good sense of (e.g. San Pedro's 'El mayor bien de quereros', 124^v); (6) in other contemporary texts, and in similar literature in Latin, Provençal, French, Italian, and English, the same or a similar abstract vocabulary (e.g. 'will', in Shakespeare[32]) serves for a euphemistic vocabulary relating to sexual activity; (7) many of these same poets also compose overtly obscene verse (e.g. San Pedro's 'Más hermosa que cortés', 226^v); (8) interpreters of both Provençal and Spanish poetry have relied on the distinction made by Andrew the Chaplain between *amor purus* and *amor mixtus*, a distinction which there is very good reason to suppose the troubadours of Provence knew nothing of; (9) the traditional acceptance of Provençal verse as a poetry of 'pure' love (excluding the possibility both of sexual consummation and of marriage) has been refuted with very cogent arguments during the last ten years.

I have suggested that in trying to arrive at a just assessment of *cancionero* verse, the modern critic cannot afford simply to rely on his modern sensibilities, which are likely to lead him to single out Florencia Pinar and ignore Quirós; that there is perhaps something odd about metrical restrictiveness's being accompanied by a restriction of the vocabulary, which appears to lead to diffusion of the semantic content; and, consequently, that it may not be unjustifiable to suspect the presence of euphemisms in this verse. It could be argued that it would also be slightly odd if Spanish fifteenth-century verse were unique in its period and tradition in celebrating 'pure' love. But the nature of euphemism is such that one can only rarely be completely certain that the second meaning is present: it would not be impossible to insist that even 'estando en la cama' could be entirely innocent and not in conflict with Denomy's view of 'courtly love'. And there are certainly contexts in which this possibly euphemistic vocabulary must be taken at its face value. We need a detailed study of the incidence and contexts of such terms as *gloria* throughout the *cancionero* verse of the period. Meanwhile we have a hypothesis which may explain the alleged vagueness of some love-poetry, the wholesale usage of this limited range of abstract terms, and the difficulty of interpreting some poems, and which certainly brings this 'insipid' verse very much alive.

[*Filología*, 13 (1968–69 [1970]: *Homenaje a Ramón Menéndez Pidal*), 361-81, in Spanish translation]

Notes

1. The table of contents says 'ciento y cinquenta y seys', but the fifteenth, on folio 122^v, is only the first four lines of the *canción* by Cartagena which is given in full on 130^v. I have used, of course, the facsimile *Cancionero general (Valencia, 1511)* with introduction and indexes by Antonio Rodríguez-Moñino (Madrid, 1958). On the peculiar difficulties of counting accurately either poets or poems in the *Canc. gen.*, see Roberto de Souza, 'Desinencias verbales correspondientes a la persona *vos/vosotros* en el *Cancionero general* (Valencia, 1511)', *Filología*, 10 (1964 [1967]), 1-95, especially pp. 7-8.
2. The glosses, and sometimes also the *canciones* glossed, are by Rodrigo Dávalos (or de Ávalos), 95^v (2 *canciones*) and 96^r; Tapia, 178^v; Pinar and Florencia Pinar, 185^r, 185^v, 186^v, 187^r, 187^v, and 188^r; Alonso de Cardona, 193^r and 194^r; Francés Carroz Pardo, 195^v and 196^v; Mosén Crespí de Valdaura, 198^r and 198^v; Francisco Fenollete, 199^r and 199^v (2); Mosén Narcís Vinyoles, 201^r; Juan Fernández de Heredia, 202^r; Mosén Gazull, 203^r; Gerónimo de Artés, 206^r; Quirós, 211^r; and the Comendador Estúñiga, 215^r. The authors of the *canciones* glossed are usually left unidentified.
3. *La Poésie lyrique espagnole et portugaise à la fin du moyen âge*, II: *Les formes* (Rennes, 1953), pp. 263-90.
4. By Mosén Fenollar, 205^r. I have excluded this atypical variant from the count above.
5. *Métrica española* (Syracuse, NY, 1956): 'Canción trovadoresca', pp. 117-20. Other works on Spanish versification have even less detail on the *canción*.
6. How far inversions in the order of the rhymes are simply compositors' errors or the result of earlier manuscript miscopying is a point to be borne in mind. The *canción* 'Desconsolado de mí' as quoted by Rodrigo Dávalos (95^v) has the regular rhyme-scheme abba cddc abba, but as quoted by Pinar (187^r) has the last two lines of the *vuelta* inverted, to make equally good sense, and give the pattern abab. Similarly Dorothy Clotelle Clarke, in 'Imperfect Consonance and

Acoustic Equivalence in *Cancionero* Verse', *PMLA*, 64 (1949), 1114-22, has noted irregularities in rhyming which, at least in the case of Fray Íñigo de Mendoza, an examination of the manuscripts and the earliest printed editions shows are mere errors of reproduction.

7. Marcelino Menéndez Pelayo, *Antología de poetas líricos*, Ed. Nac. (Santander, 1944-45), III, 161, suggests that the Juan Manuel of the *Canc. gen.* is 'más probablemente el caballero castellano favorito de Felipe *el Hermoso*', but there is a Portuguese poet of the same name who writes in Castilian (with lusisms which may be scribal) in the *Cancioneiro de Resende*. Robert de Souza, p. 37, classifies him as '¿Portugués?'.

8. This cannot be mathematically exact. I have counted as rhymes only, not repetition of a rhyme-word, rhymes like 'contento/descontento'. There are also numerous cases in which we may have to do with misprints; so, for instance, in a *canción* by Carasa, 126^r-126^v, we find 'los casos de amor' in the opening statement, and 'las cosas de amor' in the *vuelta*.

9. Since the section of *canciones* constitutes a very restricted corpus, there is no point in reproducing the complete analysis; but those involved with *cancionero* poetry may be interested to see how the list continues: dessear, Dios, fuerça, galardón/gualardón (13 each); cuidado, desamor (12); merescimiento, mudança, querer, señora, victoria (11); ausencia, bevir/bivir (10); hora, merced, perfectión/perfición, peligro, tiempo (9); cuerpo, culpa, condición, mundo, ojos, perdición, seso, sospiros (8). Fifty-one nouns, therefore, account for 1142 of the 1630 occurrences of nouns. 124 nouns occur only once.

10. I have elsewhere expressed my misgivings about this possibly unconscious bias of modern criticism, in *Spanish Literary Historiography: Three Forms of Distortion* (Exeter, 1968), especially pp. 12 and 15 [pp. 100 and 102, above].

11. *Antología*, X, 209. Strictly, the despective epithets of Don Marcelino were intended for the traditional poetry of Boscán, but the succeeding remarks, 'estos versos lo mismo pueden ser de Boscán que de cualquier otro caballero galante y discreto de la corte del Rey Católico', may justify the intention I have lent them. They can certainly be matched throughout the chapter on the *Canc. gen.* (*Antología*, III, 125-220), if less coherently: 'una pasión tan falsa como todos los amores del *Cancionero*' (p. 135), 'insípida y artificial galantería' (p. 137), 'convencionalismo' (p. 153), 'poesía artificiosa y amanerada' (p. 159), 'una afectación pueril y alambicada de pensamientos que de puro sutiles se quiebran' (p. 160), etc., etc. Literary historians tend to repeat these judgements. So Juan Luis Alborg, *Historia de la literatura española* (Madrid, 1966), I, 183, writes of 'una poesía artificiosa y convencional, basada en sutilezas y habilidades de ingenio', etc.

12. 'Courtly Love in the Spanish *Cancioneros*', *PMLA*, 64 (1949), 247-301.

13. I refer to the *canción* by Nicolás Núñez, 'porque pidió a su amiga un limón', included, along with Florencia Pinar's partridges, among Menéndez Pelayo's selection of six *canciones* (*Antología*, V). A more sophisticated critic might pitch

on something like the ingenious and amusing *canción* by Lope de Sosa, 'Quien me recibió por suyo', 124^r, but only because it is 'different'.

14. [The research to which this sentence refers led to the publication by Brian Dutton, with Stephen Fleming, Jineen Krogstad, Francisco Santoyo Vázquez, and Joaquín González Cuenca, of the *Catálogo-índice de la poesía cancioneril del siglo XV*, Bibliographic Series, 3 (Madison: Hispanic Seminary of Medieval Studies, 1982). An amplified catalogue with indexes and edition of texts is in course of publication: Brian Dutton, with Jineen Krogstad, *El cancionero del siglo XV, c. 1360–1520*, Biblioteca Española del Siglo XV, Maior, 1-7 (Salamanca: Universidad, 1990–91).]

15. Of Quirós himself nothing appears to be known. Roberto de Souza classifies him as '¿valenciano?', possibly on the strength of the name. The Quirós, however, were a well-known Asturian family (lords of Quirós, near Lena, Oviedo) who produced poets in the sixteenth and seventeenth centuries, and to which it would not be unreasonable to suppose our poet belonged. [See note 33, below.]

16. In all quotations from the *Canc. gen.*, I have retained phonemic contrasts while modernizing certain orthographic conventions (u/v, h, y/i) and supplying accentuation.

17. If one combines *muerte* and *el morir* (without counting the verb *morir* or participle *muerto*) the idea of death ranks third among the nouns; while *vida*, which ranks first, sometimes includes, as in this *canción*, the idea of death, through such phrases as 'perder la vida', 'no tener vida', etc.

18. There is a most instructive chapter (the tenth), 'Amor as a God of Death', in Edgar Wind, *Pagan Mysteries in the Renaissance* (New Haven, 1958). Although Wind is concerned with sundry exotic notions of which it is unlikely any of our *cancionero* poets were aware, the fact that the association should be made in this particular form is striking.

19. See, for a digest of the relevant information, since the original texts are not always easy of access, John L. Lowes, 'The Loveres Maladye of Hereos', *Modern Philology*, 11 (1913–14), 491-546, or Bruno Nardi, 'L'amore e i medici medievali', in *Studi in onore di Angelo Monteverdi* (Modena, 1959), pp. 517-42.

20. For associations of the types 2, 3, and 4 see the numerous references (indexed under 'Death') given by Otis H. Green, *Spain and the Western Tradition*, I (Madison, 1963), or Peter Dronke, *Medieval Latin and the Rise of European Love-Lyric* (Oxford, 1965–66).

21. Bernard de Ventadour, in *Bernart von Ventadorn: Seine Lieder, mit Einleitung und Glossar*, ed. Carl Appel (Halle, 1915), p. 186.

22. *The Italian Madrigal* (Princeton, 1949), II, 541-43.

23. The poem is probably early twelfth century, and is also to be found, without variants, in Vatican MS Reg. lat. 585, fol. 5^v, from which it may have been copied. It is printed by Peter Dronke, II, 449.

24. Obviously 'sibi moritur' also carries the connotations of (3); but in this case the

'dying to oneself' is directly associated with love-making rather than love, and in context it comes as the climax of such lines as 'Nec radii vultus paciuntur lumina figi / nec glacies carnis lubrica stare manus. / Hec annos si ducta magis quam docta sequatur / et quo ducit amor nec docet usus eat, / unius si lateri latus unaque membra reformans / ducat in alternas absque labore vices [. . .]'.

25. See John M. Hill, *'Universal vocabulario' de Alfonso de Palencia: registro de voces españolas internas* (Madrid, 1957), p. 199ab.

26. The reader will doubtless recall Calisto's use of the term in Act XIV of *La Celestina* and Juan Ruiz's in *Libro de buen amor* 387c (for commentary see Otis Green, 'On Juan Ruiz's Parody of the Canonical Hours', *HR*, 26 (1958), 12-34), but there are numerous other instances, in the *Comedia Thebaida* etc.

27. The meaning of the term is studied, with a survey of the earlier writing on the subject, by A. J. Denomy, ' "Jois" among the Early Troubadours: Its Meaning and Possible Source', *Mediaeval Studies*, 13 (1951), 177-217; but as Moshé Lazar points out, in *Amour courtois et fin' amors dans la littérature du XIIe siècle* (Paris, 1964), p. 117: 'Toutes les explications données du *joi* ont systématiquement tendu à effacer l'élément de jouissance érotique [. . .] son sens premier.' Lazar's chapter, ' "Joi": joie d'amour et jouissance', pp. 103-18, establishes, with completely convincing quotations from the poetry, that, while *joi* has metaphorically extended meanings of 'love' and even 'the beloved', its primary meanings are (1) the sensation of happiness deriving from the lady's approval of the lover (I paraphrase), and (2) the erotic enjoyment of sexual possession. *Gloria* appears to have these primary meanings plus, at times, the sense of 'glorious martyrdom'.

28. In English *serve* is restricted to the mating of domestic animals (like Spanish *cubrir*), but there appears to be no evidence for *servir* having had this particular meaning in Spanish. There are a number of ambiguous cases in medieval Latin (ambiguous in that a stubborn critic could insist that *servire* carries no more than its primary meaning in the context), and the clearest case I have found (Dronke, p. 419) depends, unfortunately, on the correct resolution of an obscure abbreviation. In Provençal, however, there are innumerable unequivocal examples: Peire de Valeira, 'a Deu prec que mi don vida / per servir son bel cors gen', etc. (ed. Martín de Riquer, *La lírica de los trovadores* (Barcelona, 1948), p. 128).

29. One is reluctant to accept Pierre Guiraud's thesis of three levels of meaning (the third level nauseatingly obscene) in Villon's *Testament*, if not in the *Ballades de la Coquille* (see *Le Jargon de Villon ou le gai savoir de la Coquille* (Paris, 1968)), but if the French have in some cases gone too far, perhaps hispanists have not gone far enough.

30. I have said something about this in the introduction to *La Comedia Thebaida*, ed. G. D. Trotter and K. W. (London, 1969), especially pp. xxv-xxvii, as well as in *Spanish Literary Historiography*, pp. 19-23 [pp. 104-06, above]. Alfred Jeanroy and Father Denomy, who have contributed so much to the study of

so-called courtly love, are among those who have mistranslated or suppressed the evidence in the texts before them. Throughout the critical literature one finds such statements as '[courtly love] is a love divorced from physical possession' (Denomy, *'Fin' amors*: The Pure Love of the Troubadours, its Amorality and Possible Source', *Mediaeval Studies*, 7 (1945), 139-207, at p. 147); 'the desire for sexual union is sublimated' (A. F. M. Gunn, *The Mirror of Love: A Reinterpretation of 'The Romance of the Rose'* (Lubbock, Texas, 1952), p. 429); 'platónico era el amor' (Francisca Vendrell de Millás, ed., *El cancionero de Palacio* (Barcelona, 1945), p. 87).

31. This is the first remedy suggested by Valescus of Taranta in his *Philonium*. See Lowes, 'Loveres Maladye', and my introduction to the *Comedia Thebaida*, p. xl.

32. See Eric Partridge, *Shakespeare's Bawdy* (London, 1947).

33. [The Corrigenda sheets included by Keith Whinnom in offprints of the Spanish version of this article include a final note which reads (in translation): After completing this article I read the MA dissertation of A. J. Foreman, 'The *Cancionero* Poet, Quirós' (Westfield College, University of London, 1969, supervised by Professor A. D. Deyermond). The following points should be added to the information I give:

    1. In the 1514 *Cancionero general*, where some 'Coplas de Diego Núñez de Quirós' are printed, the rubric adds: 'porque ay otro que abitaua en Valencia'; according to Foreman our Quirós would have been in Valencia from 1503 to 1509.

    2. In the *Cancionero llamado vergel de amores* (Zaragoza, 1557), in the *canción* 'Dos enemigos hallaron', line 3 has 'prendieron' in place of 'perdieron', so that the *canción* becomes fully typical.

    3. To the list of suspect words that could be euphemisms should be added: satisfazer, conosceros, igualaros, merescer, expender, dispender, tesoro, presunción.]

8

Nicolás Núñez's Continuation of the *Cárcel de Amor* (Burgos, 1496)

to Edward Wilson

Nicolás Núñez's continuation of Diego de San Pedro's *Cárcel de Amor* was first printed in Burgos in 1496, by Fadrique de Basilea, in the second known Spanish edition of that novel, and survives in a unique copy in the British Museum (IA. 53247). There is some confusion among the bibliographers, and various secondary sources cite as the first printing the *Cárcel de amor con el complimiento de Nicolás Núñez* which was done by Arnao Guillén de Brocar in Logroño in 1508. This is due, one supposes, to the fact that the existence of Núñez's sequel is not indicated on the title-page of the 1496 edition nor in the British Museum's *Catalogue of Printed Books*.[1] The fact, too, that the continuation is a superficial insertion—in as much as Núñez employs San Pedro's original concluding phrases for his own conclusion ('llegué aquí a Peñafiel', etc.)—may also have contributed to conceal the work from hasty investigators. But while Hain and Copinger (No. 12545, s.v. Pedro), Simón Díaz (No. 6245), the B.M. Catalogue, and Sir Henry Thomas (*Short-title Catalogue*) are silent, its presence was accurately recorded by Haebler (No. 604), Vindel (Burgos No. 43), and Palau (No. 293344). It was also printed, before the edition of Logroño 1508 by Pedro Hagembach in Toledo in 1500. The sole surviving copy of this edition is in the Huntington Library, San Marino, California.[2]

The collation of the splendidly illustrated[3] quarto edition of Burgos 1496 is A–H8, I4, and Nicolás Núñez's contribution occupies the gatherings H and I. G8^v is blank, and H1^r is headed: 'Tratado que hizo niculas [*sic*] nuñez sobre el que sant pedro compuso de leriano y laureola llamado carcel de amor' and the continuation concludes on I4^r. The only modern reprint of the continuation is that done by Menéndez Pelayo for his *Orígenes de la novela*,[4]

a badly misprinted version which looks as though it may have been based
on the inferior text printed by Jorge Coci in Saragossa in 1523, the earliest
copy of the text of the continuation in the possession of the Biblioteca
Nacional, R-31062.[5] But this is the seventh known edition of it, and if
Menéndez Pelayo did make use of it (nowhere does he indicate which edition
he did employ), he introduced yet further error. I shall quote, with minor
editorial intervention, from the 1496 edition.[6]

Although I have been unable to follow in detail the fortunes of Nicolás
Núñez's work, it is clear that it was reprinted along with San Pedro's *Cárcel
de Amor* in a great many subsequent editions—even, perhaps, in most of the
Spanish editions, although again the conflicting information supplied by
bibliographers and catalogues or their silence make the situation unclear.
According to Anna Krause (p. 128), it was translated into French in 1533
and subsequently printed with the *Prison d'amour*; but there are at least four
earlier French editions without it, and it appears to be missing from the
bilingual editions. At any rate, it is fair to say that Nicolás Núñez's
much-neglected work was frequently reprinted and must have been widely
read in the sixteenth century.

Almost no attention has been paid to it. Menéndez Pelayo deals with it
in one brief paragraph full of small inaccuracies:

> No faltó quien encontrase el final demasiado triste, y demasiado áspera
> y empedernida a Laureola, que ningún sentimiento mostró de la muerte
> de su amador. Sin duda por esto, un cierto Nicolás Núñez añadió una
> continuación o *cumplimiento* de pocas hojas, en que mezcla con la prosa
> algunas canciones y villancicos, y describe la aflicción de Laureola y una
> aparición en sueños del muerto Leriano, que viene a consolar a su amiga.
> Pero aunque este suplemento fue incluido en casi todas las ediciones de
> la *Cárcel de Amor*, nunca tuvo gran crédito, ni en realidad lo merecía,
> siendo cosa de todo punto pegadiza e inútil para la acción de la novela.[7]

Other literary historians merely repeat or paraphrase Menéndez Pelayo.
Although he tells us that 'nunca tuvo gran crédito', this statement, while
not untrue, is misleading, for the same could be said of the *Cárcel de Amor*
itself, on which one can find in the sixteenth century only despective and
hostile comment, for it is lumped by the jaundiced moralists along with
Amadís, the *Celestina*, and the *Diana*, all frivolous and unedifying reading.
We simply cannot tell whether Nicolás Núñez rode to success on the back
of San Pedro's best-seller and owed the major part of his apparent popularity
to the sheer inertia of printing traditions, or whether the success of San

Pedro's uncompromising narrative owed something to Núñez's modification of its ending. Moreover, while I should not argue that it possesses great literary merit, Nicolás Núñez (about whom we know nothing) has some more than acceptable verse in the *Cancionero general* and his continuation deserves more than this casual attention, for it is, in a mildly oblique way, the only contemporary criticism of the *Cárcel de Amor* which has come down to us.[8]

Núñez has his own preface, in which he explains his motives for writing his supplement: it seemed to him, he says, that when Diego de San Pedro left for Castile immediately after the death of Leriano, he ought to have gone to the court to tell Laureola the news. Even if that would have profited the dead man nothing ('aunque le pareciera que al muerto no le aprovechava' [51]), it would have given the author some satisfaction if Laureola had shown some sign of regret ('si viera en ella alguna muestra del pesar' [51-52]). San Pedro, he says, 'lo dexava en aquello corto' [52],[9] no doubt through the pressure of other affairs. He, therefore, has 'done it' ('lo fize') 'por saber si a la firmeza de Leriano en la muerte dava algún galardón, pues en la vida se lo había negado' [52].

'El auctor', the same character as the ambiguous author-Author of the original—but now even more ambiguous since the author is Núñez—then takes up the story. The plot, such as it is, involves no action of any consequence (to that extent it could be said to be 'pegadizo e inútil para la acción de la novela'), but is rather a device for discussing much more fully all the implications of San Pedro's story. The Author goes to Laureola, recounts the details of Leriano's death, and bitterly reproaches her for her 'mucha crueza' [53], which has caused the death of Leriano and will cause Leriano's mother's and his own. Laureola replies defending her conduct but confessing her love for Leriano. The Author returns to his lodgings, lies down to sleep and addresses in imagination his dead friend, 'como si bivo delante de mí stoviera' [56]. Then, in the Author's dream-vision, Leriano appears in a costume embroidered with a dozen *letras* (cited in detail) and consoles the Author by explaining that he was satisfied to die. Laureola appears (with nine *letras* on her costume) and attacks Leriano: loyal lovers should know how to suffer, and even if he did not know that she loved him he should not have allowed himself to die. Leriano defends himself and argues that Laureola was wrong, kisses her hands, and vanishes. Laureola laments her fate and begs the Author to stay at the court so that she can reward him as she would have rewarded Leriano. The Author wakes from his dream, contemplates and rejects the idea of suicide, seeks consolation in music with his *vihuela* (*canción* and *villancico*), and finally returns to Castile:

'llegué aquí a Peñafiel, como dixo Sant Pedro, do quedo besando las manos de vuestras mercedes' [71]. Such is the sequence of events. But there is more in the content of the discourses and in the presentation of the material which merits consideration.

Nicolás Núñez has achieved a quite remarkable pastiche of San Pedro's style; but a pastiche it remains. He has imitated his predecessor without understanding the fundamental principles of San Pedro's style, and without possessing San Pedro's rhetorical training. His discourses will not divide themselves into the *salutatio, exordium, narratio, petitio*, and *conclusio* of the manuals as San Pedro's do; his *plancti* are not proper laments; and he has seized on certain conspicuous devices which San Pedro uses with great discretion in the *Cárcel*, so that Núñez's style more often resembles that in *Arnalte y Lucenda* than that in the *Cárcel*. The final proof that it is a question of a deliberate attempt to imitate San Pedro and not merely a coincidence of similarities in a contemporary writer lies in the fact that Núñez borrows phrases and sentences from the text of the novel itself. But if Núñez has botched an attempt to reproduce faithfully San Pedro's style, he has also in the content of his continuation grossly betrayed or misunderstood (as I shall argue) his model's intentions.

In his supplement Nicolás Núñez proceeds to clear up, at least to his own satisfaction, three questions which have caused difficulty for some modern critics of the *Cárcel de Amor*: was Laureola in love with Leriano? what did Leriano want ultimately of Laureola? and was Leriano right to commit suicide (or, as Bruce Wardropper would prefer to say, 'como Cristo, hacer posible su muerte'[10])?

In San Pedro's novel there is only one passage in which the question of Laureola's falling in love with Leriano is raised; she is so perturbed by Leriano's first letter (which is not, of course, an initial declaration of love, since she had been forewarned verbally by the Author), that the Author is confused and suspects that she is in love with Leriano: 'mirava en ella algunas cosas en que se conosce el coraçón enamorado'.[11] But, as Dr Langbehn-Rohland has argued (p. 187), the Author is not an omniscient author but a fallible character within the novel, and he confesses almost at once that Laureola's subsequent behaviour showed that he had been quite wrong in his conclusions: 'Sin dubda, segund lo que después mostró, ella recebía estas alteraciones más de piedad que de amor' (p. 132 [98]). It could be argued that, since the Author is fallible, we have the right to rely on the evidence of her Ovidian symptoms ('desatinava de lo que dezía, bolvíase súpito colorada y después amarilla, tornávase ronca su boz, secávasele la boca'), rather than on that of her subsequent actions, which succeeded in disabusing the Author. But *turbación*, a symptom of love, can be produced by other emotional states;[12] San Pedro does not revert to the question of Laureola's possible emotional involvement with Leriano; and the action of his novel proceeds exactly as though Laureola were not in love with Leriano. Núñez's suggestion (perhaps not wholly serious) that San Pedro failed to mention Laureola's reaction to the news of Leriano's death simply because the pressure of affairs obliged him to bring it to a premature end, is clearly most improbable: for San Pedro, Laureola was simply the unattainable object of Leriano's affections, and his interest in her died with Leriano.

Nicolás Núñez, however, takes a very different view of things. Implicit, perhaps, in his continuation is the belief that a woman must respond to love and devotion such as Leriano demonstrated. As Justina Ruiz del Conde puts it: 'Si el varón cumple los requisitos exigidos por la época [. . .] siendo amante conforme a las leyes del amor [. . .] la mujer no tiene escape posible: ha de amar al caballero [. . .] Tales cualidades y tal conducta del caballero producen, tienen que producir amor en la dama.'[13] So Núñez not only makes Laureola proclaim her long-standing love for Leriano ('la voluntad que le tenía', H3^r [55]; 'agora juzgarás si amor le tenía', H3^v [55]; 'te quería', H8^r [64]) but argues, through Laureola, that her behaviour proved it, and, through the Author and Leriano, that her rejection of Leriano was wanton and unjustifiable. Laureola tells Leriano (H8^r [64]) that 'con sólo escrivirte bastava para desto [i.e. que te quería] asegurarte y para que conoscas que no procedía de deuda sino de mi voluntad'. Núñez seems incapable of appreciating the nice distinction between *piedad* (for San Pedro, the supreme feminine virtue) and *amor*. Moreover, he finds the *dénouement*, and Laureola's scruples about her honour, totally unconvincing. On one crucial point the text is unfortunately not incontestable: in the 1496 edition the Author attacks Laureola, saying 'Cata que las de tan alta sangre como tú son más obligadas a satisfazer al menor servicio del mundo, si dél son consentidoras, *y a guardar su mayor honra*' (H3^v [55]).[14] This would seem to reflect notions of a distinction between the 'vana honra del mundo' with its fear of gossip, and the true honour of fulfilling one's obligations. But Núñez does not dwell upon the point, and when Leriano rejects Laureola's insistence on the need to preserve her honour (Núñez has her repeat San Pedro's arguments), he states the position in terms which would scarcely have satisfied the strict *pundonor* of the Siglo de Oro: 'pues ya tu limpieza se había mostrado, nunca nadi dixera lo cierto que por dudoso no se toviera, viendo la paga que a los otros havía dado' (I1^v [66]). His exemplary punishment of one set of calumniators would have given him and Laureola licence to behave, it would seem, as they chose. Laureola has simply been wantonly cruel: the Author refers (H1$^\text{v}$ [52]) to 'la crueldad que usó contra quien tan merecido el galardón le tenía', and Leriano, even after hearing her expressions of love and repentance, goes so far as to say: 'creo que si [Laureola] pudiera otra vez verme bivo, tornaría a darme más pena' (H6$^\text{r}$ [60]).

Núñez's Laureola is, then, in love with Leriano, and promises just a little more than San Pedro's. She is quite clear that Leriano could never have married her: 'Leriano, según mi estado y linaje, por muger no me merecía' (I2$^\text{v}$ [68]), but she tells the Author in general terms that 'con la vida se puede alcançar lo que con la muerte se desespera' (H3$^\text{v}$ [55]), and, more specifically, that if Leriano had not killed himself they could at least have seen each other: 'trabajara con el Rey mi señor su libertad [. . .] para que entrase en la corte y hoviera lugar de verme' (I2$^\text{v}$ [68]).

All this now creates for Nicolás Núñez further problems: was Leriano's death a quite pointless tragedy? And this brings us to the central point of Núñez's continuation: the sustained debate about the justification of Leriano's suicide. 'Nunca deviera él perder la esperança', says Laureola (I2$^\text{v}$ [68]) in her final speech to the Author; but it would seem that the *esperança* to which she refers is not the hope of some specific *galardón*, but that Hope of which the loss constitutes the theological sin of Despair. Núñez is well aware that Despair is the unforgivable sin, and it is only the thought of falling into that sin which restrains the Author from suicide: 'muchas vezes de mi desesperada vida con la muerte tomara vengança, si pudiera fazello sin que por desesperado me pudiera culpar' (H3$^\text{v}$ [56]). And if the Author expresses the pious hope that Leriano is in Heaven ('Agora si tú supiesses el arrepentimiento de Laureola, trocarías la gloria celestial, si por dicha la tienes, por la temporal' (H3$^\text{v}$-H4$^\text{r}$ [56])), Núñez himself makes it clear that Leriano is in torment: 'te certifico', says Leriano, 'que por esto que fago, aunque es poca la habla, espero mucho el tormento' (H6$^\text{r}$ [60]), and the dream-spectre is finally summoned by a lugubrious voice, 'una boz muy triste', which calls: '¡Ven, Leriano, que tardas!' (I2$^\text{r}$ [67]).

There is, nevertheless, a certain ambiguity about Núñez's attitude to suicide, for to choose damnation is, for him, not self-evidently wrong. San Pedro put it in extreme form in his *Sermón* when he told the faithful lover that 'si tu amiga [. . .] quisiera condenarte, vete al infierno en cuerpo y en ánima. ¿Qué más beneficio quieres que querer lo que ella quiere?'[15] And there are hints of a similar attitude in Núñez. The Author, the good and faithful friend, might have been prepared to damn himself if it could have helped Leriano in any way, but 'como pensé que con mi muerte [i.e. suicide] no se cobrava la vida del muerto, vi que era yerro perder el alma' (I3$^\text{r}$ [69]), and, until Laureola convinces him temporarily of the contrary, he begins by believing that Leriano's suicide justified itself simply by making Laureola sorry: 'Si Leriano pudiera alcançar a saber el arrepentimiento de Laureola, diera su muerte por bien empleada' (H1^r [52]) and (to Leriano): 'si con la muerte ganaste la voluntad que agora muestra, por bien empleada la deves dar' (H4^v [56]).

Núñez, obliged to concede that suicide is to be condemned on theological grounds, is nevertheless prepared to argue the merits of choosing damnation for the sake of some higher good. Clearly, there is an element of mere amorous conceit in the notion that the sufferings of unrequited love are worse than the torments of Hell, but in the end Núñez does acquiesce in the rightness and inevitability of Leriano's suicide, and though, as Otis Green notes, 'the problem is complex',[16] there is some evidence here to support the thesis of Erna Ruth Berndt that suicide was not invariably regarded as inexcusable in the late fifteenth century.[17] Professor Green finds only some very few works—*Siervo libre de Amor, Cárcel de Amor, Tragedia Policiana*—in which suicide is presented 'without condemnation or extenuation' (p. 224); but there are examples to add: the dialogues of Diego Ramírez Villaescusa cited by Dr Berndt and the tale of María Coronel which, while it is also retold by the dying Leriano of San Pedro's novel, derives from the entirely laudatory account of her suicide given by Juan de Mena in the *Laberinto*, st. 79.

In any event, Núñez fails to condemn Leriano's suicide. In the earlier part of the continuation, although Laureola (in the flesh) argues in rather vague terms that 'while there is life, there is hope', the Author finds his death amply justified in producing Laureola's repentance. When the dream-ghost of Leriano appears, the Author sees only that he is finally at peace: 'vile el gesto tan hermoso que parecía que nunca pesar havía passado' (H5^v [59]). Leriano himself tells the Author that his death was inevitable ('ni yo, según el principio levava, podía escusar de llegar a este fin' (H6^r [60])), that he no longer wants anything from Laureola ('sus mercedes ya no las quiero', *ibid.*), and that there was simply no point in his going on living: 'fuera bien bivir para servilla, aunque no para gozalla; pero como nunca supe de su respuesta de lo que más se servía [. . .] dexéme morir' (H6^v [60-61]).

The debate swings in the other direction when Laureola (in the Author's dream-vision) attacks Leriano, to the extent that the Author is temporarily won over: 'como sus razones a mi pensar parecían justas, nunca creí que Leriano tuviera ninguna cosa que le responder' (H8^v [64]). But Leriano's reply answers Laureola's accusation point by point. The essence of his argument is that he had only one purpose in life, to be of service to Laureola: 'no codiciava bivir sino para servirte' (I1^r [65]), that there was nothing further he could do for her except allow himself to die, that it was not a question of reward since he was already amply rewarded: 'con sólo mirarme, cuanto te pudiera servir me pagavas', and that he was unworthy of her: 'de lo mucho que merescías se me membrava, y de merecerte estava dudoso' (11^r [65]). He simply could not have believed, without her expressly saying so, that there was anything to live for: 'cuanto mayor era la merced, tanto menos la creía, y con esto hize la obra que vees' [65-66]. But he goes on to dismiss as trivial the reasons she had given for her silence, and asks one final boon: 'que me des las manos que te bese, porque desta gloria goze en la muerte' (11^v [66]). Leriano, then, is in no way at fault, and the blame is to be placed squarely on Laureola, whose reasons for terminating their relationship (Núñez fails to refer explicitly to the correspondence and secret intimate conversation which San Pedro's Laureola refused to continue) are dismissed as invalid.

Núñez has accepted part of San Pedro's position—that Leriano had, apparently, nothing left to live for—but by refusing to believe that Laureola could have remained unaffected by his devotion, has turned San Pedro's idealized heroine into a careless trifler. And there is perhaps a little more to it than that. The fact is that many fifteenth- and sixteenth-century readers were incapable of accepting the uncompromising feminism of San Pedro or of subscribing whole-heartedly to the ideal of selfless devotion. Like the Italian translator of *Arnalte y Lucenda,* who added a preface roundly to abuse the innocent heroine of that story,[18] Nicolás Núñez has no real respect for the lady and her unique individuality, but believes, one feels, that she ought to be grateful for the attention shown her. We have, in fact, a fundamental failure of comprehension. Whereas San Pedro displayed a perfect lover accepting without reproach his inevitable fate, since he had attached his constant love to an unattainable object, Núñez insists on the pathos rather than the dignity of Leriano's death and finds a culprit not in the complex but neutral circumstances of his situation—which nothing could alter—but in a woman over-scrupulous about negligible gossip, who failed to appreciate the intensity of her lover's passion, who failed to succour him in his hour of need, and whose excuses are merely frivolous: 'con lo que te escusas, más te condenas' (11^v [66]). Who can say that Núñez's distortion of San Pedro's feminist extremism did not render the *Cárcel de Amor* more acceptable to contemporary audiences?

[*Studies in Spanish Literature of the Golden Age Presented to Edward M. Wilson* (London: Tamesis, 1973), pp. 357-66]

Notes

1. So Regula Langbehn-Rohland, *Zur Interpretation der Romane des Diego de San Pedro* (Heidelberg, 1970), p. 15, n. 48, rejects Palau's notice of it on the grounds of the B.M. Catalogue's silence. Actually, the Catalogue also has the collation of the book wrong, printing 'l' for 'i'.

2. The same copy, identifiable by the signatures of its owners, was described by Gallardo, III, col. 970, No. 3229. The colophon begins: 'Acabose el presente tratado intitulado Carcel de amor que hizo Nicolas nuñez'. Gallardo notes only that it lacks the title-page, fol. A1, but Anna Krause, who reported its existence in California in 'Apunte bibliográfico sobre D. de S. P.', *RFE*, 36 (1952), 126-30, describes it as rather more seriously defective, with missing pages replaced by manuscript. By failing to mention the date ('a dos dias de junio en el año de nuestro Saluador Mil y quinientos'), she has misled Dr Langbehn-Rohland into supposing that it is undated and that its anteriority to Logroño 1508 is not certain.

3. Fadrique Alemán employs the very superior wood-engravings of the Catalan translation, published in Barcelona in 1493. They may be seen, greatly reduced, in Vindel.

4. *Orígenes*, II, NBAE, VII (Madrid, 1907), pp. 29-36.

5. This volume may have been assigned a new catalogue-number. Simón Díaz gives it as R-13346: No. 6251 in *Bibliografía*, III, 2, revised ed. (Madrid, 1965).

6. [Page-references to Keith Whinnom's edition, in *Dos opúsculos isabelinos* (1979), are given in brackets.]

7. In the Edición Nacional, II (repr. Santander, 1962), 43. The Edición Nacional of the works of M. P. does not reprint the texts.

8. A generation later we have very brief and prejudiced comments from Vives and Valdés which need not concern us.

9. Menéndez Pelayo has 'en aquella corte'.

10. 'El mundo sentimental de la *Cárcel de Amor*', *RFE*, 37 (1953), 163-93, p. 176.

11. San Pedro, *Obras*, ed. S. Gili Gaya, Clásicos Castellanos (Madrid, 1951), pp. 131-32. [Page-references to Keith Whinnom's 1972 edition of San Pedro's *Cárcel* are given in brackets; here, 98.]

12. See B. W. Wardropper, 'The Unconscious Mind in Calderón's *El pintor de su deshonra*', *HR*, 18 (1950), 285-301, pp. 287-89.

13. *El amor y el matrimonio secreto en los libros de caballería* (Madrid, 1948), pp. 122-23.

14. Later editions, and Menéndez Pelayo, have '*que* a guardar [. . .]'.

15. Ed. Gili Gaya, pp. 105-06 [*Obras*, II, ed. Whinnom (1973), 178].

16. 'Suicide', in his *Spain and the Western Tradition*, III (Madison and Milwaukee, 1965), pp. 204-24.

17. *Amor, muerte y Fortuna en 'La Celestina'* (Madrid, 1963), pp. 112-14.

18. Bartolomeo Maraffi describes Lucenda's behaviour as 'una lunga, grave e insolita ingratitudine (anzi inhumanissima crudeltà) d'una donna di sangue, certamente

nobile, ma di costumi rudissima', and speaks of 'innumerabili discortesie verso un splendido e valorosissimo cavaliere Arnalte nominato'. All Italian ladies are urged to vituperate Lucenda and be kind to their lovers, for 'questa è la vera pietà'.

9

Fray Íñigo de Mendoza, Fra Jacobo Maza, and the Affiliation of Some Early MSS of the *Vita Christi*

It was Mr F. J. Norton who drew my attention to a forgotten little quarto volume of which the title-page runs as follows:

> Tractato pervtile & deletabile no-|minato amatoriũ acto ad ordi|nare lo amore humano alli de|biti virtu & deuiario [*sic*] de om|ne illicito amore in che | solũ cõsiste virtu no|uamẽte *com*posto da | frate Jacobo ma|za de rhegio ad | instantia de | Dom ramũ|do de Cardona: Uice re del regno | Neapolitano.[1]

The colophon indicates that it was 'Impresso in Napoli per Madona Caterina qual fo mogliere de magistro Sigismondo Mayr. Nel anno del Signor .M.D.XVII. a di XXX. de Decembre'. I have been unable to discover anything about the author beyond the information which he himself supplies at the end of his so-called 'Prologus' (which comes, in fact, at the end of the book). There he writes: 'fratre Iacobe Maza de la cita de Regio & prouincia de Calabria & ordine minore de la obseruãtia: lo quale molti fatighi pigliai ĩ cõponere la dicta opera. ad utilita de li degenti & ad honor de Dio lo quale in secula secul*orum* sia laudato.'

This curious moralizing work, in which Fra Jacobo supports his points with quotations from a wide variety of sources, may well merit further study; but for the present I confine my attention to a passage which occurs at the conclusion of a chapter entitled 'Como la bona cõuersatione pr*e*serua lhõ del las. amore' (Part II, Book V, Chapter 5). Here Fra Jacobo thought it apposite to quote from the work of his fellow Franciscan of the Observance, Fray Íñigo de Mendoza: 'Certi uersi che un fratre spirituale nominato fratre Ynigo de Mendoza Castigliano me li parse qua ponere: & non transposti adteso omne lingua ha alchuna cosa propria che non ha unaltra: & pero absurda pare omne cosa per bona che sia facta in la sua lingua trasposta in altra lingua' (fol. Q1^r).[2]

Fra Jacobo then proceeds (fol. Q1^{r-v})to quote eight stanzas from the *Vita Christi*. The mangled form in which they appear can no doubt be attributed to Fra Jacobo's handwriting, a compositor who knew little or no Spanish, and the failure of the author, usual in this period, to proof-read his work. I transcribe them as they are printed (resolving the abbreviations of *que*, *qui*, and the nasal, and changing only the long *s*) and print alongside them the reconstructed Spanish from which I assume them to derive.[3] I give these stanzas the numbers which they have in the critical edition of Rodríguez-Puértolas.[4]

16. Co tenor dela maldat	Con temor dela maldat
del uitio q*ue* aq*ui* non nombro	del uicio que aqui non nombro
en tan flacca humanidat	en tan flacca humanidat
sempre la uergindad	siempre la uerginidad
este la barua e nellombro	este la barua en ell ombro
che las q*ue* quieren guardarse	que las que quieren guardarse
de enturuyar ta*n* claro nombre	de enturuyar tan claro nombre
asi deuen enterrarse	asi deuen encerrarse
q*ue* puedan marauellarse	que puedan marauellarse
qn [*sic*] uieren algund ombre	quando uieren algund ombre.

18. La estoppa no*n* esta segura	La estopa no esta segura
in ablas con los tizones	en ablas con los tizones
ni la uirgindad tura	ni la uirginidad tura
in la muger q*ue* procura	en la muger que procura
la abla con los uarones	la habla con los uarones
ghaylla q*ue* non esperalla	huylla que no esperalla
tal guerra de mi conseyo	tal guerra de mi consejo
do ualen menos sinfalla	do ualen menos sin falla
los arnesos de mi salla	los arneses de Misalla
che las armas del coniyos	que las armas del conejo.

17. La liepre per non encouarse	La liebre per no encouarse
alaueyes perden la uida	a uezes pierde la uida
la uergen por demostrarse	la uergen por demostrarse
hauemos uisto tornarse	hauemos uisto tornarse
de uergen encorumpida	de uergen en corumpida

por saglir de la barrera
muchos muren tristamente
la uergen mucho placyera
es impossible q*ue* fuera
no*n* quiebre elasa elafrente

Prosegua poniendo exemplo de Dina
fiya de Iacob: & de Bersabe i muyer
de Vrias.

Exemplo.
19. Ca / Dina sy non saglera
aser de gentes mirada
ny deser uirgen pierdiera
ny menos per ella fuera
tanta sangre derramada
Bersabe syse lleuara
de no la uiera Dauid
ny el con ella peccara
ny ad su marido mactara
con mano agena en la lid

Otro Exemplo.
20. Sela formosa Thancar
su hermana de Absalon
leemos perse apatar
a solo dan de yantar
aotro su herman Amon
ser del dicho fortada
y con grand auyltamyento
luego presto desechada
ca dela qual errada
fue su myo appartamyemto

21. Es en gratioso partido
el q*ue* trahen todas ya
de traher por appellido
y las mas dellas fingido
primo aca: primo acculla
pues sy deudo tam certano

por sallir de la barrera
muchos mueren tristemente
la uergen mucho plaçera
es impossible que fuera
non quiebre el asa e la frente.

Prosigue poniendo exemplo de Dina
fija de Iacob: & de Bersabe muger
de Vrias.

Exemplo.
Ca Dina sy non salliera
a ser de gentes mirada
ny de ser uirgen perdiera
ny menos per ella fuera
tanta sangre derramada
Bersabe sy se lleuara
do no la uiera Dauid
ny el con ella peccara
ny a su marido matara
con mano agena en la lid.

Otro Exemplo.
Dela fermosa Thamar
su hermana de Absalon
leemos per se apartar
a solo dar de yantar
a otro su hermano Amon
ser del dicho [Amon] forcada
y con grand auyltamyento
luego presto desechada
causa dela qual errada
fue su nezio apartamyento.

Es un gracioso partido
el que trahen todas ya
de traher por apellido
y las mas dellas fingido
primo aca: primo aculla
pues sy deudo tan cercano

a Thamar fiyo burlarse
es un conseyo muy sano
con el mas lexos que hermano
ni con el nunca appartarse

a Thamar fizo burlarse
es un consejo muy sano
con el mas lexos que hermano
ni con el nunca apartarse.

22. Por que parentera dama
segundes nuostra castilla
en acha que de nuestrama
que enla tama que en la fama
siempre regostiue manyilla
cha o / tiega o / perde el tiento
fasta dar consigo emonguas
orrestiue detrimento
en su fama y casamento
con lo che diyen las lenguas

Porque parentera dama
segund es nuestra Castilla
en achaque de nuestrama
que en la cama que en la fama
siempre resciue manzilla
ca o ciega o pierde el tiento
fasta dar consigo en menguas
o rresciue detrimento
en su fama y casamiento
con lo que dizen las lenguas.

24. Assi que dieue euitar
con esquidao continente
la doncella por casar
el parlar y el carrear
del pariente y no pariente
pero la uergen doncella
en que uien tales ademanes
fallan buena cara en ella
desde entonces fiar della
un bon bacho de alacranes

Assi que deue euitar
con esquiuo continente
la doncella por casar
el parlar y el cartear
del pariente y no pariente
pero la uergen doncella
en quien tales ademanes
fallan buena cara en ella
desde entonces fiar della
un buen saco de alacranes.

Apart from the fact that Fray Íñigo de Mendoza is now another name to be added to the list of Spanish writers known and quoted, copied, or imitated in sixteenth-century Italy, the discovery of this fragment assumes an unexpected importance when it is set in the context of the several known versions of the *Vita Christi*. It clearly does not derive from any of the printed editions, and, as I shall show, an inspection of the variant readings appears to oblige us alternatively to posit yet another redaction of that seemingly much reworked poem, or, still more surprisingly, to isolate three of the earliest MSS in a stemma which would have to be regarded as aberrant and unreliable.

It is well known that, even though the work was never completed, there are four distinct versions of the *Vita Christi*, which for the moment I identify as *a*, *b*, *c*, and *d*, to avoid confusion with my subsequent hypothetical renumbering.[5]

a) In the primitive version, which is most nearly represented by the text in the *Cancionero de Oñate-Castañeda*,[6] Fray Íñigo confused and made one episode of the Presentation in the Temple (Luke 2: 22-39, in which the priest is named as Simeon) and the Circumcision, even identifying the circumcising priest as Simeon: 'Esse cultre, Simeon, / un poco solo deten'.

In addition he included two violent and remarkably explicit diatribes, one attacking by name Enrique IV, the Archbishop of Toledo, and many of the grandees, and the other assailing the Dominicans for their refusal to accept Franciscan views on the Immaculate Conception.

b) In the second stage of the text's history, the offensive stanzas about the grandees were excised. This version is represented by two MSS, Bibliothèque Nationale, Paris, MS Esp. 305, and British Library, MS Egerton 939, although the scribe of the Paris text, presumably later, also had access to a manuscript of the primitive version, since he was able to copy the deleted stanzas at the end of the poem, with a note to indicate where they were to be inserted.

c) A third and more thorough-going revision is represented by MS Escurialense K-III-7.[7] The Presentation and the Circumcision are now clearly distinguished, there is an apology to the Dominicans instead of an attack on them, and there are many additional stanzas, changes in the order of the stanzas, and evidence of extensive rewriting.

d) A final version, with further sundry changes, was given to the press of Centenera in Zamora in 1482 (Biblioteca Nacional, Madrid, Incunable 1290). All later editions are simply copies of this.

There are, of course, other MSS of the *Vita Christi*: in the *Cancionero de Vindel* in the Library of the Hispanic Society, New York (an extract of seventy-one stanzas), another in the Library of the University of Salamanca, one in the Biblioteca Nacional (MS 4114, a fragment), and one in private hands; but no one has as yet attempted to ascertain to which of the redactions *a*, *b*, *c*, or even *d*,[8] they should be assigned.

In his critical edition of the *Vita Christi*, Rodríguez-Puértolas distinguished clearly the three major stages, grouping as *a* (*a*, *a*1 and *a*2) my *a* and *b*. Being denied access to Oñate-Castañeda, he used the earliest printed edition as his base text and noted variant readings in Paris, Egerton, and Esc. K-III-7. However, while he established beyond doubt the relationship of the Paris and Egerton manuscripts and clearly defined the stages through which the *Vita Christi* passed, he did not attempt to work out a detailed scheme of affiliation. In order to determine, however, whether the Fra Jacobo fragment derives from the *a*, *b*, *c*, or *d* redaction of the work, we are obliged to examine closely the variant readings; and the most cursory inspection shows that we are faced with some surprising difficulties.

In the first place, there can be no question but that the fragment quoted in the Italian *Tractato* belongs in one respect to stage *a* or *b*. The sequence of stanzas, 16, 18, 17, 19-22, 24, with the inversion of 17 and 18 and the omission of 23, is precisely what we find in Oñate-Castañeda (*a*), and in Paris and Egerton (*b*). It is in redaction *c*, represented by the Escorial manuscript, that we first find them as 16-24 of the later printed version. But in a series of very distinctively different readings Fra Jacobo's fragment agrees with Escorial and Zamora (the first printed edition) against Oñate-Castañeda, Paris, and Egerton.[9] For example, in 16-7, 'de *enturbiar* tan *claro* nombre' is what we find in Esc. and Za, whereas OC, P, and Eg. have '*densuziar* (OC) / de *suziar* (P) / de *ensuziar* (Eg.) tan *limpio* nombre (all)'. We might, therefore, propose a scheme of affiliation and series of redactions like this:

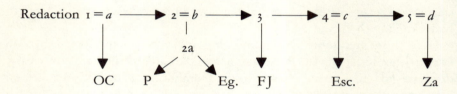

Redaction 1 = *a* ⟶ 2 = *b* ⟶ 3 ⟶ 4 = *c* ⟶ 5 = *d*

2a

OC   P   Eg.   FJ   Esc.   Za

The variant readings will support this hypothesis, provided we introduce into the schema a MS (which I have labelled 2a) between the second redaction and the MSS P and Eg., which share several readings which conflict with the readings of OC and FJ. But this superficially simple solution has two very unsatisfactory features. One is the number of separate redactions of the work which we must posit. Fray Íñigo was a busy preacher, and later courtier, who found time to compose a number of other quite substantial works,[10] and it is difficult to believe that he would have spared time to rewrite his original no fewer than four times, while not extending his life of Christ beyond the Massacre of the Innocents. It is equally difficult to suppose that when, for instance, he drafted redaction 4, he would have adopted certain readings from redaction 3 if redaction 3 had been the work of someone else, an inaccurate copyist, or even a presumptuous friend who thought he could improve on his original. And the second difficulty is that, although some of the variants are substantial enough to rank as significant (e.g. 'de ensuziar tan limpio nombre' / 'de enturbiar tan claro nombre'), the retouching viewed as a whole does not, in FJ, constitute a substantial revision of the text of redactions 1 and 2, the changes are not obviously improvements, and it is again hard to understand why Fray Íñigo should have rewritten a very long poem of almost 4,000 lines in order to make such very minor changes.

It is, of course, not impossible that, if someone had requested a copy of the work, Fray Íñigo might have written in some minor emendations in his own copy of the poem before lending it for copying, and used it when it was returned as the basis for redaction 4. The hypothetical affiliation I have set out above cannot be definitively discarded. But there is another possible scheme which will solve our immediate problem of the variant readings, as well as some others, even though its consequences are somewhat disconcerting.

The scheme I shall propose (to which the reader will at once perceive one major objection) is as follows:

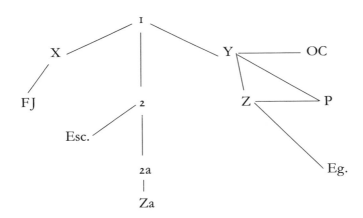

I shall return to the variants in a moment. While this scheme will account for the data provided by stanzas 16 to 24, the one major discrepancy which requires explanation is the deletion from P, Eg., and Esc., but not from OC, of the stanzas attacking the grandees. The only way of accommodating this anomaly is to suppose that the offending stanzas directed against the grandees were twice excised independently, by the copyist of the hypothetical Z, and by Fray Íñigo himself when he drafted redaction 2. A closer inspection of the facts suggests that there are sundry points which favour this hypothesis.

The hypothetical Z, represented by Eg. and by P (minus the appendix of excised stanzas which must derive from a different source), gives us the simple deletion of some alarming stanzas which name, amongst others, Enrique IV ('¡guay de vos, Enrique el Quarto!' 107), the Archbishop of

Toledo, Don Alonso Carrillo (108), Pedro Girón and Juan Pacheco (115B), the Duke of Alburquerque (115C), the Count of Plasencia (115D), and the Marquis of Santillana (115F).[11] But the deletions are effected as follows: the three stanzas 107 to 109, naming Enrique IV, the Archbishop, and an unidentified 'Duque' are deleted, but then the copyist goes back to his text, conserving the more generally worded 'reprehensiones' (from 110 on) until Fray Íñigo again begins to cite individual grandees by name. At this point the copyist does not merely excise the libellous stanzas, but gives up entirely and moves on to the next section, cutting out 115A to 115V, i.e. twenty-two stanzas, even though a majority of these stanzas are relatively innocuous, naming no specific persons. Whoever our censor was, it would seem that he began tentatively, intending to preserve the stanzas critical of the aristocracy in general, but then, either afraid of some disjointedness (though it would not have been especially evident) or simply losing patience, decided to make his task easier by removing all the remainder of the passage.

Fray Íñigo also, of course, deleted the offending stanzas, but, in the text with which we know he was certainly involved, namely redaction 2, represented by Esc., his procedure contrasts in every particular with the pruning methods of the copyist of our hypothetical Z. In the first place, he refers to the offending stanzas and offers his excuses for composing them in the first instance: 'Desculpase del auer nombrado en el primero trasunto [. . .]' (rubric to stanza 109; and note that he mentions only one earlier redaction, 'el primero'), and goes on to substitute newly composed stanzas attacking the rapaciousness, irresponsibility, and impiety of the great nobility. He has repented only of singling out certain individuals by name. Secondly, and in a similar spirit, he apologizes for his unchristian attack on the Dominicans and removes those stanzas also.

The stanzas about the grandees which Fray Íñigo was persuaded to delete are alarming. Even a modern reader must sense the temerity of his uninhibited condemnation of some of the most powerful figures in the land, and it is not hard to imagine that the copyist of Z, possibly transcribing the *Vita Christi* for an aristocratic patron, was sensitive enough to exercise his own censorship—which in the event did not coincide with Fray Íñigo's own. If he knew that the Dominicans were also grievously offended (162 to 162E: '¡O frayle preycador / daqui comiença a temblar!', etc.), he clearly did not care. One may fairly conclude, I believe, that the independent, and not entirely identical, removal of some of the stanzas attacking the grandees does not lead us to a scheme of affiliation involving an intimate relationship of P, Eg., and Esc. We have, of course, no means of knowing whether Fra Jacobo read these stanzas in the MS to which he had access, but on the scheme of affiliation proposed above it must be supposed that he did.

Before examining the variants proper, we need to consider which it is legitimate to take into account. As is well known, copyists' practices vary widely. Some will quite uniformly impose their own spelling-preferences; others will slavishly follow their text; while a majority fall somewhere between these extremes. The number of alternative spellings available in the fifteenth century—and even in the seventeenth—are such that total coincidence of the orthography of two texts is conclusive evidence of the dependence of one upon the other.[12] On the other hand, enormous orthographic discrepancies will not serve to demonstrate that two texts are unrelated. If, therefore, FJ is a crucial document for reconstructing even a fragment of the original redaction of the *Vita Christi*, we must distinguish the layers of interference. First, although the compositor employed by Madona Caterina Mayr is almost certainly guilty of some typographical errors, it would be fair to assume that, since his copy was in a foreign language, he would have followed it more closely than a Spanish compositor; but how far we can distinguish his errors from Fra Jacobo's is not easy to determine, even though Fra Jacobo allows it to be inferred that he was familiar with Castilian. To one or other of these Italians we must attribute such Italianisms as *che, saglir, nuostra, ad, in, tristamente*, etc., the rendering of intervocalic *i/j* as *y* (*conseyo, fiya, coniyo*) and the misreadings of long *ʒ* as *y* (*fiyo, veyes, manyilla*) and of *c* as *t* (*tiega, rrestiue, tama, fortada*). But it might be unwise to attribute to Fra Jacobo or the Italian compositor other inconsistencies or departures from normal Castilian orthography, word-division, and phonology. Even the ultracorrections like *dieue* and *pierdiera* could be attributed to an earlier Catalan scribe, and there are other features which seem to point to the hypothetical MS X's being of eastern provenance. The vowels of *vergen, maravella*, etc., could be ascribed to Catalan influence, and *per* certainly occurs with some frequency in Castilian texts copied in Aragon in the fifteenth century. It is also suggestive that in one style of Aragonese hand current around 1500 it is difficult and sometimes impossible to see any difference between *t* and *c*, and that some Aragonese copyists will as frequently write *alcanca, lanca, pieca*, etc., as *alcança, lança, pieça*, etc.[13] Since Fray Íñigo himself was unequivocally Castilian, almost certainly born and brought up in Burgos,[14] we shall be justified in ignoring all variants which can be attributed to interference by Aragonese or Italian copyists or compositors. I therefore reconvert the Spanish which can be reconstructed from the FJ fragment to a neutral Castilian in what follows.

The scheme of affiliation I have proposed leads us to assume that in his original redaction of the *Vita Christi* Fray Íñigo wrote: stanza 16, Con temor de (line 1), que las que quieren guardarse (6), de enturbiar tan claro (7), asi deven encerrarse (8), quando vieren algun ombre (10); stanza 18, en fablas (2), la virginidad no tura (3); stanza 17, muchos mueren tristemente (7); stanza 19, a ser de gentes mirada (2), levara (in error for *lavara*, 5), ni su marido (9), con mano agena (10); stanza 20, a otro su hermano Amon (5), luego presto desechada (8); stanza 21, es un gracioso partido (1), de traer por apellido (3), ni con el nunca apartarse (10); stanza 22, la muy parentera dama (3), que en la cama que en la fama (4), ca (6); stanza 24, Asi que deve esquivar (in error, by anticipation of *esquivo*, for *evitar*, 1), con esquivo continente (2), en quien tales ademanes (7), desde entonces fiad della (9), un buen saco (10).

The copyist of X, from which the FJ fragment derives, altered 18-3 from 'la virginidad no tura' to 'ni la virginidad tura', in 19-5 emended 'levara' incorrectly to 'llevara', inverted lines 1 and 3 of stanza 22, in 24-1 made the intelligent change from 'esquivar' to 'evitar', and in 24-9 altered 'fiad' (or possibly 'fiat') to 'fiar'. The copyist of X was, in short, remarkably faithful.

It would take too much space to list all the variants of OC, P, and Eg., but the relationship of these three extant MSS and the hypothetical Y and Z can be adequately illustrated from the first stanza of our fragment. In 16-1, Y, OC, Z, and P correctly copied 'Con temor', while Eg. miscopied it as 'Por temor'. P, on the other hand, made nonsense of 16-2 as 'del vicio que qua qua no nombro'. 16-6 was correctly copied by Y and OC, but miscopied in Z, and consequently in P and Eg., as 'ca las que [. . .]'. Y, and consequently all the texts dependent on it, changed the original reading of 16-7 to 'de enturbiar tan limpio nombre'. And so one might continue stanza by stanza.

In the whole of the passage we have been examining there are only two details in the whole list of variants which do not fall automatically into place. Instead of the logical 'lavara' for David and Bathsheba in 19-6, P has 'levara', uncomfortably close to FJ's 'llevara'; and in 24-7, Eg. has 'quando', as in Esc. and all the printed editions, in place of the 'en quien' of FJ, OC, P, and so also the hypothetical X, Y, and Z. But if these readings are not regarded as purely coincidental, no scheme of affiliation will accommodate them. Certainly the hypothesis of five redactions helps us here no more than the scheme I have argued for.

The consequence of all this is that the primitive version of the *Vita Christi* which Rodríguez-Puértolas reconstructed from P and Eg. and printed alongside the final revised version in his critical edition does not appear to be valid, or, to rephrase that conclusion in a way which does more justice to Rodríguez-Puértolas's invaluable labours, his otherwise legitimate reconstruction appears to be invalidated by the fresh evidence afforded by

OC and FJ. There are still four MSS to take into consideration which so far no Mendozan scholar has even looked at, and it may well be that some yet more complex system of relationships will have to be worked out. Meanwhile, since no one has even suggested a scheme of affiliation, I offer this tentative solution to the problem.

Manuel Criado de Val has argued that in editing medieval works which went through successive stages of elaboration (he refers specifically to the *Poema del Cid*, the *Libro de buen amor*, and *Celestina*), we should devote our attention to the final definitive version.[15] But there are also cogent reasons for paying some attention to a writer's first redaction, and in the case of the *Vita Christi* the problems presented by a series of revisions can be drastically reduced if we are able to discard the interventions and errors of a series of copyists. The whole problem is less daunting if we can suppose that there was one primitive redaction of the *Vita Christi*, one second and thorough-going revision, and what amounts to only some rather minor tinkering (2a) with the text which was given to the press. In the elucidation of these problems, it may well prove that an obscure Italian Franciscan had a not insignificant role to play.

[*Annali di Ca'Foscari*, 16 (1977 [1979]), 129-39]

Notes

1. I am indebted to Mr Norton not only for informing me of his find but for xeroxes of his own copy of it. There is a specimen in the British Library, 232.g.13, and there are doubtless others in Italian libraries, but it is not to be found either in the Bibliothèque Nationale, Paris, or in the Biblioteca Nacional, Madrid. Neither is it noticed by Benedetto Croce, *La Spagna nella vita italiana durante la Rinascenza* (Bari: Laterza, 1915, 4th revised ed. 1949); by Arturo Farinelli, *Italia e Spagna*, 2 vols (Turin: Bocca, 1929); by J. L. Laurenti, *Relaciones literarias entre España e Italia: ensayo de bibliografía de literatura comparada* (Boston: G. K. Hall, 1972); nor Franco Meregalli, *Presenza della letteratura spagnola in Italia* (Florence: Sansoni, 1974). I have not attempted to search further.

2. Fra Jacobo acknowledges his source as 'sancto Thomasi: xxxviii. distintione capitulo. Loquitio', but I have been unable to locate this. St Thomas Aquinas expresses similar ideas (deriving from I Cor. 14) in his *Summa theologica*, I, q.39, 3 ad 2, and II-2, q.176, 1.

3. Note that I have made no emendation in the Spanish which is not absolutely necessary, leaving orthographical inconsistencies, the imperfect rhymes -at/-ad,

and some possibly surprising forms such as *per*, *vergen*, *forcada*, etc., about which I have more to say below. I have changed *non* to *no* where the syllable-count demands it, but only because this particular error yields no useful information about the origin or affiliation of our fragment. No doubt some minor points of my reconstruction may be arguable, but I base no arguments on such points.

4. Julio Rodríguez-Puértolas, *Fray Íñigo de Mendoza y sus 'Coplas de Vita Christi'* (Madrid: Gredos, 1968). The numbering here corresponds with the order of the stanzas in the early printed editions.

5. For a very much fuller account see Rodríguez-Puértolas, pp. 84-117, and his most useful table of concordances, pp. 285-86. I have not followed Rodríguez-Puértolas's system of *siglas* for reasons which will soon become apparent.

6. It should be noted that Rodríguez-Puértolas was most unfortunately denied access to the *Cancionero de Oñate-Castañeda*, which was in private hands when his book was printed, and indeed came to light in a Sotheby's sale after his manuscript was handed to the printer. *Oñate-Castañeda* is now in the Houghton Library of Harvard University, but since the microfilm to which I had access lacked folios 315^v and 316^r because of a photographing error, I am indebted to the kindness of Michel Garcia of the Casa de Velázquez for a transcription of the relevant stanzas in that codex.

7. For a more detailed description see my 'MS Escurialense K-III-7: el llamado *Cancionero de Fray Íñigo de Mendoza*', *Filología*, 7 (1961 [1963]), 161-72 [English original, pp. 36-45, above].

8. As I have shown elsewhere (see note 7), the other works of Mendoza copied in Esc. K-III-7 derive from printed sources. The proof lies not merely in the coincidence of the readings but, more unusually, in the scribe's scrupulous following of the compositors' orthographic preferences.

9. From this point on I refer to the various texts by the following abbreviations: OC, Oñate-Castañeda; P, the MS in the Bibliothèque Nationale, Paris; Eg., the British Library MS in the Egerton collection; Esc., MS Esc. K-III-7; FJ, Fra Jacobo's fragment; Za, the first printed edition by Centenera of Zamora.

10. For Fray Íñigo's life and other works see Rodríguez-Puértolas, Cap. I, 'Biografía', pp. 13-65, and Cap. II, 'Obras', pp. 66-83.

11. I follow Rodríguez-Puértolas's system of identification: he employs letters for the stanzas in P and/or Eg. which cannot be matched in the printed editions.

12. See note 8. The best illustration of the use to which a study of compositors' spelling-preferences can be put is undoubtedly Robert M. Flores, *The Compositors of the First and Second Madrid Editions of 'Don Quixote' Part I* (London: Modern Humanities Research Association, 1975).

13. An unpublished piece of fifteenth-century fiction, *La coronación de la señora Gracisla*, the recently acquired Biblioteca Nacional MS 22020, provides abundant evidence to support these assertions (*per*, *forcada*, etc.). [The text was published at the same time as this article, in Whinnom's *Dos opúsculos isabelinos* (1979).]

14. See Rodríguez-Puértolas, especially pp. 37-38.

15. 'Las condiciones de la redacción juglaresca en función de la edición de textos medievales españoles', in *Actele celui de al XII-lea Congres Internaţional de Lingvistică şi Filologie Romanică* (Bucarest: Editura Academiei Republicii Socialiste România, 1971 [1977]), II, 43-51.

10

'*La Celestina*', 'the *Celestina*', and L2 Interference in L1

Given that '*LC*', standing for '*La Celestina*', is the abbreviation adopted by this excellent journal for the [*sic*] *Tragicomedia de Calisto y Melibea*, it may well seem churlish, and will in all probability prove profitless, to protest that '*La Celestina*' is incorrect in both English and Spanish: unless one prefers the lengthier but more precise titles of the early editions, the book should be called quite simply '*Celestina*' or, in Spanish, 'la *Celestina*'.

The potential ambiguity which eponymous heroes, or heroines, consistently create is, in fact, negligible in English, since Celestina may be distinguished from *Celestina* as easily as Hamlet from *Hamlet*. Modern Spanish removes even this possible source of confusion by some perfectly clear and simple rules: 'Se antepone el artículo [. . .] con los nombres que son títulos de obras; como EL *Edipo*, LA *Raquel*' (Real Academia Española, *Gramática de la lengua española*, nueva edición reformada, Madrid, 1931, §78 (b)); or, possibly even more explicitly, 'cuando una obra tiene por título un personaje, pues se dice "el *Otelo*" aunque en la obra sea solo "Otelo"' (Niceto Alcalá-Zamora, 'Observaciones' to §§865-68 of Andrés Bello and Rufino J. Cuervo, *Gramática de la lengua castellana*, Buenos Aires, 1945). It is true that these rules are not scrupulously observed by all modern Spanish-speaking critics, and that one can readily find numerous examples not only of '*La Celestina*' but also of the converse solecism (unnoticed, to my knowledge, by the grammarians), which consists in removing an article which properly belongs to the title and preposing it as a qualifier, as, for instance, in 'la *Vida es sueño*'. But a number of careful scholars (Menéndez Pelayo, Foulché-Delbosc, etc.) do invariably refer to 'la *Celestina*'; and just as 'el *Otelo*' translates back into English as '*Othello*', so 'la *Celestina*' should be translated simply as '*Celestina*'.

It may be important to emphasize that, despite sundry modern editions, the unofficial substitute title of the *Tragicomedia* was not originally *La Celestina* but *Celestina*. While we may perhaps disregard an early edition of the Italian translation entitled *Celestina: Tragicomedia di Calisto e Melibea*

(Venice, 1519), the Spanish Golden-Age editions which use this title have no article: Alcalá 1569 (copied in Antwerp in 1595 and 1599) is *Celestina: Tragicomedia de Calisto y Melibea*, while the expurgated edition of Madrid 1632 is *Tragicomedia de Calisto y Melibea vvlgarmente llamada Celestina*. But long before 1569 the title of *Celestina* was in widespread use. Although his Latin does not constitute evidence for the non-use of the article, Luis Vives calls it 'Celestina' in his *De institutione feminae christianae*, I, 5 (1529) and in his *De causis corruptarum artium* (1531). But later examples are unequivocal. In 1534 Feliciano de Silva published his *Segunda comedia de Celestina*; in 1535, in his *Diálogo de la lengua*, Valdés speaks more than once simply of 'Celestina': 'el autor de *Celestina*', etc.; in 1536 Gaspar Gómez entitled his sequel *Tercera parte de la tragicomedia de Celestina*; in 1539 Guevara, in his well-known attack on profane literature in *Aviso de privados y doctrinales*, writes of the 'libros, que es afrenta nombrarlos, como son *Amadís de Gaula*, *Tristan de Leonís*, *Primaleón*, *Cárcel de Amor* y *Celestina*'; in 1540, in his *Diferencias de libros que ay en el universo*, Alejo de Venegas, 'para dar a entender que todo género de perversidad se encerraba en ella', called it *Scelestina*; and so it goes on. In 1605 López de Úbeda in *La pícara Justina* is still saying 'en *Celestina*'. I cannot find a 'la *Celestina*' before the seventeenth century (Quevedo, Gracián, Salas Barbadillo), and then, although one might contend that the evidence is not entirely unequivocal, the references are clearly to the work and not the character, and I believe that we may legitimately suppose that in each case these writers are anticipating the modern rules ('la *Celestina*') rather than Amarita or Cejador ('*La Celestina*').

There are, of course, two other possible Spanish uses of the article which may have helped to confuse the issue. One, with a proper name, is seen in such forms as 'la Gómez' (which might be translated as 'the Gómez woman' or 'the Gómez girl') or, as in Correas's proverbs, 'la Marikita'. Except in the case of professional women—actresses, *prime donne*, or novelists ('la Guerrero', 'la Callas', 'la Pardo Bazán')—the article appears to have a mildly pejorative or despectuous function. But I see no justification for its use with 'Celestina', who in the text of the work is never referred to (if we may ignore 'madre', 'puta vieja', etc.) except as 'Celestina'. The other occurs when a proper name becomes a common noun, so that one is obliged to refer, with the article, to 'la celestina de un prostíbulo', 'the madam of a brothel', but, while conceivably a contributing factor to the confusion, this is logically irrevelant to the present problem.

The reluctance of editors, and even compositors, to accept these simple facts is curious, and in various articles and books in which I have alluded to *Celestina*, the title of the work has emerged in print as '*La Celestina*'. '*La*

Celestina', although I believe it is wrong, is, however, as nothing in comparison with the barbarism of 'the *Celestina*', which is no more and no less than a blatant hispanism, demonstrating the interference of L2 in L1.[1] Indeed, I am moved to offer this modest protest primarily because I have the impression that this gross solecism is spreading with virus-like rapidity. Alongside such old-established forms as 'the *Laberinto de Fortuna*' and 'the *Cárcel de Amor*' (for which it might be possible to make some sort of feeble case) we now have not only 'the *Quijote*' and 'the *Celestina*' (for which see any bibliography of *Celestina* or some previous numbers of *Celestinesca*) but also 'the *Diana*', 'the *Lazarillo*', 'the *Guzmán*', and so forth. No one speaks of 'the *Hamlet*' or 'the *David Copperfield*', and while there exists a very obvious explanation for terms like 'the *Quijote*', namely unthinking literal translation from the Spanish, there is surely no possible justification for it. If I am wrong, I should be most grateful if someone would tell me why.

[*Cel*, 4, no. 2 (Nov. 1980), 19-21]

Note

1. For this and other phenomena of linguistic interference see my forthcoming article (in which I cite 'the *Celestina*' as one example), 'Non-Primary Types of Language', in [*Logos semantikos: studia linguistica in honorem Eugenio Coseriu 1921–1981*, V: *Geschichte und Architektur der Sprachen* (Berlin: Walter de Gruyter; Madrid: Gredos, 1981), pp. 227-41].

II

The Problem of the 'Best-Seller'
in Spanish Golden-Age Literature

The problems of assessing the merits of 'popular literature' and of placing it within the concept of literature have been looming ever larger in recent years.[1] It is a development which may be attributed in part to modern egalitarian notions—a denial of the élitist nature of literature—in part to the necessity of broadening the concept of literature and its criteria in order to accommodate and evaluate the products of modern mass culture, and possibly in some measure to critical examination by educational theorists of methods of presenting literature to the young. In the study of Spanish literature of the Golden Age we have seen increasing attention being paid to the *pliegos sueltos* and the *literatura de cordel*, popular anecdotes and the books of *facecias*.[2]

'Popular literature' is a vast and difficult topic, and I intend to touch on only one aspect of it, by looking at some Golden-Age best-sellers. This limits our difficulties in three ways: first and most obviously by restricting the time and place of our inquiries; secondly by confining us to the examination of whole books and allowing us to ignore the fortunes of individual tales, jokes, and shorter rhymes; and, thirdly, by construing 'popular' simply as 'widely diffused', and not as implying something produced by or for the populace, a distinction which is in any case, in this period, of somewhat dubious validity.

Again like all Gaul, what might be referred to in broad terms as 'the problem of the best-seller in the Golden Age' divides itself into three parts. Our first, fundamental, and possibly unexpected difficulty lies in establishing precisely which books did lead in the Golden-Age popularity stakes, and I should like to spend some time on that. A second problem arises when we try to account for the popularity of a best-seller. Since we are trained to recognize and appreciate literary merit, we tend to assume that the works we study have gained a place in the history of Spanish literature by virtue of their literary value. But the best-seller leads us instantly into much deeper waters. Literary excellence—even when it exists—is a manifestly inadequate explanation, and we can find ourselves driven into some very dubious territory indeed. Ultimately, perhaps, we can offer no more than pseudo-psychological and pseudo-sociological explanations which are largely un-verifiable, but the effort, I think, must be made, and I shall return to this difficulty before I conclude.

We have a third problem, to which I am not prepared to offer any solution, in the discrepancy between what the readers, and writers, of former generations preferred to read, and what we, as professional critics and historians, choose to study and make our students study. I am not going to argue that our syllabuses should be dictated by a statistical examination of the frequency of manuscript copying or by the numbers and sizes of editions,[3] and there is probably no reason for us to feel very serious concern about the recovery of forgotten masterpieces which made no impact when they were first written; but it is hard to suppress some feeling of unease about the quantity of critical attention lavished on works which patently held little appeal for contemporary readers—two glaring examples are *Tirant lo Blanc* and *La Lozana andaluza*—and if at the same time we consistently ignore or pay scant attention to writers and works which at one time everyone read with enthusiasm, I cannot help feeling that as historians we must be failing in our task.

By and large, modern histories of Golden-Age literature probably achieve a better balance than those of the nineteenth century. But it could also be reasonably maintained that not every shift of emphasis has been in the right direction. It is illuminating to look at early histories of Spanish literature and see how differently they placed their accents, histories in which, as Professor Frank Pierce has had occasion to point out, the drama is virtually ignored, and pride of place goes to the Renaissance literary epic.[4] The truth is that so long as histories of literature remain uncontrolled by more objective criteria than they are, they will tend to reflect our own contemporary ethos rather than that of the age whose literary history they purport to narrate. Despite the work which is now being done by certain scholars, it is undeniable that we still tend to underrate or neglect the literary epic, Guevara, the chivalresque romances, and the *cancionero*-style verse which persisted with barely diminished popularity up to the time of Gracián; but at least we seem to be aware that they were once important.

The fact remains that, even though the distortions of emphasis may not be very serious, even though they may be slowly being put right, we are just not in the habit of doing our sums. Most of us tend to ignore the simple statistical data of book-production in the sixteenth and seventeenth centuries, and most of us would be hard put to it to provide the answers to some rather elementary questions: which Spanish work of imaginative literature was most frequently reprinted in the Golden Age? which work, composed in Spanish, saw most editions? which work in Spanish translation achieved unequivocal status as a best-seller? And so on. I really do not know what we ought to do with the answers when we have got them, but I am sure that we ought at least to know what the answers are.

Perhaps I might illustrate with a simple example the value of statistical evidence, the value of even the easiest kind of sum. Professor A. A. Parker, in that superbly condensed piece about Spain which he contributed to the Thames and Hudson volume on the Renaissance, observed that with the Council of Trent and the beginning of the Counter-Reformation, Spain 'was on the threshold of the greatest vitality and creativity that she had ever shown in religion—theological speculation, spiritual literature, mysticism, art.'[5] Leaving aside the value-judgements—since he goes on to rank San Juan de la Cruz considerably higher than Erasmus—one might legitimately suppose that this 'spiritual Renaissance', this period of greatest creativity in theological speculation and devotional literature, produced more religious books than the earlier half of the sixteenth century. Several years ago, though his results were unfortunately never published, Professor R. O. Jones looked into this in some detail. He took several volumes of Vindel and did some simple counting. What emerged was that many more books were printed in the second half of the sixteenth century than in the first half. Book-production increased greatly, and, with it, the number of religious works published. But the proportion of works classifiable as religious—theological speculation, moralizing and devotional treatises, hagiography, religious verse—quite notably declined. So far from the Counter-Reformation's producing a spiritual Renaissance, it positively inhibited theological speculation and coincided with an efflorescence of profane literature. And, of course, these facts do, on reflection, make sense. The decisions and recommendations of the Council of Trent did put a stop to a number of theological controversies; it is well known that the censors of the Inquisition were much more alert to doctrinal error in avowedly religious works than to what might be said in profane works of literature; and we know that for some Inquisitors, like Jerónimo de Zurita, the literary merit of the work in question was of paramount importance. Obviously we cannot now tell to what extent the Inquisitorial censorship may have deterred profane authors; but we can say that, given the book-production figures, it becomes a little hard to justify the thesis that the Counter-Reformation produced a spiritual Renaissance.[6]

*   *   *

As I said before, establishing the league-table of Golden-Age best-sellers is no easy matter; but I think that an examination of just why it is so hard to arrive at any accurate and useful figures is itself highly instructive.

First of all, any modern best-seller defines itself by the number of copies sold. If, indeed, we insist that we cannot speak of best-sellers without knowing the sales-figures, then we cannot talk of Golden-Age best-sellers at all. So far as the fifteenth, sixteenth, and seventeenth centuries are concerned, we cannot use as a criterion the size of the editions, and this crucial factor we have simply to ignore. In only a few cases does a chance document tell us how many copies were printed. In the early part of the sixteenth century the average edition seems to have been somewhere between two hundred and two hundred and fifty copies; but the *Cancionero general* of 1511, a lavishly produced and extremely expensive book, had—contrary, one might think, to all expectations—a first edition of 1,000 copies. At the risk of labouring the obvious, I might point out that five editions of 200 put no more copies on the market than one edition of 1,000. An unverifiable variable of this magnitude cannot be lightly dismissed. Moreover, while the early Spanish printers found it hard to compete with the mass-production of books in centres such as Lyon or Venice, in the second half of the sixteenth century they were better able to hold their own, and sizes of editions accordingly steadily increased.[7] In spite of all this, the only realistic criterion which we can usefully employ in defining our best-sellers is the number of editions through which they passed.[8]

But this is only the beginning of our difficulties. The second major problem lies in determining the number of different editions which were published. Perhaps the only edition one can be quite certain of is one which one has seen and handled. Catalogues, whether of libraries or book-sellers, have to be assigned to a second rank. And in third place come bibliographies and monographs. Some of these, but only a few, are clearly as impeccable as such works can be; the majority sin by errors of omission and commission, and often abound in phantoms, created by careless note-taking or simple misprinting. It would be absurd to suggest that professional bibliographers are not thoroughly well aware of these hazards. Both Simón Díaz and Palau, for instance, indicate which editions are extant in major libraries, which items they have taken from older bibliographers or book-sellers' lists, which editions they suspect to be phantoms. But they do not make things easy for the investigator in a hurry.

In his otherwise exemplary bibliography of Hispano-classical translations, Theodore S. Beardsley uses the most severe criteria of reliability, and, in consequence, produces figures for numbers of editions much smaller than they might otherwise have been.[9] For any given text, the largest number of editions cited by a given bibliographer may be due to very different methods and criteria. In monographs on individual authors it may be due to more painstaking investigation, while in some literary historians, such as Cejador, it can be attributed to uncritical acceptance of the data of previous writers and even perhaps—dare one say it?—to sheer mischievous invention. And the discrepancies among the bibliographers can be alarmingly large. For example, Beardsley, for purposes of comparison with his translations, gives figures for original Spanish works, and for *Celestina* cites a total of 39 Golden-Age editions;[10] but Palau lists 48, Simón Díaz has 84, and J. Homer Herriott claimed that he had information about 187 editions of that work, not even in the Golden Age as a whole, but datable before 1600.[11] Even if this includes translations—and he certainly does not say or imply that it does—and even if one makes some allowance for phantoms—which he does refer to—this seems an impossibly high figure. But Beardsley is equally certainly wrong. Perhaps paradoxically, the higher figures offered by bibliographers with less strict criteria of reliability are likely to be much nearer the truth. Anyone who has worked on the affiliation of fifteenth- or early sixteenth-century texts will know how often it is essential to posit lost editions, of which there may be no note anywhere in the bibliographical literature.

The only way of coping with these discrepancies that I have found is to assume that, for the purposes of this exercise, a given bibliographer, Vindel or Palau or Simón Díaz, maintains approximately the same criteria of reliability throughout his work, and, therefore, that comparisons within that work will be broadly valid. But even while we work on that comfortable assumption, we must recognize that it is, unfortunately, insecurely founded, for at least two quite different reasons.

One is that the survival-rate of small books is much lower than for large books. Rodríguez-Moñino has shown that literally millions of copies of *pliegos sueltos* have vanished.[12] Palau is well aware of it, and makes the point himself in a paragraph of comment on the first printed edition of the Spanish translation of Aesop. Indeed it is obvious enough and is confirmed by modern experience: a large, lavish, expensive tome will be more highly prized and hence better preserved than a small, cheap, possibly unbound volume. Whether it is a question of the size of the book or the cost of the book is perhaps not important, since size does correlate well enough with price— which is fortunate, since, although we can attach prices to many Golden-Age books, we cannot do it for all of them. As Palau notes, because Aesop was a comparatively short text, regularly produced in small format, there were certainly many more editions than those he records; but, of course, it is we, and not Palau, who must make some sort of adjustment for the shorter texts which appeared in small octavo or duodecimo editions.[13] In Beardsley's rigorous—and for my present purposes over-rigorous—bibliography, this factor is not taken into account at all.

There is a further fairly consistent distortion in all the general bibliographers who work on a scale which obliges them to rely on second-hand information; and it arises from the interest that we, collectively, have taken in specific works and authors. We can be fairly sure that we do know of all the existing library copies of, say, *Diana* or *Lazarillo*. But what of the works that none of us bothers about? Let me cite one specific instance. Some years ago, the attention of Antonio Pérez Gómez was drawn to a manuscript copy of a curious little work by Francisco Ledesma entitled *Documentos de criança*.[14] Sundry devotional poems and prayers were added to and deleted from it over the years, but its nucleus is 72 *redondillas* giving admirable advice to a boy: keep your elbows off the table, use your handkerchief when you want to wipe your nose, don't forget to wash your ears, don't chatter in class, help your mother about the house, and so forth. It was first printed in 1599, and Palau records four reprintings of it. But by assiduous inquiry Pérez Gómez was able to locate copies of no fewer than sixteen editions of it. In the seventeenth century it achieved a wider diffusion than, for instance, any work by Gracián or Góngora. I will readily concede that it may not be an important literary text; my point is that the general bibliographers who must rely on the work of others will inevitably record unduly low figures for books to which the historians and critics have paid no attention.

Until we have a really reliable general bibliography of Golden-Age printing, our table of best-sellers must remain very provisional indeed. And I have not done with the complications we face. Given that we can make some use of what figures we can muster, we shall get full value from them only if we spread them along a time-scale. Ideally we need some sort of graph rather than arithmetic totals, but I have not been able to devise any satisfactory system. The only practicable solution seems to be to break up the larger periods into smaller time-spans. Beardsley gets some interesting results in this way. Among other things, he is able to show, for instance, that while the reign of Isabella is a peak period for the printing of Spanish translations of the classics, almost all the translations were actually done earlier in the fifteenth century, and that the humanist scholars who might have been expected to be producing them were in fact engaged in supervising editions in the original language. An inspection of the dates of the reprintings of the expurgated *Lazarillo* lends support to Fernando Lázaro Carreter's suggestion that such mild success as *Lazarillo* enjoyed was due to printers who were hoping to cash in on the sensational success of *Guzmán*, and perceived between it and *Lazarillo* some kind of generic resemblance.[15] Only by keeping publication dates in mind can we see that *Don Quixote* had no observable effect on the vogue of the chivalresque romance, that the sudden cut-off of editions of *Amadís* and its continuations in 1588 might just coincide with external political events, and so on.

Finally, we must recognize that counting editions of individual books can produce a limited and possibly misleading picture. We must not lose sight either of the author or of the genre. Guevara's style, Guevara's erudition and pseudo-erudition, Guevara's peculiar sense of humour, Guevara's attitudes, were made public not through one book but through half a dozen. It is true that his *Marco Aurelio* appears to rank second among Golden-Age best-sellers written in the Golden Age, and if we also total the whole production of individual authors, Guevara appears to be surpassed only by Fray Luis de Granada. But even a writer as prolific and successful as Castillo Solórzano will fail to appear in the list of the fifty best-known works if we look only at individual volumes.

The problem of a genre is still more complex. With the exception of Alistair Maclean's *Breakheart Pass*, not since the days of Zane Grey has any individual Western novel come anywhere near the category of 'best-seller'; but a glance at any station bookstall will serve to demonstrate that one very particular formula can be endlessly repeated by successive authors, and that the Western genre as a whole looms large on the para-literary scene. And we have a close analogue in the sixteenth century. *Amadís de Gaula* did well in its own right. Its two dozen editions put it more or less on a par with Pedro Mexía's *Silva de varia lección*, Guevara's *Epístolas familiares*, San Pedro's *Cárcel de Amor*, and Cervantes's *Don Quixote*. But if we include the sequels, by sundry different authors, the Amadís story leaps to a total of almost ninety editions, and into second place in the popularity charts, overshadowed still, of course, but only by the most astonishingly successful book of the entire Spanish Golden Age.

To summarize what information it is possible to glean from the general bibliographies is no easy matter; not all the information is reliable; it is virtually certain that I have missed several best-selling works;[16] and if I cite figures, I have said enough to indicate that this apparent preciseness is quite spurious. Nevertheless, it is not impossible to arrive at some broad conclusions, which it is unlikely that further more detailed research will undermine.

The most striking fact, of course—although I am not going to labour the point any further now—is that the chart of the books most frequently reprinted in the sixteenth and seventeenth centuries bears only a rather distant resemblance to the panorama of Golden-Age literature which we habitually present to our students.

Leaving that on one side, probably the most impressive fact about the sixteenth century is that, despite the legion of new writers, the book-production of that period is dominated by fifteenth-century writers. *Celestina* —without counting its sequels and imitations—leads the way, but Mena's *Laberinto*, the anonymous fifteenth-century verse translation of Aesop, Jorge Manrique's *Coplas por la muerte de su padre*, Fray Juan de Padilla's *Retablo de la vida de Cristo* (of which there is no complete modern edition), Diego de San Pedro's *Passión trobada*, his *Cárcel de Amor*, Montalvo's *Amadís*, all achieved best-selling success, and among Mena, Rojas, Montalvo, San Pedro, and company, only six sixteenth-century authors make any showing at all.[17]

Whichever sets of figures one uses, *Celestina* was quite clearly the most successful piece of fiction in the entire Golden Age, eclipsed only if we allow *Amadís* to embrace its sequels. Second and third in the fiction class come *Guzmán de Alfarache* and Montemayor's *Diana*. Tailing behind these, equal fourth with *Amadís* and *Cárcel de Amor*, comes *Don Quixote*. Although there have now been published perhaps nine hundred Spanish editions of Cervantes's masterpiece, we should not forget that in the seventeenth century its two dozen editions indicate that it was much less widely read than *Guzmán*, with thirty-nine. In fact, *Don Quixote* and *Diana* slip two places further down the list—and *Guzmán* one—if we also class as the fiction they are two works which pretend not to be. One is Guevara's *Marco Aurelio*, which ran to almost fifty editions, and the other is Ginés Pérez de Hita's *Historia de los vandos de los Zegríes y Abencerrajes*, better known as the *Guerras civiles de Granada*. Its thirty-five editions put it well ahead of *Don Quixote* and only just behind *Guzmán*.

Volumes of profane verse scarcely make a showing. Of the Golden-Age poets, Garcilaso did best, but not as well as Juan de Mena, or the verse translations of Aesop and Virgil's *Aeneid*. His nearest sixteenth-century rival appears to be Ercilla, with his *Araucana*, but the *Araucana* is itself over-shadowed by the fifteenth-century narrative religious poems I have mentioned.

One amazing book stands quite alone, with almost twice as many editions as its nearest rivals, that is, *Celestina*, Guevara's *Marco Aurelio*, and Aesop. This is Fray Luis de Granada's *Libro de la oración*, which ran through well over one hundred editions between 1554 and 1679. Its success is even more astounding when we look at its history in detail.[18] It went through twenty-three editions in the first five years of its life, and might have continued to break all records, had not Melchor Cano, despite having been a friend and fellow-student of Fray Luis, fought to have it placed on the Index as a banned book. After protracted disputes, after Fray Luis succeeded in getting the Pope and the Council of Trent to approve it, and after the Spanish authorities had insisted on a series of corrections, it appeared in print again and went through another eighty editions. It is, of course, an instructional manual on how to pray; and it is not easy to see how it could be fitted into a course on sixteenth-century literature.

But if we are going to concentrate on 'pure literature'—which is an entirely justifiable and perfectly legitimate choice—we ought at least to remember that for every work of pure literature there was at least one other book which was more widely read. *Celestina* was outdone by the *Libro de la oración*, *Diana* was overshadowed by Fray Luis de Granada's *Guía de pecadores*, *Don Quixote* saw fewer editions than Pedro Mexía's *Silva de varia lección*, Lope's *Arcadia* does not match Guevara's *Epístolas familiares*. And, as I have tried to indicate, while we may have arranged our works of literature in some order of merit, we have done so without taking their contemporary popularity into account.

Even when we look at individual authors, we find that the histories of literature and the writers on those authors frequently ignore the relative popularity of the books they wrote. Lope's most popular work was his *Arcadia*; Quevedo's was not *El buscón* or the *Sueños* but *La política de Dios*. It is true that Fray Luis de Granada's famous *Guía de pecadores* was more popular than *Diana* or the works of Garcilaso, but it cannot compare with his *Libro de la oración*. As for Guevara's *Menosprecio de corte*—which I would guess is the work of his most familiar to most Hispanists—it is quite insignificant in comparison with his *Marco Aurelio*, *Epístolas familiares*, and *Monte Calvario*, and even minor works like his *Oratorio de religiosos* achieved greater success.

As for translations of the classics, since Beardsley has a whole book on the subject, I need do no more than remind you of some of his findings. The most frequently translated and reprinted work was Aesop's *Fables*, done initially from the Latin version of Lorenzo Valla. There were in all five different translations, which went through a total of at least forty editions. Given that it was a small book, and given Beardsley's rigorous criteria of reliability, it seems probable that Aesop surpassed *Marco Aurelio* and rivalled *Celestina*. Aesop is followed by translations of Virgil's *Aeneid*, which saw at least thirty editions, which means that it was better known even than Mena's

Laberinto or Montemayor's *Diana*. And in third place comes Ovid's *Metamorphoses*, with over twenty editions, ahead of *La política de Dios*, *Araucana*, *Lazarillo*, Guevara's *Reloj de príncipes*, and Huarte de San Juan's *Examen de ingenios*.

The fact that the three leading classical translations could all be classed as imaginative literature is mildly misleading. As Beardsley notes, among the 216 translations he lists, with almost 600 editions, imaginative literature does not figure conspicuously, and the interests of the translators, printers or reading public clearly lay primarily in moral, philosophical, scientific, and historical works. Broadly, the same applies to original Spanish works. Despite the success of a limited number of imaginative works, Golden-Age printing in Spanish is dominated by prose non-fiction, by devotional, moralizing, and historical works. And, of course, imaginative literature pretended to instruct: Fernando de Rojas claimed to have a moral purpose; Mateo Alemán quite clearly did have; Montalvo insists in the preface to his *Amadís* that it is a mine of 'enxemplos y doctrinas'; Aesop's *Fables* were read in conjunction with their morals; and the tales of the *Metamorphoses* were similarly equipped with moral and allegorical interpretations, a tradition going back to such medieval works as *Ovide moralisé* and continued into the Spanish seventeenth century.

Despite this heavy emphasis on moral lessons, it would be wrong to conclude, I believe, that the reading public of the sixteenth and seventeenth centuries was in any really basic way different from the reading public of our own day. In his history of Golden-Age prose and poetry, R. O. Jones attempts to explain the huge success of Pedro Mexía in terms of 'the curiosity of Renaissance Europe, its appetite for sheer fact'.[19] But we need only look around us to see that same appetite for 'fact'. We may choose to lecture and write about literature, but the addiction of academics to the reading of so-called 'news'-papers is a phenomenon which can be observed at any conference.

A second point—before I embark on a still more general conclusion—is that it would seem that we need not concern ourselves with the cultural level of the reading public. On the one hand, Daniel Eisenberg has argued that we have been grossly misled by Cervantes's picture of the reapers in the field gathered to hear a reading of a chivalresque romance.[20] He has pointed out not only that the romances of chivalry were normally very expensive volumes, far outside the reach of the ordinary purse,[21] but also that their authors habitually dedicated them to scions of the aristocracy. This does not mean that we must exchange the notion of a 'popular' audience for that of a cultured one; we have no reason to suppose that they did not appeal to all levels of society. Again, on the other hand, we hear repeated complaints in the late sixteenth and early seventeenth centuries, studied by Professor Otis Green,[22] about the increasing power and influence of the *vulgo*, of their taste for sensationalism, of their insistent demand for novelty, of their liking for extravagant conceits and for linguistic and rhetorical elaboration. It is an extraordinary set of reproaches, for by the standards of the more sober stylists, Góngora and Calderón would have to be classed as vulgar writers. And earlier in the sixteenth century, when moralists castigated the public which read with avidity *Cárcel de Amor*, *Celestina*, *Amadís*, and *Diana*, they made no distinction between the nobility and the *vulgo*. I conclude—with Caro Baroja—that we cannot usefully distinguish an upper and lower class of reading public even in the seventeenth century.[23] The purchasers of books must have belonged to the more well-to-do families; but there is little evidence that the tastes of the majority of them did not reflect the tastes of the population at large.

I imagine that we can take it as axiomatic that there is no literature without language. Rather more interesting is the converse proposition, that there is no language without literature. This is not a matter of definition but of empirical fact. We know of no society, however primitive, which does not possess its literature of stories, songs, riddles, and proverbs. However inconclusive the exercise, it cannot be quite profitless to speculate on why this should be so.

It is daunting, of course, to note that a great many sophisticated minds have applied themselves to the construction of a satisfactory 'theory of literature', and have succeeded in imposing themselves on several metres of shelf-space in any moderately well-stocked academic library, without having produced any generally accepted set of propositions. I am, however, emboldened to offer some crude suggestions precisely because I have always suspected that the theorists of literature have made things impossibly difficult for themselves by persistently thinking of literature in terms of the highest exemplars of imaginative literature—Virgil, Dante, Shakespeare, Cervantes —and by failing to observe that their cultured colleagues are science-fiction addicts, consumers of thrillers, and devourers of newspapers and magazines.

One basic function of language is indubitably informative. (I am not unaware that the philosophers have broken this down into sundry sub-categories.) And it is easy to see this as a function not only of non-fictional literature but of fiction and poetry also, in so far as they provide vicarious experience, and lessons of behaviour can be drawn from the experiences of other people, real or imagined. This is a deliberately crude statement of one 'theory of literature' which has been thoroughly worked over, with much subtlety, by many writers. One function of language and of literature is—must be—the transmission of knowledge in the broadest sense: literature provides guidance for the individual to adjust to the world and the society around him.

But one does not have to look far to see that this is a less than adequate explanation of a great deal of world literature. The information purveyed is too frequently useless information. Let me take first the rather marginal case of Marco Polo. Ramusio's account of the travels of Marco Polo was staple fare in the Siglo de Oro. There were several different Spanish translations, but the most frequently reprinted was Santaella's, which first appeared in the fifteenth century.[24] (In popularity, incidentally, Marco Polo is ahead of Boethius, *El buscón*, Ribadeneyra's *Flos sanctorum*, and Guevara's *Menosprecio de corte*.) One might have expected that Spaniards would have been more interested in the Indies, and narratives of the conquest and descriptions of America were certainly widely diffused. But individually Marco Polo holds his own against any *historiador de Indias*. Now, the extraordinary thing is that, although modern scholarship has abundantly vindicated the veracity of the Italian traveller, the translations which were so eagerly read are nonsense. Almost all the proper names—apart from Venice—are so grotesquely distorted that from the moment we quit Babylonia, that is, Babilun, Cairo, to travel to Asia, which is an unintelligent emendation of Saia, a Genoese colony in the Crimea, we are in Wonderland. Indeed, Sir John Mandeville's wholly fictitious travels were devoured with equally uncritical enthusiasm. We may argue, of course, that for Golden-Age Spaniards, the information purveyed in these books was unverifiable. But one might also contend that they consumed, with relish, information and misinformation about worlds which did not and could not impinge on their day-to-day living.

Even more striking is the case of *The Book of Secrets* attributed to Albert the Great, which went through over eighty editions in Renaissance Europe.[25] It deals with the virtues of sundry herbs, animals, and minerals, and the bulk of it consists of crazy recipes and remedies. To catch fish, for instance, all you have to do is to anoint your hands with the juice of nettles and houseleek, wade out into a stream, and the fish—if there are any about—will come to be taken. Well, there is a sort of saving clause there, but consider the recipe for making yourself invisible: take an opal, wrap it in a leaf of laurel or bay, and hold it in your hand. No one will be able to see you. Repeatedly the anonymous compiler alleges that 'this has been proved'; in the case of the recipe for invisibility we are told that it was regularly and successfully employed by the Emperor Constantius. Probably the only recipe in the entire book which could have been successfully proved experimentally is the formula for gunpowder. And yet, people possessed themselves eagerly of this verifiably inaccurate misinformation. Is this, in the end, basically different from the way in which people who really do know better take time to read the astrological predictions in the *Observer*, or, even, basically different from the way in which we devour quite useless information and mis-information in the daily newspapers?

Literature appears to be the product of two distinct factors. On the one hand it appears to fulfil some deep-seated human need for narrative, for learning of the experiences of other minds, no matter whether the material be real or imagined. I firmly believe that there is less distance than one might suppose between primitive myth and modern magazine. And, on the other hand, literature is clearly a disease of language—a product, like foie-gras, musk or pearl, pathological in its origins. Language bears no one-to-one correspondence with reality, and its units can be shuffled around to make statements about alternative, fantastic worlds as easily—indeed more easily—than about the 'real world'. Language may assist us to survive in the limited world we live in; but its by-product is perhaps more important: it provides us with other worlds to inhabit.

When we talk about literary texts, we all, it seems to me, give the impression that we feel that by discoursing on their literary merit—their structure or style—we are absolved from having to explain why they should have been popular. When we look at the best-sellers of the Golden Age it is hard to believe that literary merit alone suffices to explain their success. Perhaps it is time that we should bend our efforts to explain that success in other terms, in terms which might simultaneously account for the success of works which rarely or never figure in our courses of literature. I do not imagine that one single formula will explain everything, but it is time we had some ideas about it, and time that we took more seriously *all* the best-selling books of the Spanish Golden Age, books which must hold the key to the spirit of a remarkable epoch.

[*BHS*, 57 (1980), 189-98]

Notes

1. What follows is the text of a lecture delivered on 31 March 1978 at St Catharine's College, Cambridge, to the annual conference of the Association of Hispanists

of Great Britain and Ireland. In these notes I have supplied some basic bibliographical references and added a few explanatory comments. The lecture was given, of course, before the appearance of the superb article by D. W. Cruickshank, ' "Literature" and the Book Trade in Golden-Age Spain', *MLR*, 73 (1978), 799-824, to which I could not otherwise have failed to refer.

2. One might note in particular Edward M. Wilson, 'Quevedo for the Masses', *Atlante*, 3 (1955), 151-66; 'Samuel Pepys's Spanish Chap-Books', *Transactions of the Cambridge Bibliographical Society*, 2, 2 (1955), 127-54; 2, 3 (1956), 229-68; 2, 4 (1957), 305-22; 'Tradition and Change in Some Late Spanish Verse Chap-Books', *HR*, 25 (1957), 194-215; and *Some Aspects of Spanish Literary History*, The Taylorian Lecture, delivered 18 May 1966 (Oxford, 1967); Antonio Rodríguez-Moñino, 'Construcción crítica y realidad histórica en la poesía española de los siglos XVI y XVII', in *Literary History and Literary Criticism: Acta of the Ninth Congress of the International Federation for Modern Languages and Literatures* (New York, 1965), pp. 30-49, reprinted separately with a foreword by Marcel Bataillon (Madrid, 1965); and *Diccionario bibliográfico de pliegos sueltos poéticos (siglo XVI)* (Madrid, 1970); Julio Caro Baroja, *Ensayo sobre la literatura de cordel* (Madrid, 1969); M. C. García de Enterría, *Sociedad y poesía de cordel en el Barroco* (Madrid, 1973); Maxime Chevalier, *Lectura y lectores en la España de los siglos XVI y XVII* (Madrid, 1976); and *Cuentecillos tradicionales en la España del Siglo de Oro* (Madrid, 1975); Alan Soons, *Haz y envés del cuento risible en el Siglo de Oro* (London, 1976); Donald McGrady, 'Notes on the Golden Age *Cuentecillo*, with Special Reference to Timoneda and Santa Cruz', *JHP*, 1 (1976-77), 121-45.

3. Ten years ago, in *Spanish Literary Historiography: Three Forms of Distortion* (Exeter, 1968), I alluded (p. 18) to the histories of literature 'which devote more space to Fray Luis de León—whose private poetry was not even available in print—than to all the romances of chivalry put together'. In his review in *BHS*, 46 (1969), 52-54, E. M. Wilson objected to my inferred conclusion, arguing that Fray Luis fully deserved his place, mentioning his importance as a prose-writer, inquiring whether, after Sir Henry Thomas, there was anything left to say about the romances of chivalry, and refusing to concede that literary merit is no concern of the literary historian. It may not be easy to resolve the conflict inherent in our dual role as critics and historians, but we have an abundance of histories of literature which consist solely of pieces of literary criticism of selected texts strung together, and I have no doubt that it would be useful to have at least one purely objective history which analysed what was produced, what was read and by whom, what was influential, etc., and spared us value-judgements. That most of us might be reluctant to remove the poetry of Fray Luis from our undergraduate courses seems to me quite a different problem.

4. *La poesía épica del Siglo de Oro*, transl. J. C. Cayol de Bethencourt, 2nd ed. (Madrid, 1968), pp. 9 and 31-215, *passim*.

5. 'An Age of Gold: Expansion and Scholarship in Spain', in *The Age of the Renaissance*, ed. Denys Hay (London, 1967), pp. 235-48, at p. 240.

6. There is a mass of literature on the Inquisition and the iniquities of its system of censorship. For a well-documented but typically hostile account see Henry Kamen, *The Spanish Inquisition* (New York-Toronto-London, 1968), especially Chapter 5, 'Silence Has Been Imposed', pp. 74-108. Some relevant texts are conveniently assembled by José Simón Díaz in 'Algunas censuras de libros', in his *La bibliografía: conceptos y aplicaciones* (Barcelona, 1971), pp. 269-308. E. M. Wilson, 'Inquisitors as Censors in Seventeenth-Century Spain', in *Expression, Communication and Experience in Literature and Language: Proceedings of the Twelfth Congress of the International Federation for Modern Languages and Literatures* (London, 1973), pp. 38-56, concludes that (for Góngora) 'greater harm was done by corrupt reprinting by commercially minded printers'. For a detailed exposition of the proposition that the impoverished circumstances of printers produce bad literature, see Cruickshank, 'Book Trade', pp. 818-24. It seems to me impossible to demonstrate that the quantity and quality of profane literature were adversely affected by the censorship of the Inquisition, however much we may deplore in principle the censoring of literature.

7. For the subsequent seventeenth-century decline in Spanish book-production, coinciding with general economic decline, see Cruickshank, 'Book Trade', and 'Some Aspects of Spanish Book-Production in the Golden Age', *The Library*, 5th ser., 31 (1976), 1-19. It can be fairly safely assumed that the under-capitalization from which the industry suffered led to a decrease in the size of editions of books, as well as to an unhealthy increase in the production of ephemera, aimed at the poorer mass audience and geared to rapid turnover of investment.

8. Drama, of course, comes out of this rather badly. For plays, the figure for the total number of performances, if that could be ascertained, would be much more informative than the total number of printed editions which, for any individual play, turns out to be relatively insignificant.

9. *Hispano-Classical Translations Printed between 1482 and 1699* (Pittsburgh-Louvain, 1970).

10. In fact, there may be an error here. While Beardsley says (p. 114) that he relied on Palau, he does not say explicitly that he has applied his own criteria of reliability to the editions listed by Palau. The discrepancy could be explained in another way if he had used the listing under *Celestina* (III, 1950) and not included the additional items which appear under Rojas (XVII, 1965).

11. J. Homer Herriott, *Towards a Critical Edition of the 'Celestina': A Filiation of Early Editions* (Madison-Milwaukee, 1964), p. vi: 'So far the list in a bibliography that we are preparing contains 187 items dated before 1600. However we have not been able to locate a considerable number of these, and others represent bibliographical errors.'

12. See his *Diccionario*, p. 14.

13. Survival-rates, given the variable of the size and cost of the book, must clearly correlate with the sizes of the editions. Cruickshank, 'Book Trade', p. 816, makes

the interesting point that the age of the book is a factor we need not take into account: against the toll of time we can balance the fact that the older book, precisely because of its age, commands a respect which leads to its better conservation. In other words, the loss of so many incunables and early sixteenth-century editions is due to the small sizes of the editions rather than to their greater age.

14. Antonio Pérez Gómez, 'Un tratadito de urbanidad del siglo XVI: textos y bibliografía', in *Homenaje a la memoria de Don Antonio Rodríguez-Moñino 1910–1970* (Madrid, 1975), pp. 517-35.

15. 'Para una revisión del concepto "novela picaresca" ', in his *'Lazarillo de Tormes' en la picaresca* (Barcelona, 1972), pp. 193-229.

16. One unexpected best-seller which I overlooked when I prepared this paper is the Marqués de Santillana's *Proverbios* (or *Centiloquio*) which appears to have gone through about 30 editions before 1600.

17. Fray Luis de Granada, Guevara, Mateo Alemán, Pérez de Hita, Montemayor, and Garcilaso (in that order).

18. See Fray Justo Cuervo, 'Fray Luis de Granada y la Inquisición', in *Homenaje a Menéndez y Pelayo* (Madrid, 1899), I, 733-43.

19. *The Golden Age: Prose and Poetry: The Sixteenth and Seventeeth Centuries* (London-New York, 1971), pp. 14-15.

20. Daniel Eisenberg, 'Who Read the Romances of Chivalry?', *Kentucky Romance Quarterly*, 22 (1973), 209-33.

21. Citing some typical wages and book prices, Cruickshank, 'Book Trade', p. 812, n. 1, concludes: 'No labourer in seventeenth-century Europe could readily afford a *book*.'

22. Otis H. Green, *'Se acicalaron los auditorios*: An Aspect of the Spanish Literary Baroque', *HR*, 27 (1959), 413-22; repr. in *The Literary Mind of Medieval and Renaissance Spain: Essays by Otis H. Green*, ed. John E. Keller (Lexington, 1970), pp. 124-32.

23. I have allowed this paragraph to stand unmodified—since it is what I said—although I am now half-converted to Cruickshank's view that Caro Baroja is wrong. Caro Baroja's thesis is that no Golden-Age writer catered specifically for the lower classes, since the popular ephemera tend to be extracts from literary works, for instance, speeches from mythological comedies by Calderón (see also Wilson's 'Quevedo for the Masses', cit. in note 2). Cruickshank maintains (1) that the complaints of writers like Lope and booksellers like Serrano, early in the seventeenth century, indicate that they recognized that there existed (and were afraid of) a distinct lower-class audience, (2) that a revolution in education had created a new literate public, (3) that a mass of sub-literature, such as the *relaciones de sucesos*, was produced for the vulgar masses, and (4) that the economics of Spanish book production, being geared to satisfy this audience, accounts for the decline of literature in the later seventeenth century. That the classes who bought books cannot be regarded as uniformly *discreto* or *vulgo*—

which is surely true—might be a safer way of phrasing the point I made at the beginning of the paragraph.

24. The earliest extant edition is Seville 1503, but Rafael Benítez Claros, *Libro de las cosas maravillosas de Marco Polo*, Sociedad de Bibliófilos Españoles, n.s., XX (Madrid, 1947), dates Santaella's completion of his translation at 1477.

25. Palau does not record separately any Golden-Age edition of the *Secretos maravillosos* (it appeared under this title in Paris, 1860) but notes: 'Bajo el denominativo de *Alberto el Grande*, y el *Pequeño Alberto*, existen multitud de ediciones populares, que el vulgo, a fin de [. . .] desentrañar los arcanos del mundo, compra a veces'. The case of the *Libro de los secretos* may well be similar to that of the *Documentos de crianza*. The material in it was certainly widely known, and crops up in, for instance, Covarrubias's dictionary; but this is inconclusive, since the *Liber aggregationis seu liber secretorum* itself resumes material from a wide variety of sources. See *The Book of Secrets of Albertus Magnus*, ed. Michael R. Best and Frank H. Brightman (Oxford, 1973), from which I quote the examples below.

12

Interpreting *Celestina*: the Motives and the Personality of Fernando de Rojas

to Peter Russell

Historians, including literary historians, do well to stick to the documented facts, or they run some risk of turning into historical novelists;[1] there are literary theorists who insist that critics should not concern themselves with the author as a person, but only with the text before them;[2] innumerable books and articles have been devoted to the interpretation of *Celestina* and no coherent explanation of the work has yet found general acceptance; one would not care to be accused of suffering from 'el ansia simplificadora del lector ingenuo';[3] and it could be argued that the basic problems surrounding the text have not been sufficiently satisfactorily resolved for us to be able to proceed from 'hack history' to 'high history'.[4] It must, therefore, be almost inexcusably temerarious to venture to discuss the 'interpretation' of *Celestina* in one short paper, and even more so on the basis of speculation about the motives and the personality of its second author, Fernando de Rojas. Moreover, even though my own view of *Celestina* owes more to Professor Russell's teaching than I am now able to distinguish and assess, and even though we share many misgivings about other critical approaches, I am uneasily sensible that he may also have misgivings about mine.

The simplest and most obvious way of approaching *Celestina* is to accept that Rojas's motives and purpose were what he says they were. In the acrostic verses he tells us that, while he was moved by a desire to offer a warning about love, procuresses, and faithless servants, he wrote for his own recreation ('es la primera [razón], que estó en vacaciones', p. 39),[5] and in order to rescue from oblivion, clearly because of its unpublishable incompleteness, the work of the first author ('la otra, que oí su inventor ser ciente' or, later, 'la otra, inventarla persona prudente').

To write for one's own pleasure and diversion is an entirely respectable motive, even in the Middle Ages, when relaxation from more serious tasks ('mi principal estudio', pp. 36 and 44) was repeatedly justified in the works of a series of theologians and moralists by the image of the bow which must occasionally be unstrung: 'Cito rumpes arcum, semper si tensum habueris'.[6] And even though Rojas makes the conventional protest that he extended the *Comedia* 'contra mi voluntad' (p. 44), we have no reason to doubt that he did enjoy his writing. Indeed, though it might be alleged that he never quite matches the first author for sheer verbal exuberance, it is clearly his simple delight in creation, together, perhaps, with a naive desire to display his second-hand erudition, which leads him again and again into what a severe critic might describe as irrelevance and verbosity. His verve, fluency, and fertile invention have conspired to produce a colourful and thought-provoking work of literature, but one must suspect that a measure of self-indulgence has also packed *Celestina* with a quantity of dialogue and incident which, however entertaining it may be, is not germane to the bald moral messages of his preliminary explanations. That Rojas concedes that writing *Celestina* was in part a vacation pastime may assist us little so far as the interpretation of the work is concerned, but it does indicate that we should bear in mind that we are dealing with a creative work of literature and not a straightforward didactic treatise, and that being so, we are entitled to inquire what conscious or unconscious motives may have inspired the creative act.

Rojas's second reason is, of course, perfectly plausible and acceptable, and need hardly detain us: we have no reason to disbelieve him when he informs us, more than once, that he felt that Aucto I deserved to be more widely known, and we can easily assume that he undertook to finish the *Comedia* partly as a duty of piety, and possibly to discharge a debt of gratitude to his patron or the first author.[7]

The stated motive which has engaged the attention of most critics is, understandably, Rojas's third. Marcel Bataillon's interpretation was a thorough and invaluable test of the hypothesis that Rojas's assertion of didactic intent in the letter, prologue, and verses is to be taken literally;[8] but it revealed that this simple approach is not entirely adequate. Apart from the numerous objections raised by reviewers like A. D. Deyermond,[9] it can be argued that there is a great difference between the refusal to believe Rojas's unequivocal statement that he did not write Aucto I (or the beginning of Aucto II), and a reluctance to accept his explanations of his own motivation. While a writer's motives may be exceedingly complex, and, in the last resort, unknowable, it is at least clear that we can at no time legitimately suppose either that he is fully conscious of them, or that they did not change as he wrote, or that he has told us the whole unvarnished truth about them. And there are further difficulties.

The theory of relaxation had a double import, for it applied not merely to the writer but also to the reader, for whom the author would mix 'utile dulci, / lectores delectando pariterque monendo' (Horace, *Ars poetica*, 343-44). We need not ourselves subscribe to such a theory of literature to accept that Rojas and his contemporaries subscribed to it, and to follow his argument that his 'burlas', 'motes y trufas' (p. 237) are simply the sugaring of the pill: 'píldora amarga [. . .] métenla dentro de dulce manjar' (p. 38). And when, for example, Fray Íñigo de Mendoza similarly excuses the introduction of comic rustics into his life of Christ, we may accept his simple explanation as genuine:

> pues razón fue declarar
> estas chufas de pastores
> para poder recrear,
> despertar y renovar
> la gana de los lectores.[10]

But the problem with *Celestina* is more complicated, for we have no way of distinguishing between what Rojas may have written purely for his own amusement ('por recreación de mi principal estudio', p. 36) and what he contrived in order to make his moralizing more palatable to his readers, and, even worse, we find it impossible to tell where the gilding ends and the medicine begins.

And, as with a great many medieval and Renaissance writers, there is a further complication. A writer of that age was taught by literary theorists that he must write to delight and instruct ('deleitables fontezicas de filosofía', 'gran copia de sentencias [. . .] so color de donaires', p. 36 etc.); but the activities of innumerable moralists, for whom all literature and history was a vast mine of examples from which multiple edifying lessons might be drawn, surely also persuaded him that whatever he wrote could be read for moral profit. They were all firmly convinced that, as the Duchess told Alice, 'Everything's got a moral, if you can only find it'. While Bernard of Clairvaux might claim that 'aliquid amplius in silvis invenies quam in libris',[11] the Book of Nature was exploited no more than other books, and Erasmus could write: 'Immo fortasse plusculo fructu legetur poetica cum allegoria, quam narratio sacrorum librorum, si consistas in cortice'.[12] Any writer, even though he might later, like Pius II, be overcome by qualms of conscience, could confidently appeal to the theory of the pith and the cortex, the grain and the chaff ('paja y grançones [. . .] grano', p. 237), thrusting the responsibility of correct moral interpretation onto his readers ('siendo discreto, verás [. . .]', p. 237).

Rojas may well have genuinely believed that there was moral profit to be derived from reading his work; the author of *Celestina comentada* may well have undertaken his monumental task in order to show 'that the *Tragicomedia* was both theologically and morally an orthodox work' and 'to provide an effective riposte to the many voices in the Spain of that time which demanded that it should be banned as immoral or worse';[13] and it would not be unreasonable to maintain that Rojas does, in broad terms, illustrate the Pauline proposition that the wages of sin is death (Rom. 6: 23); but the uncomfortable facts remain that authentic moralists did look on it as a pernicious book,[14] that it does not resemble other unambiguously moralizing works of the period, and that the story does not effectively demonstrate the specific didactic propositions of the preliminary matter.

It is, of course, not difficult to think of other obvious motives for writing. It may be, as Miguel Marciales has suggested, that Rojas seized upon an opportunity to attempt to work out his own ideas on life, death, love, fortune, and destiny;[15] but this again scarcely assists us to interpret *Celestina*, particularly when those ideas emerge so ambiguously in both the *Comedia* and the *Tragicomedia*. Then, too, it is hard to believe that Rojas had no thought of achieving literary fame for himself. For someone of his ability and circumstances there were just two roads to recognition: one was through one or other of the professions—and Rojas the lawyer did eventually hold public office—and the other was nicely described by a latter-day *converso*: 'Literature is an avenue to glory, ever open for those ingenious men who are deprived of honours or wealth'.[16] But the fact that such speculations arise reveals that we are not satisfied with Rojas's claim to be preaching a simple warning about the moral perils of love, and it is not surprising that many critics have searched for the man behind the work, to see what hints his background and biography might offer.

We know, incontrovertibly, that Fernando de Rojas was a *converso*, not himself a convert, but a descendant, probably at four or five generations' remove, of a converted Jew.[17] Although the fact has preoccupied sundry critics, it has yet to be demonstrated that it has any very special significance, at least so far as the interpretation of *Celestina* is concerned.[18] Gilman has, of course, pursued the topic at length, arguing that the typical reactions of the disadvantaged *converso*, in constant peril from the Inquisition, took one or more of three forms, which might be summed up as fear, resignation, and defiance, and finding in *Celestina* evidence of all three: the timorous reaction of self-effacement and concealment of one's thoughts and identity, in Rojas's initial anonymity; the resigned acceptance involving withdrawal from society and refusal to compete, in Rojas's enthusiasm for Petrarchan neo-Stoicism; and the bolder stance of ironic observation and sceptical commentary on the follies and injustices of the community from which one is excluded, in Rojas's critical remarks on such topics as justice and the clergy.[19]

The hypothesis may not be invalidated, but it is certainly weakened, by three major considerations. The first is that the situation of the *conversos* of Rojas's generation really does not appear to have been as bleak as Gilman has painted it. The infamous series of *estatutos de limpieza de sangre*, which debarred *conversos* from sundry offices and honours, are not of the Isabelline period, and can hardly be said to have started in earnest before the second third of the sixteenth century;[20] Rojas, as his career shows, was at no greater a disadvantage than the vast majority of his fellow-citizens. Moreover, despite the host of horror-stories which can be culled from hostile historians, it is far from evident that the *conversos* of Rojas's time lived in constant terror of the Inquisition,[21] and we too often forget that it was a group of *conversos* who petitioned Isabella to import it into Spain, in order to protect the genuine Christians, of whom Rojas was surely one, from becoming confused with the crypto-Judaizers, who did have reason to be wary of it.[22] A second major objection is that the text of *Celestina* provides only dubious and ambiguous support for Gilman's interpretation of Rojas's reactions to his *converso* status. It is not easy to detect any suggestion of timorousness in *Celestina*;[23] his enthusiasm for neo-Stoicism is manifestly odd, in as much as he perverts and misuses Petrarchan maxims for comic effect,[24] and in *Celestina* succeeds only in denying the validity of the neo-Stoic position by demonstrating that, where passion rules, reason is powerless; and his overtly critical observations on such topics as the delinquent clergy can scarcely be accounted daring at a time when a ruthless programme of reform had driven a thousand Spanish friars to seek refuge among the Muslims of Africa.[25] But perhaps the most important objection to the entire hypothesis is that we know only too well that common background circumstances can and do produce widely divergent personalities: saints and sinners, heroes and cowards, conformists and rebels; and we are in no position to uncover the real sources of these different responses. In other words, although the personality and attitudes of Fernando de Rojas may be crucial for a correct interpretation of *Celestina*, there is no way in which we can accurately deduce their nature by speculating about the psychological reactions of *conversos* in general, who did not even form a coherent or cohesive group within Spanish society.

In a recent essay, Antony van Beysterveldt also put forward a 'new interpretation' of *Celestina*.[26] Relying on a sociological hypothesis which would explain civilization (or perhaps more precisely civilized behaviour) as adherence to a restrictive, self-imposed set of rules,[27] he sees courtly love as such a code, designed to set the aristocracy apart, and interprets *Celestina* as, primarily, Rojas's egalitarian attack on the nobility, inspired by the socio-cultural wounds inflicted by his *converso* status. Although we may wish to set on one side the debatable psycho-sociological theory, as well as the explanation of Rojas's motives which rests on his *converso* descent, van Beysterveldt's primary insight, that the text of *Celestina* betrays a man deeply resentful of the aristocracy, is worth pondering.

That *Celestina* is ostensibly an attack on love is incontestable: it is said to contain 'defensivas armas para resistir sus fuegos' (p. 36), Rojas sees 'la más gente / vuelta y mezclada en vicios de amor' (p. 39), and the moral of the tale is that since 'aquí vemos cuán mal fenecieron / aquestos amantes, huigamos su dança' (p. 236), etc.; that 'love' to Rojas meant the current code of 'courtly love' has been abundantly demonstrated,[28] and the bases of Rojas's attack are perfectly clear, and as near explicit as the nature of his dramatic dialogue will allow. 'Love', despite all the protestations of the poets, is no more than lust;[29] the lover, despite what lovers claim, is not elevated and ennobled by his experience, but becomes a blasphemous sinner and a proper object of ridicule; and love is emphatically not, despite all the theorists, a malady which affects only noble minds, for servants can fall victim to it, and, as Celestina observes, there is no difference between the peasant girl and the lady except that the lady hypocritically denies her lustfulness and defers her surrender (Aucto VI, p. 109). These are the commonplaces of misogynist literature, for the enemies of love are invariably the enemies of women, just as the defenders of love, like San Pedro's Leriano, are also the defenders of women. It was not difficult for the author of *Celestina comentada*, himself a woman-hater, to find evidence to support his view of the *Tragicomedia* as a misogynist tract of impeccable orthodoxy.[30]

Rojas, however, goes further, not here disagreeing with the theorists of courtly love, to argue that the Dance of Love is a Dance of Death, and in so doing he betrays an important facet of his personality. Death, as we know, does not make a tragedy. 'Las muertes trágicas son lastimosas, mas las de la comedia, si alguna ay, son de gusto y passatiempo, porque en ellas mueren personas que sobran en el mundo, como es una vieja zizañadora, un rufián o una alcahueta.'[31] And Rojas, having killed off his *alcahueta* and a couple of servants, goes on to dispatch his pair of aristocratic lovers and call his work a comedy. In the much-discussed passage of the prologue to the *Tragicomedia* in which Rojas refers to those who had criticized his use of the term *comedia* in the title of the first version, his excuse is that 'el primer autor quiso darle denominación del principio, que fue plazer, y llamóla comedia', and his solution is to 'split the difference' ('entre estos extremos partí agora por medio la porfía') and call it a *tragicomedia* (p. 43). Whether Rojas knew Plautus's *Amphytrio* or Verardi's *Fernandus salvatus* (or *servatus*) is irrelevant; his position is indefensible.[32] We need not doubt that the first author did call it a *comedia*, not just because the work had a comic beginning (if that is what 'denominación del principio' means) but because he had not intended to turn it into a tragedy. Rojas will not concede that he has betrayed the intentions of the first author, refuses to admit that the anomaly is his own fault, rejects the label of *tragedia*, and slides away from the issue with a joke, coining the spurious term *tragicomedia* for a non-existent genre. That this may have proved a happy and fruitful accident is quite beside the point. Apart from a degree of self-assurance bordering on arrogance, the passage reveals that Rojas did not regard the deaths of Calisto and Melibea as tragic; and the text demonstrates that he did not accept the dictum that it is 'la clase baxa [. . .] la que engendra la risa'.[33] It would be easy, but it would take time, to show that Rojas's attack on courtly love is grossly unfair; but it is more important to appreciate that *Celestina* is an attack not simply on the code of courtly love but also on those who subscribed to it, namely the aristocracy.

In the reign of Enrique IV, it is possible to find writers who attack the contemporary nobility as worthless, corrupt, and undeserving of respect. (Although it is true that his ferocious stanzas were not permitted to appear in print, Fray Íñigo de Mendoza did not hesitate to name his targets.) But in the time of Isabella it is difficult to find more than restatements of the well-worn proposition of Boethius (the idea is older but we need look no further afield for its source) that true nobility does not depend on lineage, but solely on virtue and wisdom. And this notion can be passed over in silence even by authors heavily dependent on Boethius for other ideas.[34] Although the first author makes Sempronio affirm that nobility depends on virtue (Aucto II, p. 74), Rojas does not himself repeat the point explicitly,[35] but *Celestina* makes sense if we believe that he did cherish that Stoic contention, and this covert conviction even goes some way to explaining his enthusiasm for Petrarch, and in particular for *De remediis*, in which it is the theme of two dialogues. The genuine moral indignation of a genuine moralist, like Fray Íñigo, needs little explanation: any mendicant preacher was 'against sin' in any guise and in any context. But Rojas's hostility to the nobility is so heavily disguised and so speciously justified that we may be permitted to wonder about his real motives.

Fernando de Rojas was a young man of superior intelligence, who came from a family background of little culture (there were, for instance, so far as we know, no doctors or lawyers among his close relations) and, probably, of relative penury, for an unnamed patron gave him financial assistance ('las muchas mercedes de vuestra libre liberalidad recebidas', p. 35), possibly to allow him to undertake his course at Salamanca at all.[36] While he may not have been a classic *resentido*, no historical novelist would find it hard to imagine that the young Rojas both cherished an awareness of his own intellectual capacity and moral worth, and nursed a deep-seated resentment of the pampered scions of the upper classes, who paid no taxes, did not have to work, and expected deference and respect solely by reason of their parentage.[37] But from his lowly position he could launch no open attack upon them. Instead, he offers us a portrait of what he must have intended to be a typical specimen of the class: rich, idle, precious, foolish, selfish, weak, and ignoble;[38] and he sends him to an ignominious death. Rojas claims, of course, that he has demonstrated the perils of love, and of 'falsos y lisongeros sirvientes' and 'malas mugeres hechizeras' (p. 36). But Rojas had read *Cárcel de Amor* (for he copies sentences from it), so that he knew very well how the perfect lover ought to behave: Calisto behaves badly not because he is the victim of passion but because he is no Leriano; and the logic of his accidental death, unlike Leriano's, is, unless it can be construed as simple punishment by an act of God, obscure. Moreover, although the extent to which Rojas expresses his personal views while hiding behind his creations may be arguable, Celestina's egalitarian theses (pp. 83, 109, etc.) are illustrated by Rojas's showing Calisto's servants involved in the same game as their master. Pármeno is as enchanted with Areúsa, and Sempronio as besotted with Elicia, as is Calisto with Melibea. The portrait of Melibea is possibly more equivocal, in that her passion is the result of witchcraft, but she is shown to be wilful, dishonest, and careless of her own and her family's honour, and finally commits the 'grave y detestable delicto' of killing herself.[39] While Rojas might enjoy reading that true nobility did not lie in an accident of birth, his egalitarianism levels by pulling down, not by raising up, by demonstrating, that is, the baseness of the aristocracy rather than the dignity of the commoner.

We are not compelled to suppose that Rojas was a hypocrite. If he uses morality as a stick with which to beat the nobility, his moral indignation may still be genuine. But it is also rather odd. Numerous fifteenth-century love-poets and writers of romances came in maturer years ('el seso lleno de canas' like Diego de San Pedro) to disown their early works and repent of their youthful sinfulness; but to be a misogynist in one's youth argues a certain priggishness, and it is unusual to find a young man so fiercely hostile to sexual love that he finds death the only fitting punishment for procuress, servants, master, and mistress alike.

To see the author of *Celestina* as a rather objectionable young man, as an arrogant, resentful, hypocritical, priggish show-off, may be little more helpful than to acclaim him as a genius, a Columbus of literature, 'an extraordinary student of human nature', 'one of the most rational minds ever produced by the human race', etc.;[40] and I should not contend that it is necessarily a more accurate portrait. But it may help to restore some sense of perspective. One of the greatest obstacles to a proper interpretation of *Celestina* is surely the presupposition that it is a masterpiece without flaws, a wholly self-consistent work which, in spite of its manifold ambiguities, reflects a unified vision of life and one unswerving purpose. This cannot be true. If there is any magic key to the interpretation of *Celestina*, it must be the realization that there is no single magic key. And we shall make very heavy weather of understanding the book if we cannot conceive of a flawed author, an author whose logic is inconsistent; who was blinded by the euphoria of his revenge on the *jeunesse dorée* whom he hated, and failed to perceive that his *Comedia* might be regarded as a tragedy; who, having been alerted, through pride would not admit his error and through prudence could not say that, for him, Calisto and Melibea were 'personas que sobraban en el mundo'; whose sense of humour, often cruel and black, undermines his stated purpose; whose self-indulgent displays of borrowed erudition (the worst example is the prologue to the *Tragicomedia*) lead him to repeat aphorisms and ideas with which he is not genuinely in accord; whose ambiguous pessimism is an intellectual stance which does not match his intuitive positive reaction to life; who can be easily diverted from his point, so that imaginative moments of insight (Celestina on old age, Areúsa on the hard lot of prostitutes, the responsibility of masters for the disloyalty of servants, etc.) produce misplaced sympathy for a cast of unsympathetic characters; who with Pleberio's final diatribe was carried away to elaborate rhetorically a complex of *topoi* inappropriate as a summation of his work; who in a mellower version as the author of the *Tragicomedia* agrees pointlessly to prolong 'el processo de su deleite destos amantes' (p. 44); whose Centurio is a weakly conceived, unoriginal, unfunny, and quite irrelevant excrescence who can be the product only of his creator's complacency;[41] and so forth.

To acknowledge that *Celestina* and its second author might be less than perfect detracts in no way from the historical importance of the work in European literature; but it may well be that its fortuitous fruitfulness lies in its very imperfections, in its ambiguity and in its ambivalence, and in the complexity of Rojas's personality. Properly to substantiate all these propositions would, however, require a book.[42]

[*Mediaeval and Renaissance Studies on Spain and Portugal in Honour of P. E. Russell* (Oxford: Society for the Study of Mediaeval Languages and Literature, 1981), pp. 53-68]

Notes

1. 'When positive documentary evidence about him [Rojas] and his life [. . .] is exceedingly scanty and when one of the main characteristics of his literary creation [. . .] seems to be its addiction to ambiguous statement, [. . .] the literary biographer will inevitably be driven to look far afield for information that is possibly relevant. Under such conditions, the portrait of the writer as a man that emerges is liable to exhibit, to a disconcerting extent, the appearance of a historical novel', P. E. Russell, review of Stephen Gilman, *The Spain of Fernando de Rojas: The Intellectual and Social Landscape of 'La Celestina'* (Princeton, 1972), in *Comparative Literature*, 27 (1975), 59-74 (p. 60).
2. For references see René Wellek and Austin Warren, *Theory of Literature* (1949), chaps 7 and 8; I have used the third edition, reissued in Penguin University Books (Harmondsworth, 1973). They themselves assert that 'no biographical evidence can change or influence critical evaluation' (p. 80).
3. María Rosa Lida de Malkiel, *La originalidad artística de la 'Celestina'* (Buenos Aires, 1962), p. 723.
4. See Margaret Hastings, 'High History or Hack History: England in the Later Middle Ages', *Speculum*, 36 (1961), 225-53. But to formulate provisional hypotheses, provided they do not become fossilized as 'fact', is a perfectly acceptable, indeed necessary, scientific procedure.
5. Figures attached to quotations refer to the pages of the Alianza edition by Dorothy S. Severin (Madrid, 1969, 1971, 1974), but the quotations are copied from the invaluable five-volume cyclostyled critical edition by Miguel Marciales (Mérida, Venezuela, 1977). [Marciales's edition is now generally available, having been edited for the press by Brian Dutton and Joseph T. Snow: *Celestina: Tragicomedia de Calisto y Melibea: Fernando de Rojas*, 2 vols, Illinois Medieval Monographs, 1 (Urbana: Univ. of Illinois Press, 1985).]
6. Phaedrus, *Fabulae*, III, 14, 10. For sundry later instances see my 'El origen de las comparaciones religiosas del Siglo de Oro: Mendoza, Montesino y Román',

RFE, 46 (1963), 263-85 (pp. 270-71) [pp. 72-95, above, at p. 78, and n. 15, pp. 91-92], and Julio Rodríguez-Puértolas, *Fray Íñigo de Mendoza y sus 'Coplas de Vita Christi'* (Madrid, 1968), pp. 563-66.

7. While I do not doubt that the first author was Rodrigo Cota, as Rojas tells us, I do not need here to rely on that still controversial hypothesis.

8. *'La Célestine' selon Fernando de Rojas* (Paris, 1961).

9. *Symposium*, 16 (1962), 233-36.

10. Rodríguez-Puértolas, p. 381. The preceding *quintilla* uses the image of the unstrung bow.

11. See Ep. CVI, in PL, 182, col. 242.

12. *Enchiridion militis christiani* (Basle, 1518), p. 63.

13. P. E. Russell, 'The *Celestina comentada*', in *Medieval Hispanic Studies Presented to Rita Hamilton*, edited by A. D. Deyermond (London, 1976), pp. 175-93 (pp. 185-86).

14. This generalization requires only minor qualification: see Maxime Chevalier, '*La Celestina* según sus lectores', in his *Lectura y lectores en la España del siglo XVI y XVII* (Madrid, 1976), pp. 138-66.

15. *Carta al profesor Stephen Gilman sobre problemas de la 'Celestina'*, 2nd ed. (Mérida, Venezuela, 1975), p. vi.

16. Isaac D'Israeli, *The Literary Character, Illustrated by the History of Men of Genius* (1818), in *Works*, edited by Benjamin Disraeli, 7 vols (London, 1858), IV, chap. 24. While possibly not strictly a convert, D'Israeli severed all connection with the Jewish congregation and had his children baptized (*Dictionary of National Biography*).

17. Gilman's suggestion that he was the son of Hernando de Rojas, condemned in 1488 for Judaizing (see *Spain of Fernando de Rojas*, especially pp. 45-46, and the earlier article by Gilman and Ramón Gonzálvez, 'The Family of Fernando de Rojas', *Romanische Forschungen*, 78 (1966), 1-26), appears to be unacceptable for the following reasons: (1) the allegation was made by one ferociously hostile *fiscal*, unsupported by other witnesses examined, and, in 1616, improbably late; (2) if Rojas's father had been condemned as an apostate, his son, by the Torquemada decrees of November 1484, could neither have practised as a lawyer nor been appointed Mayor of Talavera de la Reina; and (3) it would be highly unusual in a *converso* family for a son to bear his own father's forename. See Marciales, *Carta al profesor Stephen Gilman*, especially pp. 65-66.

18. It is clear that a majority of *Celestina* scholars have remained unconvinced by the work of, for instance, Fernando Garrido Pallardó, *Los problemas de Calisto y Melibea, y el conflicto de su autor* (Figueras, 1957), or Segundo Serrano Poncela, *El secreto de Melibea y otros ensayos* (Madrid, 1959), while basic errors of fact leave in ruins the interpretation of *Celestina* as a Jewish allegory by Orlando Martínez-Miller, *La ética judía y 'La Celestina' como alegoría* (Miami, 1978).

19. *Spain of Fernando de Rojas*, passim, but especially pp. 3-64. See also his rejoinder

to P. E. Russell, 'Sobre la identidad histórica de F. de R.', *NRFH*, 26 (1977), 154-58, in which he gives his reasons for preferring to view Rojas as a member of a *morada vital colectiva* rather than as an individual.

20. See the fundamental work of Albert A. Sicroff, *Les Controverses des statuts de 'pureté de sang' en Espagne du XVe au XVIIe siècle* (Paris, 1960).

21. Without making any apology for the Inquisition, it must be legitimate to query the generally accepted picture of a reign of terror, at least in the time of the Catholic Monarchs: anecdotes of later date prove nothing; the list of towns in which there were localized outbursts of hostility to those of Jewish blood, although these were perhaps symptomatic of a general subjacent resentment, can be matched by a much longer list of towns in which no unrest was evident; and no satisfactory quantification of the persecution of the *conversos* has even been attempted. Such unreliable figures as we have would, admittedly at the most favourable extreme, allow us to suppose that from 1492 to 1505 (from the expulsion of the Jews to the latest possible date for the composition of the *Tragicomedia*) as many as ninety-nine out of every hundred *conversos* lived unmolested by the Inquisition; and the figure can be pushed higher if we believe that the majority of those brought to trial were in fact crypto-Judaizers and not genuine Christians, many of whom played leading parts in the persecution of apostasy. Figures may be extracted, with some difficulty, from Henry Charles Lea, *A History of the Inquisition of Spain*, 4 vols (New York, 1906–08), and from Henry Kamen, *The Spanish Inquisition* (New York and Toronto, 1965). Cecil Roth, *The Spanish Inquisition* (London, 1937), implicitly supports this interpretation as he traces the gradually increasing power, severity, arbitrariness, and corruption of the institution.

22. See Roger Highfield, 'Christians, Jews and Muslims in the Same Society: The Fall of *Convivencia* in Medieval Spain', in *Studies in Church History*, edited by D. Baker (Oxford, 1977), pp. 121-46. On the genuineness of Rojas's Christianity, see Russell, review of Gilman, *Spain of Fernando de Rojas*, pp. 63 and 72.

23. The answer to the argument based on Rojas's concealment of his own name (Gilman, p. 103) was anticipated by Lida de Malkiel, *La originalidad*, p. 15. See also Russell, review of Gilman, p. 63, and Marciales, *Carta*, p. 53.

24. See Dorothy S. Severin, 'Humour in *La Celestina*', *Romance Philology*, 32 (1978–79), 274-91 (pp. 277-81 especially). This seems to me more disconcerting than his using Petrarchan *sententiae* to transform Petrarch's message (for instance about the value of friendship) and produce an even more pessimistic view of life: see A. D. Deyermond, *The Petrarchan Sources of 'La Celestina'* (Oxford, 1961), pp. 117-18. It may be argued that 'the moral authority of a *sententia* does not derive from the person who cites it but from the whole tradition to which it belongs': see Thomas R. Hart, 'Cervantes' Sententious Dogs', *MLN*, 94 (1979), 377-86 (p. 380). When Rojas insists that those who read him aright 'las sentencias y dichos de filósofos guardan en su memoria para trasponer en lugares

convenibles a sus actos y propósitos' (p. 43) he subscribes to this view; but the
fact that his *sententiae* often serve to persuade his characters to immoral action
must have created problems for many of his readers (particularly since he requires
them to distinguish between *sententiae* and 'refranes comunes', p. 43), suggests
a facile reliance on a dubious theory, and again constitutes a denial of the writer's
moral responsibility, for he thrusts that onto his readers.

25. See Jerónimo Zurita, *Historia del Rey Don Fernando el Católico*, lib. 3, cap. 15
    (Part III of *Anales de la Corona de Aragón*), or Pedro de Quintanilla y Mendoza,
    Archetypo de virtudes, espexo de prelados, el venerable padre y siervo de Dios, Fray
    Francisco Ximénez de Cisneros (Palermo, 1653), pp. 22-23.

26. 'Nueva interpretación de *La Celestina*', *Segismundo*, 11 (1977), 87-116.

27. The theory is that of Norbert Elias, *Über den Prozess der Zivilization*, 2 vols (Basle,
    1939).

28. See J. M. Aguirre, *Calisto y Melibea, amantes cortesanos* (Saragossa, 1962); June
    Hall Martin, *Love's Fools: Aucassin, Troilus, Calisto, and the Parody of the Courtly
    Lover* (London, 1972); John Devlin, *'La Celestina', A Parody of Courtly Love:
    Towards a Realistic Interpretation of the 'Tragicomedia de Calisto y Melibea'* (New
    York, 1971); Gay Abbate, 'The *Celestina* as a Parody of Courtly Love', *Ariel*,
    3 (1974), 29-32; Theodore L. Kassier, '*Cancionero* Poetry and the *Celestina*: From
    Metaphor to Reality', *Hispanófila*, no. 56 (Jan. 1976), 1-28; etc.

29. The fullest substantiation of this proposition appears to be in an unpublished
    paper by Antony van Beysterveldt, 'La adulteración del amor cortés en *La
    Celestina*', abstracted in *La Corónica*, 4 (1975-76), 17-18.

30. See Russell, 'The *Celestina comentada*', p. 183. A still earlier commentator,
    Giovanni Nevizanno, *Sylva nuptialis* (Paris, 1521), also saw it as antifeminist: see
    Russell, review of Gilman, *Spain of Fernando de Rojas*, p. 62.

31. Alonso López Pinciano, *Philosophía antigua poética* (Madrid, 1596), edited by A.
    Carballo Picazo, 3 vols (Madrid, 1953), III, 24, quoted in Severin, 'Humour in
    La Celestina', p. 288, n. 25.

32. In her discussion of the problem the learned M. R. Lida de Malkiel, *La
    originalidad*, pp. 51-52, seems to be thinking of an equally erudite and fully
    conscious author who, 'con la indiferencia hispánica a los distingos técnicos',
    'no sin perceptible condescendencia', and perhaps influenced by the Greek
    metaphor of the 'comedy-tragedy' of life, allows 'tragicomedy' as a conciliatory
    gesture to his critics.

33. Francisco Cascales, *Tablas poéticas* (1617), edited by Benito Brancaforte (Madrid,
    1975), p. 205.

34. Boethius, *De consolatione philosophiae*, III, 3, 4, 6; see for instance, Diego de San
    Pedro, *Desprecio de la Fortuna*, in *Obras completas*, III: *Poesías*, edited by Dorothy
    S. Severin and Keith Winnom (Madrid, 1979), pp. 271-97, and my Introduction,
    pp. 72-73.

35. The passage referred to occurs at the beginning of Aucto II (obviously I accept
    the explanation of 'en la margen hallaréis una cruz' proposed by F. Castro

Guisasola, *Observaciones sobre las fuentes literarias de 'La Celestina'* (Madrid, 1924), pp. 136-37 and 188, and confirmed by Deyermond, *Petrarchan Sources*, especially p. 91).

36. The widely accepted view that he was a student when he wrote *Celestina* (see, for instance, Gilman, *Spain of Fernando de Rojas*, pp. 270-72) is scarcely tenable: *jurista*, at this date, means 'lawyer' and not 'law-student'; *socio* means 'colleague' and not 'fellow-student'; and the *quinze días de vacaciones*, while they might refer to university vacations (the Easter break was a fortnight: Gilman, p. 270), could equally well refer to the official legal holidays (Christmas, Easter, summer, and autumn). For a full discussion of the question, see Marciales's critical edition, III, 231-33. On the other hand, such meagre dates as we have (married in 1507, wife aged thirty-five in 1525, mayor in 1538, died in 1541) suggest that he could not have been a man of mature years in 1497–98, although it must also be admitted that even Marciales's early conjectural birth-date of 1465 (III, 234) creates no insuperable difficulties.

37. Although much of what he says about *Celestina* is unacceptable, Claudio Sánchez Albornoz, *España, un enigma histórico,* 2 vols (Buenos Aires, 1956), detected 'orgullo' and 'rencor' in Rojas (I, 631 and 642). José Antonio Maravall, *El mundo social de 'La Celestina'* (Madrid, 1964), sees social protest and resentment in Rojas's plebeian characters, but tends to regard Rojas as dispassionate observer rather than participant.

38. P. E. Russell, 'Literary Tradition and Social Reality in *La Celestina*', *BHS*, 41 (1964), 230-37, observes of Lida de Malkiel's analysis of Calisto's character that 'there is surely much uncertainty about his true personality [. . .] we find him in what may well be a very atypical moral and emotional situation' and 'what she says about some of the characters is only valid in terms of the provisional and transient contingencies in which we see them' (p. 235). While this is no doubt true, and is not inconsonant with what Rojas says about the effects of passion, I suspect that, while Rojas might have fallen back on this defence, he did not intend his readers to make the distinction.

39. Lida de Malkiel, *La originalidad*, pp. 406-70, did much to demolish the view of a 'modesta e inocente Melibea', 'pura', 'ingenua', 'pudorosa', 'tímida', etc. (p. 419, n. 5, for references), but her portrait is still, perhaps, too indulgent. The author of *Celestina comentada* (fol. 217[v]) unequivocally condemns her suicide.

40. 'Columbus': Gilman, foreword to the Severin edition, pp. 8 and 13; the other quotations are from George A. Shipley, 'Reflections on the Shield: Stephen Gilman's *The Spain of Fernando de Rojas*', *JHP*, 3 (1978–79), 197-238 (p. 203), and Gilman, *Spain of Fernando de Rojas*, p. 352.

41. It is, of course, possible that Centurio is not Rojas's creation. I am now almost finally persuaded (as was Marcel Bataillon before his death: private correspondence between him and Marciales) by Marciales's complex arguments in favour of the *tratado de Centurio*'s being by another hand, possibly that of the elusive Sanabria: see especially Vol. II of his critical edition. The *tratado* would

run from Aucto XIV, Scene 8 (Severin edition, p. 192) to Aucto XIX, end of
Scene 1 (Severin, p. 219). I disagree with him, however, when he calls it 'una
brillante farsa' (p. 104) and Centurio a 'soberbia caricatura' (p. 105). Having
said that, I should perhaps also point out that I regard the extraordinary, semi-
clandestine work of Marciales as some of the most important material ever
published on *Celestina*, and I am deeply indebted to him for copies of his *Carta*
and critical edition. [See note 5, above. A revised version of the *Carta* was, like
the critical edition, published posthumously: *Sobre problemas rojanos y celestinescos:
carta al Dr. Stephen Gilman a propósito del libro 'The Spain of Fernando de Rojas'*
(Mérida: Univ. de los Andes, 1983).]

42. [The final note was by the editors of the volume, explaining that they were
'aware of Professor Whinnom's view that *Celestina* rather than *La Celestina* is
the proper way in which to refer to the work', but that 'in the interests of
consistency [. . .], they [had] decided that all contributions should conform to
the latter style.' In the present reprinting, the author's view naturally prevails,
and the intrusive '*La*' has been removed, as has 'the' before other titles (*De
remediis*, *Cárcel de Amor*).]

13

The *Historia de duobus amantibus* of Aeneas Sylvius Piccolomini (Pope Pius II) and the Development of Spanish Golden-Age Fiction

to Frank Pierce

Even if we ignore the by no means negligible histories of Italian literature, studies on the Renaissance, and works on fifteenth-century humanism, in all of which Aeneas Sylvius Piccolomini perforce looms large, the monographs, prefaces to editions, articles, and doctoral theses which focus on one or other aspect of that complex personality, prolific writer and correspondent, and influential politician and churchman are dauntingly numerous.[1] A couple of sabbatical years and a remorseless programme of reading would scarcely suffice to turn the neophyte into an authority on the writings and activities of Pope Pius II. However, the student of Spanish Golden-Age fiction may be permitted to confine his attention to just one work,[2] among Hispanists perhaps more frequently alluded to than studied in detail, namely the *Historia de duobus amantibus, Euryalo et Lucretia* (also variously entitled *De duobus amantibus historia, Historia duorum amantium, Historia de Eurialo et Lucretia*, etc.), which, completed in 1444, achieved in the fifteenth and sixteenth centuries a quite extraordinary diffusion.

Check-lists of the writings of Pius II may be found in various of the books about him,[3] but a complete and reliable bibliography of his works has still to be drafted, for reasons which are not hard to perceive. There are just too many separate works (often with protean titles), in too many editions, printed in sundry different combinations, scattered throughout the libraries of Europe; to the already voluminous list of manuscripts, of uncertain affiliation, further items are constantly being added (like the Latin manuscript of *De duobus amantibus* recently discovered by Professor R. B. Tate in the Academia de la Historia, Madrid);[4] successive editions of the *Opera omnia*[5] go on adding items of dubious authenticity, which their editors claim to derive from previously unpublished manuscripts (such as the disconcerting *Practica artis amandi* collected by Hilarius Drudo, which, as Professor P. E. Russell found, alludes to 'Calixtus', 'Meliboea', and 'Coelestina');[6] and while the task might be accomplished piecemeal, there are few genuine critical editions of the individual works, and editors tend not to pursue in detail the subsequent fortunes of the text with which they are concerned. It is virtually impossible, therefore, accurately to assess the number of early editions and manuscript copies of the *Historia de duobus amantibus*. Nevertheless, some notion of its popularity may be gained from the fact that the British Library catalogues thirty-one editions printed between 1468? and 1566 (lacking several noted by Cosenza), that the bibliographers who have confined their attention to incunables list thirty-five editions before 1500, and that it was translated into Italian (twice), French, English, German, and Spanish. All the printed editions are corrupt to varying degrees, and for his critical edition, still unique, Dévay relied on five early manuscripts, all but one available to him within the confines of the Austro-Hungarian Empire.[7]

Piccolomini had various Spanish contacts, and was a friend and correspondent of Rodrigo Sánchez de Arévalo and of Juan de Lucena; and although all the incunable editions of the Latin text of *De duobus amantibus* were printed outside Spain (in Cologne, Paris, Rome, Sant' Orso, Strasbourg, Louvain, Venice, Leyden, Antwerp, Leipzig, etc.), we may assume that it, like other Italian humanist works, reached Spanish readers, and we have more direct evidence of this in the form of the anonymous Spanish translation of the story.[8] It is somewhat unfortunate that all but one of the modern editions of this translation—the transcriptions by Foulché-Delbosc and Menéndez Pelayo, the facsimile by the Real Academia Española, as well as Marciales's still unpublished critical edition[9]—have been based on the edition by Cromberger of Seville, 1512 (for which see Norton, *Descriptive Catalogue*, No. 823). The earlier and probably original edition of Salamanca, 1496, is, however, extant in the Biblioteca da Ajuda in Lisbon, and has been edited by Jean-Paul Lecertua.[10] A facsimile edition of this important text has been promised by the Ajuda (a publishing date of January 1980 was at one time indicated), but meanwhile no microfilm or photocopies are being released,[11] and, since I secured a copy of Lecertua's transcription only after completing and submitting this article, I am obliged to quote from the 1512 edition.

And I have not attempted to inspect the later Spanish editions of Seville, 1524 and 1530.

The study of *De duobus amantibus* and of its Spanish translation bristles with problems, which here I can do no more than touch on. Let me try to identify five basic questions.

At the head of the list must come the intention of Aeneas Sylvius, a problem intimately linked with the complex personality of that surprising man. The gap between the pagan sensual libertine and the austere Christian moralist has been exaggerated by some writers and minimized by others, but it cannot be denied, and was recognized by Piccolomini himself when he declared, in his oft-quoted phrase: 'Aeneam respuite [or 'rejicite'], Pium respicite'. But the motto is misleading, for it suggests a sort of Pauline or Augustinian palinode, a change of heart marked by his ordination (March 1446), elevation to the bishoprics of Trieste (1447) and Sienna (1450), appointment as cardinal (1456), and election as Pope (1458). But neither his voluminous memoirs nor his equally voluminous correspondence supports that simple interpretation:[12] he displays moral preoccupations (and a keen interest in Church politics) while leaving scattered around Europe (including Scotland and England) the bastard offspring of his numerous love-affairs, while, although he repudiated *De duobus amantibus*, he could never bring himself to condemn his beloved Roman writers, who inspired it. Views on the enigma range from that of Voigt (still perhaps the most important authority on Piccolomini), who called his 'conversion' a *Bordell-Comödie*, through that of J. G. Rowe, who saw tragedy in our author's total inability to reconcile humanism and Christianity, to that of Di Francia, who regarded the 'distinzione fra l'umanista ed il papa' as exaggerated and unjust, perceived no essential difference between Piccolomini and his contemporaries, and transferred the problem to that of interpreting the age, 'l'età corruta', in which they lived.[13] And this basic problem also impinges on the interpretation of *De duobus amantibus*. In the preface to his friend Mariano Sozzino, who had asked him to write a love-story, he protests that the request is improper ('repugnante' and 'vergonçoso', A1^v), that he will not invent when he can tell the truth ('Quien es tan maluado que mentir quiera podiendo con verdad defenderse', A1^v), that his tale will be a moral warning to both youths and maidens ('oyan pues las moçaluillas y auisadas deste casamiento empos de los mancebos no se vayan mas a perder. Enseña tambien la ystoria a los moços [. . .]', A2^r), but he promises simultaneously to make his friend's ageing loins itch with lust ('Et hanc inguinis aegri canitiem prurire faciam', euphemistically translated as 'yo porne comezon en essas tus enfermas canas', A2^r), and while the story itself is larded with moralizing reflections, it contains passages which border, at the very least, on the pornographic. Nor does the outcome of the affair provide a convincing moral warning to philandering youth, for while it is true that Lucretia, abandoned by her lover, pines to death, Eurialus is soon consoled when the Emperor finds him a wife ('a ninguna consolacion dio lugar hasta que de la sangre y alto linaje de los duques de alemania el cesar le dio vna virgen en casamiento: rica prudente y muy hermosa', C12ʳ). And finally, of course, despite Piccolomini's insistence on the profit to be derived from his story, Pius II did all in his power to suppress it, and, albeit posthumously, achieved some measure of success in this, for most of the copies of the various editions of the *Opera omnia* held by the Biblioteca Nacional lack *De duobus amantibus*, dutifully excised by friars who countersign the mutilation and quote the Papal authority for their censorship.

A second problem relates to the historical accuracy of the story. Aeneas Sylvius not only tells Sozzino that it is true, but in the dedication to Gaspar Schlick (not translated into Spanish) he appears to insinuate that Eurialus is Schlick disguised: 'Res acta Senis est, dum Sigismundus imperator illic degeret. Tu etiam aderas, et, si verum his auribus ausi, operam amori dedisti. [. . .] Ideo historiam hanc ut legas precor, et an vera scripserim, videas; nec reminisci te pudeat siquid huiusmodi nonnumquam evenit tibi; homo enim fueras'. But Eurialus is scarcely a flattering portrait of Schlick; and the notion of Zannoni, that the letter to the dwarf Sozzino ('homuncio est', he writes to Schlick) is a piece of pure malice, since Lucretia was Sozzino's wife (and Sozzino, therefore, the miserly and suspicious Menelaus), seems even more implausible.[14] And, of course, even if the basic situation were founded on fact, the details (the letters, the dialogue, the soliloquies) must be fictional clothing for the bare bones. But belief in the factual accuracy of the story was, and remained, widespread, and affected the title of the Spanish translation, which advertised itself as the *Hystoria muy verdadera de dos amantes*.

That translation in its turn poses two major related problems, concerning the technique of the translator and his identity. The principal difficulty stems from the fact that no simple comparison of the Latin and the Spanish is possible, since we do not know what text the Spaniard used (but see note 15 below). As with earlier Latin works (Aesop, Seneca, Boethius, and so on), we face the problem of determining not what the original author wrote but what our translator read. For this purpose the excellent critical edition of Dévay is near useless, for the variants among the many corrupt printed editions are legion. To cite only one notable example, while Dévay (and almost certainly Piccolomini) has Eurialus quivering with lust, 'Euryalus, visa Lucretia', the *Opera omnia* text prints 'Eurialo viso, Lucretia'.[15]

And, finally, there is the question of the importance of *De duobus amantibus* in the development of Spanish Golden-Age (and, indeed, of European) narrative fiction. The *a priori* case, given the huge diffusion of the work, must be strong, very different from the cases, say, of the *Libro de buen amor* or *Siervo libre de amor*; and no one familiar with *De duobus amantibus* can read texts from the period of the Catholic Monarchs without noting innumerable, if often trivial, echoes. In the brief letter to Adolfo Bonilla y San Martín which serves as a preface to his 1907 edition of the translation, Foulché-Delbosc observed confidently, but without adducing concrete evidence: 'No dejará V. de notar la influencia inequívoca que ejerció en algunas obras castellanas de singular fama, y la importancia que su estudio puede tener para el conocimiento de los orígenes de la novela en España'. In *Los orígenes de la novela* (1910), Menéndez Pelayo identifies these works of 'singular fama' as *Cárcel de Amor* and *Celestina*.[16] But again specific details are sparse. He notes (II, 9) that 'influyó en nuestros novelistas sentimentales, y especialmente en Diego de San Pedro', but does not refer again to Piccolomini when discussing *novelistas* other than San Pedro, and when dealing with the works of San Pedro picks up only one detail: the letters used at the beginning of *De duobus amantibus* were a 'feliz innovación' first adopted by San Pedro (II, 11). On *Celestina* he is only marginally more specific. The *Historia*, 'la había leído de seguro Fernando de Rojas' (III, 331): and to Piccolomini Rojas owes his plot, 'una historia de amor y muerte de dos jóvenes' (although Eurialus does not die), and the blend of comedy and tragedy ('se mezcla el placer con las lágrimas', p. 331). Other coincidences are the 'elocuencia patética de algunos trozos' (p. 332), the 'psicología afectiva y profunda' (p. 332), details of the descriptions of Lucretia and Melibea (p. 332), and the violent reception of the procuress by the lady (p. 333). And he concludes: 'No prolongaré este cotejo haciendo notar otras semejanzas de detalle' (p. 334). Farinelli (1929) noted various Spanish translations of works by Pius II, but on the subject of the influence of *De duobus amantibus* was no more specific than Menéndez Pelayo, mentioning only the letters and the tragic ending.[17] And no other reference which I have seen to the positive influence of *De duobus amantibus* on Spanish fiction in general is any more precise. On the contrary, the first detailed investigation of its possible influence on *Celestina*, by Castro Guisasola, places *Eurialo y Lucrecia* in the category of 'Fuentes de autenticidad dudosa', with the verdict: 'ninguna de las semejanzas es concluyente', while Schevill, accepting that 'the influence of the *Historia de duobus amantibus* was far-reaching', minimizes its importance in Spain in the fifteenth century.[18]

So far as *Celestina* is concerned, the most important and searching examination of the possible influence of Piccolomini on Rojas is to be found, of course, in the monumental work of María Rosa Lida de Malkiel, somewhat frustratingly broken into observations on individual points scattered throughout the book.[19] Many of the parallels she quotes are classed by her merely as 'antecedentes', and since they are almost invariably cited alongside numerous similar antecedents, they are to be regarded, we must suppose, as inconclusive. But while she agrees with Castro Guisasola that the evidence adduced by Menéndez Pelayo is too slight to be significant ('estos influjos [. . .] los impugnó con razón', p. 389), she has already concluded (p. 361) that 'No cabe duda de que sus autores [Rojas and the author of Act I] conocían la sensual *Historia de duobus amantibus* de Eneas Silvio Piccolomini'. Nevertheless (and not foreseeing that it might be suggested that Rojas was the translator), she criticizes Castro Guisasola for using the Spanish text of the *Historia*, goes back to 'the' Latin (apparently the critical edition of Dévay: see p. 389), and finds, not merely parallel situations, but an impressive series of fairly convincing verbal reminiscences (especially pp. 391-92). Her definitive view on the whole problem appears to be that Rojas and the author of Act I certainly knew *De duobus amantibus*, but that they reacted to it not merely by improving on it (the consistent theme of *La originalidad artística*) but by reversing or inverting situations and traits of character: 'la *Historia* ejerció en la *Tragicomedia* una influencia no escasa, aunque totalmente negativa, en el carácter de los enamorados y en algunas escenas en que intervienen' (pp. 389-90), so that, for instance, 'es Calisto el reverso de Euríalo' (p. 391).

To her detailed analysis of parallels, verbal reminiscences, and possible influences, I can find to add only the name of the faithful servant, 'Sosias' in *De duobus amantibus*, 'Sosia' in *Celestina*, really scarcely more significant than the 'Lucretia/Lucrezia' contributed by Menéndez Pelayo and rejected by Castro Guisasola;[20] and, possibly, the scenes in which Eurialus and Calisto soliloquize, suddenly conscious of possible dishonour, until their obsession with their mistresses establishes itself once more (*Celestina*, Act XIII; *Hystoria muy verdadera*, B8ᵛ-C1ᵛ). No one who wishes to pursue the topic of the influence of Piccolomini on the authors of *Celestina* can afford to ignore Lida de Malkiel's work; but if we take a step back from inspecting the trees in order to survey the forest, her general conclusions may be modified and expanded. First, however, there is the question of Piccolomini and San Pedro.

I believe (although I should eschew the impersonal 'no cabe duda') that Diego de San Pedro had read the *Historia de duobus amantibus*. But it is virtually impossible to demonstrate. We must surely concede that the use of letters in the works of both writers is an inconclusive coincidence.[21] And all the direct verbal reminiscences which I have noted provide equally ambiguous evidence, since every unequivocal coincidence is attributable to a common source. As Dévay has shown, *De duobus amantibus* (most particularly when the author digresses to comment on his tale) is a tissue of skilfully blended quotations from Ovid (at the head of the list), Seneca, Virgil, Propertius, Juvenal, Plautus, Terence, Quintilian, Valerius Maximus, and the Old Testament.[22] San Pedro, at the beginning of his preface to *Cárcel de Amor*, writes: 'puesto que assí lo conozca, aunque veo la verdad, sigo la opinión';[23] Lucretia in Piccolomini's story complains: 'conozco lo mejor, y apremiada sigo lo peor' (A4[r]), or: 'Scio quod sit melius, quod deterius est sequor'; but Ovid (*Metamorphoses*, VII, 20) had made Medea say: 'Video meliora proboque, deteriora sequor'. And so it goes on, throughout the text. And if it is not inconceivable that a thorough-going statistical analysis might show that the coincidences were improbably frequent to be attributable to independent reading, quite certainly an intuitive subjective impression is that the quantity of trivial and inconclusive coincidences is such that it really cannot be due to chance. And once one allows the hypothesis that San Pedro had read Piccolomini, a multitude of relatively minor details acquire significance: for instance, one oddly discordant realistic note in *Cárcel de Amor*, after the Author's unexplained and inexplicable translation to Macedonia and the world of allegory, is his concern about linguistic barriers (even though he has had no trouble in conversing with Leriano and Deseo, and though he never does state that he had learned the language of the country); and Eurialus the German, having already sent one letter by way of a procuress (which, torn up and then repieced, is duly read by Lucretia) is also, disconcertingly for the reader, grieved and frustrated by his ignorance of Italian: 'aflegiale el no saber lengua ytaliana' (B1[r]). And similar examples could readily be multiplied. But in pursuing such details we are surely losing sight of the main issue, for, as Lida de Malkiel argues in the case of *Celestina*, *Cárcel de Amor* is a work radically different from *De duobus amantibus*.

It would be easy to expatiate on the fundamentally different attitudes and intentions of Piccolomini, San Pedro, and Rojas, but in the space remaining to me I should like to concentrate on the question of narrative technique. *De duobus amantibus* is a landmark in the history of European fiction, and, in its own way, a masterpiece. While it has clear antecedents in the Italian *novella*, of Boccaccio and Poggio, it is not a story whose point lies in its conclusion,[24] and its simple plot is expanded and extended by the close analysis of the emotions and internal debates of the main characters, by letters and speeches, by the introduction of a gallery of well-defined minor personages, by an extraordinary variety of incident, by near-*costumbrista* scenes, by the historical and topographical detail of Sienna, 'civitas Veneris', and by sundry authorial digressions (on the power of passion, on jealous husbands, on the nature of true nobility, on the foolishness of the feminist debate, and so forth). The essential plot, given Boccaccio and Poggio, is scarcely innovatory; after *Fiammetta* the interior struggles and the repeated allusions to classical analogues cannot be described as novel; and Ser Giovanni Fiorentino had often expanded a scene for its own sake, for its intrinsic interest. But when we look at *De duobus amantibus* as a whole, we see that Piccolomini has taken a major step away from the *novella* towards the novel. And he has for this purpose employed the most basic, obvious, and ultimately most fruitful of narrative techniques, namely that of the omniscient author who follows the fortunes of a character (here two characters) to some logical or inevitable conclusion: the story must stop, despite the postscript on Eurialus's reaction, with the death of Lucretia.

What is astonishing in the history of Spanish Golden-Age fiction is that, even before this elementary novelistic technique had succeeded in establishing itself, Spanish writers launched themselves into experimental modes of narration not unworthy of comparison with the experiments of twentieth-century novelists, while perpetuating and elaborating older medieval modes. Although any student of Spanish Golden-Age fiction could readily produce his own catalogue, it may not be wholly otiose to list some of the more important departures from the simple third-person narrative.

In longer fiction, the omniscient author survives in the chivalresque romances, but the naive narrative device of 'Meanwhile, in another part of the forest' (or 'back at the ranch') had already been elaborated in the course of the Middle Ages to a point at which it merits a special label, and in *Amadís de Gaula*, the Golden-Age model for chivalresque fiction, 'interweaving' sustains a series of parallel narratives which touch and diverge and converge again in a complex structural unity which has been described as 'the most elusive ever devised'.[25] But in a different experiment in longer fiction, in *Celestina* and the Spanish descendants of Italian humanistic comedy, sometimes called 'novels in dialogue', the omniscient author vanishes, such comment as we have is ambiguously provided by the characters themselves, and any narration or description is fragmentary and handled obliquely within the dialogue. And the rediscovery of Heliodorus and the Byzantine novel provided the inspiration for another complex but not especially fruitful form, essentially episodic, and heavily dependent on intercalated short stories to achieve its length.

Meanwhile, shorter fiction departed drastically and dramatically from the form of the Italian *novella* in sundry different ways. Third-person narration is almost wholly displaced by first-person narration: Flores's Grimalte tells his own story, as does Arnalte to San Pedro, but that first-person narrative is set within the frame of San Pedro's own first-person tale, while in *Cárcel de Amor* the narrator himself intervenes in the story of Leriano and Laureola. The increasing use of letters in such forms of fiction culminates in the first true epistolary novel, Juan de Segura's *Processo de cartas de amores* (Alcalá, 1548). Indeed, it is difficult to think of any narrative device with which Spanish writers of the late fifteenth and the sixteenth centuries did not at some time play: with first-person and third-person narration, with pseudo-autobiography in which the 'author' is clearly not the author, with tales within tales, with flashbacks and temporal displacements (starting *in medias res* or even at the conclusion), with episodic narrative held together only by a character or characters, with letters and diaries, with internal monologue, with stories told solely through dialogue, with *Rashomon*-style perspectivism (the same events described from the differing viewpoints of different characters), with 'objective' (and unselective) reporting, and so on.[26]

The story with a beginning, a middle, and an end, told by an omniscient author, 'undoubtedly the traditional and "natural" mode of narration',[27] the form which, in an overwhelming majority of cases, 'the modern novel' was to take, is conspicuous by its absence. Schevill, noting that 'the development of the short story, genuine in everything that regards the true psychology of sentiment and character, was to be put off to a still distant future' (p. 113), opts for an unlikely sociological explanation: the absence of a bourgeoisie, a centralized monarchy, well-defined aristocratic traditions, etc.; but this scarcely affects the question of narrative technique. It is hard to believe that the Spanish experimentation (which Schevill disregards, seeing only the perpetuation of medieval modes) is attributable to a negative reaction to the work of Aeneas Sylvius Piccolomini; but it may not be implausible to suggest that the search for novel narrative modes could not have been pursued except from the springboard of that 'traditional and "natural" ' model, widely diffused and so much admired that writers felt they could surpass him only by doing something quite different. I offer this notion only as a possible answer to a problem which indubitably exists, and to which I can find no other solution.

[*Essays on Narrative Fiction in the Iberian Peninsula in Honour of Frank Pierce* (Oxford: Dolphin, 1982), pp. 243-55]

Notes

1. While it is not my purpose to provide a bibliography of works on Pius II, it may be useful to note some of the less specialized and most frequently cited books about him: Georg Voigt, *Enea Silvio de' Piccolomini als Papst Pius der Zweite und sein Zeitalter*, 3 vols (Berlin, 1856–63); M. Bargellini, *Della vita e degli scritti di Enea Silvio Piccolomini* (Sienna, 1870); A. Weiss, *Aeneas Sylvius Piccolomini als Papst Pius II: Sein Leben und Einfluss auf die literarische Cultur Deutschlands* (Graz, 1897); W. Boulting, *Aeneas Sylvius: Orator, Man of Letters, Statesman and Pope* (London, 1908); Cecilia M. Ady, *Pius II (Aeneas Silvius Piccolomini), the Humanist Pope* (London, 1913); Gioacchino Paparelli, *Enea Silvio Piccolomini: l'umanesimo sul soglio di Pietro* (Bari, 1950; reprinted Ravenna, 1978); E. Dupré-Theseider, *Enea Silvio Piccolomini umanista* (Bologna, 1955); Berthe Widmer, *Enea Silvio Piccolomini, Papst Pius II: Biographie und ausgewählte Texte aus seinen Schriften* (Basle-Stuttgart, 1960); Rosamund Joscelyne Mitchell, *The Laurels and the Tiara: Pope Pius II, 1458–1464* (London, 1962); Berthe Widmer, *Enea Silvio Piccolomini in der sittlichen und politischen Entscheidung* (Basle-Stuttgart, 1963); L. M. Veit, *Pensiero e vita religiosa di Enea Silvio Piccolomini prima della sua consacrazione episcopale* (Rome, 1964); G. Ceserani, *Pio II* (Milan, 1965); Giuseppe Bernetti, *Saggi e studi sugli scritti di Enea Silvio Piccolomini, Papa Pio II (1405–1464)* (Florence, 1971); G. Ugurgieri della Berardenga, *Pio II Piccolomini, con notizie su Pio III* (Florence, 1973).

2. His bawdy humanistic comedy, *Chrysis*, sometimes mentioned as a possible source for *Celestina*, has attracted much attention, but was not printed and exists in only one manuscript, Codex 462 of the Prince Lobkowitz Library, Prague. Two modern editions, by Ireneo Sanesi (Florence, 1941) and Enzo Cecchini (Florence, 1968), provide ample bibliography on the subject. See also Bernetti (note 1), pp. 129-52.

3. Paparelli (see note 1) provides a chronological list with a useful select bibliography on each work, pp. 265-69.

4. MS 9/2176. I am indebted to Professor Tate for the information and for photocopies. This manuscript contains the dedication to the Imperial Chancellor, Gaspar Schlick (here miscopied as 'Nich'), which does not appear in the Spanish translation.

5. The first edition appeared in Basle, 1551 (Bib. Nac., Madrid, I/11336). It has been reprinted in facsimile by Minerva GMBH (Frankfurt, 1965).

6. Private communication: Professor Russell has not made public this unnerving item of news. However, since this *Opera omnia* also contains a truncated version of Leonardo Bruni di Arezzo's *Poliscena* (attributed, of course, to Piccolomini), its authenticity must be exceedingly doubtful. The edition referred to by Marcelino Menéndez Pelayo, *Orígenes de la novela*, III, NBAE, XIV (Madrid, 1910), p. lxxiv, by María Rosa Lida de Malkiel, *La originalidad artística de 'La Celestina'* (Buenos Aires, 1962; 2nd ed. 1970), p. 37, and by Professor Russell is

that of Amsterdam, 1652. Mario Emilio Cosenza, *Dictionary of the Italian Humanists and of the World of Classical Scholarship in Italy, 1300–1800*, 5 vols (Boston, Mass., 1962) refers to an edition of 1651 by 'Drudo Hilarius'.

7. *De duobus amantibus historia*, edited by Josephus I. Dévay (Budapest, 1904). The MSS in question are: Codex Vindobonum 3148 (Imperial Library, Vienna); Codex Vindobonum 3205; Codex Béldianus (Archbishop's Library, Zagreb); Codex Gervasii (Budapest); and Codex Bambergensis B.III.41 (Bamberg). A more accessible edition may be found in *Der Briefwechsel des Eneas Silvio Piccolomini*, edited by Rudolf Wolkan, 4 vols, Fontes Rerum Austriacarum, 61, 62, 67, and 68 (Vienna, 1909–18), I, 353-93.

8. I do not intend to pursue here the suggestion that the translation is in fact the work of Fernando de Rojas. This idea was first (to the best of my knowledge) adumbrated by Clara Louisa Penney, in *Symposium*, 16 (1962), 237-38, while reviewing A. D. Deyermond, *The Petrarchan Sources of 'La Celestina'* (Oxford, 1961). It has been resurrected, quite independently, by Miguel Marciales, *Carta al profesor Stephen Gilman sobre problemas de la 'Celestina'* (Mérida, Venezuela, 1975), especially pp. 16-18: 'se desprende del texto castellano un inconfundible olor y sabor rojano'. Marciales is working on a critical edition in which, no doubt, his suggestive but as yet inconclusive stylistic evidence will be set out in detail.

9. *Historia de dos amantes*, edited by R. Foulché-Delbosc (Barcelona, 1907); edited by M. Menéndez Pelayo, *Orígenes*, IV, 104-23 (note that the text is not reprinted in the Edición Nacional (Santander, 1943; reprinted Madrid, 1962)); *Historia muy verdadera de dos amantes, Euralio* [sic!], *franco, y Lucrecia, senesa*, facsimile, with an introductory note by Agustín G. de Amezúa (Madrid, 1952); I am grateful to Professor Marciales for sending me a draft of the text of his critical edition. All these scholars used the copy of Seville 1512 in the Biblioteca Nacional (R/3647), but others are extant in the British Library (C.63.c.13) and in the Hispanic Society of America.

10. Although this copy is grossly defective, lacking not only the final page with the colophon but various works advertised on the title-page (*Remedios contra el amor*, a life of Piccolomini, and 'ciertas sentencias y proverbios de mucha excelencia del dicho eneas'), the place and date of publication are almost certainly those of the volume of identical content noted in the Colombine *Registrum*. Salvá (the former owner of the Bib. Nac. 1512 copy, see Salvá, No. 1678) also possessed a fragmentary copy (quite possibly the Ajuda copy) of this older edition, and believed that its typographical characteristics did fit Salamanca 1496. Amezúa (see note 9) is inaccurate and misleading, giving the date as 1495, and alleging that 'tanto Haebler como Vindel estiman que debió ser impreso en aquella ciudad, basándose para ello en sus caracteres tipográficos'. But Konrad Haebler, *Tipografía ibérica del siglo XV* (The Hague, 1903–17; reprinted New York, n.d.), No. 2, copies Salvá and says specifically that the copy has been lost, while Francisco Vindel, *El arte tipográfico en España durante el siglo XV*, 9 vols (Madrid,

1949–54), II, No. 67, copies Salvá and Haebler, states that he has not seen a copy, but mentions that one is extant in the Ajuda. See also J.-P. Lecertua, 'L'Estoria de dos amantes . . . , traduction espagnole de la *Historia de duobus (se) amantibus* (1444) d'Aeneas Sylvius Piccolomini (Pape Pie II)', *Travaux et Mémoires: Publications de l'U.É.R. des Lettres et Sciences Humaines de l'Université de Limoges: Collection Études Ibériques*, 1 (1975), 1-78.

11. I am deeply indebted to Don Eugenio Asensio for his efforts, albeit fruitless, to secure for me microfilm of this text.

12. His memoirs, *Commentarii rerum memorabilium quae temporibus suis contigerunt*, are not in the *Opera omnia* and were first published in Rome, 1584. Voigt, II, 359-77, added a thirteenth book. There is an English translation by Florence Alden Gragg, with an introduction and notes by Leona C. Gabel, *The Commentaries of Pius II*, 5 vols (Northampton, Mass., 1936–57) and an Italian version by Giuseppe Bernetti, *I commentari*, 5 vols (Sienna, 1972–73). The *Epistolae* appeared in earlier editions (Milan, 1487, etc.) and figure in the *Opera*, 500-962. Weiss (see note 1) added 149 previously unpublished letters, and other scholars have gone on adding to the corpus, which cannot yet be regarded as complete. A useful selection, *Selected Letters*, has been translated by Albert R. Bacca (Northridge, California, 1969).

13. For Voigt see note 1; J. G. Rowe, 'The Tragedy of Aeneas Sylvius Piccolomini (Pope Pius II): An Interpretation', *Church History*, 30 (1961), 288-313 (Rowe also dwells on his inability to reconcile the often conflicting interests of Church and State, and to determine his primary allegiance); Letterio di Francia, *Novellistica*, 2 vols, Storia dei Generi Letterari (Milan, 1924), I, 305-17. Sundry other rather superficial 'profili' also discuss the matter. For his early religious preoccupations see Veit, *Pensiero e vita religiosa* (cited in note 1).

14. G. Zannoni, 'Per la *Storia di due amanti* di Enea Silvio Piccolomini', *Rendiconti della Reale Accademia dei Lincei*, 4th ser., 6 (1890), 116-27; and 'Per la storia di una storia d'amore', *La cultura*, 11 (1890), 85-92. For a survey of the facts see A. Frugoni, 'Enea Silvio Piccolomini e l'avventura senese di Gaspare Schlick', *Rinascita*, 4 (1941), 229-49.

15. Many years ago I undertook to analyse the translator's technique, grouping the discrepancies between the Latin and the Spanish under three headings: (1) errors attributable to the compositor, (2) errors due to the translator's misunderstanding of the Latin, and (3) deliberate amplification or modification of the sense. But every category shades into the next, I was not properly aware of the gross corruption of the texts available to our translator (see note 4 above), and could come to no useful conclusion beyond the *perogrullada* that the anonymous translator had allowed himself some licence. Miguel Marciales (see note 8) has gone a great deal further, tentatively identifying the Latin original as Incunable 2175 of the Biblioteca Nacional, and suggesting that sundry stylistic modifications betray the hand of Rojas. We must await his fuller presentation of the evidence. Lecertua, for his analysis of the translator's

modifications and misunderstandings of the text, has relied on the *Opera omnia*.

16. He also shows (Ed. Nac., III, 111-12) that Pius II was a source for the *Libro de los dichos y hechos del rey don Alfonso* (Valencia, 1527), but this work is simply Juan de Molina's translation of Antonio Beccadelli, *De dictis et factis Alphonsi, regis Aragonum et Neapolis*.

17. Arturo Farinelli, *Italia e Spagna*, 2 vols (Turin, 1929), I, 232-34 and 400. He also alleges that the *Historia* is 'indubbiamente' reflected in Gonzalo Céspedes y Meneses, *Varia fortuna del soldado Pindaro* (Lisbon, 1626), a claim I have not attempted to investigate. Lecertua's preliminary study of the work alludes to treatises on love, the form and content of love-letters and speeches, the epistolary novel, and exemplary literature of scandalous content.

18. F. Castro Guisasola, *Observaciones sobre las fuentes literarias de 'La Celestina'* (Madrid, 1924), pp. 145-47; Rudolph Schevill, *Ovid and the Renascence in Spain* (Berkeley, 1913; reprinted Hildesheim, 1971), p. 113.

19. See note 6. For page-references (fifty-six of them, if we include observations on the 'imitations') see the index, s.v. Piccolomini.

20. I dare not affirm that Lida de Malkiel did not note somewhere the coincidence of 'Sosias' and 'Sosia', but I cannot find the place.

21. For a host of common antecedents see Charles E. Kany, *The Beginnings of the Epistolary Novel in France, Italy and Spain* (Berkeley, 1937).

22. Schevill (see note 18) has analysed in detail the Ovidian quotations and reminiscences in *De duobus amantibus*, pp. 107-13. Lecertua has identified further quotations missed by Dévay.

23. *Cárcel de Amor*, edited by Keith Whinnom (Madrid, 1972), p. 79.

24. For a useful analysis of the techniques of Piccolomini and his predecessors see Wolfram Krömer, *Kurzerzählungen und Novellen in den romanischen Literaturen bis 1700* (Berlin, 1973), now available as *Formas de la narración breve en las literaturas románicas hasta 1700*, translated by Juan Conde (Madrid, 1979). The earliest Spanish writers to whom Krömer pays any attention are Montemayor and Timoneda.

25. Eugene Vinaver, *The Rise of Romance* (New York-Oxford, 1971), p. 81. See also Frank Pierce, *Amadís de Gaula* (Boston, Mass., 1976), especially pp. 43-79, for ample discussion of the technique and further references.

26. I must take it that substantiating references, which would take up too much space, can be readily supplied by my readers.

27. René Wellek and Austin Warren, *Theory of Literature* (first printed 1942; I have used the Penguin edition of Harmondsworth, 1973), p. 222.

14

Autor and *Tratado* in the Fifteenth Century: Semantic Latinism or Etymological Trap?

in memory of Harold Hall

That words can change their meanings is a truism which no one would attempt to dispute. For students of older literature this fact poses a problem with distinct facets. On the one hand we are obliged to learn the now obsolete senses of a very extensive list of words (and it is surprising that more scholars have not fallen into the trap of reading modern meanings into a medieval text), while on the other hand we need to know precisely when a word ceases to carry the connotations it once possessed. But, to complicate matters further, we must also attempt to determine the instances in which a writer revives an archaic meaning, or employs a Romance word not in its contemporary vernacular sense but with semantic overtones of its Latin etymon.[1] It is this latter aspect of the problem of semantic change which will concern me now. While it would clearly be rash to ignore, in any medieval or Renaissance text, the possibility of semantic latinism, I intend to suggest that some critics, specifically of the Spanish sentimental romance, who have based interpretations on what they believed to be the etymological senses of certain words, most particularly *autor* and *tratado*, have fallen into what might be termed the etymological trap.

To assist us in determining whether or not we have to do with semantic latinism, there are three tests which it is possible to apply, even though none of them can always be conclusive. First, we can ask ourselves whether we are faced with a latinizing writer, that is to say, one who simultaneously uses Latin-based neologisms, imitates Latin syntax, and displays, by erudite allusion or periphrasis, some acquaintance with Latin literature, history, and mythology. This test does not, of course, rule out either the possibility that our latinizing author is using a word in its ordinary Spanish sense (as Mena, in contrast with Góngora, does with *glorioso*) or the possibility that a less cultured writer has accepted as Spanish the etymological connotation of a word revived by an earlier latinizing author. But by and large the probability of semantic latinism is linked with more readily identifiable features of latinizing.

Secondly, we can go on to ask ourselves whether the text makes proper sense if we insist on reading a word in its normal contemporary Spanish meaning. If it does not, we may be driven back to the Latin to find a satisfactory interpretation of, say, *generoso*, 'of high lineage', or *presunción*, 'noble bearing'.[2] A curious sub-category of semantic latinism is created by bad translation. An enormous amount of Spanish Renaissance literature, from Mena on, quotes or paraphrases authors such as Ovid, Virgil, Lucretius, Seneca, and Boethius. If the derived Romance vocable is used to translate a Latin word, we may suspect that the translator intends us to read it in its Latin sense, in which case it is straightforward semantic latinism. But when other errors of comprehension show us that our translator is less than competent, as in the anonymous Spanish version of Piccolomini's *Historia de duobus amantibus*,[3] we are bound to suspect that he has been misled by some *faux ami*: while the text may make proper sense only if we treat certain words as semantic latinisms, we must also recognize that the translator may not have intended them as such.

Finally, if we are still in difficulties, we must undertake to inspect the entire semantic field of related terms and possible synonymous substitutes.

If we look at the problem of *autor* (also *auctor* and *actor*), we find that in Classical Latin itself AUCTOR presents us with some etymological puzzles. In the first place, it is the agent noun derived from the verb AUGĒRE (cognate with English *wax*), which has the primary meanings of 'to grow' (intransitive) and 'to augment' (transitive). (In the manuals of rhetoric it has a secondary meaning synonymous with AMPLIFICARE, 'to embellish' or 'to enrich'.) It does not mean 'to instigate'. Nevertheless, the primary meanings of the agent noun AUCTOR are precisely those of 'instigator', 'ancestor', 'founder' or 'creator'. A further set of meanings appear to derive not from these primary senses of AUCTOR but from its early confusion, well attested in the texts, with ACTOR, the agent noun derived from AGĒRE, 'to drive', 'to govern', 'to perform', 'to transact', 'to do', etc. However, from a multiplicity of possible senses of AUCTOR, we need concern ourselves only with two, namely those of 'author', 'writer', and 'model', 'exemplar' (although it may be worth noting in passing that in Medieval Latin probably the most frequently documented sense of the word is neither of these, but the reciprocal of EMPTOR, namely 'vendor').

The meaning of AUCTOR is also affected by that of AUCTORITAS. Although we can now easily see that the philological progression, even if we cannot assign dates to the derived words, can only be: verb (AUGĒRE), agent noun (AUCTOR), and abstract noun (AUCTORITAS), this obvious fact seems to have been less evident to some Latin grammarians. Servius Honoratus and Probus (and doubtless others if one cared to search) attempt to establish a distinction between AUCTOR, feminine gender, and AUCTRIX.[4] They prescribe that AUCTRIX should be reserved for the literary authoress, and that AUCTOR, feminine, is the word to be used for a woman holding AUCTORITAS in its prevailing significance, which I take to be 'authority', 'reputation', plus, possibly, 'liberty', 'independence', 'freedom of action' or even 'status of one to be admired and imitated'.

Over fifty years ago, in a brief note which has, through frequency of citation, acquired something like the status of a classic, M.-D. Chenu argued that, starting in the thirteenth century, AUCTOR, 'author', by association with the term AUCTORITAS, 'authority', gained a new meaning, designating someone who, by virtue of some kind of recognition or endorsement, has had his views validated, so that they are thereafter accepted as part of the great chain of 'authority', reaching back ultimately to the Scriptures.[5] It is also well known that the study of rhetoric, that is, of the rules in the manuals of rhetoric, went hand in hand with the study of AUCTORES, by implication 'the best authors', 'models' for imitation. And while Virgil and Ovid may at first have been grammatical and stylistic models, medieval commentators soon converted them into 'philosophers', writers whose works enshrined incontrovertible and even Christian truths.

When, in the fifteenth century, Juan de Mena tells us that his friend Enrique de Villena was an 'autor muy sçiente' (*Laberinto*, st. 125), it matters little whether we take this to mean that Villena was a 'very learned writer' or a 'most learned authority'. But the semantic problem acquires crucial importance when a writer applies the term to himself. Joseph F. Chorpenning, for instance, claims that in *Cárcel de Amor* Diego de San Pedro 'is an *auctor* exercising his *auctoritas*',[6] and even though Barbara F. Weissberger flatly contradicts him (San Pedro is 'an *auctor* without *auctoritas*'), she writes that 'traditionally, the *auctor* functions primarily as the representative of *auctoritas*, of impersonal, universal, objective truth'.[7] There is a subsidiary problem here in that the vast majority of fifteenth-century occurrences of the term *autor* are to be found in rubrics: 'habla el autor', 'el autor buelve a la estoria', and so on, and the notorious instability of rubrics in medieval manuscripts and early printed editions does seem to suggest that copyists and compositors felt free to insert, delete or modify them.[8] But we can scarcely doubt that a great many writers did refer to themselves as *'autores'*. Did they really mean to imply that they regarded themselves as the representatives of AUCTORITAS, 'received truth'?

It is helpful to look at the problem in conjunction with that of *tratado* (and *tractado*). The Latin word TRACTATUS is a post-verbal formation from (originally, obviously, the past participle of) TRACTARE (the frequentative of TRAHĔRE), which has the primary meaning of 'to drag' or 'to pull about', and the secondary metaphorical meanings of 'to manage' and 'to discuss'. The primary meanings of TRACTATUS are 'handling' (literal and meta-phorical), 'consideration', 'treatment', 'discussion'. It is true that the term is later applied to works to which we should now apply the labels of 'treatise' or 'sermon', but critics seem to have overlooked the fact that even in Latin, and even in the twelfth century, the use of the term is not confined to discursive factual works, but is also used for fiction, allegory, and satire.[9] Moreover, the *tractatus* was not a recognized literary form, and is not listed as such in the manuals of rhetoric. I can find in these manuals no use of the term except in the sense of 'handling' or 'treatment', so that, for instance, *tractatus loci communis* is not to be translated as 'a treatise on the commonplace' but as 'how to use commonplaces convincingly in a discourse'.[10]

It was Anna Krause who first argued that the term *tractado* used by Diego de San Pedro and other writers of sentimental romances meant that their works were not novels, but 'treatises', composed with didactic intent.[11] Samonà attacked this interpretation in 1960, and Wardropper in 1965,[12] but it has found favour with many critics of the *novela sentimental*. Armando Durán allowed various intermediate steps from the 'pure' *tractatus*, through Rodríguez del Padrón, Flores, and San Pedro, to the epistolary novel of Segura,[13] but Dinko Cvitanović has insisted on the 'tratadismo' of the genre.[14] Chorpenning, while clearly aware that the *tractatus* is not a set form, since he proposes the *oratio* as the rhetorical model for *Cárcel de Amor*, nevertheless subscribes to the view of its didactic purpose; and Barbara Weissberger, while also aware that 'more than to any particular literary form, the term [*tractado*] refers to certain rhetorical techniques', states that 'the writer of a *tractado* is by definition an *auctor*', and explicitly rejects my own earlier suggestions, admittedly unsubstantiated, that in the fifteenth century *autor* and *tratado* had lost whatever 'etymological' force they might once have had.[15]

Clearly our conception of the nature of the sentimental romance must be affected if we assume that *autor* implies a self-proclaimed 'authority' and that *tratado* means 'didactic treatise'. How, then, is it possible to determine who is right?

The first test which I proposed, that of the otherwise latinizing writer, is inconclusive. Nicolás Núñez, for instance, while he could scarcely be called a learned or latinizing author, uses *autor* and *tratado* in precisely the same way as San Pedro, from whom he may well have borrowed them, along with various other poorly assimilated latinizing traits.[16] But in any event, even when we do have a latinizing author, it is not legitimate to suppose that he employs every Spanish word in the sense of its Latin etymon. The second test is little better: while some critics would argue that we are losing the full implication of the terms, there is no context in which *autor* does not make perfectly satisfactory sense if it is translated simply as 'author', 'writer' or even 'narrator'.[17] In the same way, I can find no sentimental romance, or reference to a sentimental romance, in which *tratado* does not make sense as 'story'. But while the contexts at no time oblige us to posit semantic latinism, that fact alone does not prove that it is wrong to do so. I fall back on the third test, which involves semantic fields. What, we must ask ourselves, were the alternatives available in the fifteenth century to a Spanish writer who wished to say 'writer' or 'story'?

Auctor, *autor*, and *actor*[18] can be dealt with fairly simply. A long list of fifteenth-century writers, whom it would be otiose to detail, refer to themselves, or are described in the rubrics, as *autores*. Occasionally we find that writers in search of synonyms to refer to other writers may call them *sabios* or *filósofos*, but these terms clearly cover a different and broader semantic area, while *estoriador* and *orador* would seem to be more specialized than *autor*;[19] Rojas also calls his *primer auctor* an *inventor*, a term which is certainly synonymous with *auctor*, but which is extremely rare, is a blatant semantic latinism, and carries no overtones of 'authority';[20] and Juan Manuel's *obrador* appears to be quite obsolete.[21] One possible synonym, *poeta*, which in a handful of texts seems to carry no more than its etymological connotation of 'creator', 'author', 'prose-writer', is very infrequent and was rapidly contaminated by its obvious association with *poesía*.[22] Finally, what might seem an obvious synonymous alternative to *autor*, namely *escritor*, is conspicuous by its rarity, and when not set in an unequivocal context or accompanied by an adjective intended to remove its inherent ambiguity, as in 'los antiguos escriptores' (Rojas, prologue), means 'scribe', 'copyist': Montalvo, for instance, complains that the text of *Amadís* was corrupt 'por falta de los malos escriptores'.[23] It is worth noting that later fifteenth-century writers similarly eschew the verb *escribir*. Although, as we shall see, *escritura* is regularly used as an alternative to *obra*, *estoria*, and *tratado*, fifteenth-century literary works are almost never *escritos*, but *hechos* or *compuestos*. There is no question, therefore, of *autor*'s 'becoming simply an alternative to *"escritor"* ',[24] or at least, not as early as the fifteenth century. With the possible exceptions of *poeta* and *inventor*, there was no satisfactory alternative, no simple synonymous term for 'writer', 'author'. While it might be argued that Spanish did in fact lack such a basic neutral term, the supposition would seem to be, *a priori*, improbable, and it is contradicted by certain texts: the *autor* of *Cárcel de Amor*, for instance, is fallible ('without *auctoritas*'), and when Flores uses the persona of Grimalte as his narrator ('Grimalte como auctor', etc.), he is clearly lending him no 'authority'.

Furthermore, the 'etymological' argument requires closer scrutiny. It is alleged that in the thirteenth century Latin AUCTOR was affected by association with AUCTORITAS. This proposition must be more accurately restated: one sense of AUCTOR may have been contaminated by one sense of AUCTORITAS. The abstract noun retained throughout the Middle Ages a concrete primary sense of anything which was 'authored', that is, 'product', 'production', 'invention', 'creation', and it was also synonymous with AUCTOR in the sense of 'producer', 'inventor'. (One might note that Berceo, whom Weissberger (p. 208) quotes to support Chenu, never uses the word *auctor* (or *autor*) but always *auctoridade* or *autoridad[e]*.[25]) It would not be difficult to maintain that AUCTOR trails some implications of 'authority' in several of its meanings, such as 'vendor', 'witness', 'agent', 'spokesman', 'trustee', possibly even 'ancestor' and 'founder', and certainly in Medieval Latin 'judge', 'teacher of law'; but in others the overtones of 'authority' would seem to be minimal: 'instigator', 'performer', 'investigator', 'writer'. Servius Honoratus and Probus explicitly attach no sense of 'authority' to AUCTRIX, 'female writer'.

In sum, I cannot see that there is any evidence of substance that, in the fifteenth century, any writer who calls himself an *autor* is either laying claim to *auctoritas* or pretending to a place in the canon of the classics. What the texts show is that any writer who writes a book is an *autor* who *compone* or *faze* . . . almost anything except a *libro*.

It is true that when Queen Isabella purchased a book she did buy a *libro*,[26] and that the term appears in the title of a few fifteenth-century works, such as *Libro del esforçado cavallero don Tristán de Leonís* (Valladolid, 1501);[27] but the term leads a double life as the name of a division of a book: *Los quatro libros de Amadís*, and so forth. And while the alternative names for the divisions of a book (which include *tratado*, as in *Lazarillo* and late editions of *Celestina*) would lead us too far afield, it may be worth noting that in 1587 Juan Gracián called *Teágenes y Cariclea*, which is divided into ten *libros*, his *librito*.[28] So far as I have been able to determine, *libro* is applied to no sentimental romances except in the title and subtitle of the printed translations of *Fiammetta*[29] and in the colophon of the Burgos 1522 edition of *Arnalte* ('Aquí se acaba el libro de Arnalte y Lucenda').

There are five other terms we can fairly rapidly discard. What was potentially the most useful one for the sentimental romance, namely *novela*, is listed by Nebrija as a translation of FABULA;[30] but its currency is extraordinarily limited, and the very same manuscript (Biblioteca Nacional, Madrid, MS 6052) which calls *Siervo libre* a *novella* ('Aquí acaba la novella') uses it for Diego de Cañizares's translation of *Scala coeli*, obviously in the sense of the Italian *buona novella*, 'gospel' or 'good news'. *Fición* appears in the prologues of the translation of Piccolomini's *Historia de duobus amantibus* (1496) and of the anonymous *Qüestión de amor* (1513), where it appears to mean 'work of fiction', but in *Siervo libre* (before 1440) it is clear that Rodríguez del Padrón uses it to mean 'stories from classical mythology' or perhaps even more restrictively as 'classical allusions'. *Relación* may be found in the prologue of *Gracisla* (1506?) and in the final section of Segura's *Processo de cartas* (1548) and obviously means no more than 'account'. Indeed, although in each case the works are fiction, their authors maintain the pretence of their being true, so that *relación* (the term for a legal report to a tribunal) implies 'factual account', and is hence unsuitable for 'romance' or 'novel'. In the sentimental romances *razón* is employed only for a speech within the narrative, and never for the whole work. And if we look outside the *novela sentimental*, the only other term I have been able to find besides those I discuss below is the polysemic *dezir*, for instance in *Tristán de Leonís* (conclusion).

The available terms in frequent current use are *obra*, *escritura* (*escriptura*, *scritura*, etc.), *estoria* (*historia*), and *tratado*. It can easily be shown that *obra* and *escritura* are archilexemes which mean no more than 'work' and 'piece of writing', and we find them applied indiscriminately to fiction and non-fiction, prose and verse. *Obra* implies a work of certain substance, not for instance a *canción*, but embraces a very broad semantic field, and it is of little significance that it should be used for *Arnalte*, *Cárcel*, *Grimalte*, Núñez's *Cárcel*, *Gracisla*, *Qüestión de amor*, *Processo de cartas*, etc. *Escritura* (rather less frequent) is employed internally in the prologues of *Cárcel de Amor* and *Gracisla*, and applied externally to *Arnalte* (*Cárcel*, prologue) and *Fiammetta* (*Grimalte*, prologue).

When we search for the relevant hyponyms of the superordinate *obra* and *escritura*, we find that the only terms remaining are *estoria* and *tratado*, and note with some astonishment the total disappearance of the once common *cuento*.[31] While the texts (*Siervo*, *Arnalte*, *Cárcel*, *Grisel*, *Eurialo*, etc.) suggest that *estoria*, in the sense of 'story', can always be substituted for *tratado* in the sense of 'story', the converse is not true, and the terms are only partially synonymous. Again rather curiously, we discover that the old (and modern) ambiguity of *historia* does not lie primarily in the confusion of '(factual) history' and '(fictional) story'. In the latter half of the fifteenth century, genuine histories are called, in decreasing order of frequency, *crónicas* (*corónicas*), *anales* or *tratados*; and *estoria* refers to factual history only when it is the biography of an individual.[32] Since many of the romances of chivalry are entitled *estorias*, there is no way (since *vida* is equally ambiguous) of distinguishing between factual and fictional biography, except by adding a qualifying adjective; and the force of *verdadera* is repeatedly undermined by the pretence that fiction is fact, as in *Estoria muy verdadera de los dos amantes*. There are other curious, if rare, uses of the term,[33] but the real ambiguity which arises with *estoria* is that, again and again, in the middle of an *estoria*, we find that the author, after some digression, 'vuelve a la estoria', that is to say, to the main line of the narrative. *Estoria*, in fact, in the period which concerns us, normally implies the continuous narration of the 'story' of an individual character or pair of characters. Its hyperonymous use (for instance in the titles of *Grisel* and *Eurialo*) is synecdochic.

It is undeniable that, in many contexts, *tratado* might properly be translated as 'treatise'. It should be noted, however, that we need to be especially careful about titles, since many modern bibliographies, histories of literature, and even editions are quite misleading: works are repeatedly entitled *tratados* when the original manuscript or edition provides no warranty for this label. So, for instance, Diego de Valera's *Tratado en defensa de las mugeres* is in reality *Dos trabajos en defensa de las mugeres*; Fray Íñigo de Mendoza's *Tratado de las ceremonias de la misa* is simply *De las ceremonias de la misa*; Fray Hernando de Talavera's *Tratado de cómo vestir* is *Commo en el vestir y calçar comúnmente se cometen muchos peccados*; Martín de Ávila's *Tratado de la cargosa vida* is *De la cargosa vida y trabajoso estado y angustiosa condición de los príncipes*; and I have collected at least sixteen other examples of this incorrect, if convenient, insertion by modern scholars of *tratado* in the titles of works which do not originally have it.[34] It is true that an at least equal number of works, which could be described as treatises, do genuinely have *tratado* in their titles, but it is interesting that so many 'treatises' do not make use of the term.

Furthermore, as with *tractatus*, the use of *tratado* is by no means confined to works which we should normally think of as treatises. Valera's *Tractado de Providencia contra Fortuna* is no more (or less) a 'treatise' than Boethius's *De consolatione Philosophiae* or Petrarch's *De remediis*; Pulgar's *Tratado de los reyes de Granada* is a series of biographical historical sketches; the Archpriest of Talavera referred to Juan Ruiz's *Libro de buen amor* as a *tratado*;[35] Rodríguez del Padrón applied the term to Ovid's *Heroides*;[36] and when we turn to works of fiction we find that *Siervo libre* (prologue), *Arnalte* (title, prologue, rubrics, and colophon, plus a cross-reference in *Cárcel*), *Cárcel* (title, plus cross-references in Núñez's continuation), *Grisel* (subtitle, first rubric, and colophon), *Grimalte* (subtitle), Núñez's *Cárcel* (title), *Eurialo* (prologue and colophon), and *Qüestión de amor* (prologue) are all *tratados*. But among what might be broadly classified as sentimental romances, there are three interesting exceptions: *Gracisla* and *Processo de cartas* are described as *relaciones*, not *tratados* (the evidence is flimsy but might indicate the mutually exclusive use of these terms), and, much more significantly, the 1523 edition of the translation of *Fiammetta* is entitled *Libro llamado Fiameta porque trata de los amores duna notable napolitana*, etc. There seems little reason to suppose that there is any distinction to be made between a *tratado* and a *libro que trata de* any subject at all, factually or fictionally, didactically or otherwise. The only essential qualifications for a *tratado* are that it should be written down,[37] that it should, at least in the latter part of the fifteenth century, be in prose, and, possibly, that it should be of a certain length.

We are, of course, left with the disconcerting fact that, before the rise of *novela*, Spanish possessed no unequivocal term for prose fiction. And yet there may be an answer to the curious problem posed by this apparent lacuna. Given that the 'meaning' of a polysemic word is context-bound and that synonyms are not synonymous in all contexts, and given that on the one hand *estoria* meant 'historical biography' and 'fictional story' while on the other *tratado* meant 'treatise' and 'fictional story', then, if the terms are in fact used synonymously, the juxtaposition or evident interchangeability of the two (*Siervo, Arnalte, Cárcel, Grisel, Eurialo*, etc.) would have served to remove the ambiguity, and to neutralize the semantic overload carried by each word separately. However that may be, I must contend that, on the evidence available, there exist no adequate reasons for insisting that the term *tratado*, when applied to a sentimental romance, must be translated and interpreted as 'didactic treatise'.[38]

All this does not mean that a sentimental romance may not be allowed to have a didactic purpose;[39] it means only that the demonstration of the author's didactic intent must derive from a proper analysis of the text.

[*BHS*, 59 (1982), 211-18]

Notes

1. For bibliographical references and sundry incontestable examples of semantic latinism see Manuel Alvar and Sebastián Mariner, 'Latinismos', in *Enciclopedia lingüística hispánica*, II (Madrid, 1967), 3-49, espec. §28, 25-26.

2. Both examples occur in San Pedro's verse panegyric of Isabella; see Diego de San Pedro, *Obras completas*, I: *Tractado de amores de Arnalte y Lucenda; Sermón*, ed. Keith Whinnom (Madrid, 1973), p. 97.

3. See Jean-Paul Lecertua, 'L'*Estoria de dos amantes, Eurialo y Lucrecia*: Traduction espagnole de la *Historia de duobus (se) amantibus* (1444), d'Aeneas Sylvius Piccolomini (Pie II)', *TRAMES: Études Ibériques*, 1 (1975), 1-78. It should be noted that Lecertua collates his Spanish with the Latin text of the *Opera omnia* of Basle, 1571, and that it is probable that the translator used a much more corrupt text; there must remain, nevertheless, a substantial residue of plain mistranslations. See also my 'The *Historia de duobus amantibus* of Aeneas Sylvius Piccolomini (Pope Pius II) and the Development of Spanish Golden-Age Fiction', in the forthcoming homage-volume to Frank Pierce, edited by R. B. Tate [pp. 191-203, above].

4. Servius Honoratus, *Ad Vergilium*, ad XII, 159. There are innumerable editions from the fifteenth century on; I have used the Teubner Classics text, *Servii Grammatici qui feruntur in Vergilii carmina commentarii*, ed. Georg Thilo and Hermann Hagen, 3 vols (Leipzig, 1878–1902), in which the note referred to may be found in vol. II. Probus, in *Grammatici latini*, ed. Heinrich Keil, 8 vols (Leipzig, 1855–80), p. 1452.

5. '*Auctor, actor, autor*', *Bulletin Du Cange: Archivum Latinitatis Medii Aevi*, 3 (1927), 81-86.

6. 'Rhetoric and Feminism in the *Cárcel de Amor*', BHS, 54 (1977), 1-8, at p. 4.

7. ' "Habla el auctor": *L'elegia di Madonna Fiammetta* as a Source for the *Siervo libre de amor*', JHP, 4 (1979–80), 203-36, at pp. 214 and 205. She also quotes with approval (p. 212) the observation of Stephen Gilman, *The Spain of Fernando de Rojas: The Intellectual and Social Landscape of 'La Celestina'* (Princeton, 1972), p. 52, that when Rojas prefaces his closing verses with the rubric 'Habla el auctor', he does so to indicate to his audience that 'in this role he will provide briefly the standard piety, the mention of Christ, and the moral admonishment that are so conspicuously lacking in Pleberio's lament'.

8. José Luis Gotor, 'A propósito de las *Coplas de Vita Christi* de Fray Íñigo de Mendoza', *Studi Ispanici* (1979), 173-214, points out that the proliferation of such rubrics, even in manuscripts, is a late phenomenon: 'antes de la imprenta no existe esa conciencia textual' (p. 184, n. 10).

9. See, for instance, *Tractatus Garsiae; or, The Translation of the Relics of SS. Gold and Silver*, ed. Rodney M. Thomson (Leyden, 1973), which is, simultaneously, all three. On this work see María Rosa Lida de Malkiel, 'La *Garcineida* de García de Toledo', NRFH, 7 (1953), 246-58, and Francisco Rico, 'Las letras latinas del

siglo XII en Galicia, León y Castilla', in *Abaco*, 2 (1969), 9-92, at pp. 42-50. It should be noted that, while *tractatus* appears in Thomson's base manuscript, it is not used in all.

10. See the rhetoricians cited by Heinrich Lausberg, *Handbuch der literarischen Rhetorik: eine Grundlegung der Literaturwissenschaft* (Munich, 1960), translated by José Pérez Riesco as *Manual de retórica literaria: fundamentos de una ciencia de la literatura*, 3 vols (Madrid, 1966), especially §§408 and 854.

11. 'El "tractado" novelístico de Diego de San Pedro', *BH*, 54 (1952), 242-75. The article repeats and amplifies pp. 29-32 of her doctoral dissertation, 'La novela sentimental española, 1440–1513', University of Chicago, 1928.

12. Carmelo Samonà, *Studi sul romanzo sentimentale e cortese nella letteratura spagnola del Quattrocento* (Rome, 1960), p. 42, n. 50: 'nulla ci autorizza a pensare che il valore di quel termine *tractatus* vada oltre la lusinga di una qualifica dottrinale, in cui si è ridotto a etichetta il senso dell'originario *tractatus* latino-medievale.' Bruce W. Wardropper, '*Don Quixote*: Story or History?', *Modern Philology*, 63 (1965), 1-11, p. 1.

13. *Estructura y técnicas de la novela sentimental y caballeresca* (Madrid, 1973).

14. 'El tratadismo en Juan Rodríguez del Padrón', *Cuadernos del Sur*, 11 (1969), 25-36, and *La novela sentimental española* (Madrid, 1973), espec. pp. 63-80.

15. Chorpenning, 'Rhetoric'; Weissberger, pp. 206, 207, and 209. She refers to my introduction to San Pedro, *Obras completas*, II: *Cárcel de Amor* (Madrid, 1972), pp. 47-48; but see also my *Diego de San Pedro* (New York, 1974), p. 145, and my translation, *Diego de San Pedro, 'Prison of Love' (1492) together with the Continuation by Nicolás Núñez (1496)* (Edinburgh, 1979), p. 101. In *Juan Rodríguez del Padrón, Siervo libre de amor* (Madrid, 1976), the editor, Antonio Prieto, explains *tratado* (p. 65, n. 2) as 'discurso largo'.

16. See my 'Nicolás Núñez's Continuation of the *Cárcel de Amor* (Burgos, 1496)', in *Studies in Spanish Literature of the Golden Age Presented to Edward M. Wilson*, ed. R. O. Jones (London, 1973), pp. 357-66 [pp. 133-42, above].

17. Professor Wardropper, in a private communication commenting on my *Prison of Love*, objected to my translation of *autor* as 'narrator', on the grounds that it closes down an option and removes an ambiguity which it is important to preserve. It is an argument which has some force. Weissberger would also, no doubt, dispute my suppression of a piece of linguistic evidence, since she argues as follows: 'What we have in the *Cárcel de Amor*, then, is a curious *desdoblamiento* —an *auctor* without *auctoritas*. The phenomenon would be impossible, it seems to me, if "auctor" in 1492 did not retain most or all of its traditional etymological weight' (p. 214).

18. The variant *actor*, the least frequent of the forms, is probably a straightforward borrowing from Classical Latin; while it could not be a Spanish phonetic development from *auctor*, it might also be explained as a hypercorrection of *autor* (cf. *acto/auto*). Gotor suggests that there may be a difference between 'el *autor* como narrador y *actor* como referente de autoridades' (p. 184); but even though

certain rubrics in Mendoza's *Vita Christi* appear to lend some support to this interpretation, such a distinction does not seem to have been generalized. In general, and despite Weissberger (pp. 209-10), in narrative religious verse (Mendoza, San Pedro, etc.), the 'autor' rubrics signal precisely the passages which lack biblical authority and indicate that the poet is providing his own gloss.

19. The cases of *sabio* and *filósofo* seem to be clear enough, so that it is pointless to cite references; but *estoriador* and *orador* might repay more detailed investigation, since, not altogether appropriately one might think, Fernán Pérez de Guzmán calls Enrique de Villena an *estoriador* (*Generaciones y semblanzas*, ed. R. B. Tate (London, 1965), p. 33) and Rojas calls Petrarch an *orador* (prologue to the *Tragicomedia*). Francisco Rico, prologue to Joan Roís de Corella, *Tragèdia de Caldesa i altres proses*, ed. Marina Gustà (Barcelona, 1980), p. 18, argues that *orador* is precisely equivalent to the later *humanista*.

20. See the acrostic verses, *Comedia* version: 'oí su inventor ser ciente' (*Tragicomedia*, 'inventarla persona prudente'). Quintilian repeatedly uses *inventor* (e.g. 3, 7, 18) as a synonym for *auctor*, while *inventio* (Cicero, Quintilian, *Rhetorica ad Herennium*, etc.) is a standard rhetorical term (see Lausberg, §§260-442) which might be translated as 'creative imagination', even though the manuals describe mechanical methods to assist 'invention'.

21. In *Libro de los estados*, ed. R. B. Tate and I. R. Macpherson (Oxford, 1974), p. 65, *obrador*, applied to God, is clearly 'creator'; but in *El conde Lucanor*, ed. Herman Knust (Leipzig, 1900), p. 268, it means 'writer'.

22. Rodríguez del Padrón refers to his 'poético fin' (p. 68); Rojas (prologue to the *Tragicomedia*) calls Petrarch a 'poeta', although it is evident that he knew only Petrarch's prose; the author of *Fiammetta* is advertised in the editions of the Spanish translation as a 'poeta' (see n. 29, below); the anonymous author of *Gracisla* says that it would take a greater 'poeta' than himself adequately to describe the festivities: see my *Dos opúsculos isabelinos: 'La coronación de la señora Gracisla' (BN Ms. 22020) y Nicolás Núñez, 'Cárcel de Amor'* (Exeter, 1979), p. 5; and even Alemán refers to Guzmán de Alfarache's 'poética historia'. In other writers, however (e.g. Juan Manuel, Santillana), *poeta* does seem to mean 'poet'. Note that *poema* is not documented in Spanish before the seventeenth century (Corominas, s.v. *poeta*).

23. *Amadís de Gaula*, ed. Edwin B. Place, I (Madrid, 1959), 9. The use of *escritor* for 'copyist' must be linked with the shift of *escribano* to 'lawyer's clerk', 'notary', but it is not easy to attach dates to these changes. *Escritor*, of course, regains the sense of 'writer' in the course of the sixteenth century (cf. *La comedia thebaida*, Segura's *Proceso de cartas*, etc.).

24. Weissberger, p. 209; it should be noted that she is advancing a hypothetical argument with which, for quite different reasons, she does not concur.

25. I have used the concordance to the works of Berceo prepared by Professor Brian Dutton, which should shortly be available on microfiches.

26. See, passim, *Cuentas de Gonzalo de Baeza, tesorero de Isabel la Católica*, ed. Antonio and E. de la Torre, 2 vols (Madrid, 1955–56).

27. Contrast the earlier *Cuento de Tristán de Leonís*, MS Vaticana 6.428, and see below my remarks on *cuento*.

28. Juan Gracián, the printer, contributed a preface to the work; see *Historia etiópica de los amores de Teágenes y Cariclea traducida en romance por Fernando de Mena*, ed. Francisco López Estrada (Madrid, 1954), p. 10.

29. Salamanca, 1497: *La Fiometa* [sic] *de Juan Vocacio*; on the verso of the title-page we read: 'Aqui comienza el libro intitulado Fiameta compuesto por Juan Vocacio poeta florentino. El qual libro es partido en nueue capitulos o mas verdaderamente nueue partes'. Seville 1523 has for its title: *Libro llamado Fiameta porque trata de los amores duna notable napolitana llamada Fiameta. El qual libro compuso el famoso Juan Vocacio poeta florentin.*

30. Nebrija, *Lexicon ex sermone latino in hispaniensem* (Salamanca, 1492); the term remains extremely rare throughout the sixteenth century.

31. Professor Roger M. Walker has supplied me with copies of his detailed notes on narrative formulae employed in *El libro del cavallero Zifar*: 'cuenta la estoria' occurs 4 times, 'dize la escriptura' 16, and 'dize el cuento' 33. The later aversion to *cuento*, while obviously only a temporary phenomenon, does not appear to have been noticed previously, and is not easy to explain.

32. I have relied primarily on *Bibliography of Old Spanish Texts (Literary Texts)*, 2nd ed., compiled by Anthony Cárdenas, Jean Gilkison, John Nitti, and Ellen Anderson (Madison, 1977); note, however, that it is essential to check the STIT (specific title) of works listed in the index by their GTIT (general title: 'the title by which the work is generally known'). See below my remarks on *tratado* in titles. J.-P. Lecertua argues (pp. 16, 16a, 16b) that *estoria* also implies didactic purpose, but relies on early fourteenth-century testimony (in fact Don Juan Manuel) to support his contention.

33. We may ignore the old sense of 'picture', but Alan Deyermond points out to me that, soon after 1450, *estoria* ('la estoria deste santo apóstol') is used for II Corinthians by Teresa de Cartagena, *Arboleda de los enfermos; Admiración operum Dey*, ed. Lewis J. Hutton, *BRAE* anejo 16 (Madrid, 1967), p. 62.

34. *BOOST* (see n. 32) lists 77 MSS or editions under the GTIT of *Tratado*, but reference to the STITs shows that almost half of these titles are 'unavailable', and that for those available and assignable to the second half of the fifteenth century, only half are genuine *tratados*. The works I have mentioned are numbers 1849, 1481, 1754, and 876. The modern use of *tratado* also extends, of course, to works composed later than *BOOST*'s limit.

35. Weissberger is in no way disconcerted by this fact: 'The Archpriest's work [. . .] can fruitfully be considered a mock-*tractado*' (p. 208).

36. See Olga Tudorică Impey, 'Ovid, Alfonso X, and Juan Rodríguez del Padrón: Two Castilian Translations of the *Heroides* and the Beginnings of Spanish Sentimental Prose', *BHS*, 57 (1980), 283–97, at p. 296 (n. 34).

37. This part of the definition tends to go by default, although it is clearly regularly assumed. It is explicit in *Vocabolario degli Accademici della Crusca*, 5 vols (Naples, 1746–48), s.v. *trattato*: 'Discorso compilato e messo in iscrittura'.

38. To complete a proper structural semantic analysis of the term *tratado*, it would be necessary to examine at least French *traité* (*traicté*), English *treatie* (*treaty*), *treatise*, *tract*, and Italian *trattato*; doubtless (if I may quote one of my favourite footnotes), 'il y a une belle thèse à écrire là-dessus'. But preliminary soundings seem to indicate that the use of these terms to refer to works of fiction first appears in translations from the Spanish (for instance, *Petit traité de Arnalte et Lucenda*, *A Certayn Treatye Most Wyttely Deuised*, *A Small Treatise betwixt Arnalte and Lucenda*, *Picciol trattato d'Arnalte e di Lucenda*, etc.), thus providing yet another example of L2 interference in L1.

39. I find almost nothing to quarrel with in Bruno M. Damiani, 'The Didactic Intention of the *Cárcel de Amor*', *Hispanófila*, no. 56 (Jan. 1976), 29-43; but he does not rely on the interpretation of *autor* or *tratado* as semantic latinisms.

Index

The index is not exhaustive, but it lists all the significant references to authors and their works, terms, topics, and scholars. The abbreviation 'crit.' indicates a critique or rectification of fact or interpretation. References concerning authors or works as best-sellers (pp. 159-75) are listed together under 'best-sellers'.